Students, Teachers, and Leaders Addressing Bullying in Schools

Students, Teachers, and Leaders Addressing Bullying in Schools

Edited by

Christa Boske
Kent State University, USA

and

Azadeh Osanloo
New Mexico State University, USA

SENSE PUBLISHERS
ROTTERDAM/BOSTON/TAIPEI

A C.I.P. record for this book is available from the Library of Congress.

ISBN: 978-94-6300-146-5 (paperback)
ISBN: 978-94-6300-147-2 (hardback)
ISBN: 978-94-6300-148-9 (e-book)

Published by: Sense Publishers,
P.O. Box 21858,
3001 AW Rotterdam,
The Netherlands
https://www.sensepublishers.com/

Printed on acid-free paper

This book provides the reader with the missing voices of students, educators, and families in the national dialogue on bullying. The telling of stories by those who have been marginalized due to race, gender, class, ability, sexual orientation, or gender expression is one of the truest forms of activism in our time. This incredible book helps us to understand the impact of taunting, teasing, and micro aggressions targeted at student identities that result in identity-based bullying. This book will help the reader to develop a critical understanding of the systematic injustice of bullying in order to better support and create welcoming and culturally competent schools.

– Johanna Eager, Director of Welcoming Schools, A Project from the Human Rights Campaign

Boske and Osanloo have demonstrated the gift of "story catching" in this book and offer readers a bricolage of voices on bullying. The editors demonstrate craftiness as bricoleurs as they weave stories of sadness, bravery, and triumph to create an agenda that shifts the overall voice of the book into an agenda for action. This literary work of art virtually stands alone as it places the voices of all stakeholders – children, families, community members, practitioners, and scholars – at the forefront of a current crisis that, if not addressed, will continue to cause devastating losses of life and community.

– Whitney Sherman Newcomb, Professor at Virginia Commonwealth University

With increased attention to violence in and around schools, this book provides a systemic analysis by going directly to the source: young people, their families, and involved educators. Boske and Osanloo dig beyond media portrayals and knee-jerk reactions to uncover the oppression that shapes bullying, from a range of powerful voices. This book is a must read for educators, social workers, and concerned professionals dedicated to educational solutions to our deepest forms of oppression.

– Christopher Knaus, Professor and Director, Educational Leadership at the University of Washington Tacoma

School bullying is one of the most detrimental and violent scourges on education. It undermines learning and destroys lives and communities, yet the voices of bullied students and educators continue to be marginalized or completely suppressed. Drs. Boske and Osanloo gathered a collection of powerful and important narratives that give voice to the bullied. In this book we find vignettes penned by a diverse group of educators, scholars, students and community members that explore problems associated with bullying and possibilities for effecting positive cultural change, protection and caring relationships in schools.

– Jeffrey S. Brooks, Professor of Educational Leadership at Monash University

Bullying is happening repeatedly across the country and in a variety of schools. The challenge is not taking a myopic approach, rather, one that takes into account the intersection of factors and contexts in which bullying occurs. Boske and Osanloo take an approach with this volume that goes beyond a simplistic frame of perpetrator versus victim and instead promotes reflection, articulation, and change. They illustrate and affirm bullying hurts us ALL. Boske and Osanloo present the complexity of this issue and the insufficiency of "good intentions." They invite readers to explore new possibilities and responses.

– Noelle Witherspoon Arnold, President of the University Council for Educational Association and Associate Professor at the University of Missouri-Columbia

This books captures the essence of one of the gravest challenges facing our schools – the daily realities of bullying. While bullying has become part of the rhetoric of schools, there is the perception that bullying happens "other places" or that it is "part of growing up." Boske and Osanloo's book provides authentic voices that present vivid accounts about bullying. In short, this books makes the compelling case about why all schools, all communities, and all leaders must substantially engage with their local school cultures that allow and perpetuate bulling. Bullying is not other people's problem, it is all of our responsibility to tackle. Our vulnerable children depend on us to do that. This is an important book!

– George Theoharis, Department Chair of Teaching and Leadership at Syracuse University

LGBT youth deal with bullying in the form of harassment, violence and attacks. One of the most common reasons for bullying is actual or assumed sexual orientation or gender identity. It's unfortunate that so many young people have felt unsafe at school due to bigotry. This book addresses this important topic to help put bullying to rest.

– Deidre McPherson, Founder of Sistah Sinema Cleveland

TABLE OF CONTENTS

MICHELE JOSUE

FOREWORD

When I was asked by Christa Boske to write the foreword for *Students, Teachers, and Leaders Addressing Bullying in Schools*, I was suprised, but incredibly honored. As a close friend of the late Matthew Shepard, who was murdered in one of the most brutal and notorious hate crimes in our history, the issue of bullying and intolerance is one I am very passionate about.

I had met Christa after a very emotional screening of my documentary *Matt Shepard is a Friend of Mine*, which explores Matt's life and death through the point of view of his family and friends. The screening event, hosted by the wonderful educational organization Facing History and Ourselves, was one of deep reflection and discussion. The audience, comprised mostly of students, educators, and advocates, was committed to asking tough questions and examining their own community.

That evening's discussion gave me great insight into the complex issues Matt's story brings up—issues of hate, ignorance, fear, and social injustice. However, this book, as an important collection of significant voices and perspectives on the implications of bullying in schools, also provides invaluable insight into those same issues.

Matt's story demonstrates bullying's most extreme and tragic outcome. Our film presents the devastating reality that extraordinary people in the U.S. and around the world continue to fall victim to the hate and ignorance that persists in our society today. But beyond that, our film also shows that bullying and intolerance has a ripple effect that causes pain not just for the victim, but for their friends, family, community, and even the bully themselves.

In our film, it would've been impossible to show this ripple effect had it not been for the willingness and courage of Matt's family and friends to stand up and share their point of view. This book takes the same approach by compiling varied and important perspectives on the issue of bullying in schools.

Students, Teachers, and Leaders Addressing Bullying in Schools helps us explore the way we deal with bullying as a society and encourages tough questions and open and honest discussion. This book is a clarion call to students, educators, families, and community members to work together to create not only safe and inclusive classrooms, but a safe and inclusive society.

I believe that by learning about people like Matt and their experiences, and listening to different voices, like the ones in this book, we can begin dialogues that have the power to create a more accepting world; one in which we can talk about difference and similarities, and recognize pieces of ourselves in others.

Ending bullying in our schools is no simple task. But *Students, Teachers, and Leaders Addressing Bullying in Schools* is a huge step forward in the fight against an epidemic of violence that has in some way touched each and every one of us. This book and its collection of courageous voices inspires the safe, inclusive, and respectful educational environment every young person deserves.

By Michele Josue
Director, Matt Shepard is a Friend of Mine

CHRISTA BOSKE AND AZADEH OSANLOO

UNCOMFORTABLE TRUTHS

An Introduction to Bullying in U.S. Schools

Christa received an emergency alert from her daughter's elementary school. Family members were asked to attend a meeting in the early afternoon as they announced a death in a child's family. When she arrived, the room was filled from wall to wall with family members. All of the children were huddled in the center of the room at their desks. The teacher announced a classmate's sibling passed away from a "tragic accident." Christa remembered hearing those words on two other occasions during her 18 years in public education. In both situations, young men had stepped in front of trains and committed suicide. One was a middle school student and the other was a high school student. These students were taunted and harassed for their gender expression and perceived sexual orientation. Their peers often used names such as "faggot", "gay", and "homo" towards them. Both students left letters for their families informing them they could no longer deal with the on-going bullying they faced.

   Much like the two events Christa recalled from her past, this student too experienced a "tragic accident." The students cried. Christa held her 11-year old daughter in her arms as she wept. She said, "Mama, I don't understand how this could have happened. It's so sad. He was so young…just a kid. It just doesn't make any sense." The child's parent attended the classroom discussion. The mother and Christa hugged one another. They cried and spoke briefly. She wore a picture of her son on a chain around her neck. The student's mother shared his recent role in a theatrical production, love for dance, passion for singing, and the family's wish to "not share any of the details." During the funeral, one of the speakers announced the child's "love for Taylor Swift" and his "ability to know every word and sing every note." The speaker also announced the child was "not normal and like the other boys." Family members and friends of the family continued to speak of his "testimony" and "love of God" as well as his leadership positions in the church. He was further described as "kind, caring, loving, and looked out for all of kids who didn't have friends." Letters were read aloud from his peers who described him as "loving", "funny", and "a good listener." His family shared stories of his "cleanliness", "obsession with his hair", "good taste in fashion", "singing that often annoyed his siblings", "theatrical nature", and how often he shared his love for his family. Again, the speakers announced the unfortunate circumstances surrounding this "tragic accident" of a young adolescent male; however, this was not an accident.

It was a tragedy, period. No one spoke of the alleged bullying he experienced for years, because of his gender expression and perceived sexual orientation. He committed suicide at the age of 13. *That* is the tragedy.

It was surreal for Christa to sit in a church with hundreds of people who may not have wanted to hear the unbearable realities this young person faced. The way in which this person's life was described calls into question everything presented regarding the life and death of this child. The child's tragic and untimely demise may have been fueled by his gender expression and perceived sexual orientation.

After attending the funeral and discussing the tragic loss of the family's son, two more stories emerged from the headlines. First, parents of a 12-year-old shared the tragedy of their son Ronin Shimizu, who committed suicide due to relentless bullying in elementary and middle school (see http://www.nydailynews.com/news/national/bullied-boy-cheerleader-12-found-dead-calif-home-article-1.2035167). In sixth grade, the bullying became so difficult to manage, Ronin's parents homeschooled him. Their son enjoyed participating on the cheerleading squad. They shared stories of his love for fashion, art, and cheering. They advocated not only for prevention measures in school, but the need to understand cultural responsiveness, acceptance, and understanding in children's homes. Second, Leelah Alcorn, a teenager from the Cincinnati area, was hit by a tractor-trailer at the age of 17. The death was declared a suicide after reading a suicide note hoping her death would "mean something." The suicide note shared Leelah's experience of coming out to her parents as transgender, their reactions to her identity, and being assigned to conversion therapy to "change her." After bouts of depression and isolation, Leelah grappled with the realization of her parents choosing not to accept her. In her closing lines, she noted, "Gender needs to be taught about in schools, the earlier the better. My death needs to mean something…Fix society. Please." (see http://www.wlwt.com/news/hundreds-attend-candlelight-vigil-for-leelah-alcorn-other-transgender-teens/30519342).

As parents, educators, and community members, we can neither imagine the hopelessness these young men felt and experienced nor stand by as these "tragic accidents" become innumerable. They were simply being themselves; and yet, they were ridiculed, humiliated, and ostracized for being who they were as young people. This book is dedicated to the young people who took their lives, those who endure bullying in schools, and children who interrupt hostile school environments in an effort to create safe and nurturing schools for all children. We hope, by offering a platform for their voices, their lives will continue to matter. The authors of this book are courageous individuals, who hope their stories, insights, and research will be tweeted and retweeted, shared and reshared on Facebook, posted and reposted, so one person's story becomes 10 and exponentially, becomes 10,000.

BRIEF OVERVIEW OF BULLYING

Although state laws have little consistency regarding what is meant by bullying, accepted definitions by mental health professionals suggest bullying involves verbal and//or physical aggression. Some of these aggressive behaviors include may physical, verbal, social, reactive, and *e*forms (i.e., electronic forms) of bullying (Espelage & Swearer, 2004). Physical bullying includes hitting, kicking, pushing, and fighting. Verbal aggressions may include name-calling, discriminatory comments, public humiliation, harsh teasing, and name calling. Social bullying focuses on excluding individuals from peer groups through threats, rumors, isolation, and other forms of intimidation. Reactive bullying refers to individuals who were bullied and responded to their victimization by bullying others. These aggressive behaviors are considered bullying when they are repeated over a period of time. Such behaviors involve an imbalance of power between the victim and aggressor(s). Power may be characterized by an individual's or group's social status over the victim to exert power and cause harm. These aggressive behaviors (e.g., name calling, rumors, gossip) may also include electronic media (e.g., Facebook, Twitter, email, text, instant messaging, chat rooms, blogs or other social media), which is referred to as cyber bullying (Schneider, O'Donnell, Stueve, & Coulter, 2012). Although bullying is often thought as taking place... about taking place between K-12 children at school, bullying can also occur within the work place. Adults may be verbally abused, experience sabotaging work relations, and/or abusing authority/power. This systemized and reinvigorated bullying pandemic has long-lasting and widespread impact, which may affect multiple stakeholders including students, parents, educators, medical professionals, and the community. It is incumbent upon educators to not only address bullying from a systemic manner, but also attend to the needs of both bullies and victims (Osanloo & Schwartz, 2015).

Statistics on bullying suggest 30% of students in grades 6-10 either identify as bullies or have been the victim of bullying. In regards to cyber bullying, approximately 16% experienced this type of bullying within the past year with 75% documenting they have been a victim of this form of harassment in their lifetime (Goodwin, 2011). Many times, educators underestimate how often bullying occurs in schools. Although schools may report incidents of bullying at 4%, only one third of victims report their experiences of being bullied to an adult in school with families being aware of their child's experiences only half of the time. In regards to adults, more than 40% of American workers report being bullied in the workplace. More than 90% of working women are undermined by other women at some time in their careers.

Bullying can also have significantly negative outcomes on an individual's well-being, and in the cases noted at the beginning of this chapter, life itself. Those who bully other children have a greater risk for engaging in delinquent behaviors, dropping out of school, and involving themselves in substance abuse (Fekkes, Pijpers, & Fredriks, 2006). For those who are bullied, victims tend to develop or increase their anxiety, depression, social isolation, academic issues, and frequent absences (Menesini, Modena, & Tani, 2009). For adults, victims in the workplace may experience more absences, less work satisfaction, reduced job performance, and higher turnover (Duffy & Sperry, 2014). In regards to the risk of suicidal thoughts and actions, for either the bully or the victim, both are at risk. This risk seems to be higher for victims who identify as girls, while there is a tendency for suicidal thoughts and actions for boys who identify as bullies and victims who experience bullying over time. However, for boys, the frequency of suicide attempts in boy bullies and victims seems to increase even when bullying is not consistent over time.

In order to help better understand student needs, educators might consider becoming more aware of the differences between normal conflict and bullying. Students in K-12 schooling will experience normal conflict throughout their education. Normal conflict is when two peers of equal power, who may even be friends, clash or have a one-time disagreement. Often these conflicts are resolved with each person taking responsibility for what happened (Osanloo & Schwartz, in press). Whereas, the concept of bullying (as previously mentioned above) underscores three integral components described as intentional, imbalanced, and repeated. Meaning, the behavior is *intended* to cause harm; there is an *imbalance* of physical or psychological power or strength among the parties, and the behavior occurs *repeatedly* over time (Garrity et al., 2000; Olweus, 1993).

CREATING SAFE SCHOOLS

There is currently no federal law that directly addresses bullying. Policies often overlap it often overlaps with discriminatory harassment, which is covered under federal civil rights laws enforced by the US Department of Education and Department of Justice. Federal anti-bullying legislation and policy is under works via the Office of Safe and Drug Free Schools (Osanloo & Schwartz, in press). In fact, President Obama held the first-ever anti-bullying conference in 2011. At this event, he stated:

> If there's one goal of this conference, it's to dispel the myth that bullying is just a harmless rite of passage or an inevitable part of growing up. It's not. Bullying can have destructive consequences for our young people. And it's not something we have to accept. As parents and students, as teachers and members of the community, we can take steps – all of us – to help prevent bullying and create a climate in our schools in which all of our children can feel safe; a climate in which they all can feel like they belong.

The Anti-Defamation League sent the President many recommendations regarding establishing guidelines to address bullying. Three of the seven recommendations, most connected to this research, were: (1) Establishing a comprehensive anti-bullying policy for all schools; (2) Providing training and technical support for school administrators on anti-bullying programs; and (3) Analyzing the impact of bullying on social and emotional health and academic achievement. Obama strongly advocated for a federal anti-bullying policy to ensure effective anti-bullying and cyber bullying programs ("United Effort to Address Bullying," 2011). Lastly, an interagency collaboration was developed to further conversation and policy initiatives in the area of bullying. The Departments of Education, Health and Human

Services, Justice, Defense, Agriculture, and Interior banded to establish the Federal Partners in Bullying Prevention Steering Committee. This steering committee is charged with ways to explore and provide guidance for individuals and organizations in combating bullying ("United Effort to Address Bullying," 2011).

There are a myriad of ways to address bullying in schools, which may include, but are not limited anti-bullying legislation, student handbooks aligned with negative consequences for bullying, and promoting culturally responsive schools. Unfortunately, legislative measures remain somewhat problematic. Often times, legislation mandating bullying prevention is perceived as expensive to taxpayers (Ferrell-Smith, 2003). However, the Washington Institute for Public Policy discovered bullying prevention programs can save taxpayers $5.29 for every dollar spent due to fewer districts facing lawsuits. Other preventative measures may include anti-bullying policy in student handbooks and school codes. These codes may constitute how bullying is defined within that school community and provide immunity to students for reporting instances of bullying (e.g., Milsom & Gallo, 2006; Swearer, Espelage, Vaillancourt, & Hymel, 2010). These handbooks may also identify how to prepare school community members for recognizing/intervening/responding to bullying and outlining possible consequences for bullying for remediation purposes. In addition to the promotion of anti-bullying legislation and school disciplinary/prevention policies, consideration may also be given to ensuring culturally responsive practices and policies are embedded throughout the school community by bridging resources, considering curriculum/pedagogy, personnel hires, and authentic community efforts (Boske, 2012). Assessing the strengths and needs of the school community, especially for those who are discriminated against due to their race, class, gender, gender expression, native language, immigration status, ability, family, and religion/beliefs/faith, is essential to uncovering many of the possible causes and sources of bullying. This assessment may include input from students, families, teachers, administrative assistants, school leaders, and community members in order to better understand the experiences of young people in schools. This information may be gathered via surveys, focus groups, interviews, town hall meetings, written/audio/video narratives, and other data collection to provide policy makers at multiple levels (i.e., local, regional, state, national) with a clear picture of the state of U.S. school communities. This rationale operates in tandem with suggestions made by Osanloo and Schwartz (in press) who advocate that, "Hate-based bullying must be identified and addressed as a unique and deleterious type of bullying. The response must be system-wide to prevent and address hate-based bullying as it happens. Since discriminations and stereotypes do not happen in a vacuum it is important to collaborate with all ecological contexts to prevent the impact of prejudice."

Together, school community members may draft pertinent and comprehensive policy that informs practices to protect *all* of our children. As families, students, educators, and policy makers at the building, district, state, and federal levels work to create safe, nurturing, and culturally responsive schools, what is most essential is to commit to doing what is in the best interest of all children, especially those who live on the margins. This effort begins with each of us looking within. We may ask ourselves: To what extent do we understand what it means to live on the margins? Who is discriminated in schools? What do we believe? What do we value? To what extent are we aware of the realities young people face in schools? Next, we may move forward by creating dialogue about our new understanding. Afterwards, we work together and move beyond refection to critical dialogue with children, families, educators, school leaders, and community members. Within these contexts, group members may problematize what bullying means and who is named as members of enumerated groups. Together, they might discuss anti-bullying measures/mandates, bullying, school safety, school climate, cultural responsiveness, and school reform. For example, questions may include, but are not limited to: 1) How are bullies and victims identified? 2) How do we address intervention? Prevention? 3) How do we understand intervention of antigay and anti-transgender taunting? and 4) What are the roles each school community member plays in promoting this work in schools? Such efforts provide a forum to imagine legislation that protects all children and promotes culturally responsive practices and policies that emulate the laws in our most progressive jurisdictions.

For those who engage in the work to protect *all* students, the authors commend their efforts. The success of schools, districts, states, and regions depends on our ability to build bridges amongst others and ourselves. These linkages can then recognize and support states with comprehensive anti-bullying laws, policies, and practices that underscore how to protect each and every child. All students deserve equal access to a safe education and equal opportunity to be their best selves. How will this be achieved? The authors of this book contend it is in their doing and your doing. It's a collective and systemic effort. Each person, no matter what age, creed, or walk of life, has a moral and ethical responsibility to be aware and to be involved in this movement. Moreover, these authors contend it is essential for all school community members to be actively engaged in understanding the influence of personal beliefs/ attitudes/actions toward marginalized populations, critical reflection, understanding impending social and political impact of bullying policies, expanding and creating instruments for reporting bullying, promoting cultural responsiveness through curriculum and pedagogy, and understanding how such efforts will improve understanding regarding how bullying translates to discrimination/harassment/ racism/homophobia in society. The elimination of bullying can be achieved if *every* child can attend school free from victimization, hallway terrorism, and with the creation and promotion of a culturally responsive environment in which all children can be their best selves.

OVERVIEW OF THE BOOK

We were honored when Michele Josue, the documentary filmmaker for "Matt Shepard is a Friend of Mine," agreed to write the introduction for this book's. Christa met Michele at a public showing in Cleveland. Michele believed in the message and supported the collaboration of voices from a myriad of authors including children, college students, community members, teachers, school leaders, organizational leaders, and scholars who prepare school leaders and teachers. Michele created a powerful feature documentary about Matthew Shepard, who was a young gay man tortured and murdered for being gay. The case became one of the most notorious hate crimes in U.S. history, leading to federal legislation. The film reviews the case with never-before-seen footage and photos regarding Matt's life. The film won four "Best Film" awards at numerous film festivals, including the 2014 Best Film at the Cleveland International Film Festival. The documentary was shown in theaters in 12 cities in the U.S. and Canada in February of 2015, following a host of film festivals in the U.S. as well as Petersburg, Russia. In the summer of 2015, Matt Shepard is a Friend of Mine hit mainstream theaters by storm.

This book is the first time K-12 children, educators, families, community members, organizational leaders, and scholars came together to share their stories, insights, and research regarding bullying. There is significance to sharing personal narratives and storytelling, especially for those who are marginalized due to their gender, race, class, gender expression, sexual orientation, religion/beliefs/faith, immigration status, native language, ability (i.e., social, emotional, physical, cognitive), family structure, gender, and other dimensions of diversity. Storytelling and personal narratives afford disenfranchised groups with opportunities to discuss their experiences within an oppressive society. Moreover, it was an imperative for the editors to include the voices of all stakeholders in this work. There is a need for people to make sense and develop an understanding of who we are in relationship to the world, especially those who are ostracized for their "differences" (Boske, 2014; Greene, 2004; Pinar, 1988). One means of understanding how children, teachers, families, and school leaders make sense is to provide them with opportunities to move beyond themselves, search for imaginative possibilities, create possible alternatives, and utilize their new ways of understanding the world (Boske, 2015, in press, 2014a, 2014b; Greene, 1988; Pinar 2011). These new understandings shape and reshape their personal narratives and stories. Their storytelling plays a critical role in countering culturally dominant stories that often send messages to marginalized populations suggesting their differences are perceived as "abnormalities," allegedly supporting why their social isolation is validated (Boske, 2015, in press; Greene, 1988; Pinar, 2011).

Personal narratives are at the heart of this work with the significance of "voice" embedded throughout. This book is divided into four sections and emphasizes voice as a common, linking thread: 1) An overview; 2) Voices from youth in schools; 3) Voices from concerned families and community members; and 4) Voices from educators and scholars in the field. The first chapter is "What's going on? Understanding Bullying in U.S. Schools." Christa Boske suggests schools shift from "anti-practices and policies" to engaging in culturally responsive policies and practices. The culturally responsive framework provides opportunities for students, families, faculty, school leaders, and community members to deepen awareness, understanding, and interactions regarding dimensions of diversity through curriculum, pedagogy, and policy making. The second chapter by Azadeh Osanloo titled "What Are You? The Hidden Curriculum and Microaggressions Associated with What It Means to be 'Different'" focuses on a personal narrative of ethnic identity exploration and how racial microaggressions can compound the negative impacts of bullying.

VOICES FROM YOUTH IN SCHOOLS

The next section, "Voices from Youth in Schools" is written by K-12 students in public schools. Chris Board, a high school student, begins with chapter three titled, "Don't Judge Me: I Was the Bully." In his chapter, he shares his story of being a young Black male raised in an impoverished community and how he was teased for living on the "wrong side of the tracks." In an effort to confront his bullies, he eventually becomes a bully and provides readers with an understanding of how he grappled with his choices to taunt and tease his peers. Next, Emily Wirth, wrote chapter four titled, "You are Worth It" and provides readers with insights regarding her experiences of being bullied and how she overcame her struggles along the way. In chapter five, Goldiea Shaw, a high school student, discusses the need for educators and peers to increase their awareness, understanding, and willingness to be involved in eliminating bullying. She wrote the fifth chapter "Does it Really Matter if No One is Around?" which exemplifies the need for advocates for children who are victims of bullying. In chapter six, Mariyah shares her experiences as a victim of bullying and how she grappled with those who harassed her in middle and high school. Next, in chapter seven, Devin McMiller, a high school student, demonstrates courage as he divulges his experiences with bullying from family members, teachers, and classmates from early childhood through high school in "I'm a Little Bit Darker." Anthony Bias, in chapter eight, a recent high school graduate and member of the Esperanza Youth Leadership group, shares his insights regarding bullying and the need for school communities to work together to provide youth with safe and nurturing spaces. His chapter "How do You Feel About Bullying in Schools" captures some of the experiences facing youth in schools. Chapter nine, written by Leah Bailey, a high school student, discusses her efforts to eliminate bullying in "Standing Up to the Popular Girl." In Chapter 10, Edward Valentin, a high school student and member of the Esperanza Youth Leadership group, shares his insights regarding school violence and bullying in schools. In Chapter 11, Aajah Chapman, a high school student, shares her experiences of being teased because some of her peers do not seem to accept the way she presents herself in "Not Black Enough." Erica Howard, a high school student, wrote Chapter 12 titled "What Makes Me Beautiful", which focuses on the need for children to address bullying through a personal strengths perspective. Chapter 13, "What the World Should Be", are the accounts of Angely Boske, an elementary student, who shares her personal experiences with being bullied in elementary school and the steps she took to promote cultural responsiveness for teachers, children, school leaders, and families. In Chapter 14, Kiara Kane, a high school student, provides a framework titled "T.H.I.N.K." to demonstrate what she identifies as essential steps to eliminating bullying in schools. Destiny Puffenbarger, a high school student, concludes this section with "You Just Get Used to It." Her story urges teachers and school leaders to consider the impact of bullying in schools on children's identity and acceptance of self.

VOICES FROM CONCERNED FAMILIES AND COMMUNITY MEMBERS

This section focuses on the voices of parents, guardians, teachers, and community members committed to eliminating bullying and hallway terrorism in schools. Bradley Sinick, a former high school teacher, who was bullied for being perceived as "gay", begins this section with Chapter 16. Bradley shares his journey of being bullied in elementary school and how one teacher inspired him to commit to this work in schools. His chapter is titled, "All I Wanted was to BE Mrs. Baker." Jennifer Turley, a parent of a child in transition from female to male, discusses the tensions her child faces in Chapter 17 titled, "Dyke! Dyke! Dyke!" and how they continue to navigate through the harassment as a parent and a child in transition from female to male. In Chapter 18, Jonathan Gill, a former member of the U.S. military and facilitator of the Lesbian/Gay/Bisexual/Transgender/Queer (LGBTQ) group in the military, wrote a poem regarding what it means to be "gay." Mother and daughter Kim Mosyjowski and Joan Mosyjowski team up in Chapter 19 in "Chaos and Order." Together, they dialogue about the lived realities facing their family as Joan discusses grappling with her bullying in middle and high school and how her mother sought support through Parent and Friends of Lesbians and Gays (PFLAG), a national organization. In Chapter 20, internet radio host Dwayne Steward, discusses his experiences with bullying in "Bullied at the Intersection: Growing Up Gay in the Black Church and Rural Ohio." Chapter 21, "Masculine of Center" depicts Logan Sherman's experiences with expressing gender in school and on the football team. In Chapter 22, Bradley Rhodes provides readers with an inside look at his experiences of being bullied in school and how those experiences continue to influence him today as an adult in "I Was Prime Pickn'." In the next chapter, Mandy Miller, a parent and former special education teacher, discusses the influence of bullying in preschool in the chapter "Bullies in Diapers." Martinez E-B, the Esperanza Youth Director and Artist, examines the influence of his inner-city roots in understanding and addressing what bullying means to youth in "Bully: The Synthetic Cool." Katie Miller, in "Katie", concludes this section with a personal narrative about her childhood experiences with bullying, coming out at as a lesbian, and how she continues to navigate through her sexual identity through advocacy.

VOICES FROM EDUCATORS AND SCHOLARS IN THE FIELD

The third and final section of this book highlights the voices of educators and scholars in the field who have dedicated (all or parts of) their work to examining issues of bullying across the PK-20 spectrum. The section begins with chapter 26, in which Bernard Oliver offers a comprehensive examination of schoolhouse bullying by students and teachers. Next, Chapter 27 "Dancers Addressing Bullying" by Kimberly Meredith uses a multiliteracies lens to share two hip-hop dancers response to bullying. Chapter 28 by Ryan Schoenfeld and Jeff Dinse discuss the significant impact a diversity enhancement program had on the school climate and community. Amanda Hudnall in Chapter 29, "The Quiet Roar" details her account from a student who was bullied to a teacher who is an anti-bullying advocate for her students. Next in this section, Laura Merry and Joanna Royce-Davis, from the University of the Pacific, expand on the notion of traditional school-based bullying to include a glimpse of bullying in higher education. In Chapter 31, Karen Tollafield sheds light on the potential of teachers acting as bullies, or as she describes it "recognizing bullying in other forms." Darla Wagner, a K-12 public school teacher, describes in Chapter 32 a comprehensive system of support provides middle school students with essential skills and supports to address issues of bullying and other facets of social and emotional concern. Next, Dickson Perry uses case study method to examine a GSA (Gay-Straight Alliance) at a public urban high school. The results are fascinating. For scholars Yoona Lee, Malcolm W. Watson, and Ki-Hak Lee, exploring the relation of physical discipline to bullying behaviors across different families and ethnicities was the anchor of their study and Chapter 34. Michael J. Sheehan and Malcolm W. Watson address bullying behavior with research implications for school policies and intervention programs in Chapter 35. And finally to close out this section, Christa Boske examines culturally responsive bridge building among schools, nonprofits, and universities to address bullying in K-12 schools.

Our concluding thoughts section was written by the award-winning documentarian, Paul Saltzman. Paul was a civil rights volunteer with SNCC, the Student Non-Violent Coordinating Committee, in Mississippi in the summer of 1965. He is also the director and producer of "Prom Night in Mississippi" and "The Last White Knight—Is Reconciliation Possible?" Also important to this work and to Paul's personal and professional mission is his organization Moving Beyond Prejudice. Paul has dedicated his life to advancing issues of equity, diversity, communication, and respect – all from a healthful and heartening perspective. We were honored, humbled, and grateful he afforded us his thoughtful wisdom in the concluding thoughts.

REFERENCES

Boske, C. (2012). *Educational leadership: Building bridges among ideas, schools and nations*. Charlotte, NC: Information Age Publishing.

Boske, C. (2014). Critical reflective practices: Connecting to social justice. In I. Bogotch & C. Shields (Eds.), *International Handbook of Social [In] Justice and Educational Leadership* (pp. 289–308). Netherlands: Springer.

Boske, C. (In press, 2015). Preparing school leaders to interrupt racism at various levels in education systems. *International Journal of Multicultural Education.*

Boske, C. (2014b). Using the senses in reflective practice to prepare women for transforming their learning spaces. In W. Sherman & K. Mansfield (Eds.), *Women interrupting, disrupting, and revolutionizing educational policy and practice* (pp. 225–253). Charlotte, NC: Information Age Publishing.

Duffy, M., & Sperry, L. (2014). Overcoming mobbing: A recovery guide for work. New York, NY: Oxford University Publishing.

Espelage, D.L., and S.M. Swearer (2004). *Bullying in American schools: A social-ecological perspective on prevention and intervention.* Mahwah, NJ: Lawrence Erlbaum Associates.

Fekkes, M., Pijpers, F. M., & Fredriks, A. M. (2006). Do bullied children get ill, or do ill children get bullied? A prospective cohort study on the relationship between bullying and health-related symptoms, *Pediatrics, 5*(117), 1568–1574.

Ferrell-Smith, F. (2003). *Tackling the schoolyard bully: Combining policy making with prevention.* Washington, DC: National Conference of State Legislatures.

Goodwin, B. (2011). Research says...bullying is common-and subtle. *Promoting Respectful Schools, 9*(1), 82–83.

Greene, M. (1988). *The dialectic of freedom.* New York, NY: Teachers College Press.

Greene, M. (2004). Curriculum and consciousness. In D. J. Flinders & S. J. Thornton (Eds.), *The curriculum studies reader* (2nd ed., pp.135–147). New York, NY: RoutledgeFalmer.

Guerra, N. G., Williams, K. R., & Sadek, S. (2011). Understanding bullying and victimization during childhood and adolescence: A mixed methods study. *Child Development, 82*(1), 295–310.

Menesini, E., Modena, M., & Tani, F. (2009). Bullying and victimization in adolescence: Concurrent and stable roles and psychological health symptoms. *Journal Of Genetic Psychology, 170*(2), 115–134.

Milsom, A., & L.L. Gallo. (2006). Bullying in middle schools: prevention and intervention. *Association for Middle Level Education,* 37(3), 12–19.

Osanloo, A., & Schwartz, J. (2015). Using social norming, ecological theory, and diversity-based strategies for bullying interventions in urban areas: A mixed methods research study. In M. Khalifa, N. Witherspoon-Arnold, A. Osanloo, & C. Grant-Overton, (Eds.), *Urban school leadership handbook.* (pp. 199–210). Lanham, MD: Rowman and Littlefield Publishing Group.

Schneider, S. K., O'Donnell, L., Stueve, A., & Coulter, R. W. S. (2012). Cyberbullying, school bullying and psychological distress: a regional census of high school students. *American Journal of Public Health, 102*(1), 171–177.

Pinar, W. F. (2011). *What is curriculum theory?* New York, NY: Routledge.

Pinar, W. F. (1988). Autobiography and the architecture of self. *Journal of Curriculum Theorizing, 8*(1), 7–35.

CHRISTA BOSKE

1. BULLIED

What's Going on?

If you didn't act like such a *faggot*, you wouldn't be in this predicament.

Who would say something like this? A K-12 principal directed this comment to a 13 year old student who came to the office for assistance in managing male students harassing him during the school day. Five girls escorted Marcus to the office (I changed his name to protect his anonymity). The girls offered him tissues to wipe away his tears. Marcus had cried long enough to leave salt marks down his cheeks. He proceeded to inform the principal he was tired of being bullied in school. Marcus said, "Kids keep making fun of the way I talk...the way I act." The girls confirmed his story with numerous examples including Marcus being pushed into lockers, his being lunch thrown away, name calling in the hallway (e.g., faggot, gay, homo, pervert), and taunted in the boy's bathroom. The principal's comment was not only perceived as advice, but placed responsibility for altering possible outcomes on Marcus. The student's self-referral was not documented in the school's disciplinary record, nor were countless other accounts of bullying, which included hate speech, harassment, and physical assault. Unfortunately, Marcus' story is not unfamiliar to issues facing children and families who identify as lesbian/gay/bisexual/transgender/queer (LGBTQ) in K-12 schools across the United States. The purpose of this chapter is to deepen understanding of who is bullied in schools, increasing awareness of disjointed bullying laws, school practices and school district policies, and possible ramifications for school practices and public policy.

Every child deserves the opportunity to attend a safe and culturally responsive school; however, some students continue to face harassment on the basis of their race, ethnicity, class, immigration status, ability (mental and/physical), religion/beliefs/faith, gender, sexual orientation, gender expression, native language and other differences. Despite the efforts of academics, organizations, and legislators to develop a universal working definition of bullying, harassment, or intimidation, most incidents of bullying are still judged on a case-by-case basis. Incidents may occur within the context of verbal/physical/cyber threats, verbal/physical assault, social isolation, and other forms of violence. Although there is no standard or universal definition for bullying, there are specific elements to consider. First, there is a pattern of behavior exhibited over a period of time in which an individual is exposed to intentional injury (e.g., verbal acts, name-calling, graphic and written statements) inflicted by one or more people. These behaviors may include, but are not limited to, cyber assaults, physical contact/injury, verbal assault, social isolation, obscene virtual/verbal/physical gestures, or other hostile acts that place the victim in fear. Next, there is a common element regarding an imbalance of power (e.g., between educator and student, student and student, student and group of students, student and group of educators), which affords one person or group of people to victim others. The imbalance of power may be verbal, physical or virtual; however, the victim is feels humiliated, threatened, and/or harmed. However, harassment does not need to include the intent to harm another or align with a specific individual or involve repeated offenses. Harassment creates a hostile environment when it is pervasive, persistent, and/or severe. The behavior may interfere or limit a child's ability to fully participate or benefit from activities, services, or opportunities afforded all children within the school. If harassment is based on race, color, national origin, sex or disability, then the perpetrator violated the laws the Office of Civil Rights enforces. Without a standardized federal definition of bullying or harassment in schools, some state legislators question what constitutes bullying in schools within their own borders. The result–fragmented definitions and interpretations that address a myriad of behaviors in schools. For example, the state of Georgia defines bullying as an intentional act occurring on school property to related school functions or activities to data/software used through local school technology that attempts or causes injury or fear (U.S. Department of Education, 2012).

The increased attention regarding bullying may stem from the tragedy at Columbine High School in 1999. This incident was the catalyst to the creation of a host of legislation focused on addressing school violence and bullying in schools. This trend may also contribute to the visibility of suicides linked to bullying and harassment (National Center for Injury Prevention and Control, 2014). Since Columbine, the extant literature documenting the consequences of bullying has grown substantially. The push for anti-bullying legislation placed pressure on national, state, and local governments and schools to develop and implement ways to address bullying. As national organizations, such as the Gay Lesbian Straight Education Network (GLSEN), and the media continue to shine more light on the harsh realities of bullying and harassment, creating safe schools is becoming a key public policy concern. In the 2014 School Climate Report, GLSEN, as well as states, school districts and researchers invested millions in deepening their understanding of bullying in schools. Some questions to consider when assessing what bullying means in your school community/region/state may include, but are not limited to: 1) Why is bullying occurring? 2) What type of bullying is happening in schools? 3) How frequent is bullying and harassment? and 4) Who is being bullied? 5) How accurate is the reporting of bullying? and 6) What can be done to eliminate bullying and harassment?

Although these questions may help shape the national discourse regarding bullying and encouraging legislatures to seriously consider the impact of bullying on children and adults, there is still a need to uncover, consider, and implement culturally responsive practices and policies as preventative measures to keep all students safe, especially those who are members of vulnerable populations (i.e., LGBTQ youth,

Children of Color, children with physical, social, and/or emotional challenges). Although this movement is an opportunity to support universal systems to protect all children, not all children are ensured of learning in a safe school. For example, No federal law has been enacted to protect the rights of LGBTQ youth from being discriminated against, threatened, or intimidated in schools. So, despite efforts to bring bullying in schools to the center stage in the public debate surrounding school legislation and policy over the past decade, there are still populations of children who go unprotected and remain invisible.

Most Americans might agree discrimination on the basis of ability, race, ethnicity, religion, immigration status, gender, sex, and/or ability is wrong. However, these marginalized groups are still targets for being bullied. So why, with over 50% of American citizens stating people who identify as LGBTQ are morally acceptable (GALLUP, 2012) are there still youth who remain an unprotected class? There is a growing need to increase awareness and actions taken to understand the shunning of members from marginalized populations in an effort to create inclusive and welcoming school environments. The groups noted early in this chapter are among the most vulnerable groups within our society, and therefore, there is a need to promote culturally responsive practices and policies and ban discriminatory practices that may target children, educators, and families, who are members of these groups.

Over the last 25 years working in and with K-12 schools, some of the following insights were shared by teachers and school leaders when discussing bullying in schools, especially for children who were bullied due to their sexuality:

> I am not about to deal with this. It's going to make us look bad if we report every little incident of what kids think is bullying. It's not bullying. It's just kids being kids and they need to get some kahunas (balls) and deal with it.

> They don't belong in school...I mean, really, this stuff is not about teaching... if a kid wants to act like this, then he has what's coming to him.

> I was not equipped to deal with this petty stuff. So what, a kid is called a name...deal with it...it's not like the kid can't deal with it like a man.

> If kids don't want to be called a dyke or faggot or gay then they need to act differently...think about how they dress...don't think people don't notice this... they do...so change and it won't be as difficult...it's not like it's out of their control.

In addition to these insights shared by educators and experiences Marcus faced in middle school, other students across the country experience tragedy due to their sexuality. In Oakland, California, in 2013, Sasha Fleischman's skirt was set on fire by a 16 year old student from another school.[1] At the start of 2014, a small Iowa community reflected on the fifth suicide over the last five years due to intense bullying at Southeast Polk High School due to a student's sexuality.[2] In October of 2014, the Los Angeles Unified School District blew the whistle on students bullying student athletes who identified as LGBTQ.[3]

At the same time youth across the United States may be enduring bullying in schools due to their perceived sexuality. In 2013, the Supreme Court overturned two highly anticipated rulings: 1) Defense of Marriage Act, which defined marriage as a union between one man and one woman, with a 5–4 vote declaring it unconstitutional; and 2) the Court decided that supporters of California's Proposition 8, which outlawed same-sex marriage, did not have standing to bring the case to the Court. During that same year, Illinois became the 16th state to some legalize same-sex marriage. However, these decisions are clearly contradictions regarding beliefs, values, school practices influencing children and families who identify as LGBTQ. What do these incidents and insights tell us about the complex state of lesbian/gay/bisexual/transgender/queer issues at this moment in the United States? What do these situations mean for children, educators, school leaders, and families in schools?

WHAT DO WE KNOW?

As of April 2013, 88% (434) of the Fortune 500 companies implemented non-discrimination policies to include sexuality, and 57% (282) included policies regarding gender identity (Human Rights Campaign, 2014). In June of 2014, 1,200 registered voters were polled regarding public support for federal non-discrimination workplace protections for LGBTQ workers. Sixty-three percent of those surveyed favor a federal law protecting LGBTQ people, while 25% oppose it (Human Rights Campaign, 2014b). However, national surveys suggest 21% of LGBTQ respondents were treated unfairly by an employer (Pew Research Center, 2013). As of 2010, 78% of participants who identify as transgender reported having experienced harassment while in the workplace, and 47% reported being mistreated in the hiring, promotion, or retention process due to their gender identity. In 2009, the enactment of the Matthew Shepard & James Byrd Jr. Hate Crimes Prevention Act provides businesses, schools, and government agencies a means to protect LGBTQ members (United States Department of Justice, 2009). Although the U.S. government has not promoted a comprehensive federal antidiscrimination protection law on the basis of sexual orientation or gender identity, policy makers have implemented tougher punishments for hate crimes or violent acts that target people due to their actual or perceived sexual orientation and/or gender identity.

K-12 schools are home to more than 55 million students from a myriad of backgrounds on the basis of race, ethnicity, family structure, native language, immigration status, religion/faith/beliefs, levels of ability and other differences. This cultural diversity reflects the increasing multicultural tapestry within American society (National Association for Education Statistics, 2014). Although the American educational system prohibits discrimination and harassment of students from these vulnerable populations, there are currently no standardized anti-bullying or anti-harassment protections for LGBTQ youth, faculty, or staff in schools. This inherent discrimination on the basis of sexuality and gender identity creates spaces for public debate regarding the nation's current discourse on the lived realities faced by children, families, and educators who identify as LGBTQ in school communities.

Despite these recent advances regarding the rights of LGBTQ populations and 49 states passing anti-bullying legislation, not all schools are safe for students who identify as LGBTQ. These are important steps to addressing serious problems regarding bullying; however, focusing on specific incidents of bullying narrowly defines the issues. Categorizing a myriad of aggressive behaviors towards vulnerable populations under the generic term bullying does not get at the heart of the lived experiences of those who are affected by this discrimination. An emphasis should be placed on the need to promote culturally responsive practices. Talking about bullies and being bullied may encourage people to understand bullying as an individual situation versus discrimination students face on the basis of gender expression, race, class, immigration status, ability, religion/beliefs/faith, gender, sexuality, native language and other differences. These groups may be marginalized in schools; therefore, offering school communities opportunities to deepen their understanding of these critical issues is essential to understanding the underlying conflicts among children, families, community, and schools.

THOSE HIGHEST AT-RISK IN K-12 SCHOOLS

Although bullying ranges from type (e.g., cyberbullying, verbal, physical) and severity (e.g., verbal assault, physical assault), there is research regarding the impact of bullying on the development and well-being of children. Bullying is of significant concern, because it is often less visible or identifiable than other academic, social or emotional concerns. For the purpose of this chapter, bullying is defined as a form of unwanted or intentional aggression, harassment, abuse or violence. It is a systematic use of power including, but not limited to, physical aggression (i.e., pushing, shoving, punching, kicking, use of weapons), verbal aggression (i.e., using degrading language towards another person, humiliation, spreading rumors, name-calling), social aggression (i.e., exclusiveness), and cyber bullying (i.e., the use of social media to embarrass, harass, or abuse) (Espelage & Holt, 2012; Olweus, 1993; Vaillancourt, McDougall, Hymel, Krygsman, Miller, Stiver, & Davis, 2008; Wade & Beran, 2011).

There is an urgency to better understand the immediate and long-term impact bulling may have on children's development, because, as noted earlier in the chapter, incidents may go unreported and the impact of bullying is often unidentifiable or invisible. The concern lies knowing most children spend at least 30 hours a week in school. The percentage of children bullied in schools for 12 to 18 year olds is approximately 28% (Robers, Zhang, Truman, & Snyder, 2012). Other studies suggest comparable percentages of students who admit to bullying peers (Wang, Iannotti, & Nansel, 2009).

Those who are bullied are among the most vulnerable populations. These groups are vulnerable due to learning differences (Rose, Espelage, Aragon, & Elliot, 2011), race/ethnicity (Cook, Williams, Guerra, Kim, & Sadek, 2010), sexual orientation (Kosciw, Greylak, Bartkiewicz, Boesen, & Palmer, 2012; Russell, Kosciw, Hom, & Saewye, 2010), gender expression (i.e., traditional, heterosexual gender norms are expected for girls and boys) (Kosciw et al., 2012; Meyer, 2008), immigration

5

status, native language, and religion/beliefs/faith. Historically, extant literature has omitted, distorted or under researched the experiences of these student groups. There is a need to examine bullying dynamics surrounding these marginalized school-age populations. Students with learning differences are twice as likely to be identified as victims and perpetrators as their general education counterparts (see Rose, Espelage, Aragon, & Elliot, 2011). These children are often perceived as having low social and cognitive skills (Rose et al., 2011) and are often socially rejected by their peers (Baumeister, Storch, & Geffken, 2008). Students who identify as LGBTQ experience homophobic teasing and derogatory language (Espelage, Basile, & Hamburger, 2012; Kosciw, Greytak, & Diaz, 2009; Poteat & Espelage, 2005; Poteat & Rivers, 2010). This group of students often encounters more victimization than their heterosexual counterparts (Espelage, Aragon, Birkett, & Koenig, 2008; Kosciw et al., 2009). Students who identify as Children of Color, specifically Black children, are less likely to report bullying and victimization; however, Black youth experience more hostile acts than their White or Latino/a counterparts (Turner, Finkelhor, Hamby, Shattuck, & Ormrod, 2011). Although these student populations experience a lack of response from educators, many school leaders, teachers, and support staff lack the training to address bullying, may not be aware of when or how to address it, and might not know ways to prevent bullying from occurring (Espelage, 2012; Tremlow, 2006).

Although teachers and school leaders may lack the necessary training to address bullying in schools, it is also important to note a number of anti-bullying programs implemented in schools are often unsuccessful. Sustainability is the key (Tremlow, 2006). Anti-bullying programs are often not successful due to the complexities associated with lack of awareness, funding, resources, and/or faculty/administrator turnover. Children realize faculty and school leaders have the ability to interrupt bullying; however, if educators witness the incidents and still continue to allow it, there is a grave concern for the safety of all children. For example, bystanders may not report bullying, because they fear retaliation or have conflicting loyalties with their peers. A canned or scripted anti-bullying curriculum for prevention and intervention is simply not enough to address these issues.

According to bullying statistics from LGBTQ communities, approximately 25% of all students from elementary school through high school are victims of bullying and harassment because of their race, ethnicity, gender, ability, religion or sexual orientation. Unfortunately, the primary reason children are bullied is due to something that may set children apart from other children in school, such as sexual orientation. The Gay Lesbian Straight Education Network (GLSEN) conducts surveys across the country asking LGBTQ youth to share their experiences in schools (Kosciw, J. G., Greytak, E. A., Bartkiewicz, M. J., Boesen, M. J., Palmer, N. A., 2011). The sample consisted of 8,584 students between the ages of 13 to 20. Students were surveyed from all 50 states, including the District of Columbia. Two-thirds (67.9%) of the sample identified as White, 49.6% were female, and 61.3% were lesbian or gay with students in grades 6–12 and most students in grades 10–11. Six out of

10 LGBTQ teens identify themselves as feeling unsafe in school. And over 80% have been verbally harassed because of their sexual orientation. In the latest GLSEN survey with over 8,000 youth participating, 65% of participants frequently heard the words "gay" and "dyke" used in a derogatory way in school (Kosciw, Greytak, Bartkiewicz, Boesen, & Palmer, 2014).

LGBTQ youth are two to three times more likely to attempt or commit suicide than any other youth group. Approximately 30% of suicides are related to a sexual identity crisis. Those who identify as LGBTQ are also at risk of missing school, because they feel unsafe. This same group of students is also at-risk of dropping out of school due to being bullied. The findings suggest teens are bullied because of their perceived sexual orientation or What is gender expression? Gender expression is the way in which an individual choose to express being a girl or a boy. In Western society, acting as "like a girl" may include specific ways of dressing, speaking, interacting, and behaving. The same may hold true for a boy. Boys may be socialized to understand what it means to be 'a man.' In regards to this survey, teens were bullied due to their appearance; in other words, to what extent boys and girls dressed or physically appeared as "boys" or "girls." Adolescents are at a pivotal point in their young adult lives in which they are discovering who they are, their beliefs, values, and ways of knowing what it means to be an adult. This time is critical to a young person's development; therefore, being bullied and/or harassed for their sexual orientation and/or gender expression could negatively influence their sense of self.

For those who identify as LGBTQ, 9 out of 10 students reported being bullied in school due to their sexual orientation. More than half of those who were bullied reported being physically harassed and another 25% indicating they were physically assaulted. Unfortunately, many adolescents who experience bullying and/ or harassment for their sexual orientation and/or gender expression are reluctant to share their experiences with educators and/or school leaders. The students' hesitation to report bullying and/or harassment was due to the lack of responses from school community members (i.e., teachers and administrators). For those students who reported a bullying incident, 30% of all students within the school community personnel did not resolve the issue. For those who identify as LGBTQ, 85% of students felt a lack of support from teachers and school leaders when they were harassed or bullied due to their sexual orientation, perceived sexual orientation, and/or gender expression (Kosciw et al., 2010). These findings suggest bullying and harassment, especially for LGBTQ populations, is more systemic and problematic for this vulnerable student population versus other populations.

THE NEED FOR CRITICAL DIALOGUE AND ACTION

What are some reasons schools may not engage in this critical dialogue despite recent advances regarding LGBTQ rights and anti-bullying mandates? Educators and school leaders may be concerned about the possible backlash from community members. As the movement continues to develop, tensions may rise from early LGBTQ liberation beginnings to more complex dialogue regarding curriculum, pedagogy, policy, and practice. There is a need for educators to deepen their understanding of the challenges facing vulnerable populations in school communities as well as their role in perpetuating the socially constructed ways in which we understand and embrace Cultural responsiveness is a call to action requiring educators and school leaders to look within, reflect on their cultural knowledge and identity, and understanding how their beliefs, values, and ways of understanding influence their interactions, decisions made, and ability/willingness to interrupt oppressive practices and policies in schools. This movement is more than teaching the parts of a cell, algebra or Roman history.

The key to promoting a movement focusing on issues of cultural responsiveness relies on building bridges among children, families, educators, communities, and society. A critical key to bridge building is acknowledging and valuing the voices of those served. Bridge building is not a solo act. And those who engage in this work successfully build authentic culturally responsive communities by promoting visibility, awareness, and meaningful dialogue among its members. Within this work, all voices are valued and recognized. For example, for those engaged in working with agendered youth (i.e., youth who refer to themselves using the term "they" as opposed to the gender normative pronouns "he" or "she") (see http://www.huffingtonpost.com/2014/06/03/chloe-aftel-agender_n_5433867.html), how often have adults participated in dialogue with youth, families, and community members committed to understanding their lived realities in schools?

For several years, I was an adjunct professor with aspiring teachers and school leaders while I was a public school leader. I worked with hundreds of candidates; however, no one worked in a school in which children, families and/or community members were asked to engage in this critical dialogue and consider the vital role community membership plays in creating culturally responsive practices and policies (i.e., curriculum, pedagogy, vision, mission, student handbook, positive behavior interventions, school policy). My eight year old daughter asked if she could address the need for a critical dialogue regarding cultural responsiveness when she presented at a regional conference to over 100 educators:

> When I was five, I learned what it meant to be a girl and what it meant to be a boy from my kindergarten teacher. On my first day of school, she separated us. Boys were in one line and girls were in another. I asked, "Why are we not allowed to be in line with one another? Can't we all get along?" The teacher replied, "Because I said so…and this is how we do it." The same teacher posted colors and their names along the whiteboard. She informed us pink was for girls and blue was for boys. I didn't understand how colors belonged to certain groups of people based on whether I was a boy or a girl. It didn't make sense to me. I liked blue. In fact, my favorite color was electric green, but I didn't want to say anything, because I didn't want my teacher to embarrass me, so I stayed quiet. When it came time for Halloween, I wanted to be Darth Vader. My teacher and the girls

in my class told me only boys could be Darth Vader. Girls were princesses and allegedly love My Pretty Pony, but I didn't. I was a HUGE Star Wars fan. My mommies were my Storm Troopers that year. I didn't listen to my teacher, and wore the costume anyway, but I was called names by the girls in my class. I didn't let it bother me. I felt sorry for them, because they were missing out in being a kid. My kindergarten teacher wasn't very nice to me. She didn't seem to understand me. I questioned why we had to use separate bathrooms for boys and girls. I didn't understand. When I was in preschool, we shared a bathroom. When I am at home, I share a bathroom. I thought school was about being a family. My kindergarten teacher said, "This is what we do here and we have always done it this way." She didn't answer my question. The same kindergarten teacher picked five boys in a row to be Star of Week. I didn't understand. My two friends and I protested on the school bus. We chanted and pounded on the backs of the school bus seats. We chanted, "We want the girls!" The boys didn't seem to know any better. Instead of asking us what we were chanting about, they just started pounding on the backs of their seats and saying, "We want the boys!" The bus driver let us protest. I came home and told my mom what happened. She asked if I had spoken with my teacher. I didn't know I was supposed to do that first. My mom spoke with the teacher, but was very disappointed to find out she wasn't going to talk to my friends and I. She didn't want to talk to us about what my mom called the hidden curriculum. The next Friday, she chose a girl. The boys booed and the girls cheered while we sat on the carpet and heard the news. I sat there quietly with my legs like a pretzel and my hands on my lap. My mom asked me why I responded in that way. I said, "I didn't think it was right to throw it in her face. I wanted to do the right thing, so I sat there quietly." I wished my teacher knew how to talk about these things. It's sad to think she is a teacher and didn't feel comfortable talking to five year olds about real things.

What is critical is building community in which no one is silenced, and being different is considered the cornerstone of an authentic, culturally responsive school. There is a need to build nurturing school communities in which children, educators, school leaders, families and community members believe they are part of something larger than themselves. At the heart of this cultural responsiveness is nurturing empathic responses, which creates space for self and communal understanding as well as for teaching critical issues aligned with honoring differences. By promoting this work in schools, teachers and school leaders may have the capacity and willingness to engage in dialogue regarding gender, sexuality, race, class, ability, as well as other perceived controversial or taboo topics. If adults are prepared for these conversations, they may be more willing to talk with and listen to children discuss these issues as well. Therefore, cultural responsiveness encourages bridge building and affords school community members with opportunities to reflect on themselves, identify critical issues, and collectively work through differences versus choosing to ignore the lived experiences of vulnerable populations.

Some means of assessing to what extent school communities engage in culturally responsive work is to review may include the following:

Policy: To what extent do educators, school leaders, families, community members, and children understand school policies and the extent of their inclusivity? To what extent do school policies protect vulnerable populations? How do we know if these policies are working? To what extent are school policies aligned with supporting culturally responsive curriculum? Pedagogy? Policy-making? Why or why not?

Anti-Bullying Policies: To what extent are vulnerable populations acknowledged? To what extent are LGBTQ populations protected under anti-bullying and harassment school policies? To what extent are LGBTQ populations protected under hate speech?[4]

School Forms: To what extent are school forms inclusive? Why or why not? Do school forms ask to identify a "Mother" and "Father" versus Family Member(s)?

Bathrooms: To what extent are gender neutral bathrooms identified within schools?

School Lines: How often are boys and girls separated according to gender-oriented lines they stand in, lunch groups, interest areas, and activities?

Media/Literature: How often are vulnerable populations represented throughout media and literature presented to the children? For example, how often are boys and girls represented on media posted within the school? To what extent are books within the curriculum empowering boys and girls? To what extent do books or media in the library interrupt gender-based stereotypes? To what extent do books or media used throughout the curriculum interrupt gender-based stereotypes? How often is race discussed in school through media/literature selections? Why or why not? In what context? How are discussions facilitated? How often are learning differences acknowledged? Why or why not? How often is native language or citizenship discussed? Why or why not?

Pedagogy: How often are vulnerable populations discussed within the school community? If yes, how so? If not, why not? For example, how often do teachers and school leaders discuss the strengths and challenges facing boys and girls throughout their learning? How often are teachers and school leaders discussing the needs of girls and boys throughout their learning? To what extent are teachers and school leaders prepared to address how gender may influence pedagogy?

Discipline: How often does the school assess who receives office referrals, classroom discipline, and/or types of referrals/issues within the school based on gender?

Committee Work: How many school-wide and/or district-wide committees incorporate children, families, and community members? How are members chosen to serve on each committee? To what extent is the process an authentic means of selecting members who represent the community's cultural diversity?

Professional Learning: How often is cultural responsiveness discussed throughout professional learning opportunities within the school and/or district? To what extent is data collected to deepen understanding regarding school practices being implemented on the basis of race, class, sexuality, religion/ beliefs/faith, immigration status, ability (mental and physical), native language, gender, family structure, gender expression, and other dimensions of diversity?

School Organizations: To what extent do school offerings embrace inclusive membership? To what extent do student organizations empower all children to participate? To what extent do student organizations focus on empowering students deepen their understanding of social justice, including Gay Straight Alliances (GSAs)?

Community Outreach: To what extent does your school community reach out to local, regional, state, national, and/or global organizations (i.e., Gay Lesbian Straight Education Network, National Association for the Advancement of Colored People, Esperanza, Honor Good Deeds, Human Rights Campaign, Welcoming Schools, Teaching Tolerance, American Civil Liberties Union, National Fair Housing Association, Center for Media Justice, Race Forward, National Urban League, National Council of La Raza, Community School Coalition)? Why or why not? To what extent are these relationships with organizations contributing to creating safe and culturally responsive spaces within your school community? Why or why not? To what extent are they contributing to revising curriculum, pedagogy, expectations, beliefs, values, mission, vision, policy, and/or school practices?

WHAT IS CULTURAL RESPONSIVENESS?

How and what we learn are at the heart of what it means to be human. It is through learning that we deepen understanding of self, recreation of self, and capacity of self in relation to others. An individual's ability to systemically think of oneself in relation to others within a learning organization is critical to supporting them in better understanding themselves as well as the world around them. Therefore, learning is ultimately a shared vision and mission that fosters a commitment to build upon individual strengths, develops a larger picture of what lies beyond individual selves, and unearths possible shortcomings in an effort for people to play a vital role in the generative process of learning (Boske, 2011; Boske, 2012; Boske & Diem, 2012; Tooms & Boske, 2010).

In order to further develop an intrinsic sense of connection among ourselves, those we serve in school communities, and communities-at-large, there is a need for learning organizations to examine their expansive patterns of thinking, learning, and doing to promote an authentic collective in ways for us to learn about one another as well as with each other. To engage in this process may involve an individual's need to become more culturally aware and responsive to communities-at-large. Engaging in cultural responsiveness bridges meaningful relations among children, families, schools, and communities by valuing and embedding lived sociocultural realities throughout learning (Boske, 2011b; Boske, 2012).

Culturally responsive teaching and leading is complex. Although there may be a cry for change throughout educational settings, specifically in creating safe learning spaces for all school community members, members may be incredibly resistant to change. Not only are students deepening their understanding of self, but educators and leaders are developing their intellectual, emotional, social, and political learning through cultural referents (Boske, in press 2015; Ladson-Billings, 1992). One means of addressing a school community's capacity for learning as a collective is assessing a school community's cultural responsiveness (i.e., teaching, leading, practice, and policy). Geneva Gay (2010) suggests culturally responsive teaching is holistic, because a teacher considers the whole child (i.e., sociocultural experiences, cultural identify, and heritage). A culturally responsive teacher uses a student's strengths by building on cultural knowledge, prior lived experiences, and diverse learning styles to engage students in appropriate and effective learning. The practice legitimizes cultural heritages of diverse ethnic groups affecting a student's attitudes and dispositions throughout the formal curriculum. For example, Children of Color have opportunities to have their culturally valued knowledge acknowledged, valued, and embedded within the curriculum content (Hollins, 1996). Children's cultural excellence is celebrated and all children are encouraged to engage with their peers as extended family members who assist, support, and nurture ideas as well as each other (Ladson-Billings, 1994).

These practices not only involve teachers and holistic approaches, they include curriculum development, context, climate, relationships, pedagogy, and assessments. Culturally responsive teaching is inclusive. Students are actively engaged in their learning, performance, and outcomes. Therefore, students are empowered to increase their academic competence, self-efficacy, and collective accomplishments. For those who engage in culturally responsive teaching, there is a need for the implementation of a student-centered process encouraging critical democratic pedagogy for self and social change (Shor, 1992). Students understand growth as an active process in which authentic collaborations and social process is aligned with an individual's ability to grow (i.e., develop critical curiosity, develop habits of inquiry, and promote social change).

Culturally responsive teaching encourages teachers to respect the culture and experiences of diverse groups as viable resources for teaching and learning. The strengths and accomplishments of all students is essential to deepening students' ways of knowing. For example, story-telling may be a unique lived experience among Black students. These interactions are perceived as a gift and may be used to teach writing skills. James Banks (1991) suggests some Students of Color may want to participate in cooperative learning or study in small groups. Therefore, culturally responsive teaching has the potential to provide educational opportunities that empower vulnerable populations. The key to promoting these practices as transformative involves the children and their capacity to develop, reflect, and make decisions that influence their personal, social, political, and economic actions. The implementation of cultural responsiveness may lead to liberating learning experiences, especially for Students of Color (Asante, 1991/1992; Au, 1993; Erickson, 1987; Gordon, 1993; Lipman, 1995; Pewewardy, 1994; Philips, 1983), because the practice guides students in understanding there are multiple versions of truth due to the myriad of lived experiences. Students who engage in cultural responsiveness may expand upon their insights, interconnections among self and others (e.g., individual, local, regional, state, nationally, internationally), renewed knowledge base, and understanding knowledge is continuously evolving (Chapman, 1994; M. Foster, 1995; Hollins, 1996; Hollins, King, & Hayman, 1994; Ladson-Billings, 1992, 1994, 1995a, 1995b; Lee, 1993; Lee & Slaughter-Defoe, 1995). Although culturally responsive teaching often focuses on the Students of Color (Gay, 2010), there are elements of this educational process that can transfer to the highest at-risk LGBTQ populations in schools (Boske, 2011a).

PROMOTING COMPREHENSIVE CULTURALLY RESPONSIVE PRACTICES AND POLICIES FOR THE HIGHEST AT-RISK STUDENT POPULATION

Over the last decade, legislatures worked to formally address bullying in schools; however, they have often fall short of protecting LGBTQ populations in schools. Although states have anti-bullying and anti-harassment laws, these laws did not include sexual orientation and/or gender identity as explicit categories alongside other vulnerable groups on the basis of race, ethnicity, religion, ability, and national origin. Although it is an ethical responsibility to ensure all students have the opportunity to learn in a culturally responsive environment, part of this responsibility involves advocating for legislation and policy designed to not only eliminate bullying in schools, but to foster culturally responsive practices and policies. Despite sharing the research findings, providing examples of ways to prevent bulling in schools, and the need to promote anti-LGBTQ bullying, legislators remain reluctant to mandate all states and schools to protect LGBTQ populations. Because LGBTQ students may attend schools without comprehensive laws and policies, they continue hearing words such as gay, dyke, homo, and faggot in school. The generic anti-bullying laws are directed at policing harassment by prohibiting these behaviors from occurring in schools. Schools put out fires and at times react to the negative consequences of bullying; however, schools do very little to move toward preventing bullying. The rate at which students are being bullied and/or harassed continues to remain constant unless the school implemented a comprehensive anti-bullying policy. In those cases, there were no reported increases in bullying or harassment, which may suggest these comprehensive policies made a difference in the lives of students.

Families who attempt to protect their children from bullying wonder how school staff can ignore bullying or choose not to resolve these issues. And that is the question at hand, isn't it? How do we create schools in which children, families, educators, and community members' contributions are valued, cherished, appreciated, and nurtured? Although the legal rights of children and families from vulnerable populations may be shifting, creating spaces for critical dialogue for these advances in curriculum, pedagogy, and policy to enhance school climate is essential to this process. However, for those who work in schools, homophobia, racism, classism, and other forms of oppression are alive and well. And for those who identify as progressive schools, there is still a need to create nurturing spaces for all school community members who do not conform to society's gender and sexuality norms. The question remains: How do we move forward?

Educators and policy makers promoting safe schools need comprehensive anti-bullying and anti-harassment policies that clearly outline the school's responsibility to eliminate bullying practices. Building bridges among families, children, teachers, school leaders, community members, and organizations is essential to creating a collaborative to ban bullying and create a climate in which culturally responsive practices and policies are conducive to improving student learning for all students, especially those who are members of vulnerable populations. When students are attending schools with comprehensive bullying laws (e.g., LGBTQ populations are included as an enumerated group), students reported hearing less homophobic remarks versus states in which no law or generic anti-bullying/anti-harassment laws were implemented (Kosciw et al., 2011, 2014). Furthermore, schools that incorporate comprehensive bullying policies were also more likely to offer culturally supportive on-campus alliances (i.e., GSAs, diversity clubs, global learning) which provided safe, affirming, and responsive spaces for students who identify as LGBTQ (Kosciw et al., 2011, 2014). These schools were more likely to publicly announce safe spaces throughout the school, which suggested students could find support among staff, teachers, and school leaders (Kosciw et al., 2011, 2014). Such efforts provide LGBTQ students with support at the state and local levels and help students feel safer in school. This holistic approach to addressing cultural responsiveness, especially with LGBTQ populations, is essential to creating safe spaces, encouraging critical dialogue, developing meaningful relationships, and promoting policies that improve the social, emotional, and academic experiences of all students.

Several years ago, my colleagues and I worked together to address the disparities facing our middle school. We created the Multicultural Task Force in an effort to provide spaces for educators and school leaders to become more aware of critical issues facing vulnerable populations. One of the most difficult conversations involved the discussion of LGBTQ populations. I was quickly reminded that although teachers and school leaders wanted to make schools safe for all children, those who identified as LGBTQ were not safe at this middle school. I was also alarmed, because my colleagues did not know I identified as queer. LGBTQ populations were not a protected group in the state in which I worked. There were no personnel policies protecting me from being fired. I was not in a position to come out to my colleagues, and after listening to their reactions to the discussion of LGBTQ youth, I was not willing to take a risk and come out. Some teachers' comments ranged from "Those kids don't belong here" to "It's alright as long as I don't have to see it" to "It's against God's word" to "I am a Christian and those kids are going to hell" to "Not in my classroom…I will have none of that" to "If those boys just acted like real men, they wouldn't have this problem" to "I am not talking about sex in my classroom" to "I could see myself getting fired and hauled in by the union for talking about this stuff" to "Those poor kids must have been molested and lost their way" to "I don't know how anyone could hire one of them as a teacher, because they could be child molesters." It was a difficult conversation, but it was even more difficult facilitating how to make schools safe for LGBTQ teachers and staff. No matter how often we discussed the need to interrupt classroom discussions regarding gender stereotypes and homophobia, overall, my colleagues were not comfortable engaging in that critical conversation. We emphasized the need for a nurturing environment; however, when discussing LGBTQ populations, the conversation did not align itself with protecting this vulnerable population. Creating a protective community for LGBTQ adults and children in school was not a priority.

I spent several years working with school leaders and teachers within a large urban school district regarding the need to promote culturally responsive practices and policies for all children. Some teachers wondered, "What might a culturally responsive school look like for both children and adults?" There would be a need to assess the school community's understanding of vulnerable populations, their lived experiences, and collect data regarding student learning and academic success. We discussed the role of the union in supporting educators emotionally and professionally as they engaged in new practices. We emphasized the need to build bridges among ourselves, families, and community-at-large. This collaboration had the potential to mobilize families and foster meaningful relationships to discuss critical issues facing children and families on the basis of race, class, gender, sexuality, immigration status, native language, ability (mental and physical), religion/faith/beliefs, and other differences. Teachers, school leaders, and staff members conversed about the need to provide learning opportunities through curriculum assessments, review of pedagogical practices, school policies, cultural student groups, school vision and mission, and biases.

There was a need to examine current practices and move beyond celebrating specific cultural groups through holidays and heroes/heroines. The new focus–to integrate the lived experiences of marginalized populations through a myriad of perspectives in an effort to foster critical dialogue and social change. In order to promote cultural responsiveness, agreeing to reframe the school's focus was the first step. This refocus was a call for everyone to approach school practices and policies in new ways. For example, we examined the math, science, social studies, language arts, and specials' curriculum. We assessed to what extent specific vulnerable groups were identified within content areas. Educators documented disparities among content areas, grade levels, and opportunities for learning for all students. School leaders and teachers did not integrate a curriculum that integrated the contributions, history, struggles, or critical issues in the day-to-day school practices across all subject areas. For example, no one addressed literature reflecting diverse families including single headed households, blended, adopted, bi/multiracial, and/or LGBTQ families. There was a need to consider how school practices aligned with this new lens to understanding the existence of a broad range of families. When considering school application forms, the forms identified "mother" and "father" versus "family member(s)." Educators reconsidered their approach to activities regarding Father's Day, Mother's Day, and family lineage assignments. School leaders and educators recognized how often children were affected by how the school district perpetuated oppressive school customs.

Other educators noted the need to "queer the curriculum" by providing spaces for students to critically examine the impact of LGBTQ authors, musicians, and poets have on American and world-wide culture (e.g., Francisco Alarcon, Oscar Wilde, Charles Rice-Gonzalez, Tennessee Williams, Virginia Woolf, Ricky Martin, Wanda Sykes, Langston Hughes, Angelina Weld Grimke, Emily Dickenson, Ehtel Waters, Gertrude Rainey, Frank Ocean, Meshell Ndegeocello, Bessie Smith, Countee Cullen, Josephine Baker, and others). Some teachers suggested including the Lavender Scare, Stonewall Riots, overturning Defense of Marriage Act (D.O.M.A.), and the LGBTQ acceptance into the military as pivotal historical events. However, integrating LGBTQ histories in K-12 curriculum may not be easy to promote.

BUILDING BRIDGES IN NORTHEAST OHIO TO PROMOTE CULTURALLY
RESPONSIVE PRACTICES AND POLICIES

My line of research focuses on how teachers and school leaders understand the promotion of culturally responsive practices and policies under the umbrella of social justice and equity. I began collecting data on the schooling experiences of children, families, teachers, school leaders, and community members to fill a critical void in the extant literature regarding how K-12 US schools served vulnerable populations. Despite cultural shifts in demographics across schools, children still receive the overwhelming message from society that members of the cultural majority (i.e., White, middle/upper class, English speaker, heterosexual, able body and mind, Christian, two-parent heterosexual family, American citizen) are in positions of power to decide what is and is not deemed appropriate. It is not uncommon to hear a myriad of debates from politicians, preachers, and/or officials to debate whether or not we live in a post-racial society and/or whether to perceive LGBTQ protections as civil rights.

16

Because the national conversation around anti-bullying and harassment seems framed around Title VI of the Civil Rights Act of 1964 (i.e., prohibiting discrimination on the basis of an individual's race, color, or national origin with regards to programs and activities receiving federal financial assistance), Title IX of the Education Amendments of 1972 (i.e., prohibits discrimination on the basis of sex), and Section 504 of the Rehabilitation Act of 1973 and Title II of the Americans with Disabilities Act of 1990, Americans might assume all children are members of a protected class; however, little movement has occurred to protect a child's sexual orientation or gender identity, which needs to be conceptualized as another protected class of citizens.

Findings from studies throughout school leadership preparation programs, teacher leadership preparation, as well as urban, suburban, and rural school communities suggest a lack of knowledge and understanding of cultural responsiveness and the need for action to create safe and affirming schools for all children, especially those from vulnerable populations (Boske, 2011; Kosciw et al., 2011; Vossekuil, Reddy, & Fein, 2000). Over the last 25 years in K-12 schools and higher education, I continue to commit myself to building bridges among the university, K-12 schools, and nonprofit organizations in an effort to promote culturally responsive practices and policies in schools. There is a need to create spaces for culturally responsive work in schools as a response to the number of children who experience harassment and/or bullying in schools, because they are members of vulnerable populations. Over the last two years, several organizations and educators have committed to promoting this work in Northeast Ohio: National Association for the Advancement of Colored People (NAACP), Gay Lesbian Straight Education Network (GLSEN), Parents Friends of Lesbians and Gays (PFLAG), Honor Good Deeds, Sistah Sinema, American Civil Liberties Union (ACLU), Beyond Borders, Ambition Limitless, Welcoming Schools, Northeast Ohio Diversity Center, Esperanza, Dare2Care, Human Rights Campaign (HRC), Equality Ohio, Arts-Inspired Education, Lesbian Gay Bisexual Transgender Community Center (LGBT), professors, teachers, school leaders, K-12 students, and other community members.

There is a need to question, interrogate, and rethink why schools engage in oppressive practices and policies that isolate marginalized populations. The myriad of authors in this book who range from children to teachers to school leaders to community organizations to scholars assert the need for a prophetic voice. This voice questions why Children of Color, children who identify as lesbian/gay/bisexual/transgender/queer (LGBTQ), children who receive special education services, and children who are identified as outliers continue to undergo discrimination based on their identity. The authors emphasize the need for revitalization, reform, and revolution. This movement begins with each of us looking within and examining how we understand dimensions of diversity. Their narratives remind us of the power of a voice. Although their voices have gone unheard, this book provides a vehicle to not only question current school policies and practices that perpetuate disparities among vulnerable populations, but a means to propose and redesign an agenda for systemic reform.

17

Together, we propose a framework for the field of education preparation focusing on activist-oriented practices with an embedded prophetic and a pragmatic voice. And activist-oriented mindset centers on doing this important work in schools by promoting social justice and equity (Bogotch, 2002). By prophetic, we emphasize a framework that challenges and calls for a revolutionary response in how schools empower marginalized populations, and in this case, those who are often the victims of bullying. This message encourages those who engage in this work to consider how to utilize courage and personal knowing to interrupt oppressive practices and policies within various educational levels in school communities.

This call may be considered radical, and even dangerous, in some contexts, because those who serve are committed to making substantive changes to educational practices and policies. Educators will position themselves in places and spaces to disrupt the discourse and facilitate a prophetic discourse questioning current power structures with K-12 US public schools. The necessary outcome—eliminating oppressive practices and policies and rebuilding authentic, meaningful relationships. Such efforts have the capacity to promote democracy, equity, and social justice throughout schools to create safe and culturally responsive learning environments. In order to meet the challenges associated with this daunting task, those who engage in this work are held accountable for asking critical questions, assessing the impact of current learning spaces, proposing new ways of understanding, and creating and sustaining equitable learning spaces for all children.

This calling also encourages school community members to be actively involved in proposing and designing an agenda of reform to rid the system and writ large, oppressive policies and practices that often lead to shameful discriminatory results. As important as it is to create safe spaces for all children, especially for those who live on the margins, it is not merely enough to add school or state policies (i.e., sexual orientation or gender identity), and for those who promote preventative measures, mandating legislation can be perceived as costly (Ferrell-Smith, 2003). For those who are victimized, adding these enumerated groups to already in-place anti-bullying policies or erect policies that simply outlaw bullying is not effective. To effectively address anti-bullying and legislation addressing anti-bullying, proactive, holistic, and systemic elements (i.e., attitudes, beliefs, interactions towards marginalized populations, curriculum, pedagogy, school practices, cultural responsiveness, community involvement, local/regional/state/federal policies) should be considered.

NOTES

[1] Sasha identified as an agendered youth. An agendered youth is someone who identifies as gender neutral; in other words, it is a term to describe someone without gender. This person can be any physical sex, but the person's body does not necessarily correspond with their lack of gender identity. The student who seriously burned Sasha was charged as an adult with two felony hate crimes.

[2] http://www.pasadenastarnews.com/social-affairs/20141014/lausd-blowing-the-whistle-on-bullying-and-hazing-of-lgbt-student-athletes

[3]   http://www.huffingtonpost.com/news/bullied-gay-teens/
[4]   http://www.nydailynews.com/news/national/school-staff-bullies-lesbian-student-anti-gay-slurs-calls-
      lawsuit-article-1.1560922

REFERENCES

Asante, M. K. (1991/1992). Afrocentric curriculum. *Educational Leadership, 49*(4), 28–31.

Au, K. H. (1993). *Literacy instruction in multicultural settings.* New York, NY: Harcourt Brace.

Baumeister, A. L., Storch, E. A., & Geffken, G. R. (2008). Peer victimization in children with learning disabilities. *Child and Adolescent Social Work Journal, 25,* 11–23.

Boske, C. (2011a). My name is Michelle: A real-life case to raise consciousness. *Journal of Cases in Educational Leadership on Queer Theory/Queer Cases [Special issue], 14*(2), 49–60.

Boske, C. (2011b). Sense-making reflective practice: Preparing school leaders for non-text-based understandings. *Journal of Curriculum Theorizing, 27*(2), 82–100.

Boske, C. (2012). *Educational leadership: Building bridges among ideas, schools and nations.* Charlotte, NC: Information Age Publishing.

Boske, C., & Diem, S. (2012). *Global leadership for social justice: Taking it from the field to practice.* Oxford, England: Emerald Publishing.

Chapman, I. T. (1994). Dissin' the dialectic on discourse surface differences. *Composition Chronicle, 7*(7), 4–7.

Cook, C. R., Williams, K. R., Guerra, N. G., Kim, T. E., & Sadek, S. (20 10). Predictors of bullying and victimization in childhood and adolescence: A meta-analytic investigation. *School Psychology Quarterly, 25*(2), 65–83.

Erickson, F. (1987). Transformation and school success: The politics and culture of educational achievement. *Anthropology and Education Quarterly, 18*(4), 335–383.

Espelage, D. L. (2012). Bullying prevention: A research dialogue with Dorothy Espelage. *Prevention Researcher, 19*(3), 17–19.

Espelage, D. L., & Holt, M. K. (2012). Understanding and preventing bullying and sexual harassment in school. In K. R. Harris, S. Graham, T. Urdan, S. Graham, J. M. Royer, & M. Zeidner (Eds.), *APA educational psychology handbook: Individual differences and cultural and contextual factors* (Vol. 2, pp. 391–416). Washington, DC: American Psychological Association.

Espelage, D. L., Aragon, S. R., Birkett, M., & Koenig, B. W. (2008). Homophobic teasing, psychological outcomes, and sexual orientation among high school students: What influences do parents and schools have? *School Psychology Review, 37,* 202–216.

Espelage, D. L., Basile, K. C., & Hamburger, M. E. (2012). Bullying experiences and co-occurring sexual violence perpetration among middle school students: Shared and unique risk factors. *Journal of Adolescent Health, 50,* 60–65.

Feagin, J., Orum, A., & Sjoberg, G. (Eds.). (1991). *A case for case study.* Chapel Hill, NC: University of North Carolina Press.

Ferrell-Smith, F. (2003). *Tackling the schoolyard bully: Combining policy making with prevention.* Washington, DC: National Conference of State Legislatures.

Foster, M. (1995). African American teachers and culturally relevant pedagogy. In J. A. Banks & C. A. M. Banks (Eds.), *Handbook of research on multicultural education* (pp. 570–581). New York, NY: Macmillan.

GALLUP. (2012). *Americans' acceptance of gay relations crosses 54% threshold.* Retrieved from http://www.gallup.com/poll/154634/acceptance-gay-lesbian-relations-new-normal.aspx

Gay, G. (2010). *Culturally responsive teaching: Theory, research, & practice.* New York, NY: Teachers College Press.

Gordon, B. M. (1993). African American cultural knowledge and liberatory education; Dilemmas, problems, and potentials in a postmodern American society. *Urban Education, 27*(4), 448–470.

Hollins, E. R. (1996). *Culture in school learning: Revealing the deep meaning.* Mahwah, NJ: Erlbaum.

Hollins, E. R., King, J. E., & Hayman, W. C. (Eds.). (1994). *Teaching diverse populations: Formulating a knowledge base.* Albany, NY: State University of New York Press.

Human Rights Campaign. (2014a). *Employment non-discrimination act.* Retrieved from http://www.hrc.org/resources/entry/employment-non-discrimination-act

Human Rights Campaign. (2014b). *New HRC data: American public strongly supports federal non-discrimination protections.* Retrieved from http://www.hrc.org/press-releases/entry/new-hrc-data-american-public-strongly-supports-federal-non-discrimination-p

Kosciw, J. G., Greytak, E. A., & Diaz, E. M. (2009). Who, what, when, where, and why: Demographic and ecological factors contributing to hostile school climate for lesbian, gay, bisexual, and transgender youth. *Journal of Youth and Adolescence, 38,* 976–988.

Kosciw, J. G., Greytak, E. A., Bartkiewicz, M. J., Boesen, M. J., & Palmer, N. A. (2012). *The 2011 National School Climate Survey: The experiences of lesbian, gay, bisexual, and transgender youth in our nation's schools.* New York, NY: Gay Lesbian Straight Education Network.

Kosciw, J. G., Greytak, E. A., Bartkiewicz, M. J., Boesen, M. J., & Palmer, N. A. (2014). *The 2013 national school climate survey: The experiences of lesbian, gay, bisexual, and transgender youth in our nation's schools state by state.* New York, NY: Gay Lesbian Straight Education Network.

Ladson-Billings, B. (1992). Reading between the lines and beyond the pages: A culturally relevant approach to literacy teaching. *Theory into Practice, 31*(4), 312–320.

Ladson-Billings, G. (1994). *The dreamkeepers: Successful teachers for African-American children.* San Francisco, CA: Jossey-Bass.

Ladson-Billings, G. (1995a). But that's just good teaching! The case for culturally relevant pedagogy. *Theory into Practice, 34*(3), 159–165.

Ladson-Billings, G. (1995b). Multicultural teacher education: Research, practice, and policy. In J. A. Banks & C. A. M. Banks (Eds.), *Handbook of research on multicultural education* (pp. 747–759). New York, NY: Macmillan.

Lee, C. (1993). *Signifying as a Scaffold to literary interpretation: The pedagogical implication of a form of African-American discourse* (NCTE Research Report No. 26). Urbana, IL: National Council of Teacher of English.

Lee, C. D., & Slaughter-Defoe, D. T. (1995). Historical and sociocultural influences on African American education. In J. A. Banks & C. A. M. Banks (Eds.), *Handbook of research on multicultural education* (pp. 348–371). New York, NY: Macmillan.

Lipman, P. (1995). Bringing out the best in them: The contribution of culturally relevant teachers to educational reform. *Theory into Practice, 34*(3), 202–208.

Meyer, E. J. (2008). Gendered harassment in secondary schools: Understanding teachers' (non) interventions. *Gender and Education, 20*(6), 555–572.

National Center for Education Statistics. (2014). *Enrollment in educational institutions, by level and control of institution.* Retrieved from http://nces.gov/fastfacts/display.asp?id=372

National Center for Injury Prevention and Control. (2014). *The relationship between bullying and suicide: What we know and what it means for schools.* Chamblee, GA: National Center for Injury Prevention and Control.

Office of Civil Rights. (2014). *Bullying.* Retrieved from http://www2.ed.gov/about/offices/list/ocr/whatsnew.html#2012

Olweus, D. (1993). *Bullying at school.* Oxford, UK: Blackwell.

Pew Research Center. (2013). *A survey of LGBT Americans: Attitudes, experiences and values in changing times,* Pew Research Center. Retrieved from http://www.pewsocialtrends.org/2013/06/13/a-survey-of-lgbt-americans/

Pewewardy, C. D. (1994). Culturally responsive pedagogy in action: An American Indian magnet school. In E. R. Hollins, J. E. King, & W. C. Hayman (Eds.), *Teaching diverse populations: Formulating a knowledge base* (pp. 77–92). Albany, NY: State University of New York Press.

Philips, S. U. (1983). *The invisible culture: Communication in classroom and community on the warm springs indian reservation.* Prospect Heights, IL: Waveland.

Poteat, V. P., & Rivers, I. (2010). The use of homophobic language across bullying roles during adolescence. *Journal of Applied Developmental Psychology, 31*(2), 166–172.

Robers, S., Zhang, J., Truman, J., & Snyder, T. (2012). *Indicators of school crime and safety: 2011* (NCES 2012-002/NCJ 236021). Washington, DC: National Center for Education Statistics, U.S. Department of Education, and Bureau of Justice Statistics, Office of Justice Programs, U.S. Department of Justice.

Rose, C. A. (2010). Bullying among students with disabilities: Impact and implications. In D. L. Espelage & S. M. Swearer (Eds.), *Bullying in North American schools: A socio-ecological perspective on prevention and intervention* (2nd ed., pp. 34–44). Mahwah, NJ: Lawrence Erlbaum.

Rose, C. A., Espelage, D. L., Aragon, S. R., & Elliott, J. (2011). Bullying and victimization among students in special education and general education curricula. *Exceptionality Education International, 21*(2), 2–14.

Russell, S. T., Kosciw, J. G., Horn, S. S., & Saewyc, E. (2010). Safe schools policy for LGBTQ students. *Social Policy Report, 24*(4), 3 –17.

Shor, I. (1992). *Empowering education: Critical teaching for social change.* Chicago, IL: University of Chicago Press.

Tooms, A. K., & Boske, C. (Eds.). (2010). *Building bridges: Connecting educational leadership and social justice to improve schools.* Charlotte, NC: Information Age Publishing.

Twemlow, S. W., Fonagy, P., Sacco, F. C., & Brethour, J. R. (2006). Teachers who bully students: A hidden trauma. *International Journal of Social Psychiatry, 52*(3), 187–198.

Turner, H. A., Finkelhor, D., Hamby, S. L., Shattuck, A., & Ormrod, R. K. (2011). Specifying type and location of peer victimization in a national sample of children and youth. *Journal of Youth and Adolescence, 40*(8), 1052–1067.

Vaillancourt, T., McDougall, P., Hymel, S., Krygsman, A., Miller, J., Stiver, K., & Davis, C. (2008). Bullying: Are researchers and children/youth talking about the same thing? *International Journal of Behavioral Development, 32*(6), 486–495.

Wade, A., & Beran, T. (2011). Cyberbullying: The new era of bullying. *Canadian Journal of School Psychology, 26*, 44–61.

Wang, J., Iannotti, R., & Nansel, T. (2009). School bullying among adolescents in the United States: Physical, verbal, relational, and cyber. *Journal of Adolescent Health, 45*, 368–375.

United States Department of Justice. (2009). *Matt Shepard and James Byrd Jr. Hate crimes prevention act.* Retrieved from http://www.justice.gov/crt/about/crm/matthewshepard.php

Vossekuil B., Reddy M., & Fein R. (2000). *Safe school initiative: An interim report on the prevention of targeted violence in schools.* Washington, DC: U.S. Secret Service National Threat Assessment Center.

AZADEH OSANLOO

2. WHAT ARE YOU?

The Hidden Curriculum and Microaggressions Associated with What It Means to Be "Different"

"What are you?" The number of times I have been asked that question is innumerable. It probably started when I was in my teens and has gotten profoundly worse as I have gotten older. Most likely as my features become more prominent due to make-up tricks and aging, which lead to more pronounced bone structure. And it is not just me who gets asked that absurd question. My mom gets asked that question too. However, her iteration is more often, "where are you from?" She has grown so weary of the tired, stale query that her new stock response is "from Heaven" – mostly because it makes her giggle to say that aloud. Only slightly tangentially, because of the confused look on the asker's face.

In the most colloquially defined categories, I do not exist. I am not Black; I am not White; I am not Hispanic; I am not Native American. Although I could technically (according to historical facts or geographical contexts) be considered Caucasian or West Asian, I do not in the most stereotypical of ways phenotypically look like people in either of those groups. Now, you and I know (especially since you are reading this book), that not all people look the same even if they are in fact from the same racial or ethnic group. However, that does not stop people from wanting to do what I call the "lump dump." That is to say, dumping people in clearly recognized and segregated lumps of racial groups. People like to categorize, compartmentalize, and in general, be able to slap a name on that which they know, and sometimes even on that which they do not know. Who knows, maybe by the end of this personal exploratory narrative I will leave you wondering, "what is she?"

Most recently, I have gotten "you look like one of them Kardashian girls. You know, kind of brownish, and exotic looking, but not White." I am not certain, but I think that might be what is called "making progress."

THE HIDDEN CURRICULUM AND MICROAGGRESSIONS
OF BEING "DIFFERENT"

Giroux (1983) defined the hidden curriculum as: those unstated norms, values, and beliefs embedded in and transmitted to students through the underlying rules that structure the routines and social relationships in school and classroom. Looking back on my K-12 educational experience, I recognize now the implicit lessons

C. Boske & A. Osanloo (Eds.), Students, Teachers, and Leaders Addressing Bullying in Schools, 23–32.
© *2015 Sense Publishers. All rights reserved.*

that were being taught to me regarding difference, otherness, and outsiderness. There was an "unwritten" set of rules that governed my socialization into the K-12 educational arena. Concurrently, I was being taught, albeit in an implicit manner, about hegemony, social reproduction, structural racism, and microaggressions.

Pierce et al. (1978) put forth that "the chief vehicle for proracist behaviors are microaggressions. These are subtle, stunning, often automatic, and non-verbal exchanges which are 'put downs' of blacks by offenders" (p. 66). Furthermore Pierce (1974) recognized that:

> These [racial] assaults to black dignity and black hope are incessant and cumulative. Any single one may be gross. In fact, the major vehicle for racism in this country is offenses done to blacks by whites in this sort of gratuitous neverending way. These offenses are microaggressions. Almost all black-white racial interactions are characterized by white put-downs, done in automatic, preconscious, or unconscious fashion. These minidisasters accumulate. It is the sum total of multiple microaggressions by whites to blacks that has pervasive effect to the stability and peace of this world. (p. 515)

In this same vein, Peggy Davis (1989) defined microaggressions as "stunning, automatic acts of disregard that stem from unconscious attitudes of white superiority and constitute a verification of black inferiority" (p. 1576). Microaggressions are exemplified by dismissive and often innocuous comments, behaviors, or beliefs that minimize, exclude, or render insignificant. The *Microaggressions Project* (www. micraggressions.com) routinely uploads anonymous posts that exemplify the pervasiveness of microaggressions.

Of course during the time I was a K-12 student I was unable to articulate these ideas with any lexical dexterity or the current academic jargon. However, I innately felt the interplay of the hidden curriculum and microaggressions that were circumnavigating me. The two converged, like thunder and lightening, to create a fraught educational experience. I was always able to sense that something was "not right." That in some way, I did not really fit or belong – that in fact, I was "not right." These unsettled feelings can best be explored through three narrative vignettes that capture my tenuous and fraught positionality in K-12 schools, context, and circles. Each one of the vignettes exemplifies the tangibility of the "other" and the importance of cultural awareness, responsibility, and responsiveness.

What's in a Name?

As I am sure you have seen and read, my name is Azadeh Osanloo. For some, that may be problematic, as it does not necessarily underscore gender, ethnicity, or race. For many, it begs the question "will s/he speak English?" One of my least favorite memories growing up was the roll call on the first day of school in each class. For many, the first day of school marked a shiny new year, with bright new clothes, a warm summer tan, and some physical sign that you have grown one step closer to adulthood over the summer (i.e. pierced ears, shaved legs, drugstore make-up). However, for me, it meant the dreaded "going down the roster" at the beginning of each class. I always knew when my name was coming up. The teacher, with confidence and slight indifference, would lazily singsong away at the Mary Anderson's and Brian Johnson's of the world. Then she would skip along through the Martin's, Nickelson's, and O'Keefe's. Then and only then, would she take a pregnant pause, furrow her brows, and purse her lips together in a vain attempt to pronounce the nearly impossible (for her lips had never even tried to mash together these haphazardly thrown together consonants and vowels in this unique, nearly parody-like, manner before). Before she could even aspirate the first attempt of a syllable out of her mouth, I would interrupt the butchering. "It's Azadeh," I would say. "You know, like the Wizard of Oz?" "Oz-uh-day...like a day of the week." That damn silent "h" always threw people for a loop. She would look at me confused and slightly irritated. I never knew for certain if the irritation was because I had interrupted her attempt to say my name or the fact that my name was so "weird." Truthfully, I think it was a little of both. I had gone through this "exercise" more than 50 times while growing up. The process was nearly always the same and with the same ending.

It was around this time my mom suggested I adopt a middle name – her intentions were good and she thought it would make things easier for me. We went with Farrah. You will see it noted on my writings, business cards, web page, and even my driver's license. I do not know exactly when or how it got so seamlessly adopted into my life, but it did. I am now Azadeh Farrah Osanloo. So now when I attempt to make things easier for other people, I go by Farrah. Like at Starbucks, it is almost always Farrah. However, even that at times has back-fired on me as I have gotten "Mira," "Serah," "Sarah," and once even "Feral" – as in a feral animal, untamed or wild. Truth be told, I kind of felt "feral" at that moment.

To this day, the mere pronunciation of my name baffles people. Even after I correctly and very s-l-o-w-l-y pronounce it, it takes people a few more walk-throughs before it is totally digested. After it is fully consumed is when I get the flurry of verbally sputtered adjectives. Your name is so "interesting," "unique," "different," "odd," "weird," "pretty," and "hard to say." Then it is the "what does it mean?" and "where does it come from?" barrage of seemingly friendly fire. I go through my name dance with people often, sometimes three-four times in a single day. It gets tiresome. On the days I am most tired, I simply go by my childhood nickname, Ozzy. And then when people ask how I got that name I tell them that my parents met at an Ozzy Osbourne concert and that is where I was conceived. By the way, that is not true, but it makes for fun fodder.

Just the other day I got a piece of mail addressed to ASS Osanloo. I venture to guess that the sender was probably a Kardashian fan.

Food, Food, Glorious Food

My mother is a gourmet chef. She has not won an official James Beard Award or is Michelin star-rated, but her cooking is out of this world. As an adult, I crave her home-cooked cuisine. I salivate just thinking about my favorite dishes, often wishing I lived closer so I could indulge in the sensory fireworks of taste, sight, and smell that accompany her cooking. She is to cooking what Mozart was to classical music and Michelangelo was to the Sistine Chapel. But, as a wanting-to-be-typical-American-youth in middle school I was not as impressed or willing to gush. When you're a little brown girl with a "weird" name wanting to "fit in" with American culture, food is an obvious, direct route for racial congruence and harmony.

I used to love watching my classmates as they pulled the shiny wrappers out of their lunch sacks and boxes. Bright oranges and fiery reds that indicated Doritos or Cheetos; clear cellophane wrappers that emitted a sugary sweet smell when opened and a yellow spongy tube with cream-filling inside; and white doughy bread with perfectly square pieces of tangerine-colored cheese and pinkish gelatinous meats that stood as the centerpiece of the meal. Their lunches were light and airy; sacks of happiness filled with colorful presents.

My brown paper lunch bag was always heavy. There were no crinkly wrappers with shiny colors and graffiti-like writing inside. No tube of spongy delight that squirted cream upon the first careless bite. And definitely no perfectly squared-off Wonder Bread. My bag held carrots and celery sticks; a piece of fruit (apple or banana mostly likely); some small token of home-cooking that was usually green or brown; and the pièce de résistance, the densely constructed sandwich with layers of alfalfa, thick-cut deli meat, cucumbers, and radishes, all nestled between two slices of a brown, grainy, seedy, fibrous bread. Oh, how I longed to open something…anything that held some sort of processed, food-colored enriched vending machine-like food.

When the pretty little blonde girl with the big pink bow in her perfectly coiffed cheerleader pony tail said aloud at the table "Ew…what is that? Your lunch is so weird." I knew she had only said what everyone else was thinking. My lunch was weird ergo I was weird. The little voice in my tense head screamed, "Your name is weird and now even the food you eat is weird! Can't you get anything right?" Apparently, I could not. Weirdness cloaked me like a dark dense cloud.

Today, it is ironic to think that back then all I wanted were things in wrappers, processed delights, and other American-certified "delicacies" like hot dogs, hamburgers, and pizza. I have had my full of those since I left home for college at age 18. Now, all I yearn for are those tasty, delicious, homemade meals that mirrored the gastronomy of Bacchus.

Wide Body, Lithe Body, White Body, Brown Body

"You just don't have the right body for ballet, or really, any kind of dance," she said. I was 13. I knew I did not look like either of my lithe, petite sisters or the other perfectly pirouetting lissome dancers in the studio, but I still thought I was allowed to dance. For God's sake, this was *not* Footloose. However, my shortly lived foray into dance was over. The plain-spoken instructor, an expert, had just informed me so. She told me that I was "built for other things" like sports that "boys play."

I remember being stocky and stout with big hands as a youngster. My hands were like that of a growing Great Dane puppy – comically big for my age. I still have big hands today. I was always able to catch and throw with ease; I excelled at most sports that involved balls. However, I longed to be graceful, slim, and willowy. I yearned to float in the air like a feather whose flight required only the softest wisp of air. But, as one of my coaches told me, I was "built like a Mack truck." And as we know, Mack trucks are built to last on the rough open road, not built to be prima ballerinas who are tossed into the air with ease and deft.

In addition to being w-i-d-e, I was also not white. I had dark hair, cinnamon-colored skin with red undertones, hazel or muddy brown eyes (depending on the lighting), and those dark half-moon circles under my eyes that never go away (except now with the best camouflage of make-up – see Cle de Peau). I looked different from the majority of my female classmates – with their lily-white skin, blonde hair, and blue eyes. The peach-fuzzed golden hair that donned their arms and legs stood in stark contrast to the homely brown hair that covered my limbs like Kudzu. I remember wishing for the turquoise trails of veins against the palette of snow-colored skin that ran down the arms of my classmates. Even the latest, coveted fashions I donned from Forenza and Outback Red were droll cloaks that could not hide the fact I looked different.

Everything about me was different – my name, the foods I ate, and the way I looked. I learned early in life that "different" was synonymous with bad, wrong, incorrect, deficient, defective, and inferior. Different. Different. Different. Different. Even now the word elicits a subliminal, charged, and palpable reaction from me.

THOUGHTS ON NURTURANCE

I know that the work that I do today is largely influenced by my experiences as a youth. I know that constantly being recognized and pointed out for being different has painstakingly guided my deliberate decision-making to be an advocate for social justice, transformative change, servant leadership, and multiculturally competent educators. Concomitant with this advocacy work has been the importance of recognizing that the hidden curriculum and microaggressions, which permeate difference in K-12 schools, are conduits that help illuminate the dynamics of a larger systemic issue. How can a system or institutional structure shift from a place of deficit to asset thinking, from exclusion to inclusion?

One positive step in that direction requires paradigmatic change that will move educators and educational leaders from a philosophical perspective of tolerance, acceptance, and even celebration towards the unadulterated nurturance of difference. For the purposes of this work, I focus on the nurturance of racial and ethic difference.

The notion of nurturance was keenly and adeptly captured by Dorothy Riddle's (1985, 1994) work. She designed a psychometric scale that measured the degree to which a person is or is not homophobic. While Riddle (1985) anchored her research within the lesbian, gay, and bisexual community, I examine her "Homophobia Scale" from a xenophobic or racial phobic place.

Capitalizing on the work of Riddle (1985), I offer that nurturance is an epistemological position that views racial and ethnic difference (i.e. different from the hegemonic, white normative) as an indispensible part of our society; and that racial and ethnic difference increases and diversifies knowledge bases as well as is as a requisite asset for success in school, family, and community life. Moreover, people who are racially and ethnically "different" are viewed with genuine affection and delight (Riddle, 1985), and citizens of a democratic society are willing to become genuine allies and advocates of these "different" people. So, how do we get there? More specifically, how do we as educators and educational leaders pave the way?

I offer several recommendations for underscoring racial and ethnic nurturance in K-12 schools and higher education today. These strategies are tools that I have employed in my classroom teaching (both K-12 and university), in my research and training, as well as are based upon my personal experiences as the "other." They are the result of the symbiotic blending of research and experience, which is a valuable course of action for engaging with issues from a holistic perspective. *First*, issues of and pertaining to race and ethnicity should be taught at the elementary school level. The earlier we discuss these topics with children, the better chance we have of demystifying the "elephants in the room" that are race and ethnicity. From an earlier research study I conducted with elementary students (Osanloo, 2012), it was clearly evident that children are not only aware of racial issues, but they are ready, willing, and able to discuss them. From a nascent perspective, they understood topics like racism, bias, prejudice, and difference, and were able to articulate their thoughts on these issues while contextualizing the concepts in current and historical examples. Discussions on race and ethnicity should go beyond the mere "celebration" of different ethnic groups (i.e. food, festival, and fetishizing), and dive into the politics and polemics of racial and ethnic difference in this country as well as globally.

Second, crucial conversations about race and ethnicity should include educators and students as well as family and community members. These discussions should not be void of larger scale goals that are inclusive of bettering and building a democratic community of conscientious citizens. Schools and universities should not be the only sites for transformational change. Other places, like homes, places of worship, and community centers are ideal pipelines for the transference of racial and ethnic awareness, knowledge, and information. Racially charged travesties, like the deaths of Trayvon Martin and Michael Brown and subsequent incidents in Ferguson, need to be deemed more than "teachable moments," but rather "climacteric opportunities" in which in-depth conversations about the delicate, yet powerful intricacies of racial and ethnic relations in this country can occur.

Third, curriculum choices at all levels, pedagogical and andragogical, should include works written by racial and ethnic minority scholars, as well as offer non-hegemonic views of history, politics, religion, and other topics that are rooted in the "Westernization myth" and devoid of racial and ethnic controversies. This type of intentional curricular choice opens the doorway for other important pluralistic decisions, like adhering to culturally responsive teaching and leadership (Ladson-Billings, 1995). Ladson-Billings advocates for the term culturally responsive – she stated, "Only the term culturally responsive appears to refer to a more dynamic or synergistic relationship between home/community culture and school culture" (1995, p. 467).

Social justice and equity building are natural alliances with the nurturance of racial and ethnicity issues in education. By embracing purposive choices in curriculum, the notion of teacher as researcher is uplifted. Furthermore, this can lead to racially and ethnically responsive practices; these practices in turn lend themselves to social justice and equity building in schools and universities.

Building on the first three suggestions, the *fourth* recommends that educators and educational leaders should be trained in cross-cultural communication. Too often in my personal and professional experiences one manner of speaking has been privileged over another. Most often, the privileged manner is that which is akin with "speaking white." And as we know "speaking white" is often linked with the notion of "acting white" (Fordham & Ogbu, 1986). As Fordham and Ogbu (1986) pointed out "speaking standard English" is one of the ways that Black students at an urban high school in Washington D.C. adopted as a method for "acting White." There a numerous ways in which race, ethnicity, and culture impact linguistic styles, techniques, and dialectics. Passion is not always aggression; proper is not always perfect; and strong is not always inappropriate. As I once wrote (2014):

> It has interested me to know when the word "strong" became a pejorative in relation to women faculty members in education - whether the term is used in relation to dispositions, personality, or tone. I wonder, was there ever an option for a space invader, like me, to not be strong? Would I be sitting at the same table as you, watching you as you curiously watch me, if I were not strong? Pervasive sexist and racist systems perpetuated by the hegemonic exclusionary elite require strong action. It is this type of action that will help me push past the liminal space, into a more solid realm. I do not have the luxury to be passive. (p. 61)

People must be able to express themselves in a manner that is consistent with their cultural sense of self. If not, we are asking for inauthenticity, academic spectacle, and the performance of self through the obfuscated lens of whiteness. Of course, it is often important to remain collegial and respectful; however, no one should be asked or encouraged to perform "whiteness as rightness."

And finally, my *fifth* recommendation is really more of a suggestive thought – don't just invite "different" people to the table, but welcome them. For example, many of my ethnic minority colleagues and I discuss the sad reality that we must consistently "prove" that we should be in the racialized spaces of academia. While we are all properly degreed and pedigreed, there remains a burden of impossible proof that does not rest in our accomplishments, research, teaching, or service, but rather in the eye of the beholder. I feel the endless ebb and flow of the liminal space in which I exist in academe, and the constant watchful eyes waiting for me to make a mistake. As Puwar pointed out:

> Due to the existence of a racialised form of surveillance, there is also a racialised reason for wanting to succeed. Knowing that they are in a precarious situation and that the most minor of mistakes could be taken as evidence of incompetence, women and racialised carry what might be termed the "burden of representation." (p. 62)

I often tell my ethnic minority doctoral advisees as they embark upon their post-graduate academic journey, "just because you are sitting at the same table as 'them,' does not mean that 'they' want you there. And it definitely does not mean that they want to hear what you have to say." Unfortunately, that reality has rang true for many of them since their youths, just like me.

These five recommendations come from a long history of being different, working within difference, and working towards the nurturance of difference. The recommendations are not static, but rather the dynamic embodiment of what it means to be different today. They should be moveable, massaged, and molded as the idea of "difference" in this country and around the world continues to evolve.

DIFFERENCE AND ANTI-BULLYING WORK

The implications of importing the recommendations above into the K-20 educational pipeline and ancillary sectors, is that they may have a positive impact on bullying. In a study I conducted with my colleague, Jon Schwartz (2015), we focused on the role of diversity and student experiences in the understanding of bullying and being bullied. Generally, we found that kids in middle schools are bullied for being "different."

To assess the relationship between diversity and bullying we surveyed two ethnically similar middle schools in the southwest. We gathered descriptive data on issues of perceived safety, bullying experiences, school belongingness, strategies to deal with bullying, and experience with diversity based bullying. The two middle schools consisted of approximately 1400 children, equal rates of males and females. Overall, both schools had a higher rate of bullying (34%) then the national average (15–25%). The majority of the children at the two schools were Hispanic (58%) followed by White (40%) followed by equally small numbers of African Americans, Native Americans, and Asian Americans. One of the most revealing questions on the survey asked – Have you ever witnessed bullying related to: (1) Race/Ethnicity; (2) Family Income/Wealth; (3) Sexual Orientation; (4) Appearance; (5) Religion; (6) Disability; and (7) Other. The responses for each school site were as follows:

School Site One - Have you ever witnessed bullying related to: (1) Race/Ethnicity – 46.7%; (2) Family Income/Wealth – 22%; (3) Sexual Orientation – 31%; (4) Appearance – 49%; (5) Religion – 23%; (6) Disability – 26%; and (7) Other – 12%.

School Site Two - Have you ever witnessed bullying related to: (1) Race/Ethnicity – 37.7%; (2) Family Income/Wealth – 16.7%; (3) Sexual Orientation – 24.2%; (4) Appearance – 40.3%; (5) Religion – 17.7%; (6) Disability – 24%; and (7) Other – 6.3%.

Although there were notable differences between the two schools, overall this data demonstrates a high rate of witnessing bullying based on perceived differences. Based on the data gathered at these two schools, we offered that capacity building in the area of diversity must occur for school sites to be healthful places for student learning. Our data demonstrated that building diversity skills is essential to better understand bullying behavior. Every school has a unique ecological context, thus the diversity climate of every school will also be unique. To prevent hate-based bullying it is vital to address the climate of diversity and difference at each school. This can be conceptualized as a box of "normal" behavior, with any behavior that strays outside of the box becoming a target for bullying. Strategies for increasing the size of that "box" must be tailored to the school diversity climate (Osanloo & Schwartz, 2015).

FINAL THOUGHTS

I was truly honored when Christa asked me to co-edit this volume with her. Not only because she is an amazing, conscientious, and thoughtful scholar, but also because this work sheds a bold light on the pandemic of bullying. It does so by allowing a safe platform for the many voices within the bullying cycle to be heard. The chapters written in this compendium by students, parents, advocates, allies, and teachers are powerful, painful, and scarring. This work is decolonizing in that it is not merely researchers "doing work on/in bullying" but rather focuses on the experiences of the people most impacted by bullying. Christa and I have vowed to do work *with* people and not *on* them. Moreover, what these stories did most for me was bring me back to a time in my childhood that had been buried beneath degrees, jobs, and other masks. The venial microaggressions of my childhood, captured by the vignettes, still reside in me, at my core. And I still know, can even feel, when someone looks at me and thinks "different." However, by theorizing the ideas at the underbelly of difference (and essentially doing work like this), I now have a better foothold when asked, "what are you?" because I know that for me, the more audacious, important question is, "what do you stand for?"

REFERENCES

Bonilla-Silva, E. (2009). *Racism without racists: Color-blind racism and the persistence of racial inequality in America*. Oxford, United Kingdom: Rowman & Littlefield.

Davis, P. (1989). Law as microaggression. *Yale Law Journal, 98*, 1559–1577.

Fordham, S., & Ogbu, J. (1986). Black students' school success: Coping with the "burden of 'acting white.'" *Urban Review, 18*, 176–206.

Giroux, H. (1983). Theories of reproduction and resistance in the new sociology of education: A critical analysis. *Harvard Educational Review, 53*, 257–293.

Ladson-Billings, G. (1995). Toward a theory of culturally relevant pedagogy. *American Educational Research Journal, 32*, 465–491.

Osanloo, A. (2012). Bridging transformational leaders and youth activists: Human rights pedagogy for social justice. In C. Boske (Ed.), *The practice and pedagogy of building bridges in school leadership.* (pp. 35–48). Charlotte, NC: Information Age Publishing.

Osanloo, A. (2014). The invisible other: Ruminations on transcending "la cerca" in academia. In W. Sherman (Ed.), *Continuing to disrupt the status quo? Young and new women professors of educational leadership.* (pp. 55–64). Charlotte, NC: Information Age Publishing.

Osanloo, A., & Schwartz, J. (2015). Using social norming, ecological theory, and diversity based strategies for bullying interventions in urban areas: A mixed methods research study. In M. Khalifa, N. Witherspoon-Arnold, A. Osanloo, & C. Grant-Overton (Eds.), *Urban school leadership handbook* (pp. 199–210). Lanham, MD: Rowman and Littlefield Publishing Group.

Pierce, C. (1974). Psychiatric problems of the Black minority. In S. Arieti (Ed.), *American handbook of psychiatry* (pp. 512–523). New York, NY: Basic Books.

Pierce, C., Carew, J., Pierce-Gonzalez, D., & Wills, D. (1978). An experiment in racism: TV commercials. In C. Pierce (Ed.), *Television and education* (pp. 62–88). Beverly Hills, CA: Sage, 1978.

Puwar, N. (2004). *Space invaders: Race, gender, and bodies out of place*. New York, NY: Berg Publishing.

Riddle, D. (1985). Homophobia scale. In K. Obear & A. Reynolds (Eds.), *Opening doors to understanding and acceptance*. Boston, MA: Unpublished essay.

Riddle, D. (1994). The riddle scale. *Alone no more: Developing a school support system for gay, lesbian and bisexual youth*. St Paul, MN: Minnesota State Department.

Sue, D. W., Capodilupo, C., Torino, G., Bucceri, J., Holder, A., Nadal, K., & Esquilin, M. (2007). Racial microaggressions in everyday life: Implications for clinical practice. *American Psychologist, 62*, 271–286. doi: http://dx.doi.org/10.1037/0003-066X.62.4.271

PART 1

VOICES FROM YOUTH IN SCHOOLS

CHRIS BOARD

3. A YOUNG MAN'S JOURNEY

First off, I need you to know this is the first time I have ever done something like this. I do not put my feelings on paper for the world to see. I keep them bottled up. But this time, I decided to take a risk. No one ever offered me an opportunity like this. You know, to make a difference by sharing my experiences. I decided to write this chapter so people could see the world through my eyes. I am taking a risk and telling you about something that has bothered me for many years. I am ready to share my story and tell you how I was the bully and yet, I turned things around. This is hard for me to do. I mean, telling you I was the bully a book and about the need to stop bullying, but I need you to hear my story. I am afraid you might judge me, but please know that as I share my experiences, I am stumbling to find the right words.

As I get older, I look back and realize how much I have grown. I was an arrogant kid. I thought I knew it all, but I learned I had some real growing to do. As a young Black man, I have a different perspective on the world. I learned the hard way not to judge a book by its cover. Let me make this clear—I am not a bully now. I do not criticize or push people around with my words or actions any more. I have learned to love all people and accept people for who they are. I hope you find value in my story and understand people can change, but what they need are opportunities to think about why they do what they do. And they need people in their lives to help them learn to see the world differently. Maybe this is why I am writing this. Maybe you can learn from my life too.

OUTCAST CHRIS

In elementary school, at the age of seven, I was picked on in school. Kids made fun of me because of the clothes I wore and the way I talked. I used to get picked on every day in school. Either my clothes weren't cool enough or my vocabulary was too big. No adults intervened. They let things slide.

I did not want to go to school. Each day grew harder and harder for me, because I knew what was waiting for me once I left my home. I rode the school bus every day. My stomach would turn as I waited for the bus to arrive. As we got closer and closer to school, I got more and more nervous. I was the kid who sat by himself. I did not have a lot of friends. I became a loner, not because I wanted to be alone, but because kids did not want to be my friend. I wore clothes too big or too small for me. My shoes were not the name-brand shoes everyone else might have been wearing.

C. Boske & A. Osanloo (Eds.), Students, Teachers, and Leaders Addressing Bullying in Schools, 35–39.

My shoes were messed up. They had scuff marks on them and my laces were not torn. What I wore was all we could afford. My mom did her best to provide for all us. There were five children and this was a lot of responsibility for my mom. She watched over us and made sure we had what we needed.

Kids at school were mean. They cracked jokes on me the moment I walked into school. It was as though they were just waiting to intimidate me and make me feel small. They said,

You're gay!
You're broke!
Your mom and dad do not live together! You don't know who your dad is!

They cracked on me constantly, but the teachers did not seem to hear it. I do not know how that was possible, but they seemed to ignore what was right in front of them. Some teachers might ask me or the other kids what was going on, but the kids would laugh it off. I would not say a thing. I did not want to have kids make fun of me even more than they did.

In the yearbook, kids drew glasses on me or "xed" out my face out of the class pictures. I remember crying when I saw this. I did not want anyone to see me cry, so I either cried in the bathroom or waited until I got home. I tried to deal with the bullying on my own. The hurt kept building up inside of me until I could not stand it anymore.

No one at home knew anything about what was happening at school. I did not tell my mom. I did not want to seem soft or like a tattle tale. As a boy, I learned at an early age, you are supposed to be tough. When you are tough, nothing should bother you.

As a man, you should be able to handle your own business.
As a man, you should be able to brush it off.

I thought I must not be like most boys. I had feelings. I had anger inside me. I was hurt. At times I felt broken. I thought I was different. I pretended to be tough. I thought I needed to keep to myself. Doing this was difficult for me.

Crying by myself was hard.
I just wanted to share it with someone.
I didn't have any friends or anyone to talk to about any of this.

Maybe my teachers and mom did not notice me, because academically, I was doing just fine. But mentally, I was depressed. I felt alone. I felt like no one really cared about me. I never told my parents about this. Remember, I wanted to be tough, just like a boy "should" be. I thought I was strong enough to deal with the bullying on my own. In elementary school, I thought about suicide. I often wondered what it would be like if I was not around. I was not sure it would have made that much of a difference. I did not attempt suicide, because I decided killing myself was not an option. But for some reason, it weighed heavy on my mind. The thought of suicide kept my mind busy. I continued to think about taking my own life until fourth grade.

CHRIS THE BULLY

I moved to a different school in fourth grade. This was a fresh start for me. I decided to save myself from being hurt by getting back at people. I decided to try being the bully. I tried to be cooler. I changed the way I spoke. I changed how I interacted with my family and how I spoke with teachers. I was a different person. I started saying negative things about the clothes people wore, wear someone lived, or how students talked.

I was not going be the target.

I would say things like, "You're ugly!" or "This is why you ain't got no money." I tried to be one step in front of the other kids. I thought if I came at them first, if I lashed out first, then I could get them out of the way. They would not be able to bother me, because I stood up first. It might not sound right, but this was the only way I understood how to protect myself. I was doing what was done to me. I was known as a prankster.

The attention I received was not what I anticipated. Teachers and students thought I was a negative person. They did not know the old Chris. They only knew the new Chris, and the new Chris just wanted to make fun of other kids so he would not get bullied. The more I tried to be like the cooler kids, the more they would smile at me and approve of the choices I made. But inside, I need to tell you I felt horrible. I knew this was not Chris Board. I knew who I really was deep inside. I just tried to be a bully, so I could stop anyone from thinking they could bully me. I felt horrible every time I did it. I did not like how I felt inside. It got so uncomfortable for me, so I decided to change my ways.

CHRIS IN TRANSITION

In fifth grade, I moved again. I decided to change my ways. This time, I decided it was time to move from being bullied to being the bully to being someone who helped others. I moved a lot, so I took advantage of these chances to start over again. I had to think about why I was doing what I was doing. I did not understand why I kept putting kids down for living just like me. I needed to make a change.

My mom started giving me more responsibilities at home. I think her help made me realize I could do good in the world. She helped me see I needed to change. I was the oldest. She expected great things out of me. I could no longer continue acting as I did in fourth grade. My mom asked me to watch my younger siblings. I was also in charge of going to the store and watching the house in my mom's absence.

In sixth grade, I moved again. One day, I was beat up on my way home from school. I was jumped by kids, because of the shoes I wore. My mom got me some Jordan's for my birthday. I was walking home. Some guys punched me. They tried to take the shoes off of my feet! Some older guy got out of his car to help me. I held on tight to my shoes. I ran home as fast as I could. I told my mom what happened.

She said, "This isn't safe. We have to move again." My mom moved us to the town we live in today. At first, I lived my grandparents, but later on, I moved again into an apartment with my mom. I have been living with my mom ever since.

My mom helped me think about the needs of other people. I could no longer think of only myself. I was given responsibilities to watch over my family. I took this very seriously, and it helped me grow. I spent more time with my family and this made a difference in how I saw myself. My mom believed in me. Now, I needed to learn how to believe in myself and like me too. I wanted to learn how to be the person my mom saw in me at school, at home, and when I was by myself.

CHRIS, THE WISER MAN

High school can be a difficult time for young people. I remember one incident from my freshman year. It changed my whole outlook on bullying in schools. I went to school with a girl named Gina (I changed her name for this chapter to protect her identity). Every day kids called her "gay", "weird", and "crazy." I could name more, but I hope you get the idea. They constantly called her names and bullied her. Every day I tried to talk to her and make her feel welcome in our school. Gina was a kind-hearted, genuine person until she was filled with rage. She seemed to get upset easily. One time, she stabbed someone with a pencil. Another time, she choked a student. Her parents decided to place her in a mental institution. Kids thought she was crazy. I did not. I thought there must be more to her rage or how she reacted to people. I remember feeling that kind of rage, but I did not act on it the way Gina did. I saw her trying to fit in and being a part of the "high school society." Her efforts never worked in her favor. She was still considered an outcast.

I received a phone call from our school. I heard the recording—Gina hung herself from a rope in her bedroom. I sat the phone down and remained in shock for a bit. I never knew Gina would reach the point that she would have taken her own life. As an upcoming high school graduate, we refer to Gina's life as an example of bullying gone too far. We will always remember her. It takes tremendous strength to deal with the stress of being picked on. The whole situation made me feel realize life is precious. It should never be taken for granted. Gina's death made me realize every life is sacred. I was so upset. Gina was a beautiful person and took her own life based on the hostility and ignorance of others.

At school, I zone out sometimes. I breeze through the hallways. I do not really like a lot of people. I do not think we are on the same maturity level. So many kids seem to think about school differently. They do not seem to understand how important school is or the need for us to treat each other with respect. I try to stay away from these kids, because I do not want to surround myself with stupidity. There seem to be so many cliques. And these cliques divide us, not unite us. One group sticks together and believes other kids are not as good as them. In my high school, there are three groups: sports players, cool kids, and smart kids. If you do not belong to one of those three groups, then you are an outcast.

I think I have always been an outcast. I was bullied when I was younger and then I became the bully. And now, I do not feel I can relate to most people my age. I try to be different by respecting everyone and not belonging to a clique. I talk to everyone in school–kids who are picked on or who are considered outcasts. I never wanted to be a part of a group of people who acts as though they are better than anyone else. I realize I can stand on my own two feet. I need my family and recognize I need to stay focused on being there for others.

In my opinion, people who are called "odd" or "weird" are the most intellectual and exciting people to talk to and be around. It kills me when I see some people act as though they are better than others. Just because someone talks or acts a certain way does not mean one group of people is better than another. I spent my childhood experiencing what it meant to be an outlier. I was bullied because of it. I spent two more years bullying other kids, because they were outliers. Through it all, I needed to realize being an outlier was something kids just made up. We don't have the authority to judge someone and isolate them because we may not agree with them or behave differently. The thought of being picked on and talked about, because someone is an individual, leaves a knot in my stomach. I will not make that mistake again.

Now, I am a senior. I am grateful for the experiences I had as child. I can look back and take away something positive from being bullied. I used this situation as a way to find myself. I am not condoning bullying. I used those horrible experiences to grow stronger. I became the man I am today because of the experiences I had when I was younger, and many of those involved being bullied and bullying. Looking back, I gained knowledge about myself, grew to love who I have become, and learned to respect others.

I learned to stay true to myself. It is high school. People grow and change. We will gain new friends and lose friends who no longer value what we value. You might think these people will be with you forever, but these same people might become a distant memory. We are learning how to live and work with people who are not like us. I am glad to be the way I am. I am learning to cherish my experiences, family, and people who value themselves and others. At 18, I see the world differently, and owe so much of this to her. I enjoy meeting people who are often ignored in school. I like being around kids who are called "weird." When I see kids being picked on, I stand up for kids and talk to them, because they are real people.

I dedicate this chapter to my mom–the most important person in my life. My mom is proud of ME. She is my inspiration. She is my everything. Her love helps me focus on what I need to do and what it takes to get where I want to be.

EMILY WIRTH

4. YOU ARE WORTH IT

Did you know bullying is the third leading cause of death with over 100 people attempting to commit suicide and more than 4,000 succeeding every year? It is a serious situation facing thousands of young people. If you or anyone you know is considering suicide, please seek help immediately. Let an adult know what is happening so they can help you. Do not manage this alone, because there are people who can help. If you are being bullied, you need to know YOU ARE WORTH IT!

I wonder if people who are bullies think it makes them cool? Does it make them look tough to everyone? It is important for anyone who thinks they can intimidate, threaten, or do harm that it is cool. I cannot think of a situation in which it is okay to do harm to another person with the intention of hurting them. I want young people to remember we are human first. We are different from one another. It is never okay to harass, ridicule, or physically harm another because they do not share the same ideas, color of skin, groups of friends, or live in the same neighborhood. I consider this bullying and is NOT okay.

The purpose of this chapter focuses on my bullying story and coming to terms with understanding my story matters. I was 12 when my bullying started. Students were calling me names. I do not feel comfortable sharing those in this chapter, because I cannot say them out loud. These horrible things were not only said to my face, but they were shared over the internet and in school. I found myself in the middle of having rumors spread about me on bathroom stalls to Facebook pages. Their words hurt me. I could not stop crying.

I tried to separate myself from how I was perceived by people who did not know me from the truth. I promised myself I would not allow these students see me upset. I knew they wanted to see me fall apart. That would give them great satisfaction. I was determined not to allow them to get the best of me. However, as the rumors continued in school and online, I felt worse.

I coped by isolating myself. I went home and cut myself with anything sharp I could find. I would cut myself in places on my body that nobody would see. I thought, "If they could not see it, then those bullies would never know how much they were hurting me inside." I wanted someone to see the pain they were putting me through, but I did not want the bullies to know.

After one year of being bullied and keeping the situation to myself, I went into a deep, dark place. I believed committing suicide was the only answer. It was my only way out of this horrific situation. I believed that leaving this world would bring me

C. Boske & A. Osanloo (Eds.), Students, Teachers, and Leaders Addressing Bullying in Schools, 41–43.

peace, because the bullying would stop, right? After thinking about this for some time, I realized killing myself might erase my pain, but my death would create new pain for my family. This was not my intention. I am getting the help I need, but it was not an easy road. Changes cannot just take place with the person being bullied. Changes need to take place in the bully as well as in the school.

Educators tell us they want to make school a safe zone– a place to get away. However, school was not my safe zone. My family and home was my safe zone. School was actually the place I avoided. Even though I am no longer contemplating suicide, I am 16, in 10th grade, and hate going to school. I think school is my danger zone. I witness people walking the halls acting as though they own the school, pushing people around, acting big and bad, and pretending everything is alright when an adult comes around. I cannot believe the teachers and principal do not know what really happens in and outside of school. We cannot begin to address the problem if we do not realize what bullying looks like, sounds like, and feels like by all of those involved.

I witnessed too many adults stand there, listen and watch versus doing something about bullying behavior. I do not understand why they do not do the right thing and stand up for the students who are being isolated or harassed for being different. What stops them from doing something about it? I thought they were teachers who became teachers because they care about students. Most adults seem to walk right past students who are acting out. I want teachers to know their actions could save a student's life. In my experience, too few adults, and you know who they are, stand up and do the right thing. I want you to know students know who you are. We know who cares and who does not. Just remember, the power of caring can save the life of a student.

Whether they realize it or not, teachers play a big role in stopping bullying. Sometimes teachers are bullies. They yell and scream at kids. I hear teachers cuss at students, tell them they are lazy, and what a disappointment they are to the school. It is sad for me to watch teachers, who are supposed to be well-respected adults, pull students down. I remember sitting in my math class. My teacher overheard a conversation with a peer. The teacher started screaming and cursing at us in front of the class. I could not believe the names the teacher called us. I would never have expected this kind of behavior from a teacher. I was humiliated. People in class laughed. I think they were laughing at me. The situation made my heart drop to my stomach. I considered that teacher a bully. I am a student. That person was a teacher. I cannot say anything to this teacher, because I will get in trouble. However, I am supposed to respect this teacher? I think teachers should be role models for students. I do not understand why some teachers feel it is okay to pick on students or embarrass them. They have students looking up to them, so it is not okay to take advantage of the situation.

If you are reading my chapter and know someone who being bullied, STAND UP! Make a difference. Do not stand there and watch things happen. I realize it might be difficult to jump in and do something, but remember you might be saving someone's life. Look what I went through. If you are being bullied, please know I am very sorry. Nobody deserves to be treated the way you are being treated. Reach out to someone. Do not give up. There are family members, friends, and maybe even teachers, principals, or coaches who will help you. I found a teacher who made a difference in my life. She is the only person in my school I feel safe sharing things with or even talking to when I was upset. She was my safe haven. She continues to help me realize my potential in life. Bottom line? Bullying is a big deal.

STAND UP, MAKE A DIFFERENCE, and realize YOU ARE ALL WORTH IT!

GOLDIEA SHAW

5. DOES IT REALLY MATTER IF NOBODY IS AROUND?

Everyone hears bullying is bad. We are informed through advertisements, school lectures, or sometimes, our families. Some of us choose to ignore it, because it does not pertain to us. Unfortunately, I must admit, I was one of those people. I did not think bullying mattered. I saw it happen all around me. I watched it happen. I did not seem to care about what happened to others. I saw kids bullying other kids in the hallways. I watched people snicker and laugh at certain kids constantly. No one seemed to care except the person who was being taunted. Believe it or not, I fell victim to the constant name calling, but I dealt with it, by not dealing with it. I thought I was strong enough to just let it go. I did not think anyone would care if I hurt inside. I looked like I was happy, and everyone left me alone. When I was a sophomore, everything came to a head. It hit home, and the experience changed my life.

I never had a lot of friends, so going to school was simply just attending school. I was there to learn and return home. I recall the day things changed for me. It was a typical day at my high school. I moved from class to class. I was known as a quiet, very shy, short, brown hair, blue-eyed girl. I squeezed through everyone in the hallway, because they seemed too small for all of the students to move through from class to class. We brushed up against one another just to get by and be on time to class. I moved through, but I accidently bumped into someone. She gave me a disgusting look and yelled, "You are ugly!" Puzzled and confused, I walked away. I wondered, "Did she mean what she said? Is this just a thing she did because she just had a bad day?"

Unfortunately, there were no teachers around. Everyone seemed to move in the direction they originally intended. It was almost as though it did not happen, because nobody responded to what they heard, especially me. I walked away. And I realized people my age do not seem to care about anyone, so I did not really expect anyone to stand up for me. I hoped an adult would have been there to hear it and say something to that student. I decided to let it go and move through my day.

I did not realize this would happen again and again from the same girl. Every day for over one month, the same person found me in the hallway and yelled at me. She told me how ugly I was, laughed, and walked away. Because I was a quiet and shy person, I did not know how to handle the situation. I could not find one adult in the hallway. And no one my age ever said anything to the girl or asked me if I was

C. Boske & A. Osanloo (Eds.), Students, Teachers, and Leaders Addressing Bullying in Schools, 45–47.
© *2015 Sense Publishers. All rights reserved.*

okay. These people seemed more consumed with their lives, and could not take time to intervene.

The girl's yelling and name calling started to get to me. It was as though she knew I would not do anything about it, so she continued to yell at me when she had the chance. I went home and thought about it. I could not the words out of my head. I started to think something was wrong with me. She must have picked on me, because it was true. The girl did not choose anyone else, so, was it me? It devoured me. I could not focus. I grew more and more anxious going to school. I did not know when she might pop up and intimidate me. I felt so small.

All I could think about was her yelling at me, calling me ugly, and watching other people laugh at me. It tore me apart. I could barely get out of bed. I started going to school later and later. I could not focus in school. I became more anxious as the class ended, because I knew I needed to use the hallway to get to my next class.

I did not want to go to school anymore. I felt so small and helpless. Sometimes I would cry in school. My self-image changed and I actually believed I was ugly and deserved to be treated this way. My self-esteem was definitely at an all-time low.

If you have not experienced something like this, know, it is intimidating to have someone humiliate you in front of other kids, yell at you, and laugh. The more difficult part of enduring this is trying to explain what is happening to you. You start to believe you deserve to be treated this way, so it is almost as though you should not say anything to an adult.

Sometimes I think the only way people might understand this is to experience it themselves. It is almost like people remove themselves from these situations. I think of it as a blind person listening to a movie on tape. The person can hear the movie, but is limited, because the person cannot get the full experience—seeing the actors and pictures.

I was being bullied, and I did not know how to handle the situation. I was paralyzed. It was horrible. I was miserable. I did not want to talk about the experiences with anyone. I was embarrassed, humiliated, and believing the words had some validity to them. With all of this happening, and burying everything deep inside, I was growing more and more stressed. I could not deal with it anymore.

I was stressed and depressed. I never thought I would have been one of those kids who would even care about something like this, but when it happens to you, it helps you realize the seriousness of bullying. That girl needed help. And I needed someone to stand up for me and help me confront what was happening. It was a new and unexpected experience for me. I felt like a failure. I did not know what I could do except keep to myself and stay away from school. I wanted this to stop.

The girl won the daily battles. I needed to win the war. How would I do this? What steps would I take? I knew turning the other cheek helped me take the high road, but did I actually win the war? Just knowing I was more mature by walking away did not seem to help me. I never confronted the girl. She continued to yell at me and call me names. I continued to walk away. Months went by and eventually, she must have found someone else to pick on, because she stopped bullying me.

The experience will always be in the back of my mind. I never told anyone what happened until now. I never felt comfortable talking with a teacher or principal. No one seemed to care, because no one was out there to watch over us. Teachers did not seem to notice I was more quiet than usual. I did not have many friends, and for those I had, I did not want to burden them with my stress.

I hope teachers and principals reading this will realize there are students who are not comfortable telling adults what is going on in their lives, because they do not think any of them care. Teachers did not ask about our day or weekends. And adults were not present in spaces where students gathered. I do not want something like this to devour a kid or make them upset. I hope they have someone they can turn to and reach out. I did not feel comfortable doing that, but my first choice would have been to turn to someone.

I handled this situation on my own, but there was a cost involved. I was stressed, anxious, and unfocused in school. I became more and more depressed as the yelling continued. I was able to see the light at the end of the tunnel, because my bully decided to eventually leave me alone. I might be one of the lucky ones.

I am not sure why someone chooses to bully others. I just wanted to go to school, learn, and return home. I try to make people happy. This is why I did not understand why someone would do this to me. I meant no harm, but obviously, this girl thought she could do this to me. Although I experienced this, I did not take my anxiety out on other people. I continued to try to make people smile and make them feel special. I give out at least 10 compliments a day. If I can help make someone smile, I know I did something good that day.

I hope teachers and principals reading this chapter realize we need them. We all look up to at least one of our teachers. Do you know if we look up to you? Do you know if you are one of those teachers we count on? We know who we can go to and we know who not to go to. We do not want to share with teachers who make it clear they are only there to teach. We want teachers who care about us. We want teachers who listen to us, give us advice, and support us. These teachers help us work through difficult situations, such as bullying. I did not have anyone at my school, but I hope you are someone students can turn to for help. This makes all the difference in the world, because what happens to students DOES MATTER, even if no one else is around.

MARIYAH

6. I WAS THE SHY AND AWKWARD GIRL

First off, I am not known as the beauty queen or most popular girl in school. Being popular, well, is being friends with *everyone*. Popular people seem to have the self-confidence that screams, "We can take on the world!" All my life, however, I was the *shy and awkward girl*. Today, I still work on my confidence, but please know, I have grown tremendously. A few years ago, I would not have had the courage to write about my life. And for the purpose of this chapter, I am writing about being bullied in school. Because of my hard work in counseling and focus on developing myself, I have the confidence to share this important part of my life.

As I talked about the bullying and shared my experiences, I grew to see myself as a strong, young woman. I can overcome any obstacle. I just need to focus, believe, and put my effort into overcoming it. Part of my strength comes from my belief in God, who I believe loves me and made me who I am. Throughout my experiences of being bullied, I realized I did not need to impress anybody. People who are true to me, love me for who I am. Today, I can stand before you and tell you–I am a strong, young woman. I have overcome a lot in my life. Because I am opening myself up to all you as a reader, I also need to protect myself, so I decided to choose to only use my first name as the author of this chapter.

I attended a small school and moved to a bigger school my freshman year. I barely knew anyone. In a matter of months, rumors spread like wildfire. I allegedly slept with a guy who I did not know. Girls and boys whispered my alleged sexual escapades in all of my classes. In my new town, I was known as "that girl." I had people who I did not know me, approach me, and ask if the rumors were true.

The more I heard, the more I grew scared. People left threatening notes in my locker. I was scared. All day, I constantly reminded myself of the rumors. I grew more and more upset. I was stressed out. It was hard to concentrate in school. I could not sleep. I started losing my hair. My mom knew something was wrong. She thought I was depressed. I went from being a happy, active young person, who wanted to socialize with people her age, to someone who did not want to get out of bed or do her hair. My mom took me to get my hair cut. She discovered something was seriously wrong. My hairdresser asked if I was pulling out my hair. My mom seized the moment. She asked me what I was experiencing at school. I told her what happened. The rumors tore me up inside. They went against my character.

My family made the decision to move me from one school to another one. My father did not seem to understand how this experience was impacting me. He seemed

C. Boske & A. Osanloo (Eds.), Students, Teachers, and Leaders Addressing Bullying in Schools, 49–51.
© *2015 Sense Publishers. All rights reserved.*

unaware of the seriousness of having being exposed to rumors about my sexual conduct. All in all, my father did not understand I was being bullied. He considered the rumors "girl drama," however, it was much more than that.

I was diagnosed with depression. I remember looking in the mirror and crying. I did not like what I saw. The rumors I heard continued to run through my head. Students yelled, "You are such a slut!" Others commented, "Why would anyone want to be with you?" and laughed. Some said, "You are fat." Others said, "You are ugly." I could not stop their hurtful words from running through my head. Unfortunately, I believed what I heard. I started to bully myself and became my worst enemy.

Over time, and in working with my counselor, I realized the impact their bullying had on my life. I started cutting myself. For those of you who do not know what this means, it is a form of physical self-harm. It is often done are people's arms, wrists, legs, and shoulders. At the time, I thought it was a way for me to release the pain of being bullied. I turned to cutting myself for several months.

One week before my birthday, I attempted suicide. It was one of the darkest moments of my life. I needed to know there was a light at the end of the tunnel. The scariest part for me was thinking there was no way out of being bullied. I tried overdosing with pills, but my body rejected it. My mom saw what was happening. I was rushed to the hospital and spent time focusing on keeping myself safe. I spent my 16th birthday with my family. It was at that moment, I felt I had a fresh start. If I could go back in time, I would have stood in front of myself and told myself that I could overcome the bullying without doing harm to my body and risking my life.

When I returned home, I fantasized about going back to school. I wondered if the people who bullied me would care about what I experienced. What I did not realize while being admitted into the hospital, is that you cannot make people be compassionate towards others. Returning to school was hard and nerve-wracking. On my first day back, I came home crying. I could not understand how people could be so mean. I was bullied again and again. The jokes were nonstop and at my expense. People would say hurtful things like, "Why don't you go kill yourself?" and laugh. I wanted to return to the hospital. It was a safe space. I thought when I came back to school, I would be safe. I thought the bullying would end. However, I was not safe. People did not change. I realized I needed to change.

I asked my mom, "Why can't I just run away and be myself?" I did not understand how people could be so cruel. I could not change the people around me, but I figured out I could change myself. I needed to increase my self-confidence. My junior year started off rough. I was bullied again. No one seemed to care or wanted to do anything about it. I felt hopeless, like there was nowhere for me to go. I cried almost every day in school. I started cutting again. On November 27, 2013, I attempted suicide. I gave up. I wanted to give up more than ever before.

I was rushed to the hospital. I stayed there for a week. This time, the staff reminded me going back to school would not be a safe bubble like the hospital. I grew more and more nervous about going back to school. I also grew scared to face myself.

They allowed me to go back to school and confront the bullying. I was ready to use the skills I learned in the hospital.

This time, I faced a new reality returning to school. I finished the semester. I ignored the bullies. I started off the semester with great grades. I also made amazing friends who supported and loved me. Today, I am living life with an authentic smile on my face. I have a new self-confidence, and it is slowly growing each day. I learned I have people around me that love me. I also learned that if people are meant to be in my life, then they will love me for who I am. In writing this chapter, I have gained a deeper understanding of what I have experienced and what I have overcome with bullying. I am proud of myself and where I am now. I love myself and love waking up every morning getting to start a new day.

I dedicate this chapter to my Mom—my everything.

DEVIN JONTEZ MCMILLER

7. I'M A LITTLE BIT DARKER

When I started writing this chapter, I initially kept to the facts. I quickly realized, after sharing my chapter with people my age, I needed to tell my story. I was bullied at the age of seven. I lived it. It is the use of force, threats, abuse, intimidation, or aggression towards others to try and overpower them. There are many different types of bullying. Some kids physically hit people; some verbally make fun of kids; others lie or spread rumors; and sometimes those same lies make their way onto the internet, which is called cyber bullying. For this chapter, I will talk about my experiences of being verbally and physically bullied. I experienced being bullied by my family members as well as people spreading rumors about me. It was sad, because I was just a kid. I did not have anyone to turn to, because I was just a kid; and I guess, it was supposed to shake it off, especially because I was a boy. I did not know what to think at the time, but I knew I felt sad every time I was called out of my name, made fun of, or had rumors told about me.

It hurt EVERY time it happened.

No one knew about it. I did not talk to anybody. I was afraid of being judged by my family, friends, and teachers. I did not want anyone to think I was crazy for telling people my feelings were hurt or let them know I was sad. My friends would have judged me. They would not have understood why bullying bothered me. I was expected not to let stuff like that get to me. If kids let names and rumors get to them, then they stand a good chance of being a target. It sounds crazy, but if I told my friends and family their words and actions hurt me, I would be blamed me for being hurt. It is almost like telling someone that if you are bullied, well, it is your own fault, because you should not let stuff like that bother you. It excuses the bullies. It is not right, but that is what happened. In writing this chapter, I want everyone to know words do hurt.

Ever since I could remember, I was always targeted for my dark skin color. It is not just because I am Black. It is because my skin is much darker than most Black people I know. Throughout my childhood, I was always made fun of because my skin was darker than other Black people's skin color. Children at my school said things like, "Ewe…you're as black as night," or "You look like a TV when it's turned off," or "You look a burned piece of meat." I said stuff back to them. I laughed. But I laughed, because I had to hide the hurt inside. I thought, "Wow, I can't believe they just said that to me" on the inside. I did not understand why anyone would ever say stuff like that to anyone, especially another Black person.

Some people might not consider this bullying, but it was. I was made fun of every day. I felt so small. I wonder if students saying these things to me thought they were bullying me or not. I wonder, because I laughed. And because I laughed, did they think it didn't bother me? But what was my other choice? To cry? Laughing, for me, took the pain away.

I tucked away the pain in my heart. I held onto it for years. I thought I let it go, but the more I grew up and thought about it, the more it hurt. Even though it weighed heavy on my heart, I never told anyone until now. Writing this chapter is the first time I am sharing what I experienced when I was bullied. I did not tell my teachers or principal, because I was convinced they would think I was foolish. What teacher is going up to pay attention to a kid telling them these two guys or two girls are making fun of me because I am darker than them?

I decided to write this chapter, because it was a chance to write down my feelings. I journal every so often, but I never shared my thoughts publicly, as I have in writing this chapter. I am taking a risk by telling you about being bullied by my family and friends. I decided to do this to show people they can do something to stop bullying. I know there are people who will not tell you what they are really thinking, but maybe teachers and principals could give students a chance to write it if they are in pain, especially if they feel bullied.

I saw what happened to me as bullying. There was absolutely no reason why someone should have said those things to me or to anyone. It was constant. The more that was said, the smaller I felt. Just because my skin was darker than other Black people did not give anyone the right to talk about me in a negative way. I am not sure if someone said those words to them, if it would hurt or not, but it hurt me. It hurt me deeply. When I see people get made fun of, it does not always seem like it gets to them. However, they might be hurting on the inside. I just realized in writing this, they might be just like me. They might hold onto the pain even though it might bother them.

I don't think people understand how much it hurts to be taunted, to be ridiculed, to have someone degrade you. It is like losing somebody. When I lose someone important to me, I feel like I lost everything. When someone hurts me, I feel like I lost a part of myself. Every school I attended, every party, every sporting event, every time I went out with my friends or my family members, I was called a name, or made fun of because I had dark skin. My family would laugh at me, but I was not going to show them their words hurt me. The same thing happened with my friends. And when you are made fun of by your family and your friends, who are you going to turn to?

I think that some of this is because of how I was brought up. I was taught what it meant to be a man. My dad, grandfather, and brother always told me to be tough, not to get pushed around, and not to let things bother them. I never saw anything get to them. I wonder how often my dad cried as a kid or as an adult. I wonder if he cries to himself. I wonder if he goes to a private place and lets it all out. I also wonder what hurts my grandfather. I wonder what hurts him? Who does he talk to? Where does the hurt go?

Today, I'm 17 and a senior in high school. People still make fun of me, but it does not affect me as much as it did when I was a kid. I think I just became used to it. My heart still hurts when people say mean things about my dark skin, but I try not to let their words get to me. The key is having one person you can tell everything. I met him 1 ½ years ago. He is my best friend. I feel safe talking to him about these kinds of things. He is not going to pass judgment on me. My best friend understands me and believes no one has the right to degrade anyone.

As I spoke with my best friend, I became more aware of how bullying affected me. It impacted me emotionally, academically, and socially. First, I came home every day after school. I would lie on my bed and cry. My parents asked me if something was wrong. I would not tell them the truth. I would simply say, "Nothing." I never told my parents anything, because I did not like to express my feelings. Second, bullying not only affected my inability to share with other people, it also affected me mentally. Their words weighed heavy on my mind. I found it hard to concentrate on what was really important, like school, and my sports. Bullying affected me mentally and academically, because I could not concentrate. I was not able to focus on my school work, pass my classes, or do my best in my sports. Third, bullying influenced me socially. I stopped hanging out with some of my friends. I did not want to tell anyone how I felt, so I thought it would be best to stay away from people. I did not seem to have a care in the world. My friends acted like they did not care about what was happening in my life or how much they hurt me. I knew if I went to them, they would laugh at me. I saw it happen with other people, so I knew I would not be any different. It seemed that staying to myself was the best option.

I was not the only person bullied in school. I remember a girl I knew since I was four years old. Her name was Mariah (I changed her name for this chapter to protect her anonymity). She was skinny. Mariah was made fun every single day, because of her weight. There was a point in time when she starved herself and threw up things she ate. She said she did this, because people made fun of her. Mariah had a difficult time dealing with people taunting her. She was called names like "twig", "toothpick", and "kick stand", just to name a few. I reached out to her, because it hurt me to see her in this kind of pain.

All the way up until July 16, 2010, when we were talking, she told me she could not take the hurt and pain anymore. The next day, her mom called me. She said Mariah committed suicide. I cannot begin to tell you how sad I was to lose my friend. I hope, after hearing Mariah took her life, that for every person who bullied her, they would realize the hurt they caused. I hope those individuals feel terrible inside for the damage done. They may not have seen Mariah as valuable or important, but she was my childhood best friend. And I was Mariah's only friend. I wish she was still here, so I could show her everything would have worked out in the end. I wanted to help her to ignore the negative people in her life. I wanted her to know she had a friend in me. I still miss my childhood best friend.

I think bullying is one of the worst things someone can do to another person. For Mariah, it led to her death. For me, it continues to hurt my heart, but I have someone to talk to—my high school best friend of 1½ years. I learned to take those experiences that had a negative impact on me and turn them into a positive. For me, being bullied was negative, because it hurt my heart. It was positive, because I never had the courage to express myself as I am in this chapter.

I never thought I would be an author of a chapter in a book to prepare teachers, principals, students and families to understand the effects of bullying. This opportunity helped me find the courage within to share publicly about what happened to me. I look at this chapter as a way to reach out to others—students or adults who work with children. I do not want children being bullied to think they deserve to be treated in that way; I want adults to learn how to listen to children and care about what they may or may not say; and I want those who think it is okay to bully other children the impact their actions have on someone's spirit. Adults and students need to take action and do something about bullying in and outside of school.

> For those who might be bullied, I want you to know this:
> No matter who you are
> how you look
> or what someone might say about you,
> YOU can be whatever you want to be.
> Live up to your dreams!
> Whatever you have going on with yourself,
> don't let anyone take that away from you.
> Focus on the positives in your life.
> Forget the negatives, because they aren't worth it.
> Believe me.

When I finally shared my experiences with adults, all they told me was to let it go. The adults acknowledged the issues I shared, but they failed to take action. They did not attempt to protect me or say anything to the person bullying me. They heard my words, but chose not to get involved. What happened? I continued to be bullied. Adults need to know we count on them to do something. They need to learn to be present. They need to learn to be there. What happened to me was unacceptable. I did not ask for much. I asked for a helping hand. I asked for someone to stand up for me. I asked for someone to stop hurting my heart. If you are an adult and work in schools, you are supposed to DO SOMETHING about it. So, please do something. Show children you care. And in the end, I need you to know I realize BLACK IS BEAUTIFUL.

ANTHONY BIAS

8. HOW DO YOU FEEL ABOUT BULLYING
IN SCHOOLS?

Bullying is possibly one of the easiest things to deal with; however, it is also a very traumatizing event in a child's lifetime. When a child is bullied, it often leads to low self-esteem, depression, and in serious cases, suicide. According to studies done at Yale University, it is estimated that bully victims are 2 to 9 times more likely to consider suicide then non-victims. When a child is bullied in school, it can also lead to low grades and antisocial behavior.

When I was in middle school, I was bullied because of my race and my weight. I was called everything from racial terms like "cracker" and "honky" to things like "snowflake" and "Santa Claus", just because I was White and overweight. I became depressed and my school work showed it as well. When asked by my teachers what was wrong, I would lie or say nothing, because I didn't think they could help me without making it worse. I took three years of bullying, both physical and mental, just because I was scared of them. That's something nobody should have to go through. I'm a senior in high school and about to graduate in four months. I'm not afraid to help someone who I see is getting bullied or give them an ear to listen to if they want to talk.

Honestly, I feel if you're bullying someone in your school, no matter who they are, you don't belong in that school. You might be better off being homeschooled, since you don't know how to treat other people. A child who is being bullied doesn't function the same as someone who has never experienced it. The victim who is being bullied often has a troubled look on their face, is paranoid, has low self-esteem, and often keeps to themselves.

There are multiple ways to resolve being bullied but, of course, that's easier said than done. You can try telling an adult like a teacher or parent about the bully and let them handle it; you can try talking to your bully and finding out why they are bullying you; or you can try and ignore them and hope that he or she stops. There is one other option that most children resort to, which is fighting. Fighting your bully can either be a good or a bad way to resolve your issue. By fighting your bully, you are are showing her/him that you are no longer afraid of and you have had enough. At the same time though, you can get into serious trouble and be expelled or suspended from the school. So, fighting should be your last resort after trying to talk to somebody about it.

C. Boske & A. Osanloo (Eds.), Students, Teachers, and Leaders Addressing Bullying in Schools, 57–58.
© 2015 Sense Publishers. All rights reserved.

However, everyone is responsible for the bullying. The bully is responsible for harassing someone and the victim is responsible for not telling someone about it. It's important not to let the verbal and physical abuse go on. The school is responsible, because they either are not promoting a "bully-free" learning environment or have very little consequences to punish the children who are bullying the others. I believe the main people who are responsible for bullying, however, are the parents of the children. They're responsible too, because bullying starts at home with older, and in some cases, younger siblings bullying each other without being punished. They grow up thinking it's okay to act and treat other people that way, so they do it at school. Parents are also responsible, because if they show very little to no interest to their child, it can cause the child to become mean and hateful towards other people and causes them to take their anger out on other people. If the child is dealing with issues at home like a death in the family, their parents getting divorced, or being abused, it can confuse the child and make them act out for attention. My message to parents and teachers is this: If you suspect your child or student is being bullied, encourage them to talk to you and inform them that you're always there to talk to them.

Anthony Bias
Esperanza Inc.
Youth Leader
Senior at Horizon Science Academy
Cleveland, OH

LEAH BAILEY

9. STANDING UP TO THE POPULAR GIRL

Mindy was a good friend of mine, well actually, she still is. We've known each other since we were two years old. You could say we were opposites. She often saw the sky as rainy. I often saw it as sunny. She loved to sing and I loved to draw. Eventually, we taught each other to think like the other. She now loves to draw. I now love to sing and act. There was a time, however, when Mindy was underestimated, bullied, and kicked aside like a rotting soccer ball.

We were at school one day, when we sat down for lunch. A tight-skirted, glossy-haired, high-heel wearing, "popular" (I hate that word) girl, named Emma, strutted up to us-posse right on her tail. Emma glanced at me, then Mindy. She smirked and began to mock Mindy. Emma made fun of the way she dressed; the way she was overweight; and the way she flipped her head and squealed. You need to know Mindy has Tourette's syndrome, which is an uncontrollable psychological disease that causes her to have repetitive movements and vocalizations called tics. Nobody, not even Mindy knew she had it.

"I…I can't control it!" Mindy sobbed. I don't know if it was my imagination, but it seemed the more stressed she was, the more tics she had. I didn't know what to do. I had never been in a situation like this before.

Emma continued to laugh along with her posse until an athletic-looking girl, sporting a worn, blue, baseball jersey with auburn hair, walked toward us. "You know Emma," The girl said. "If you keep this up, I'll tell the principal."

Emma scowled at her and said, "Why do you always have to be such a teacher's pet, Alex!?"

That seemed to have shut her up, because I saw her and her intimidated posse walk away. The girl, apparently her name was Alex, said, "Yeah, sorry about that, I wish I saved you guys sooner." I smiled and since that day, all three of us have been good friends.

It's funny, because I even made friends with Emma. She grew out of her childish ways. Alex, Mindy, and I are still good friends. Anyway, I go to a different school now. I suppose there are ways to stand up to someone like that. But I felt the need to let you all know that's how I confronted a bully in school.

C. Boske & A. Osanloo (Eds.), Students, Teachers, and Leaders Addressing Bullying in Schools, 59.
© *2015 Sense Publishers. All rights reserved.*

EDWARD VALENTIN

10. SCHOOL VIOLENCE

To think that it got so far and at the same time out of control. What is the point of
existence if at the same time, when you think about it, the people who help you only
help the people they see fit to help? I'm not one of the people selected. What does
that make me? What's the point of it all? If you're shunned and try to change your
stars and fail, does that make you more of a failure or does that make you a fool?
I learned that everyone in life who has succeeded in life has gambled everything,
including their every last dime, and came back and stood tall. I believe that in that
moment when you have failed, you realize that you're already in pain, so what's the
point in giving up? You're already in pain. You are already hurt might. You might as
well get a reward for it. So why not keep trying?

People are different from one another in many ways. So, is it the system we live
in or are we supposed to act just like everyone else? Follow everyone's tale? If they
jumped off a bridge, should we jump off too? In our society, what makes a person
cool of hip? Is it how many fights you can win, how many sexual partners you can
obtain, or simply seeing who is the baddest of the bad? What's the point in trying
to achieve self-satisfaction by hurting others? Is it because you want others to feel
what you felt? This is a question I ask myself all the time, but I never acted on those
thoughts and feelings (hurting others). Does that make me weak?

If you don't become an actor of sorts, you honestly won't be a factor in people's
eyes. The people who have their face thrown through the dirt are people who I can
relate to, because I've gone through bullying myself. I remember a teacher of mine
was talking to me about all these kid in juvenile detention centers and how he was
always trying to help the youth there. He said, "It's interesting to meet a kid who
murdered somebody, but can be the ideal son." As young people, we go through
a lot of pain. And most of the time, if not all of the time, it's because we have
dysfunctional families. Acknowledgment is what I believe people are searching for
and that's why people do the things they do. They want to be known and recognized.
I also think it's because they're lonely; through personal experiences, I know that
loneliness is one of the greatest sufferings a person can go through.

Even if it's mischief, the fact there is acknowledgment, gives them something
to strive for. They are confused and maybe they believe only people with God-
given-gifts can become "Somebody". Both youth from both parties, the ones being
bullied and the ones not, don't realize they both have potential. They need to practice
and develop their skills so they can become successful themselves. How can they

C. Boske & A. Osanloo (Eds.), Students, Teachers, and Leaders Addressing Bullying in Schools, 61–62.
© *2015 Sense Publishers. All rights reserved.*

though? They don't have a mentor most of the time or a coach who can put them on the right track. So it all comes down to the fact these young people need to want it for themselves. They got to have to want change to have it. They have to be able to devote themselves to an idea and become something much more.

And I do believe people that go through pain can change their pain into something positive, and make a difference.

Edward Valentin
Esperanza Inc.
Youth Leader
Senior at Horizon Science Academy
Cleveland, OH

AAJAH CHAPMAN

11. BEING "WHITE"

Currently, I am a ninth grader. I am an active and adventurous, young Person of Color. I love playing sports. The two sports I excel in are volleyball and track. Up until ninth grade, I have been one of the few Children of Color in school. Because there were only a few of us, I was often bullied because I acted White. "Acting White" means acting proper, listening to pop music, watching certain kind of movies, using certain words like "blouse" and the tone of your voice. Most of my friends are White. I don't really correspond with other Black students, because of how I've been treated. In fourth grade, I saw a lot of kids getting picked on, because of how they dressed, the activities they liked to do, and the way they learned. I was picked on too. I thought it was just kids being mean to one another, but when I turned ten, I realized teens and adults called that kind behavior "bullying".

The first time I really experienced bullying was during my fourth grade year, after school, in daycare. The daycare held infants and school agers up to twelve years of age and served around 20 kids. It used to be a house. From the outside, it was painted grey and it was about the size of a trailer. There were two bathrooms, one kitchen, and four rooms for the children.

The bully was a third grade girl who was nine years of age. I was excited to see her attend the daycare, because she was Black too. In the daycare, I was the only Black person in my age group, which was fine because I got along with everyone. Her skin tone was a bit darker than mine. She had thick, medium, blackish-brown hair. Lo and behold, she was not what I expected. Because I wasn't around a lot of Black people, I thought she would have been like me. However, she was rude and spoke in a ghetto accent. A "ghetto accent" is when someone talks in slang. I couldn't comprehend what she was saying to me. Both she and her brother were alike. They both bullied me.

The girl always pushed, shoved, and said mean things to me. Her brother and his friends called me peanut head after we'd get off the school bus. One day, the girl decided to slap my face. And without thinking, I kicked her in the stomach. The daycare director and our mothers disciplined us both. We both were written up, but she was suspended for a day. I was not suspended. Her mother decided not to let her children return because I was not suspended.

In fifth grade, I was homeschooled, because I'm a bit slower than others. I have Attention Deficit Hyperactivity Disorder (ADHD) and Auditory Processing Delay (APD). This makes it harder for me to focus in school. Homeschooling worked for a while, but I started to miss my friends, and the computer I used for schooling got damaged. When I returned to school in 6th grade, the bullying started all over again. My classmates made fun of my forehead. They told me my forehead was huge. They

C. Boske & A. Osanloo (Eds.), Students, Teachers, and Leaders Addressing Bullying in Schools, 63–64.
© 2015 Sense Publishers. All rights reserved.

called me LeBron James, because he had a receding hairline too. At first, I thought it was funny. I laughed along with them, but as the years passed, and as I got older, it started to annoy me. I felt self-conscious.

What really bothered me was people thinking they could walk all over me and talk to me in any kind of way. I didn't say anything back to them. They knew I wouldn't speak to them in the same, because I never acted that way towards them. When I was younger, I defended myself verbally and physically, but years later, those actions came back to haunt me. The girl I kicked never forgot and never forgave me. She lived by me. She never really said anything to me, until one day, when her cousins were visiting. She decided to show off. Her cousins and brother held my arms and legs above ground. They let her punch me in the stomach. They swung me on the ground. She told me she punched me for kicking her in the stomach.

Since then, I decided to try not to argue with people or fight them, because they could hold a grudge, say something that's hurtful, or spread rumors. And I don't want to get in trouble at school, because my education means a lot to me. I don't have time to worry about bullies or drama. I don't need to be distracted or suspended from school. Today, in school and on the bus, I feel a little sense of security, because I know bullying is not tolerated. Usually bullying starts when nobody is watching. And when a teacher or staff member confronts the bully, unfortunately, the damage is already done. In my neighborhood, I also feel a little sense of security. I am friends with all of the neighborhood kids. If an unwanted visitor comes in the neighborhood and decides to bother me, all of the kids have my back. If an unwanted visitor does come and no one is around, I'll just walk somewhere else or go home.

During school, I ignore the bullies and focus on my work. When I get bullied in school, I take it as a motivation to be better than that person and to do better in school. Sometimes the bullying makes me feel stronger. Sometimes it makes me feel weak. Sometimes I wouldn't mind it and other times, I just get annoyed. Through all of this, I learned bullies can also be my friends. People don't always mean to be a bully or offensive. Sometimes, they do things to be funny. Sometimes it is funny. Sometimes I make a joke about the comment made and crack a joke about them. Most of the time, the jokes are funny, but when jokes aren't funny, they know when to stop.

When I get bullied, I usually tell my mom. She tells me to ignore them. Sometimes my mom goes to the school or to the parent(s) of the bully and speaks to them about what happened. When she does this, sometimes the problem is solved, but sometimes a new problem happens. The bully and his or hers friends call me a snitch. They tell everyone my mom came to help me, because I can't fight my own battles. So, because of this, sometimes I don't tell my mom or teachers about the bullying.

I have been bullied throughout my life, and will probably continue to be bullied. Bullies are everywhere– at school, work, and other places. What teachers should do to make and keep a safe environment for students in school is to have a talk with students who have been bullied and ask them what they would like teachers to do to help them in their situation and talk to the bully. Maybe, teachers should ask why they are bullying and maybe figure out why it's happening. I bet they have a story too.

ERICA HOWARD

12. WHAT MAKES ME BEAUTIFUL

I was seven years old when I experienced bullying. No one likes people making fun of them, but at the time, I was the victim. Two girls were teasing and making fun of me, because they thought I was a little on the chubby side. I realized I would eventually grow, so I wasn't concerned. I also had curly hair. It was harder for me to wear certain kinds of clothes. I thought I needed to impress these girls or maybe even act like them. I hoped that if I could just change a few things, maybe they would leave me alone. I didn't realize being a little on the chubby side and having curly hair gave these girls the right to hurt me. I knew there were things going on with me and my life, but I never thought I would be bullied for being me.

When all of this started, it was a weird thing for me. I didn't know what to do. I didn't fully understand it. I always tried to be nice to people, so I didn't understand why these girls were being mean. I tried to be nice to both of them and even wanted to hear why they thought they could be mean to me.

From the very first day I was bullied. I dreaded going to school. I feared every morning what they might say to me. If both girls were at school, I knew they would make fun of me. I dreaded getting on the bus to school and going to school. However, I loved taking the bus home, because neither of those girls rode the bus after school. Being on the bus and heading home was my only safe place at school.

Finally, one day, I had enough of these girls. While we were sitting on the classroom rug, I raised my hand, stood up, and said, "Katie and Kim are being mean to me and I don't know why." Afterwards, I remember kids laughing at me. I slowly sat down. The girls eventually got in trouble by the teacher, but my self-confidence went down, way down. I started to keep my thoughts to myself. I was shy and had less self-confidence. I went from being a social butterfly to keeping to myself and sharing only a few words.

At the time, I didn't believe it was the bullying that caused me to stop sharing. I was under the impression it was because I told the teacher in front of the whole class. I didn't know at the time they were bullying me. And I didn't know how to properly handle the situation. And the teacher, well, she wasn't my favorite teacher. I didn't trust her, but she was the only teacher around when I told myself enough was enough.

The year after all this started, I met my best friend, Cassy. I made many friends through the years, but the majority of them came and left. Cassy was different. She stayed at my school. The year I met Cassy, I wasn't bullied. So, it's safe to say third

C. Boske & A. Osanloo (Eds.), Students, Teachers, and Leaders Addressing Bullying in Schools, 65–67.

grade was my favorite elementary year in school. However, the bullying started up again in fourth grade.

This time, I chose to just deal with the bullying, since I had such a horrible experience when I told my teacher I was being bullied. I made friends, but none of them ever knew people bullyied me. I realize now, I dealt with the bullying through food. It wasn't my best option, but it's what I turned to at the time, and now, it's back to bite me in the butt. But at the time, food filled the hole in my heart.

In seventh grade, I experienced the worst of the bullying. For some reason, I thought high school might be the worst place where bullies are their meanest; however, it was bad in middle school.

In seventh grade, students were mandated to attend a suicide prevention program. I knew what suicide was, but I never knew why people would choose to attempt or commit suicide. After the program, let's just say a new window opened for me.

I was in physical education for the marking period. A group of girls bullied me in the locker room. They would tell me in sorts of ways that I stunk. I hated PE already, because I wasn't fast or athletic. Having those girls make fun of me in the locker room made it even worse.

One day, they took it too far. I hit my breaking point. I wanted to get away from their evil words, so I considered ending my life. I wanted them to feel sorry they ever did or said those horrible things to me.

When I was younger and someone was mean to me, I either drew a picture of them and ripped it or wished they would leave. I sat across from Cassy and told her I thought about killing myself. She started to cry. I still feel guilty about sharing that with her to this day.

Cassy told another student and the other student told a school counselor. I was called down to the counselor's office. The counselor and I had long chat. I had a good cry. I told him about the girls and what they were doing to me. I trusted him. I just needed to let my feelings spray out.

The counselor called my parents. I told my parents everything. That night, I was listening to Christina Aguilera's song "Beautiful." That song made me feel a bit better. There was another song that made me even happier. Yes, a song actually helped me feel a bit happier about myself. The song was called, "What Makes You Beautiful."

There were five teenage boys on my screen singing why I was beautiful. That's not something that happens every day. Their song made me smile. I didn't stop smiling the rest of the day. They were like magic. I still use their song when I'm feeling bad about myself.

I went back to school the next day feeling a bit better. One of the girls told me she was sorry for saying and doing those things to me. I knew I had heard those words many times before and again, they were just words, but I felt like she actually meant them. She didn't make fun of me again. She is nice to me now and she is someone I call my friend.

In eighth grade, there were people who were mean to me, but I stopped caring. I just wanted to build a wall between myself and the bullies. I actually succeed. Their words never got to me again.

As a freshman in high school, I don't get bullied any more. I made friends and my self-confidence is going up. I am trying to be less shy, but I realize that might take a while. My self-esteem is not the highest, but it's better than before. I'm still a little awkward in social situations, but I'm okay with that for now.

I get the impression it's wrong or weird to be shy and awkward in social situations. It's almost like thinking that if someone is shy, they need to see a therapist or something. What people really need is someone to be their friend. Everyone has their own story. There are reasons why people became the person they are today. It's important to get to know the person versus judging them.

People say high school is where most bullying occurs, but I don't think that's true. I think it's too late to wait until high school. Look at me. I was in elementary school. I was just a kid.

I still hate school, but now I can say it's not because of bullying. I hate school, because it's normal for teenagers not to like homework and just want to sleep. I can tell you for the first time in school, I have a super cool teacher I can count on to help me with any problems. That is the best thing a student can ask for: a teacher who cares about you.

That super cool teacher helped me come out of my shell a little bit. I am still a work in progress, but I am growing stronger every day. You know, all students need to have a teacher they can go to with a problem in their life, not just in school.

I try to forget my memories of being bullied, but I am not sure I want them completely out of my head. As much as I hate those memories, they can actually help me sometimes. They help me with working towards my goals. They help me remember life has up and downs. And even though I had a lot of downs, I always came back up.

Just writing this chapter about my experiences is making me feel better. I needed to let my feelings and share my experiences. Some of these feelings and experiences were bottled up for seven years! And for some memories, they are still hard to talk about. Too often people who bully other people need to realize they can leave scars. Some scars heal over time, while others stay fresh forever, never to heal.

ANGELY BOSKE

13. LEARNING TO LOVE ONE ANOTHER

My Mom asked me years ago if I would be interested in contributing a chapter to a book someday. I was surprised, because I was just a kid. Actually, I was only five years old at the time. I didn't know if I could handle it, but my Mom knew I could. She believes all children are valuable, and she believed in me and wanted me to use my voice. Using my voice is about being heard. It's not about being heard literally, it's about using your advantages to educate people. For example, I have the advantage of having a Mom who is a writer, a professor, and teaches people how to be good leaders. That gives me an advantage, because she teaches me to be fair and to understand the world and how we should act toward one another. Another advantage is I get to publish my work. We can write with each other and I have the chance to put my work in art exhibits that focus on leading for social justice. I have also been able to read books about Brown v. Board and it helps me understand what happened when Black and White people were separated from each other. I use all of these experiences when I am in school, especially in social studies. By using my voice, I learned I can reach people and help everyone love one another. I raised funds during one of the Leading for Social Justice Art Exhibits for books for my school so children could understand that differences should be celebrated. I bought books about boys who felt like girls on the inside; about families with two Moms or two Dads; about girls who were leaders; children from different countries; people who changed the world, because they fought for human rights; and children who spoke a language other than English.

When we put people in categories, we shut people down, because being different for some reason is bad. People are not just the color of their skin or who they love or what they look like or who they live with. People are much more complex than that. We should be thinking about differences in a positive way. I don't know if I am right or not, but I think children need to believe in themselves and children need adults to believe in them too.

In this chapter, I want to talk about what principals should do to make sure children feel welcome: 1) All children need to be loved and valued; 2) We need Brown children and White children going to school together; 3) We need to be a family when we are in school; 4) Children's families should be seen as something special and welcomed; and 5) Make learning fun and mean something.

C. Boske & A. Osanloo (Eds.), Students, Teachers, and Leaders Addressing Bullying in Schools, 69–75.

A. BOSKE

ALL CHILDREN NEED TO BE LOVED AND VALUED

I have been to a lot of schools since I was two years old. I can only remember one principal who made a difference. I had a horrible experience with my first elementary principal. She was mean and didn't seem to like children. I was bullied for almost a year and she wouldn't do anything to help me. I cried in school. I visited the nurse several times a day. I needed to get out of there. I just wanted to go home and be away from those girls. It got so bad that I got sick to my stomach. I thought I was going to throw up. I wouldn't eat my lunch or my snacks.

At night, I started grinding my teeth. I took off a layer of my teeth. I had terrible headaches from grinding and clinching my teeth. I didn't even know what stress was at seven, but my dentist knew something was very wrong too. My Moms shared all of this with my principal and my teachers. They explained how bullying was affecting my health. My teachers wouldn't do anything about the bullying and neither would my principal. When my Moms went to school over and over again to help them understand what was happening, all my principal would do was make things harder and harder for me. She sent out these spies to watch me on the playground. It was crazy. They actually stood outside with little notepads and wrote down what I was doing. I felt like I was under so much pressure. I just wanted it all to stop. I wanted these girls to stop pushing me on the playground, calling me names, making fun of me because I was Latina, and trying to make other children stay away from me. It was a bad time in my life. It got so bad that I told my Moms I didn't want to go to school anymore. What kid doesn't want to go to school at seven?

My Moms called the superintendent and the Board members. No one would help. They heard about a principal in the district. They went and spoke with the principal about my situation and being bullied. She welcomed my Moms to her school. She gave them a tour of the building and let them sit in on classes. My Moms were impressed with the teachers and the principal. We went to some family events and I interviewed students my age to find out what they thought of the school. They loved the principal and all of their teachers. They felt like their teachers and principal really cared about them. The principal even gave me a water bottle and a card welcoming me to their family. I saw her at a summer blues concert at the art museum before school even started. She saw me, came over, and asked my Mom if she could dance with me. I was all red in the face. I was so excited to see my new principal and that she remembered I was going to go to school there. She was so much fun and thanked me for the dance. I thought she was so special. And then my teachers at my new school sent me letters to my home! They told me how excited they were to have me in their classes. They also told me something about themselves and their families. On my first day of school, I made sure I picked flowers from our garden for my principal and my new teacher. I couldn't believe how much they already showed me that I mattered. It was so different than my other school.

70

So, what did I learn? I think principals and teachers need to show how they love all of the children or they shouldn't be allowed to work in schools. I think principals and teachers need to be standing at the front door every morning and giving everyone a hug. I actually had this happen when I went to my new school. Every day two of the ladies who worked in the office were outside and so was the principal and my teachers. Why? They wanted us to know they loved us. They wanted us to feel welcome. It wasn't just about getting an education; it was about my teachers and the principal and the two ladies loving us and wanting us to do our very best.

Children need to know they are loved and valued by their principals and their teachers. We were greeted every day. They asked us every day how we were doing. They looked out for us. When they hugged us, they knew right away if something just wasn't right. It made me feel special. They treated you like every day was their last day with you. It was a special place. That principal is no longer at my old school. She retired, but my teachers and the two ladies made sure they hugged every child every morning and showed them how much they cared.

WE NEED BROWN CHILDREN AND WHITE CHILDREN IN SCHOOL TOGETHER

I thought about what it might take to make a school welcoming for everyone. First of all, there needs to be a mix people of Brown, Black, and White children. I was the only Latina child in my elementary school before I went to my new elementary school. When I went into fourth grade, there were a couple of children adopted from Guatemala. I didn't know them, because they were younger than me, but I knew I wasn't the only Latina. I am in a new school now for 5th grade. I am the only Latina child, but there is a student in my class who is bi-racial. She is Black and White, but I can only think of one other Black student in a lower grade and some children who are Asian. We need to think about how we are going to change what schools look like, because right now, there are a lot of White people, but that's not how every school looks at all.

If we are going to learn about each other, then there have to be opportunities for everyone to be with someone from another race. Teachers and principals need to make this happen. The more we learn about each other, the more we can stick up for one another. I want to know about different people and understand their perspectives. We all come from different walks of life, but I can't learn something about someone if I don't get to know them as people.

I want to end this section by saying, it's important for White people to know Brown people, not just White people. They need to realize Brown people are not different and are not people to be afraid of. By spending time with each other, you get to know them. You get to learn with them and create with them. Just think, what could we accomplish if we had the chance to work together and do something to make schools better places?

CREATE A SENSE OF FAMILY

Schools need to do a better job at making kids feel like they are in a family when they are in school. Families are spaces where people are loved and cared for. At home, family members live with you. You know you are loved and this is where you belong. So in school, to create a sense of family, teachers, principals, and students need to learn about each other, love each other, and should know people will be there for them. Children who love school and feel like a family would probably not want to leave school, because they enjoy the people they live with during the day. If they had to choose a second family, children would say school is their second family.

To make a family, you need to act like a family. It can't just be words. Like my Mom always says, it's my actions that speak louder than my words. The same holds true for my teachers and principals. Every child should be greeted by the teacher, principal, and everyone who works there. Compliments should be given to each child. Every child should hear one positive thing about themselves at least once a day. How hard would it be to say to a child, "You will do a fantastic job today!" or "Good luck on your test today! You studied so hard". How difficult is that?

I am a firm believer in showing people you love them. Every child needs at least one hug a day from a teacher. It tells us we are cared for and cared about. It shows us we are loved. This is important to a child.

Every child should greet one another. Maybe we could begin talking about what saying hello means to us. Maybe we could learn how to say or give a "hello" in a different language. Maybe every child could give one another one compliment to start the day. Receiving a compliment raises a child's spirit. They will get excited about the rest of the day, because you are reminding children they are important. And without them, children's lives might be sad. I mean, I know I can live without certain people, but I appreciate my friends and appreciate them in my life. I want them to know and to feel they are important to me and all of those around them.

Another way to make sure children feel like school is a family is for teachers and principals to let them visit with them. Maybe students could go to the teacher's home one night and let the teacher know how great this teacher is and what this teacher means to the children. They would celebrate the teacher. That's an idea.

When you are in a family, you feel like you are important. Your family members tell each other this every day. Maybe students could have a bucket in their classroom. Every time the teacher does something kind or if the children admire something about her, then the child might say, "I really like how you taught us multiplication" or "you did an awesome job teaching us about…". I think we should stay away from compliments about their shirts or the way they dress, because we should be focusing on what they are doing. I think too often we put too much emphasis on what people look like, what they wear, or how they do their hair, and teachers need to know what kids appreciate about them. I know every student would pay close attention to what everyone is doing and put the compliments in the bucket.

INCLUDE OUR FAMILIES

If you want people to feel welcome, then you have to want to know who I call my family and what they mean to me. It's more than telling them my grades or telling them to come to open house. Schools should come to families. The school should not always expect the adults to come to the school. I think teachers and principals need to leave the school and visit our neighborhoods. If they want to understand us, then they should come and visit our families.

If students are having trouble on homework, I think teachers should help adults at home understand how to help their child. Or maybe let them have a way to keep in touch with them, so if they have a question, they can get help.

Instead of having an open house, where everyone just goes class to class and no one really talks to each other for more than five minutes, teachers and principals go to students' homes and meet their families. Maybe they can give them a card with a piece of candy attached to it. Teachers would let the families know what they appreciate about their child and what their child brings with them to school.

Maybe principals and teachers could begin the year by visiting students at home. They could send a letter to every family letting them know how excited they were to have their child in their class. There would be a piece of candy tied to the card. When the teacher came to the family's home, the teacher would find out more about the child would like to learn and how the child learns best. Maybe a child needs to work on more math facts, then the teacher would know this and the family would know the teacher is going to work with their child throughout the year.

I think it would be helpful if everyone met everyone's family. I think it's important, because you would know each other and feel safer if you go to their home or spend time with them. When you meet someone's family, you learn their character traits. You learn what makes them who they are. Like, if they are kind or what they like to do. You will feel so much safer when you know someone's family. My mom would feel better and so would I if my mom knew them and realized she could leave me alone with this family.

Teachers and principals need to know families are not all the same. Every time my Mom registers me for school, I hear here laugh and cross out the word "father." She reminds them I have not only two Moms, but two other people I consider my family, and one I consider another Mom. Families can be Mom and Mom or Dad and Dad or Mom and Dad or Grandma and Uncle or Aunt and Cousins; because, not one family is like another. They could include animals, aunts, uncles, and grandparents. You understand your family is not the only way to be. This helps me know people can be different, and different is okay.

I think families should be invited to school. Family members could eat lunch with you or come and spend time with you after school in an activity. School should be a place where everyone is welcome. Families need to feel welcome in school. They need to feel safe and accepted.

Teachers and principals should talk to each other about what all of this means before they do anything. They need to figure some things out. What counts as family? I want to know people are good people inside. I am looking for people with a good heart, kind-spirited, caring, loving, respectful, honest, fair, and unique-you don't try to be like everyone else.

MAKE LEARNING FUN AND MAKE IT MEAN SOMETHING

Teaching kids about loving one another is more than talking about it. We need to make sure we are really learning this in school. It has to be something that is part of every day, not an assembly we see and no one talks to us about it. I think we of course we should teach math, science, and language art, but I think we need to learn how to share our feelings, how to talk to one another, how to work things out with one another, how to be respectful, and how to believe in yourself, so you can stand up for who you are and be friends with everyone.

If we want to learn about differences, then students should have opportunities to work with partners or small groups. These groups or pairs would be picked randomly, so you work with someone different most of the time. We should take time to tell each other after working in a pair or small group, one thing each person did well.

I think there should be times when all students get a chance to play games that help them learn how to talk about their feelings or what is on their mind. It's important, because you don't want kids to explode. You learn how to communicate and talk to people in healthy ways. It's kind of like counseling.

You need to play games and sing songs to learn. There are many ways to learn, and everyone is going to support one another. So, if you need more time, you get more time. Some things may be harder for other children than others, and we need to be patient and help one another until we get it. We can play games in the gym to learn a concept, like tic-tac-toe math, and put math facts on a bean bag game. Every time they hit the x or o, then they would need to know that math fact or they don't get the x or the o.

All students should do projects in class in all of their subject areas, so whatever you are doing, you are helping your community. I think your homework should be about taking care of our community. Every 10 weeks, we should work together and try to help another part of the community. Maybe one time we work with animals, the next time you work with children who need books, and maybe the next time, you help elderly people. Students need a focus and need to constantly be thinking about how to organize and come together and make the community better. I think we should celebrate each of these projects by talking about what happened and how we came together to make a difference.

I think all of this could be included in language arts by providing feedback or asking the community for feedback and reflecting on what this meant to them. I think that feedback should be shared with the student's family. I think students would learn how to bring people together and make change.

Some community projects might include helping people who are hungry and learn about homelessness in math, social studies, and write about this in language arts. You could use technology to get people to pay attention to this.

Maybe a school helps a small business by helping them with a new marketing plan. We could learn about the economy in social studies, learn about their money making challenges in math, and write about this in language arts…and make new advertising to catch people's eyes…and the art department would work with us.

In order for this to work, my teachers need to work together. Math teachers cannot only work with teachers in math. They need to work with each other on these projects or figure out what they have in common.

We just can't do this work during school. We have to continue it at home. Homework would be with the projects we are working on and would not only include other students, but it would include our families and community. It would not stop for at least 10 weeks. This would make it fun and make us learn what we need to learn, because it is real and students will want to do more. They want to do more, because it would be fun, and I am not just worrying about myself. I learn to be concerned about my community and make a difference.

Imagine, if you did all these projects kindergarten through high school, you are not only making a difference, you are getting a chance to be part of something, you feel good inside and proud, and realize you did great things, and what it is like to have a job. They would feel happy and proud. They would realize how many lives they touched because of the work they did. Maybe they helped thousands of people or animals. Students would be proud of their work. And once they graduate, they will keep doing this work.

MY FINAL THOUGHTS

I don't think teachers give us enough credit for what we do or think we can do what we can do. It's almost like they are surprised when we do more than they expect, but we can do things. One time, a teacher of mine told my Mom "enthusiasm wasn't required" for her class. Really? I don't think principals and teachers understand what we are capable of doing and I am not always sure they know how to talk about this stuff either. I don't know how accepting my teachers and principals are of my family, my skin color, my abilities, my questioning everything, or who I am. I am ready, but I am not sure they are. I think that's sad, because there is so much more we can do together. They just need to believe in us and our families and give it a chance.

KIARA KANE

14. T.H.I.N.K.

I thought bullying was something that was all around school. I think teachers and students may not know that what they are seeing or hearing is bullying, because, unfortunately, the students in school are used to that being part of their natural environment. I think bullying is a very important topic and it should always be taken seriously.

Bullying comes in a few different ways. One of those ways is physical. You may see some students messing with another student. They are pushing them around or attempting to knock their belongings out their hands. You might think they're just messing around, but there is a chance that it is not just for fun. We see it, but teachers may not. Some students just play along with it so other people might not notice. Sometimes students just want to fit in with those people, because they would do anything to be one of them. Everyone wants to fit in somewhere and not be the one that people think are way too weird to hang out with.

Another form of bullying is cyber bullying. This usually takes place through social networking like Facebook, Instagram, and Twitter. Often times, people who are doing the bullying online don't understand there is a living, breathing human being reading what they're sending out. They don't understand the impact of what they are saying to them. They cannot see the actual pain they are inflicting on the other person, because it's all online. I know there is the saying, "Sticks and stones may break my bones, but names will never hurt me", but those words can actually hurt someone, and they do sometimes. People think the internet is a place they are free to say whatever they want about someone, especially because it isn't to their face. It also seems like they feel more confident to say something through an Instant Messenger, because, like I said before, it's not to their face, so they don't need to deal with the person directly.

The last form of bullying is verbal. Words do hurt and can have many effects on people. It's not fun to be made fun of or called names because of the way you dressed that day or because you may not like something that everyone else likes. A lot of people call other people names and make fun of them jokingly, and maybe even get people to laugh along, but deep down inside, it might've hurt their feelings. People need to think about the things they're going to say before they say them, because it can seriously affect someone.

C. Boske & A. Osanloo (Eds.), Students, Teachers, and Leaders Addressing Bullying in Schools, 77–78.

I found a possible solution to this. Before someone says something to someone else, I think they should use this:

THINK
*Is it **True**?*
*Is it **Helpful**?*
*Is It **Inspiring**?*
*Is it **Necessary**?*
*Is it **Kind**?*

If people thought like this before they said something, better choices could be made.

Bullying can lead to a lot of things like depression, harming yourself, and sometimes even suicide. Students who are depressed are often quiet, and stay away from people and activities. This can also lead to someone skipping school to avoid being bullied and then even to a student dropping out. Many students are often scared to tell an adult if they're being bullied and just deal with it on their own. When bullying gets so bad that someone begins to do self-harm or attempt suicide, that's extreme. No bullying should ever be able to get that far.

It seems like a lot of adults don't take any kind of action, let alone prevention. I think they should do something about it. If a teacher or principal sees it happening once, then it has probably happened before. It's not new. They shouldn't assume that. What they need to do is take action. They need to take steps and tell the person bullying to leave that student alone.

It also seems like schools don't take enough action when people do bully. It's like they just brush it off. You know, acting like it never happened. Schools need to take more action, because bullying is a serious matter. It should never be taken lightly. If schools did do more about bullying it would be happening less, because more people in the school would be aware of what bullying really is and that's the first step. So, if a student sees someone bullying someone, maybe they could stand up for someone.

Bullying can happen to any student. All it takes is for a student to come off as different versus being seen as "normal." Students who are bullied are made to feel that different is bad. Being bullied because you are "different" in school can make students feel powerless, unpopular, and alone. Students feeling different or abnormal will have a hard time standing up for themselves. Being "different" can also make the students sad, lonely or nervous. It can also make students feel sick and have problems in school. And these feelings may build up, and even push the student into bullying another student.

DESTINY PUFFENBARGER

15. YOU JUST GET USED TO IT

It all started in second grade in a small, suburban town. The kids on the school bus were never very nice to me. They called me names, beat me up, threw me across the bus, and things that you may or may not imagine.

They were bullies.

They called me names like four eyes; told me I was a disgrace to humanity; called me ugly; told me I was stupid and dumb; and called me every name in the book of bad names. My life was terrible. I felt terrible about myself.

One day on the bus ride home, I had sat in the back, so I could feel cool for once. Bullying never made me feel good, so I thought I would try something new. The bus driver took a very sharp turn. I flew across the bus into another seat. I landed on one of the bullies. It didn't hurt too bad.

I was used to being beaten up.

The bus driver pulled the bus over on the side of the street. He got up out of the driver's seat and started yelling at me. The driver accused me of purposely jumping onto another seat and landing on top of another kid. The driver said I wasn't allowed to ride the bus anymore, because I caused so much trouble.

I think the driver was bullying me. I never had a bus driver be so mean to me. I wasn't a kid who caused trouble. I was quiet and kept to myself. He didn't even ask what happened. He just assumed he knew and acted on it.

As soon as I stood up to get off of the bus at my bus stop, the bus driver started yelling at me again. This time, however, he hollered at me in front of my Mom. She was very mad at him and started yelling back. My Mom started swearing and cussing up and down about how bad the kids on the school bus treated me. She told him how I came home crying every day covered in bruises. The bus driver didn't listen. He continued to blame the situation on me.

After the bus drove away, my Mom and I went home. She decided to call the police. After she talked with the police, she contacted the Board of Education and finally, the district's transportation department.

She tried and tried and tried to get help.

My Mom was sick and tired of how terribly we were being treated. A couple of years later, my Mom was able to get me off of that nasty, bully-filled school bus.

C. Boske & A. Osanloo (Eds.), Students, Teachers, and Leaders Addressing Bullying in Schools, 79–80.

Being bullied physically and emotionally made me feel like I had nobody to rely on while I was at school. I felt like I didn't have any friends, or anyone to tell about my problems. I didn't want to be in school. I always went to the nurse and made up excuses so she would call my Mom to come pick me up. I thought leaving school would help me get away from the bullying, but when I went back to school, it only got worse. After a while, my Mom figured out something was wrong.

After my Mom caught on that something was wrong, she tried to fix it. It took her three years to solve the problem, but it finally happened. I was able to switch buses. I started opening up and talking to people.

I was finally safe.

I was okay. I was able to open up to people, because nobody was bullying me anymore.

To this day, I don't know why they bullied me, but I think they may have been jealous of me. I don't know. My life got better. The bullying wasn't occurring every day. I was happier. I didn't come home crying every day in pain. My life was terrible when I was bullied. For some reason, I think things must get worse before they can get better, and if that's true, trust me, they did.

PART 2

VOICES FROM CONCERNED FAMILIES AND COMMUNITY MEMBERS

BRAD SINICK

16. BECOMING MRS. BAKER

I got into teaching to make a difference. It's that simple; however, I left the profession after two years, because I felt I could no longer be effective. Early on, I realized the field of education was not ready for someone like me. I was different, and being "different" was not something educators, school leaders, or community members embraced. That realization was hard for me. Why? I devoted my life to education. And not just attaining an education, but wanting to be an educator in order to make a difference in the world. But when I entered the field of teaching, I was immediately disheartened. I realized overcoming the obstacles I faced was no longer a possibility. I hope my story helps readers better understand the impact bullying had on me as a learner, as an aspiring teacher, and as a teacher who left the field of education in my prime. I hope one day teachers like me will be welcomed into the profession.

As a young man, I dreamed of going into education. I wanted to make a difference. I earned the necessary degrees. I spent extra time in school. I thought I did what I needed to do to prepare myself for teaching high school science. My journey, however, began because I was bullied at a very young age. When I was in elementary school, I learned I was dyslexic. Because I didn't read or write like the other kids, I was always the kid bullied and picked on. What saved me? I had a teacher who believed in me. That was the difference for me. Mrs. Baker believed in me. Her efforts to reach out to me was literally what made me go from failing all of my grade school classes to graduating high school in the top ten and earning five degrees, including a master's degree.

I had so many people from grade school who looked at me and said, "I can't believe YOU accomplished what I accomplished." Others exclaimed, "Oh my gosh! You have done more than I ever could have imagined you would have done!" People did not seem to believe in me. I want it known, I owe the beginnings of my journey to one teacher– Mrs. Baker.

LOOKING BACK

When I was a kid, I went to a private school. The school was known for its academic rigor. I was diagnosed as dyslexic and having Attentional Deficit Hyperactivity Disorder (ADHD). It was difficult for me to overcome those learning differences, let alone do well in school. Throughout my elementary experiences, I struggled with my learning differences. I attended a school in which every kid was expected to do well. It was a lot of pressure. If a student didn't do well, they were held back.

C. Boske & A. Osanloo (Eds.), Students, Teachers, and Leaders Addressing Bullying in Schools, 83–95.
© 2015 Sense Publishers. All rights reserved.

I was held back in preschool. I also failed first, third, fifth, and sixth grade. It was a difficult time. I was known as the "dumb kid." However, I was lucky to have some athletic prowess that allowed me to be good at something. But while in school, I was always the one pulled out of class. My experiences testify to the significance of inclusion. I hated being removed from class. I was one of "those kids" who had an intervention specialist. This is a person who works one-on-one with a student or in a small group to help them work through any learning challenges. However, in my class, I was the only one asked to leave. And this happened multiple times a day.

When it was time to leave to see the Intervention Specialist, I remember getting up and trying to sneak out of class. I didn't want anyone to know I was being removed from the classroom. Throughout these experiences, I learned I had to hide everything. I was already bullied for being the "dumb" kid, so this would just be another reason for kids to pick on me.

It was a very difficult time for me. I was always the one sitting by myself on the playground. No one wanted to play with the "dumb kid." This led to me being very internal. I learned to keep to myself. Over time, I became self-conscious about everything I did. The experience of being bullied, because of my learning differences influences me even to this day.

After earning five degrees, I heard people say, "Brad, you are one of the smartest people I know." And even though I heard what they were saying, it was hard for me to hear the words and accept the compliments. I still find myself deflecting or telling myself not to accept them.

It bothers my friends when I find it difficult to internalize what they are saying to me. My friends believe I have accomplished a lot. But what happened to me at such a young age, still affects me today. After hearing how dumb you are for so many years and being told you aren't capable, it's no wonder I still have a hard time accepting compliments about my intellectual abilities.

I don't consider myself an insecure person. I don't feel worthless, but obviously, my self-worth isn't the same as other people see me. I think my being bullied and picked on for my learning differences impacted more than people thought it would. It's a hard thing to overcome, but I think I did overcome these challenges over time. What got me through? People who loved me, believed in me, and accepted me. I remember that got me through numerous hard times. My Dad sat me down after I broke down in tears. I kept telling him, "I can't do it!" He replied, "Brad, if you ever want to do anything in your life, you are going to have to realize that you are going to have to work twice as hard as everyone else to achieve what they do easily." That quote matches up with one teacher I aspired to, Mrs. Baker.

A TEACHER BELIEVED IN ME

Mrs. Baker spent years, I mean years, developing and believing in me. I remember being told I was dyslexic. As a first grader, I also remember not being able to write.

Mrs. Baker asked me to write a story. She wanted me to write about being bullied in kindergarten.

Mrs. Baker wanted to submit my story to a contest. I asked, "Are you sure? You mean me? But I can't even spell." In first grade, we worked for two months on writing, rewriting and rewriting my story again. It never won any awards, but MY story was worth something to her.

My experiences moved Mrs. Baker. She found my story worthy enough to submit for a writing context. She said, "I never did this for any of my students, but I want to do this for you." This was the first time someone ever believed in me. Her efforts meant a lot to me. I realized at that moment the impact a teacher could have on a student. From there on, I always said, "I want to be just like Mrs. Baker."

Even though I didn't like being pulled out of my class, I could go there and not feel judged. Mrs. Baker was my respite. I felt like I could go there, make a mistake, and I would not be ridiculed. Her use of positive reinforcement empowered me.

I invited Mrs. Baker to my first college graduation. Even though I had not seen her in ten years, she attended. It was really sweet of her. She said, "Brad, I don't know what I ever did for you that meant this much to you." I replied, "Well, you did a lot. You literally changed my life." I continued to explain her impact on my learning when I went to junior high. I switched from a private Christian school to a public school. The public school's academics were not as rigorous as the private school. This wiggle room gave me a couple of years to really put the skills I learned in grade school into play at the middle school. When I was in grade school, I couldn't put these skills into play. I was always trying just to keep my head above water. At the public school, I could float and learn at least learn how to paddle. From seventh grade through high school, I never earned anything lower than an A. I took all Advanced Placement, honors, and college courses my last two years of high school. I studied at the University of Akron. I went from a kid who never earned an A or a B before junior high to kid who excelled in school. I believe my success was due to my Dad's advice about working harder than everyone else, and Mrs. Baker believing in me. Their advice and support got me somewhere down the road.

PREPARING MYSELF TO BE THE NEXT MRS. BAKER

I wanted to be Mrs. Baker. I wanted to do what she did for me for someone else. I decided to enter the field of education. Thinking about the impact Mrs. Baker had in my life is what got me through my difficult semesters in undergrad. I was taking biology and education courses and using all of my time for studying.

Students usually complete their degrees in four years. I was a determined and committed student. I was able to earn two degrees in four years, and I was a full-time collegiate athlete. At my university, I was an All-American and national champion, which was a full-time commitment. I learned how to balance my coursework and my athletic aspirations. During several low moments, I found myself going back and telling myself, "Remember, Brad, these degrees are not for you. They are for someone else you are going to impact later on." I reminded myself about the power of reaching out to others. This realization is what got me through my teacher preparation.

When I was student teaching, I was protected from the harsh realities of education. It sounds bad, but it's true. I was like a protected bear cub. I didn't understand or confront the realities of administration and educational politics. I focused on being there for the students and helping them learn. The cooperating teachers played Mother Bear and sheltered me from the politics of education. They encouraged me to focus on the students. After student teaching, I was still living high. I couldn't wait to get out there and work with students. I thought I was going to change the world one kid at a time.

During my teacher preparation, I did begin to experience some tensions regarding a specific group of students and families. I quickly realized professors literally skipped over certain chapters of texts. They pretended specific groups of people didn't exist. Later in my career, ignoring these groups existed would cause great tension in my life.

Throughout my teacher preparation, discussing the experiences of lesbian/gay/bisexual/transgender/queer/questioning (LGBTQQ) students, families, and colleagues did not occur. I attended a Christian college. Discussing LGBTQQ populations was something the university completely eliminated from my teacher preparation courses. I can't say LGBTQQ groups were eliminated from the texts, because they weren't physically taken out of our books. As aspiring teachers, we just didn't read or discuss chapters about kids or families who identified as LGBTQQ. Professors said, "Okay. Read chapters 1, 2 and 4." The instructors completely bypassed chapter three, which focused on LGBTQQ populations.

I never had one discussion throughout teacher education preparation that dealt with LGBTQQ populations. I was always the only student who went back and read the chapters we skipped. I remember my senior year, I took an ethics course. I was one of two people who had the courage to speak about LGBTQQ issues. The professor did not want us to debate about specific controversial topics; however, she did bring up LGBTQQ populations one time. Two of us tried to facilitate a conversation, but to no avail. Everyone in our teacher preparation was opposed to discussing anything to do with LGBTQQ populations. They defended themselves and made it very clear they did not support inclusive practices for all students, especially "those" students.

I was concerned. These people wanted to be teachers? I was literally the wounded deer in the lion's den throughout my teacher preparation. It was a class of 30, me and one other girl. One of our professors took us out to lunch after a tense class discussion. The instructor thanked us for demonstrating courage. My preparation experiences showed me the mentality of these preservice teachers and of the university. Looking back, I cannot understand why we were not exposed to understanding marginalized populations, let alone LGBTQQ populations. There was no place for this dialogue in my teacher preparation. The university as whole shied away from every aspect of LGBTQ populations. Rather than embedding these conversations throughout our coursework, the institution would rather not talk about it. It was almost like the university was thinking "out of sight, out of mind." Looking back, I don't know of any teachers I worked with in student teaching or in the field who engaged in coursework or discussions around LGBTQ populations in their teacher preparation.

MY FIRST YEAR AS A TEACHER

I remember interviewing for my first teaching position. The principal asked, "Why do you want to be a teacher?" I replied, "I want to be THAT teacher who is remembered for taking kids somewhere. You know, that person, who if it wasn't for me, the kids wouldn't be where they are today." I further explained, "I don't mean for my own recognition. I want kids to know they can make it. You know, for their own sake." I wanted to be a teacher who helped students realize they could become whatever they aspired to. I wanted to be a teacher who brought students to new levels—to a place they weren't at before. I was committed to working 12, 13 or 14 hours a day, if that's what it took to help students learn. I believed in the power of teaching, building meaningful relationships with students, and supporting their learning.

I focused on building relationships with students and knowing their strengths, challenges, and interests. One means of supporting their learning was getting to know students on multiple levels. I decided to coach three times a year in addition to teaching. I believed in the power of teaming and believed athletics provided that venue. I relied on my prior experiences with my high school and college athletic coaches. They reminded me of Mrs. Baker. My coaches "knew" me. Athletics provided my teachers with opportunities to understand their students, and I decided to utilize those spaces to do the same. I thought of coaching as ministry towards kids. It was about reaching out to them.

I remember my first day. I walked into the position thinking the world was just. My teacher preparation encouraged me to believe this to be true. They encouraged us to believe all teachers and all school leaders worked to ensure the success of all children. I was under the impression I needed to work hard, and everything would fall into line. If I committed to this work, then people would be receptive to my ideas. I thought all teachers and principals wanted to help students. I quickly learned that while that was true to some extent, it was not true within my district. There were many administrators and teachers who had political or societal biases that conflicted with my beliefs and practices. Many of them would rather see a child perish if they were from a certain sector of society, than watch students grow, develop, and flourish. Teachers' and administrators' innate prejudices interfered with students' success, just because they lived on the other side of the tracks or learned differently or just did not come across just like them.

I remember sitting in the teachers' lounge. I didn't say anything. I was approached by two male teachers. They started talking negatively about their students. One of them began berating a female student. He said angrily, "Oh, she is a blatant lesbian!" I thought, "Oh my gosh! He is talking about one of his respective students? What makes you think you can talk about her like that?" These were the same people who had innate prejudices about the way kids express their gender. They weren't culturally aware, and I wonder if they understood the impact of their daily axes to grind? The experience in the teachers' lounge impacted me as an educator. I reflected on the experience. I realized the need to build up a wall. I started to believe I couldn't really help kids. I recognized the need to protect myself from my colleagues, because I was gay, and obviously, I couldn't come out at school.

CHAPERONING PROM

During my first year, I didn't have many problems with administrators or teachers. At the end of my first year, the principal came to me. She said, "We are in critical need of chaperones for prom. It's at one of those places that if we don't have enough chaperones, then the kids can't have prom. The teachers are not willing to participate in order to move forward with prom, so we will need to cancel it if we don't have enough chaperones." The principal proceeded to ask, "Do you know anyone who could do it? Could you?" I replied, "Well, sure." She said, "Well, if you know of anyone else who is an adult and who is responsible, let me know." I said, "Sure. I think this would be a good thing for me and my partner to do." The principal did not make any remarks at the time.

I did not have the chance to attend my prom. At the time, it was only a dream. My high school did not allow for students to be out at all (i.e., gay, lesbian, transgender, bisexual, queer (LGBTQ)). Students would not protect kids who identified as LGBTQ. I realized the need to seize this opportunity to be a role model for students and help educate the community about people like me. I thought, "I couldn't go to prom when I was in high school, but now that I am older, and a teacher, it would be cool to attend." I considered it an honor to chaperone. I thought it would be a great experience for students to see one of their teachers in a quality partnership.

From that point on, things started to go downhill. My partner and I chaperoned prom. I tried to figure out how people understood our willingness to attend the prom. I watched. I listened. I tried to read between the lines. We did not hold hands or kiss each. We attended as chaperones. I could see the wheels turning when people introduced one another by stating, "This is Mr. so and so who brought his wife. And this is Mrs. so and so who brought her husband and this is Brad who brought this other guy?" At the time, I didn't think anything of it. I thought it would have been a wonderful experience for my partner and I to help out the school. I was too naïve. The following year, everything changed.

MY SECOND YEAR AS TEACHER

Students approached me about starting a Gay Straight Alliance (GSA) at our high school. Most of the teachers were quite upset. They said, "Why would we ever need something like that?" This was a school that graduates 500 students a year. They had every club imaginable from magic to juggling to ice skating to gymnastics to Japanese to Latin, but they didn't have a GSA or anything like that.

The kids thought I was different from all of the other teachers. I was a young teacher. I am not sure if they assumed I was young and opened minded, so that is why they brought their idea to me to create a GSA. I never asked. Or maybe attending the prom with my partner was discussed among the students. I do not know encouraged them to include me, but I was honored they asked.

We completed all of the proper paperwork to form an official high school club and submitted it. I was the official advisor. However, administrators did not contact me after the forms. The administrators informed the kids they could not form a GSA with me, because they thought I might have been gay myself. They said, "If you want to do this, you are going to need to find another advisor. We suggest you speak to Mrs. Donmeyer (I changed the teacher's name to protect her), who is married and has a couple of children." I spoke with her. Her and I were cut from the same cloth. Mrs. Donmoyer needed encouragement to step out and take on the role as faculty advisor.

Together, we completed the necessary paperwork again. Her and I discussed the need to name her as the advisor, as noted by the administrators, because she was a straight, married woman. The proposal was brought to the administration. They officially killed the proposal. The administrators said, "No, we can't have a club like that here."

After that experience, I contemplated leaving the school. I realized I could not have the effectiveness I wanted as a teacher. I wanted to be like Mrs. Baker, but they wanted me to remain silent, do as I was told, and be a name on a paycheck. I couldn't do that. I felt my effectiveness as an educator, as a light, was greater outside of the community than within the community. The few students who were committed to the initiation of a GSA were hurt and furious. They wanted to petition the administration, but the community was so anti-gay. The proposal was squelched quickly. It seemed as though an underlying fear from the administrators and military families played a role in the outcome. Families in this community were quite wealthy and often utilized their military leadership positions to dictate school policy, practices, and procedures.

RUMOR HAS IT

I got word from a friend who worked in the county education building office. My friend said, "People were talking about you at the county level. They said there was a new, young science teacher who was gay over at the high school." I was shocked. I could not believe it. I did not understand why they would talk about me and this was considered appropriate conversation at the county education office. They weren't discussing that I was teacher of the month my first year or that I had the lowest standardized test failure rate in the high school or the best scores on the same standardized test for my department. It was not about any of this. No, they focused on the notion I was a "new gay teacher." That realization set me back. Within that year, the administration became more and more hostile towards me.

BEING A NATIONAL CHAMPION WAS NOT GOOD ENOUGH

I was an All-American national champion in my respective sports in college. I applied to be a coach for the sport that recognized me as a national champion. I was turned down, because a physical education teacher, who had never participated in that sport, was asked to coach instead. I was a Level I certified official through the national organization. At that time, I was the youngest Level I certified coach in the United States. I was certified to coach every level up to the Olympics. I was a national champion, All-American, and the administrators chose someone who did not apply for the job and never participated in the sport. The administration chose that teacher to be the coach. I reflected on the experience. I thought, "Maybe I need to 'put in my dues' and in year 4 or 5 it will happen." I was naïve.

BEING PULLED BACK INTO THE CLOSET

Year two, like I said, was a difficult year for me. People at the county level were discussing my sexual orientation, the students' GSA proposal was not accepted, my request to coach was denied, and now I was being pulled into the office by the administration. Two administrators requested my presence in a private office. One of them began by stating, "Brad, we just want to let you know about one of our unspoken policies. If someone who works for the district just so happened to be gay and was out with their partner…let's say they were out at a restaurant, and they happened to see a student, we would expect them to leave immediately or they would no longer be working for us." I wasn't sure what to do. I replied, "Thank you for letting me know about your unspoken policy." I was shocked and scared.

That conversation took a toll on my relationship with my partner. I was in a long-term relationship. We lived together in the community in which I was employed. I know longer felt comfortable going out to dinner or to the mall with my partner. I was afraid of being fired. Our friends asked if we would join them, and many times, we decided to say home. On rare occasions, we would go out under specific conditions. I would not be seen at restaurants in our area. Some friends asked us to go to the movies, but even at the movies, and even though it was dark, I wore a long-sleeve hooded sweatshirt and covered my head. We sat in the back corner with the hood pulled over my head for the entire movie.

The stress I endured played the biggest driving force between my partner and me. We could no longer engage in any social activities outside of our house. The situation was devastating to our relationship. Unfortunately, the stressful situations continued. I assumed they would attempt to "push me out of the system until I would leave on my own accord", and that is what happened.

I worked with a student who did not complete an assignment. I gave the assignment to the student again. The student did not complete the assignment again. I reminded the student how important the assignment was towards the final grade. I gave it to the student three more times. After the fourth time, the student still chose not to complete the assignment. Because I attempted to work with the student, the course grade was now overdue by two weeks. I tried to offer the student ample opportunity to complete the work. However, I was required to submit the grade. Unfortunately, I had to enter a zero for that assignment. The student's grade went from an average score to a failing score.

The administrators contacted me. One said, "Who do you think you are enforcing school policy. Give him the grade!" The administrator said, "You are doing it this way, because I fucking said so." He commanded respect. People in the building feared this administrator. I was especially afraid of him. I went into the grading system and changed the grade from a failing grade to a passing grade. I did what he what he told me to do.

I spoke with my union representative. The representative highlighted the policy that supported my efforts in reaching out to the student as well as my job description. The union representative and administrators went back and forth regarding the situation. I was informed by the administrators "the situation was been taken care of." I did not receive an apology. I was simply informed, "It was taken care of."

About two weeks later, I was called into the office again. The administrators informed me there were allegedly pictures of me as a cross dresser or drag queen on Facebook. The assistant principal and principal told me I had to show them all of the photos on my Facebook page. I was blown away by this. I had no idea what this meeting was going to be about, and then I was told I had to show these administrators all of my photos on Facebook.

I said, "No. You can't do this. I am requesting my union representative to be here." However, I was scared. I knew I did not have any photos on my Facebook page regarding these accusations. We were able to solve the issue, because I chose to share all of my photos with the union representative. The representative, in turn, told the administrators, "He is not a cross-dresser or a drag queen." I was confused by all of this. I wasn't sure why I had to "prove" I was not a cross-dresser or a drag queen. I didn't know that if I identified as either that it somehow related to my job. What they did to me was unethical and sneaky. However, it did not end.

I remember having conversations with my Dad about the following situation. We thought this incident bordered on kidnapping. These administrators were former football players. They coached football and they towered over me, because they were the size of linemen. They administrators physically pulled me into a school closet. They stood between me and door. They said, "You are going to show us all of your photos. There is a computer in there and you are going to do it." I never feared of being injured until that moment.

They told me I needed to log onto my Facebook page on my phone. I told them over and over again, "I need my union representative." They became more and more vocal. I told them I wanted an apology from them for putting me through all of this. I told my union representative what happened. However, nothing happened. The administrators were allowed to behave in these hostile ways.

Another incident occurred in my classroom. A student wrote "faggot" eight times in large print all over my room. Luckily, I am the type of person who comes in really early. I like to be organized and be at my best. I come in an hour and half early to get "flowing", so I hit first period in stride. I was devastated when I walked in the room. I saw the word "faggot" written all over the classroom walls. I quickly turned off the lights, shut my door, and asked the first period kids to meet me in the cafeteria, because I didn't want anyone to see anything.

In the school policy, if a student wrote the derogatory word "nXXXXX" for a Black person on a bathroom stall, the student would be suspended for 10 days. The school allegedly had a zero tolerance policy for that type of behavior. I spoke with the administrators about the hate speech written on my classroom walls. They informed me, "We have no way of figuring out who would have gone into my room and vandalized it with the word faggot on your walls." The administrators said the graffiti would be cleaned off the walls; however, they said, "This is all that can be done."

There was a security camera outside of my classroom door. Right after meeting with the administrators, I immediately walked over to our security officer. I asked, "You guys have videos, right?" The security officer was not aware that I was trying to investigate who vandalized my classroom. And, he did not know the administrators were attempting to keep this "hush hush." I asked the security officer if he could review footage during a specific time during the day. He checked for my room. I saw the student and recognized him.

I brought that video footage to the administration. They immediately back peddled. The student was given a. 5 day out-of-school suspension. A week later, a student wrote the "n" word on a bathroom stall and received a 10 day out-of-school suspension for hate speech. I was taken back by the efforts I made for some type of action taken to occur when hate speech was used in my classroom towards me. The administrators' choices indicated a lack of support for me and for students who identify as LGBTQ.

Students "spread the word," and most rallied around me. They identified me as a "different type of teacher." However, my colleagues and administrators were not supportive. One teacher said, "No one should have broken into your room." And two more seemed supportive because they knew gay people. They were emotionally distraught by the experience. One of the two was in tears.

I was being bullied by the administration and now a student was allowed to do the same.

The remaining educators were not interested in addressing the elephant in the middle of the room. I was under enormous stress and contemplated whether or not I could do my job. A female student in ninth grade seemed "more masculine than other girls" in the school. This student did not attend for a week. I worried about her. I checked with the counselors and administrators. I discovered from the counselor the girl attempted suicide and was admitted into the hospital. Kids were picking on her for identifying as a lesbian. When she returned to school, I discovered who was bullying her in my class. I remember seeing it. I just stood there. I felt powerless. I could not find the strength to address the situation. I started to think about myself, and the consequences I might face versus the needs of the students. I thought about saying something, but after thinking about the possibilities facing me, I chose not to intervene. I was concerned for my own safety. I was afraid of being pulled into the closet again.

I realized I could no longer be an effective teacher. I became discontent, which led me into a depression. I had no one to talk to about being bullied and watching students bully others. I could not speak with my mentor teacher or tell anyone what happened. I could not rely on my union representative and inform him I was gay. In this state, I am not a member of a protected class of people. I could lose my job. Because the union and administration worked hand in hand, I knew the union representative would tell the administrators "off the record", that I was gay.

I lived in survival mode. I had to protect myself. I could not let anyone know I was gay. If I confirmed I was gay, I would not be allowed to work with the students. If I was going to be effective, I needed to work outside of education. I decided to leave teaching. I still have a calling to teach, but I cannot teach in a public K-12 school setting. I won't live in fear anymore.

In that school environment, there was an established culture I could not interrupt. The bullying practices were systemic, and one person could not interrupt these hostile practices. I was concerned about their agenda and the impact of their agenda on the students I served. I felt powerless as a new teacher. I was no longer effective. Leaving teaching was one of the more difficult decisions I have ever made; I wanted to be Mrs. Baker, but I had to leave for my own safety and mental health.

REFLECTING ON MRS. BAKER

Mrs. Baker does not know about my unfortunate experiences in public school or my decision to leave the profession. After much consideration, I would like to share this chapter with her, but not yet. I think she would be disappointed in the educational system and attempt to encourage me to reinstate myself in the profession. I imagine her saying, "I am sorry this happened to you. We need more educators like you in our schools."

I wish I would have had support from the administration and the school community to stay and interrupt those oppressive practices. However, I felt alone. As school community members, we need to create a culture that is conducive to caring. We need to create teachers and school leaders who are culturally aware. And not just aware, but knowing what do when things are not just. This takes courage, integrity, and awareness.

As I reflect on these experiences, I think about Mrs. Donmoyer, the teacher who decided to stand up and be the GSA advisor. She was married and had children and realized she needed to use her power and privilege to take a stand for kids who were not given a voice in our school. She knew the administrators' practices were unethical; however, she attempted to use her privilege to do right by the students. We must remember, teachers also need this type of support.

I needed teachers, administrators, and mentors who would provide me a safe place to be myself, to talk things through, and to do whatever I could to reach as many students as possible. However, I lived in fear. And when you live in fear, you function in survival mode. It is difficult to critically think about the world when you are most concerned about the next minute. I could not tell anyone about my situation, because I could risk my job. I constantly asked, "Do I tell someone? Do I let this one go?" If I told the wrong person, I realized things could get worse. I did not need more stress in my life.

When I made the decision to leave, I had colleagues spread rumors about why I was leaving. They said, "He is abusing little boys from the junior high and was forced to leave." I remember calling the principal, the superintendent, and the union about this. I told them, "This needs to stop. These false accusations could ruin my reputation and my career." They said, "We will do our best." I realized nothing would be done. I had to leave the profession.

Working in this public school system was unhealthy for me. I could no longer do what I needed to do as an educator, mentor, or school community member. After talking with my Mom and Dad, I realized working in K-12 public schools was not the only way to make a difference in the world. I took time and reflected on my experiences. I completed a graduate degree and removed myself from that conservative, abusive political educational system. I note the word "system", because I don't think other K-12 schools in this state would have supported me.

As I contemplated whether or not to leave the profession during my final days of school, I was informed by my union attorney, "Brad, this community is ultra conservative. They have their agendas. They are going to see you as a gay teacher and will not see the case." I wanted everything to go away. I was physically and emotionally destroyed. Out of all of this, I ended up losing my long-term relationship and moved back home. I did not feel I had a safe place. The judges and school communities were conservative and would not hear the case.

Since then, I spoke to other attorneys. They said, "I wish I could have been there for you to help you out." But I didn't have anyone to create a safe environment for me. Educators might speak of creating a safe environment in school, but teachers and school leaders do not seem to understand what that really means. Educators and school leaders cannot "pick and choose" who they are going to "keep safe." Those who work in schools cannot allow their bias or prejudice to interfere with their moral responsibilities.

I don't even know if most teachers and school leaders are even aware of their bias. They seem to have these "twisted ideas" of what it means to create a safe environment, and yet, they think demeaning people is a way to create a safe environment. Why would we engage in behaviors at the expense of children's lives? How many students go through school and do not feel like they have anyone they can turn to? That is not coincidence. I remember Christa Boske introducing me to a principal who engaged in culturally responsive practices. I could not believe it. Standing in front of me was a principal attending an anti-bullying conference. It was such a shock for me to see her there. That experience interrupted my stories and my understanding of what is possible for school leaders. I reflected on the impact this school leader must have due to her ability to not only be culturally aware, but to have the courage to act on it. And then I had a moment. What might happen if what Christa said could be—working with school leaders, teachers, kids, families, and community members who were culturally aware. The power of that community could play a significant role in supporting every member within the school. That needs to be the new focus. We can be effective if we reconsider what it takes to build a new culture. It's about considering the need for student to student or teacher to teacher or family to family or community to community to create spaces in which people are culturally aware and transcend this new awareness across borders.

Each of us have stories. We need to make time to hear them. We should not wait for the world to happen. We need to be the people to make something happen. We can no longer stand still. We need to do something. Doing nothing is not an option, because someone will get hurt. The key to making a difference is moving beyond what we think and say. We need to put what we learned into practice. This work goes beyond picketing or protesting. This call to action requires a commitment to others. We need to think about what it means to believe in humanity. We have a moral obligation to uphold these beliefs, because, as Christa has noted time and time again, "the real work is in the doing." And it is "within the doing, within making changes within ourselves and communities we serve, that more change will come, and eventually change the way we understand and respond to the world." Now, that's something Mrs. Baker would be proud to hear and see from me.

JENNIFER TURLEY

17. DYKE, DYKE, DYKE!

How does it feel to have a child who is gay? I've been asked that several times. Believe me, I'd rather face that question than have that ugly, accusing glare from some small-minded person who is allowing themselves to believe that I "allowed my child to choose to be gay." How can a person best describe the cross between trying to be a responsible and well-behaved adult, and wanting to choke the very last breath out of some ignoramus who stands within earshot saying despicable and hateful things about the child who you love more than your own life?

By now, many people have either read or heard about the poem by Emily Perl Kingsley entitled, "Welcome to Holland." The poem depicts the way a mother feels upon learning that her newborn child is disabled, after preparing herself for a "typical" child during her pregnancy. I believe that all mothers have certain expectations during pregnancy, and then we solidify certain expectations upon learning the sex of the baby. I suppose that could be my segue into what it's like to have a daughter who is lesbian, yes? You hear the doctor pronounce to all in the room, "It's a girl!" and you begin imagining her school dances and formals, and even a brief thought of her wedding, though it's way down the road. You have certain expectations just because the child is born with a particular set of genitalia. It's unfortunate that it all begins that way, but I know that it's common, no matter how erroneous.

WE first noticed how different Maddy was when she was a little over two years old. You could NEVER tell her that she couldn't do something. I'm not talking about dangerous things, but small, albeit, societal norms. She loved to mimic her father shaving his face in the morning. She would smear a small amount of shaving cream on her lower face, then scrape it off methodically with a popsicle stick, like an expert. She then showed great determination when trying to use the bathroom. She tried to urinate standing up, like her father and two brothers. Of course, this failed. When I tried to explain that she and I, (females), were very different from the other three (male) family members and must therefore sit down while using the toilet, she was even more resolved. "I can do it" she said with a determined face, "I will show you". Sure enough, not even two weeks after this incident, Maddy came to get me. "I will show you!" she said, grabbing my hand and leading me to the restroom. When there, she hopped up on the edge of the tub, put her hand on the wall, arched her back and peed directly at the drain of the tub. "I can do it!" she declared triumphantly. It was then I knew, I was not the mother of a "regular, typical little girl." My daughter

C. Boske & A. Osanloo (Eds.), Students, Teachers, and Leaders Addressing Bullying in Schools, 97–103.

is extraordinary. While it meant she was a very determined and creative individual, it also meant, I was in trouble.

Maddy had a little "boyfriend" during pre-school, with whom she remained close for many years. I realized after one year that Colton was not really a boyfriend in the traditional sense of the word. He was more of a best friend-someone who Maddy played tackle football with, or rode her bike or skateboarded with, or just joined to go swimming. No other boy was as close to Maddy growing up, but this is probably because Colton accepted her early on as an equal, not as a romantic inquiry.

In middle school, Maddy began dealing with a lot of antagonists. Because she was a little different from the other girls in that she didn't wear make-up, or mini-skirts, or stuff her bra, she became the target for some bullying. Boys would just make stupid comments telling her that they wouldn't date her (which made no difference to her), but the girls were much more vicious. They never missed an opportunity to make fun of her, humiliate her, or just bully her on a daily basis. Complaints got me nowhere. I ended up taking her out of the public school after the first quarter of her sixth grade year, and home-schooling her for the remainder. It was the best I could do under the circumstances.

Maddy wanted to go back to public school her 7th grade year. She was ready. After spending time focusing on just academics and adjusting to "growing up", she felt confident to begin her new journey. Though her father and I had suspected for a while that she was lesbian, the topic never came up with Maddy. She was simply...well...Maddy! She was a unique person, never really holding a sexual identity or characteristic. Maddy JUST WAS! She had male and female friends. She cared more about the welfare of others than she did for her own. The people that got to know her absolutely adored her. Her look became more androgynous. Some teachers were very confused about what bathroom she should go into, too embarrassed to ask her, or to have any inquiry. How hard is it to check someone's sex in their records?

High school was emotionally draining, to say the least. By now, I had found out that Maddy was binding her breasts, and was "out" with her friends...as well as with us. She felt comfortable talking about it. She said, "Because all your friends are gay, Mom, all your friends are gay!" Yes, the majority of them were gay. They were priceless to me!

Maddy's actual sexual identity was still a mystery to a lot of faculty. Her bound breasts, broad shoulders, short hair and swagger caused a lot of confused looks. She was a SUPERB soccer goalie, but the cruel comments that were thrown her way became too much to bare. I don't know who was more upset, Maddy or me? She had initially quit the soccer team her sophomore year. Maddy was fed-up with a lot of the issues going on; however, her team was going to the All-City Play-offs and had come to her. They begged for her to play the championship game. Maddy agreed to do it for the team. She played very well, holding the other team at minimal points, but her defensive guards were getting tired and starting to break-down. When the other team broke through and scored, they gained momentum. The crowd got more aggressive, and a group of male students from the other team gathered behind my daughter's goal and began chanting "Dyke, Dyke, Dyke!" I could see my daughter's face. I knew these people succeeded in breaking her concentration. When the game ended, she tried to pull herself together. The frustration was too much. Maddy chased after the car of male students. They sped from the parking lot. As they exited, Maddy challenged them to taunt her to her face instead of behind her back.

I emailed the principal of the school the following day to express my disappointment in the students' behavior. I stressed this was supposed to be an honorable match-up between two top teams. I stressed the boys' despicable behavior drew away from the talent and hard-work of the players in the game. He wrote me back he had spoken to each of the boys. He insisted they did nothing wrong.

My LEAST favorite soccer occurrence, by far, would have to be the indoor soccer game that my daughter agreed to play to help her friends. The goalie for the team was out with an injury. Could Maddy help them out for a game? She agreed, and we showed up 15 minutes before the match to allow her to warm-up. Maddy was in amazing physical form. She had been playing her junior year on the boys' Junior Varsity (JV) football team as a defensive end. Maddy was so strong, that many of the male players welcomed her in the weight room. She had also cut her hair very short during football season, because of the heat under the uniform and how annoying hair was under the helmet. True androgyny at its finest! She took the field with her teammates and assumed her position at the front of the goal. Immediately, the players from the other team had puzzled faces. One of them motioned for the referee, spoke to her for a few moments, and then the referee went over to our coach. Obviously, there was a question as to my daughter's gender. His face was showing disgust as he nodded Yes! Yes! to the question that had been posed. Good enough! Everyone knows females are allowed to play on MALE soccer teams, but males are NEVER to play on FEMALE soccer teams! The coach's assurance should have been enough, but the coach from the other team called the referee over to question my daughter's gender...yet again! What did they want from her? To drop trough? No boy in his right mind would EVER embarrass himself by playing on a girl's team! Our coach assured them, yet again, that Maddy was indeed supposed to be there. The game began.

I sat in the bleachers with the other parents, clapping and cheering enthusiastically. I remained upbeat until ugly remarks from the other teams' parents started such as, "Who's that boy down there?", "I didn't think boys were allowed to play on the girls' team!", and "Why is the ref allowing that boy to goalie?" I took a deep breath. I knew my daughter's appearance could be confusing to people. Maddy's physical fitness was far superior to the other players. I calmly told the group, "No, boys are NOT allowed to play on the girls' team. That is not a boy in the goal. That is a girl, and she's my daughter." I felt good. I didn't get nasty with anyone or raise my voice. I was matter-of-fact. Still the comments continued, "That really looks like a boy!", "Why are they letting that person play goalie?", and "Shouldn't someone say something to the ref?" Again, I took a deep breath, and tried to reaffirm what I had just said, "That is NOT a boy! That is a girl! That's my daughter down there! She's strong because she just got done playing football with the boy's football team!" My friend, whose daughter grew up with mine, was sitting next to me and touching my arm to get me to calm down. But then, not even five minutes later I heard it, "That goalie looks like a boy." I had to stand up. I shouted, "Look! If you insist on making ignorant comments after you have already been well-told that the goalie's my daughter, you're going to have to move or I'm going off on you!" Cue the change of seats.

I wish everything would have ended there, but it did not. There were obviously some comments made down on the soccer field. Our team was doing well, and my daughter's goalie skills were shutting out the other team, causing some pretty ugly comments from some players. Luckily, Maddy's players were there to back her up, and stood up to the haters on the other team.

After the game, which we won handily (proud Mom!) while the girls were changing out of their gear, angry parents and players were awaiting my daughter near the exit of the facility. What exactly did they think they were going to do? I rushed to where my daughter was changing, lest someone try to get into her face and cause an issue. My husband decided to confront these people proactively. He calmly said, "Listen, I don't know what your problem is, but I know your girls are upset because they lost. But let me tell you point-blank, that goalie is my daughter whom I love very much. I can assure you…that is my girl!" Several of the parents looked down at their feet, embarrassed and ashamed. A couple of the players still stood there with their hands on their hips, defiant. "Yeah right!" one scorned him. My husband just waived her off and walked away. Luckily, the crowd finally disappeared before our players came out and Momma Bear didn't have to bite off any heads!

While I understand that people who don't know Maddy don't quite understand her, I expect more from those who do know her and know how kind and respectful she is to others. During her sophomore year, she was leaving school when one of the teachers, a math teacher, was outside handing out flyers that clearly said that homosexuals were sinners and were going to burn in hell! I was furious when she came home and told me! Did she get one? "No way! I crumpled it up and threw it on the ground in front of him!" Even without the evidence in-hand, I called the school and left a complaint. I never received a reply. The next year my daughter actually had this math teacher for a class. When Maddy became eligible for an early college program, we were excited! All she needed was an A- in all core classes, which she had been able to maintain. We received the semester report card, and there was a C- in her math class. I called to inquire about this. How was she getting a C- when all of her work scored A- or higher? He made some remark about "participation", which I couldn't believe could bring a grade that low. Then they had taken a semester exam that was a cumulative test. This was to be reported as a separate grade, but he decided to average it into the classroom grade. This, of course, made my daughter ineligible for the program. When I contacted the assistant principal, she told me that this was "left up to the teachers' discretion." I got no support here.

Early in her senior year my daughter was being stalked by the girls on the soccer team who desperately wanted her to play. She had no desire to go back on the field for anyone. After the garbage she had been through, I didn't have the heart to force her to play. One of the girls on the team had a mother who worked as a teacher in the school. She loved my daughter and was trying frantically to get her back on the team. She saw Maddy in the hallway returning to class from the restroom and motioned her into her classroom. She tried to convince her one last time to join the team. While in the room, a boy in the back of the class called her a "bitch" rather loudly. Maddy simply told him, "Grow up." She left to got back class. While walking back, the assistant principal stopped my daughter and asked, "Why aren't you in class?" My daughter explained, "I went to the restroom" and she proceeded to show the assistant principal her hall pass. The assistant principal said, "That wasn't your room that you came out of." Maddy was sent to the office. When the assistant principal returned, she accused Maddy of disrupting the classroom, being out of her assigned area, and of trying to incite an altercation with the boy in the classroom who had yelled at her. The teacher, who called her into the room, came in shortly after. She told the assistant principal exactly what happened. The teacher responsibility for Maddy being in her room and explained my daughter was NOT the one who had disrupted the class. It was the boy. None of it mattered, however, because my daughter was given a day of in-school suspension. Arbitrary discipline was given for the next two months for random reasons- no reasons.

I had grown tired of my daughter being beaten down for no reason. I decided to contact a friend of mine who was on the school board. This person knew my daughter as a kind and responsible student. I explained everything from the pamphlets passed out to the students, to the discretionary grade given to my daughter that kept her from an athletic opportunity, and the arbitrary disciplinary procedures being handed out to her despite teachers coming to her defense. I gave her names of teachers who could vouch for Maddy. Long story short, after the investigation, the teacher who "gay-bashed" was relieved of all extracurricular student activities, including the National Honor Society. The assistant principal was forced to retire half-way through the school year, and by the beginning of the new school year, new administrators were hired. Because of what I have seen and experienced as both a parent and as a teacher, I have begun my own path toward becoming an administrator. I know I can do better than all the others have, because I will do it for the RIGHT reasons.

I'm happy to say that my daughter is now working somewhere that accepts her and the work ethic that she holds: the United States Army. Her Cos respect and admire her, and everyone who knows her, thinks the world of her. She has earned promotions before anyone else in her unit, and has been invited to join special forces.

Do I miss the fact that she didn't wear a sparkly prom gown to her senior prom? Do I resent the fact that she will not be wearing a big frilly wedding gown when she weds? Absolutely NOT! She is who she is, and I swear that I wouldn't have her any other way!

MADDY'S STORY

I've always known I was gay. I was never attracted to males. My "boyfriend" in preschool and kindergarten was really more of a friend. I used the term "boyfriend", because everyone else did.

I never really had to "come out" to my parents. I think they kind-of always knew. In school, I was always embarrassed to have to correct teachers and administrators who thought I was a boy. It was awkward for me and for them, especially after having to correct them.

I never really had to come out to any of my friends or co-workers either. They pretty much always knew, just like my parents. Obviously, since they are my *friends,* they accept me as I am, without any problems or issues.

When I was younger, like in middle school, people would call me "weird" or "dyke." I really didn't understand why I was so different. I was just being myself, but people treated me different. Now, as an adult, I am in the military and surrounded by people with VERY different backgrounds and VERY different backgrounds. I am cautious as to how I present myself to people I don't know. As an adult, I understand everyone is not accepting of those who are different, so I typically stand back and wait to be approached. My current best friend approached ME, because she heard about me from a mutual friend. She was open to meet me and to get to know me. She has always treated me like a "regular person" and we have typical discussions just like other "normal" people. Of course, since we're in the military, our discussions are sometimes about training, deployment, and those in our company.

Recently, I befriended someone who is a lot like me! She's in the Army, is sometimes mistaken as male, and is a lesbian. She's older, 28, and is originally from Mexico, but her family moved to Texas when she was very young. She's more outgoing than I am though. She's definitely not afraid to reach out to others, even if she's unsure how they will accept her. She was the most masculine female on the base before I got there. We laugh about that.

The most annoying thing I deal with today? The constant staring, like, "Is that a girl?" "Is that a guy?" And when my friend and I are together, we get the WEIRDEST looks! People actually stop in their tracks and turn to look at us as we pass! My friend has large breasts and a higher voice than I do, so she's obviously female. People are left with all kinds of questions about the two of us, I guess. But really, WHO DOES THAT? I mean…who physically stops in their tracks and turns all the way around to stare at someone? I could NEVER do that. It's so awkward and so disrespectful!

The military has definitely helped me mature. You learn responsibility, the importance of family, and all of the little things we usually take for granted. Right now, at 19, I'm financially stable, and I can see the benefits of my choice to join the military. They always teach that the "Mission comes First", so the little issues or differences you may have with someone must be left to the side for the good of the mission.

Words of wisdom to other LGBT youth: There's a whole community of people going through the same thing you are right now. The world is changing, adapting, and slowly becoming more accepting.

JONATHAN W. GILL

18. SOMETHING SOFT

It will have been
22 years tomorrow
and still I wonder if it meant
anything at all.

Would it have made a difference
if it had never happened?

Could a smile
have saved a life?
A hug?

I wonder where my parents would be
if they weren't changing diapers
saving up for that college fund;
were they better off?

Of course they will say yes
but I think deep down
in those private spaces
everyone wonders.

What if I had been braver
when those kids
ran a boy out of town
for the color of his skin?

Do you believe in karma?

I guess sometimes I do
but I shouldn't
I don't think people should
need fear to be good

But then I fear that I am wrong.

I've never quite fit in with others;
Vampires, aliens, and oddballs
I've always felt at home far away.

C. Boske & A. Osanloo (Eds.), Students, Teachers, and Leaders Addressing Bullying in Schools, 105–107.

When I was a little boy
I wanted to have long nails
so I begged my mother
to let me buy the glue-ons.

I put them on in the basement
so no one would see me.
I thought it was the coolest thing.
That's love.

I have a penis
so I don't know how that
makes me less of a man.

I still like to look good
and I love hugs;
rare moments when people
take off their masques
and show me themselves.

I am vulnerable
because too many
are too hard;

People need something soft.

I even fell in love with a boy once
but I don't think he loved me back.

Sometimes I fall in love with strangers
because they remind me of him
Is that wrong?

I've never been in a fight.

I used to daydream
about my funeral.
I thought it would be nice
if a lot of people showed up
or just a few.

As long as they smiled
or cried
or cared.

It seems selfish
but I just want to know
that it all mattered.

I'm not suicidal.
I'm honest.

I'll keep this hand out here
and you grab it when you're ready.

KIM MOSYJOWSKI AND JOAN MOSYJOWSKI

19. CHAOS AND ORDER

Chaos and order, calm and fury, birth and death, darkness and light, summer and winter, sound and silence, sickness and health: as the cycles of the natural world circle and spiral, powered by polarities, so too do our human lives. It is in circles that we should gather, it is in circles that we need to listen and speak, and in circles that we should form for healing and for strength; for the sum of the power of many joined together in a circle of community is always, always, greater than the sum of the power of the individuals who form its parts.

They say that hindsight is 20/20, but I still do not see conclusive signs of the severity of depression my youngest daughter, Joan, was in the midst of even with that enhanced lens. Joan had a very successful Power of the Pen competition the *Day before the Darkness*. She acted like the thirteen year old she was: happy and having fun with her friends and talkative on the way home about the day. My adult daughter, her sister, was home for the weekend. When my son, Nik, returned from work that evening the siblings spent Saturday evening watching shows and playing on the Wii and enjoying time together. The next day, Sunday, *The Day That Changed Everything*, Erika left for home, Nik went to work, I went to an art museum with a friend, and Joan went to our basement and tried to hang herself.

This is our story; a mother and daughter's journey together out of the depths of Hell after *The Day That Changed Everything*.

This part of our story was shared with the Unitarian Universalist Church of Akron in 2012 from the pulpit. The UUCA is one of the Circles we joined when I realized that Joan especially, but also me, needed to find a supportive community to counteract the toxic school environment she dealt with daily. Joan needed to hear voices of acceptance and celebration. She desperately needed a larger world view beyond the myopic, bigoted, homophobic, conservative, "Christian" views the most vocal members of the Hartville community espouse.

KIM: It has been said that in order to be saved from cold grasp of Hell one must find someone who is willing to leave his or her own safety, comfort, and daily routines behind and travel down to those dark cold depths in Hell to find you and lead you out. We have such a journey into Hell and back to share with you today, because whether you were aware of it or not, as a member of this UUCA congregation, you are very much a part of this journey.

C. Boske & A. Osanloo (Eds.), Students, Teachers, and Leaders Addressing Bullying in Schools, 109–116.
© 2015 Sense Publishers. All rights reserved.

JOAN: The journey begins at the beginning of my eighth grade year. I was thirteen. I started to realize that I was gay. From what I'd heard, it was a trait that made you subhuman, at best. When I came out to my family, I was relived at the unconditional love and support I received so swiftly and completely. My mom and I sat on the couch for hours one night as I cried with both relief and fear at the sudden realization at the different life I would lead just by being me. She gave me insight and resources to help with coming to terms with my sexuality, but even that didn't protect me from the harassment and adversity of my peers. Eventually, I broke up with my boyfriend and I came out to one of my best friends. I never anticipated that she would reject me for who I was, and I especially did not think that she would out me to my classmates. But she did, and in a few months' time, my world came crashing down and I entered into to my own circle of Hell.

KIM: I knew she was going through a tough time, but what thirteen year old doesn't? We talked. I gave her my unconditional love, and I thought I offered her the right words
You see, our words are powerful beyond imagination. They can be used to heal and...

JOAN: and also to hurt, and even kill. Over the next few months, it felt like every single person in my predominately conservative, Christian, public school knew my little secret, and no, they didn't like it. They harassed and bullied me by calling me a freak, and a loser, and a creepy, nasty, homo. I was isolated from close friends. When the bullying and name-calling became overwhelming, I began a regiment of self- inflicted harm by cutting, burning, and bashing myself. It was a way of taking the pain inside caused by bullies, depression, isolation, and my own internal homophobia, and reflecting it onto the outside.

TOGETHER: (She) (I) didn't know. (I) (She) was in the dark.

JOAN: I was in such a dark place that I couldn't find any reason to keep living a life that I hated; a life where it seemed I was so alone. I began to plan a way to leave everything behind. On March 6th, 2011, after planning for nearly two months, I tried to hang myself. I've never felt such a dark, cold void and a hopelessness that I just couldn't fill. Today, I couldn't be more thankful that the rope broke and I decided to wait another day, because I wouldn't be alive, my mom would not have found out, and I would never have found the place where I belong. I was lucky, and have been given a second chance at life that unfortunately, most youth who attempt suicide don't get.

KIM: My extreme gratitude that she failed in her suicide attempt was closely followed by confusion, and anger, but mostly I felt such profound sadness. MY. GOD. My CHILD tried to KILL herself. No one should ever have to feel that low or that alone. How could I have not known the extent of her anguish? How could I have not been there to help her? I felt like I should have a placard around my neck that said "Inadequate Mother." I certainly had that tattooed upon my heart.

While desperately searching for the immediate help Joan needed to get through this darkness, I started to spiral down into my own pit.

JOAN: I felt so alone.

KIM: I felt so confused.

JOAN: I did not know how to recover

KIM: or where to turn for help.

KIM: I forgot, momentarily, about my invisible means of support. (And no, I am not talking about my bra.)

JOAN: Through many tears, my mother helped me find a hospital program for teens, a counselor, and PFLAG; Parents Families and Friends of Lesbians and Gays. I was starting the process of healing.

KIM: PFLAG is an amazing organization. We are all actively involved in that group still. But Joan needed something more, especially since school was such a hostile environment for her at that time. I began to search for a supportive community for her. The Unitarian Universalist Church of Akron was already in my mental file, filed under the "Someday" category, as in: someday I will check this interesting church out. I moved it to the "ACTIVE" file and...

JOAN: the idea of a church was unappealing. Church? She wanted me to go to the very institution that hated me for who I am? I did not want to go. But, I couldn't have been more wrong. As soon as we set foot in the church, we were greeted with smiles, and with these simple, wonderful, words: "Welcome" and "good morning!" As we sat down in the pews for the first time, I STARED at the dais in utter disbelief at this shining beacon of hope displayed proudly for all to see; a rainbow flag. By some cosmic convergence, the first service we attended was dedicated to LGBTQ people.

KIM: As we listened to Rabbi David Horowitz, the president of PFLAG National, talk that day, we laughed, and we cried, and as soon as the service ended, Joan looked at me and said:

Joan: "Wow, a sanctuary that really is one." I knew that UUCA was going to be a safe haven and a community that embraced and welcomed us both.

KIM: We arrived at the UU Church of Akron looking very much like the wild-eyed refugees that we were. We entered this church emotionally bedraggled and seeking sanctuary. You saved us with your kindness, acceptance, and words of welcome.

Our words are powerful beyond measure, and so are our actions. Even those of you who just learned our names this morning helped save this young person's life. And by saving hers, you saved mine also. By supporting and participating in this wonderful, welcoming, loving, spiritual community, you gave her, and me, the support we needed to get through a very dark and difficult time. You have made us a part of this circle of friends and propped us up until we were strong enough to stand on our own again. For that...

TOGETHER: We thank you. ...

KIM: Each of you here right now, and all who came before you who helped make this church the welcoming congregation that it is.

JOAN: I would like to extend a special thank you to the youth of this community. You guys get it, and that is more than can be said for much of the world. Whether it's at a Youth Conference, class, retreat, Summer Institute, there is never a question about accepting into your midst an LGBTQ peer. It just happens, and that can make a difference in a youth's life. It certainly has in mine. THANK YOU for opening the doors to your church and to your heart.

KIM: We as welcoming Unitarian Universalists have the potential to save more lives like Joan's. Our LGBTQ youth are DYING for a lack of a spiritual community like this one. It is so urgent that we as UUs raise our voices and are heard over the hateful noise the right wing bigoted "Christians" are making as they tell our LGBTQ youth and citizens that they are somehow less-than, evil, or sinners because you and I know that they are WRONG! It is deadly and completely unacceptable that their voices are ever heard spewing hatred louder than ours are heard as we proclaim love, acceptance, and celebration.

JOAN: I need YOU; the positive forces of diversity, to be LOUD and PROUD and VOCAL for the youth who are silenced in oppression an even in death. I need YOU to join me and my family and this congregation in rejuvenating this church's welcoming committee, so that we may reach out and save the lives of more LGBTQ youth like me. Because now that you know me, and my mom, and how YOU are a part of our story, the real question is this: what role as welcoming and loving people will you play in saving lives and telling LGBTQ people that we are here and WE CARE.

Time passes...

JOAN: For three years, I have been doing something that I never thought I would do again; I have been living a life worth living. By some miraculous act of the Universe's kindness, I have been given a rare and incredible gift and opportunity to exist as a conscious entity and to try again to move forward. I feel reborn; aware of a life I used to live and able to use it as an example of how I should live now. I intend to soak up the beauty of every breath and to devote my life to climbing back into the icy depths of Hell to direct as many people out as I can; I wish to be a candle in the dark and a hand to hold, just as those kind souls who saved my life have been before me. These past years have been filled with triumphs and letdowns and joy beyond anything I could have imagined as an eighth grade student. Today, I am proud to be myself and thankful for this life I can live.

Going into high school, I knew I wanted to make a difference and to help other students who may be struggling to stay afloat. It can be incredibly difficult to stay positive under the rule of high school values, especially in a bubble of a small town. My heart was bursting at the seams with excitement to be leaving middle school behind me and moving under a larger microscope, though once I arrived, I realized quickly that people were still quite capable of cruelty. In the halls I was still harassed, though less frequently. I had been spat at, thrown slurs at, and once pushed into the bus lane as the busses were rolling in for holding hands with another girl. It was clear that my high school was far behind the times. I wanted to start a Gay-Straight Alliance, and began planning a way to get one when one day, I stumbled across a unique opportunity. MTV was hosting a second *It Gets Better* special and was casting teens. The summer before my sophomore year I submitted my story thus far and expressed my desire to establish a Gay-Straight Alliance. To my surprise, I was contacted by MTV representatives and asked to do a Skype interview with a casting assistant. While I was not casted to be a part of the special, it was an opportunity that I am thankful to have taken. It was a reminder that I had a story to tell, a voice to be heard, and an obligation to help others in my school.

To my surprise and elation, that year in school I saw posters and heard whispers of the first Gay-Straight Alliance in the high school led by two ambitious juniors. Quite unfortunately, the club fizzled and only a few faithful believers stuck around to ensure the club was not cancelled. At the start of my junior year, I took on the responsibility of holding the first meeting and holding elections for a new team of GSA leaders. I was elected president and my close friends were elected as secretary, fundraiser, and vice president; a brand new team of leaders hell-bent on revamping the club. As the president, I am graced with the opportunity to work with friends old and new to make our school safer for ALL students; it is a great comfort to know that what we do can change lives, and potentially save them.

Away from school, I have been and continue to be a student of many subjects. Through opportunities presented through the Unitarian Universalists of my church and beyond I have been able to expand my abilities in leadership. I became a fundraising chair of the youth group, and am now the co-chair. Through district-wide youth conferences of UU youths, I have been to leadership and chaplain trainings with inspiring and wondrous people whom I have been honored to grow with. I became the co-chair for an LGBTQ teen Pride Prom that is now becoming an annual affair. My mother and I have been granted numerous opportunities to share our story and to help to advocate for gay teens through PFLAG and Unitarian Universalists. I have been accepted onto GLSEN's Jump Start Team, an opportunity to learn more about running successful Gay-Straight Alliances. I have also been recognized by the Unitarian Universalists' Association as a Luminary Leader; one who lives their values to lead and work for change. I have been blessed with so many new and exciting changes and chances that I know will continue, and just as I know that I will have those chances, I know I will run for them, thankful to be alive.

I got to live again, that means that I got to have dreams and goals to aspire to and challenges to conquer. I got to get out of middle school. I got to have not one but THREE more birthdays with many more to come. I got to turn 16 and spend that day with friends and family that I love so dearly. Last summer I got to march in a gay pride parade after seeing my first one in Denver, CO a year before. In school, I got to read great works of literature and write whatever I wanted. I got to go to church, and I got to skip church because I wanted to sleep in. I got to kiss a girl and like it, just as Katy Perry told me I would. I got to make new friends and reconnect with old ones. As every living creature does, I got to make mistakes. As every teenager does, I got my heart broken once or twice, and then I got to shake the dust off and move on. I got to see progress in gaining equality for LGBTQ people, and I also got to witness a few steps back. I got a car. I got to travel again. I got to eat, sleep, waste time, and repeat. I got to escort my girlfriend to a school dance, and accompany her to a few others. I got to sing in a choir and bang drums in a school band. I got to fill my calendar and stress out about filling my calendar months later. I got to forget to do my homework and procrastinate on mammoth projects. I got to cry tears of pain, anger, frustration, and unfiltered happiness. I got to help others. I got a second chance and I got to live; no amount of hatred or harassment can take away my will to live again. This life is the only one I have and I intend to continue doing all that I can do to be happy and to assist others in finding their peace.

These past three years have been hectic to say the least. In such a short time I've lived the best possible life I could live, and I wouldn't trade it for anything. With every new light no matter how I wake up I thank the Universe for granting me the chance to face another day, no matter what it holds. When I awake I take time to list at least ten people and ten things I can be thankful for; my loving family, my supportive friends, the end of winter and the start of spring, the voice I've been given to sing, legs that work and take me far, and a will to live that can take me even farther. Recalling the darkest of all days, I remember the closeness of every slur; of every painful moment. But now, those words are far away, and while some days being gay can take away a smile, it can never again take away my will to LIVE.

Kim: These past three years have been eventful. My husband, Joe, and I joined the board of directors for the Akron PFLAG chapter in 2012. PFLAG is an outstanding national organization whose reach is now extending into other countries. We are dedicated to helping all LGBTQ people through advocacy, education, and support. Our Akron PFLAG chapter is well established and is run by devoted, informed, highly active community leaders, some of whom have been working for equality and justice for all for decades. In 2013 I was elected as president of their board.

The Akron chapter has seen a steady increase in the number of teens who come to PFLAG looking for support. The fortunate teens arrive with a supportive adult or family member. Some come alone. Far too many have been thrown out of their homes when their families found out they were gay. Statistics state that forty percent of all homeless teens are LGBTQ teens. Forty percent! That is too disturbing to ignore. The majority of the teens who come to PFLAG support meetings have one thing in common: they thought about committing or attempted to commit suicide. Statistics state that LGBTQ youth are two to three times more likely to attempt suicide than their heterosexual peers. I think that number is low. They speak about the overwhelming sense of isolation and the feelings that no one else shares their struggles because there are surely no other gay teens nearby. They speak about having no one to talk to, about always being afraid that someone would find out their Big Secret. These young people need help and they need it now, and they need more than one meeting a month. What could we do to help? PFLAG is excellent at offering support at their monthly meetings and helping people find resources. We educate many as we talk to schools, GSAs, teachers, doctors in training, social workers, churches, and individuals. But some of the teens needed support from peers and a safe way to meet other LGBTQ teens. They needed a supportive community like Joan and I found at the Unitarian Universalist Church of Akron.

With that thought in my mind, UUCA's Pride OUUTreach chairperson, Conni Cook-Wagner, and the new executive director of CANAPI- Community Aids Network and Akron Pride Initiative, Rebecca Callahan, and I, representing Akron PFLAG, met in July, 2013 and put our heads together, and the Teen Pride Network was born. The Teen Pride Network offers LGBTQ teens the best of the three collaborating organizations.

I am a firm believer in collaboration. With Akron PFLAG, CANAPI, and UUCA pooling our resources, our talents, and our time we can make an impact in even more lives than any one person or single organization could ever make working alone. The whole is greater than the sum of the parts. We organize pro-social events for LGBTQ teens and their allies to meet in safe, supervised, fun situations and network. Teen Pride has hosted and has planned: a hike at the Metro parks and a bonfire, a Halloween dance, an ice skating evening, a mid-winter games night, the Pride Prom, an art in the park day, event attendance at the Gay Games in Akron/Cleveland, and marching in the Cleveland Pride parade. Teen Pride Network is one way for me to express my gratitude for a second chance to watch my own daughter grow up while doing what I can to help as many teens as possible to make it through those tough teen years. Joan is my sunshine and I am prepared to do whatever I can to keep her shining. She continues to make me so proud to be her mother and so grateful she is thriving.

The Day That Changed Everything changed our entire family in positive ways. We appreciate life and each other more openly. We have discovered so many truly amazing people who are devoted to equality for all and to changing the toxic school, business, political and religious environments of LGBTQ people. We have made new friends and have grown and expanded our circles and joined new ones. Our lives are busy and rich and rewarding.

It is in circles that we should gather; it is in circles that we need to listen and speak; and it is circles that we should form for healing and for strength; for the sum of the power of many joined together in a circle of community is always, always, greater than the sum of the power of the individuals who form its parts. In this circle we give thanks to all who have touched our lives. May you live well and long. Be kind. Give thanks. Live with purpose and joy. Life is short, join hands and make it count.

DWAYNE STEWARD

20. BULLIED AT THE INTERSECTION

Growing up Gay in the Black Church and Rural Ohio

When I first walked into Mrs. Mitchell's fourth grade classroom at Carlisle Elementary School, I knew my life was never going to be the same. After landing a promotion at the Honda plant in Marysville, Ohio, my father moved my two younger sisters and me out of Columbus, Ohio's, inner city and into the small rural town of Delaware, Ohio, in order to move closer to his job and give us a "proper" suburban upbringing. Mrs. Mitchell (one of the few black teachers in the elementary school district at the time) immediately took me under her wing, likely because she knew what I was in for. I was one of just a handful of black kids in our school, one of two in my fourth grade class. And, there was an active chapter of the Ku Klux Klan just down the street whose members fed a plethora of their kids into the local school system.

Why do you use grease in your hair? Why do black girls' hair stick up like that? What's ashy? Why are all black people loud? Aren't you supposed to be *good* at basketball and football? Does your dad have a job? He does!?

My 9-year-old self scoffed at these questions. Why don't these people know this stuff? Everyone back home did? I immediately began to identify as the "other." Back in Columbus I was picked on for being too feminine. Here, I was first picked on for being black before being asked why I "acted like a girl." Ducking and dodging bullying and insults became an art form.

My father is a deacon-turned-minister in an Apostolic church. A faith I grew up in, where fear became the regular main course. Fear God. That was the motto to live by, because you could easily go straight to hell. And the one major straight-to-hell tickets, other than suicide, was homosexuality. A message the preacher decided to touch base on at the end of nearly every service. And being that my father was an aspiring minister, I was in church nearly every day. There was a Monday youth meeting, Wednesday Bible study, a second Bible study on Thursday, Friday prayer service, Saturday choir rehearsal and of course, Sunday morning and afternoon services (and don't forget Sunday school). So I heard this gay-is-bad message a lot.

So naturally when a 14-year-old boy, who's grown up in the above, one day discovers orgasms, prompted by a shirtless LL Cool J in a 90s music video, inner turmoil and self-hatred were guaranteed to follow.

C. Boske & A. Osanloo (Eds.), Students, Teachers, and Leaders Addressing Bullying in Schools, 117–122.

For me, it was first denial. This was wrong and Satan was just attacking me. It was my job to pray as hard as possible, trust God and make sure Satan didn't win which is exactly what I did for the next four years. I threw myself into being the "model" student. If my parents ever found out that I was gay, they'd still have to love me, because at least I was smart and accomplished. Right? Becoming my school's valedictorian or salutatorian became the ultimate goal. I ran myself ragged by joining every group I could. Concert band, marching band, pep band, drama club, key club, National Honor Society, I was an editor on the school paper and the year book, and to top it off, I had a part time job at a fast food restaurant. *Stay busy and you won't have to think about it. It won't all blow up in your face. They won't kick you out. God's going to save you.*

I started dating females on the popular premise that "faith without works is dead" but this presented an entirely new set of problems. Black girls weren't readily available and after being told by a mutual crush that her parents thought it was "unwise" for us to be together because they had friends and family in the KKK, white girls became off limits too.

I finally found a girl in marching band whose single mother had a biracial son. She played the French horn and thought I was the bees knees. Jackpot. We started going steady. I lost my virginity. I was in love. It was happening. God had cured me. I had a 4.1 GPA, a date for the prom and I had found the perfect face wash to clear my growing acne problem. Life was finally going my way. Well, almost.

It's funny how 16-year-olds can always sense which kids have the lowest self esteem. Despite my attempts at creating the perfect straight Dwayne that I thought God wanted me to be, my classmates routinely reminded me that I wasn't. Faggot, sissy, fudge packer. Those were my nicknames in high school often thrown my way by the "jocks" and "preps." I was pushed against a few lockers, spit on a couple times and even told I wasn't "black enough" on several occasions.

But, school wasn't really the worst part. I was strong, confident and, like most teenagers, slightly vain as a kid. Comments from ignorant bullies didn't really faze me. Looking back, it was the religious bullying from my home and church families that caused the most damage.

I have a pretty big family. That's an understatement. My family is huge. My immediate family is made up of only six (two parents, two boys, two girls), but I have 16 aunts and uncles and nearly 50 cousins. My maternal grandparents had 27 siblings between them and my paternal grandparents had 10. If we start with my great-grandparents on both sides of my family and move down, my family could probably fill a small city. A large portion lives in Central Ohio, which makes escaping them all the more difficult. Growing up with family always around made me treasure them even more. I always have and always will have somewhere to turn if I ever need help.

I say all that to say this, coming out to that many people, in the same area, in a black family, can be a little more than daunting. Most of my family has grown up in the black Apostolic or Baptist church, a community that has always frowned on "the homosexual lifestyle." The thought of all that disapproval compounded with the weekly gay doomsday speech at church kept me locked in the closet.

As you can imagine, church also gave no solace. The church I grew up in was pretty small. The members were mostly comprised of a family that my father grew up with. He dated the pastor's daughter in high school and I ended up dating her daughter in junior high. Most of the congregation lived in Columbus, but traveled two hours away out to rural Welston, Ohio, to a spacious building that was half the rent it would be in the city. If you just counted the cost of gas alone that was spent over the two decades that we attended that church, you can start to imagine how dedicated my parents were to this pastor's ministry.

Soon after discovering I was gay, another boy my age, who happened to be the pastor's grandson, discovered the same. We began confiding in each other and became fast friends. This closeness soon became misunderstood and the gay bashing messages became louder and clearer. I was forced to start participating in more masculine activities, like sports, and told to stop hanging around so much with girls. Everything from the way I walked to my handwriting needed to be modified and made less feminine. Later after we both finally came out, the hate exploded and rumors soon went rampant through the church and family that we both were HIV-positive and infecting each other and those around us with AIDS. So much for God's unconditional love. I soon left the church and went down a long road of losing my faith, believing God had rejected me. Years later I did rediscovered Him, but on my own terms.

So, I was a 16-year-old, closeted gay, black boy dating a white girl in rural America, where an active and not-so-underground chapter of the KKK resided. I was dealing with racist and homophobic bullying at school and religious bigotry at church and in the home. According to the Lifetime Movie Network, suicide should have crossed my mind more than a few times. But surprisingly it didn't. Not once.

Remember, along with homosexuality, I was taught that suicide would also send me "straight to hell." My real saving grace became my friends. A small group of girlfriends that insulated me like a mamma kangaroo's pouch from the growing depression of my situation. They all knew I was gay but respected me well enough to let me figure that out for myself. Not once did they ever ask me about my sexuality. Even though, later I learned, they were questioned by prying classmates about my disposition on several occasions. Mall trips, sleepovers, birthday parties in the park, sleuthing together on the school newspaper and impromptu road trips were the moments that kept me from the worst parts of myself. Today these girls' kids are my nieces and nephews. The fun I had with them may have been the reason I was a few spots shy of landing salutatorian but I'd take these friends over a certificate any day.

Graduating from high school also does wonders for one's growth. As soon as I left Delaware Hayes High School for Ohio University, it was like a 50-pound burden had been lifted off me. Ohio University is known for its liberal atmosphere and I felt embraced from the moment I stepped on the campus. I finally came out to my friends at the end of my sophomore year, to which all my girlfriends from high school responded with a simple shrug and "what's new?" Even then I claimed to be bisexual and continued to date females, still clinging on to some sort of hope that I'd marry a woman and have the family that was "right" in the eyes of God and my parents.

During my junior year at OU, I found a group of friends on campus that truly understood me and together we started a student organization called SHADES. It was at first a simple support group, a space where gay students of color could gather without fear of being judged by the predominately white gay culture for the color of their skin or the multicultural community for their sexual orientation. It was a space to be undeniably and unapologetically you. Soon the group began to grow and branch out. We began doing community service on campus and in the surrounding city of Athens and even sponsored major events on campus like speakers, dances and concerts. There is now a SHADES chapter at Ohio State University, and there are plans in the works to start chapters at various universities in Ohio and around the country.

Little did I know that being a part of founding SHADES was not only helping gay people of color at the various schools it's serving, but it also helped me break out of the cycle of self-hate I'd bound myself. By the time I was 21, the pieces of my damaged psyche and dwindling self worth had been put back together and I was strong enough to finally come out to my mother.

By the time I'd returned home from an internship during the summer after my junior year, the AIDS rumors at my former church had reached its peak and my mother had started asking questions. Once I arrived home for a visit, I decided it was time to set the record straight.

I remember it like it was yesterday. We were driving to a family function. I was in the passenger seat like I'd been many times before, whether we were on the way to soccer practice, Little League baseball, or rehearsal for the Spring Musical. I suddenly felt like that five-year-old she'd tote around to Boy Scouts or tap dancing lessons.

"Mom, I need to tell you something."

She got quiet for a moment. "What is it?" Just based on the way she whispered her response, I could already tell she knew what I was going to say.

I took a deep breath, nearly changing the subject out of fear. "I'm gay."

Silence.

"I knew. I've known for a long time. I was just waiting for you to tell me. It doesn't change anything. I'll always love you no matter what."

Those words did give me hope that my world wasn't going to come crashing down but only for a moment.

"But you know this is a lifestyle I don't agree with, and God doesn't either," she said after another long silence.

It was a long road back from those comments. Before this conversation, my mother was akin to a God-like figure in my eyes; perfect in every way. My main goal in life was to please her, to make her proud. After that car ride, a deep rift spread through our relationship. Every time I looked at her I could only see the hurt

120

and disappointment in her eyes. It would be a few years before we'd talk about my sexuality again. For a while, I *refused* to discuss it with her. I knew her stance. She knew mine. I didn't even tell my dad. I had her do it.

Eventually the word spread throughout my large family and many of them also replied with the "I already knew" response. (At this point I was starting to wonder why no one bothered to clue me in!) My sisters were extremely supportive and by this time one of them had come out as well. (Two gay kids out of four. Maybe God's trying to tell my dad something?)

The last person I came out to was my brother, who is the eldest of the four of us. At the time his wife had given birth to two of his three kids and I was most afraid of being cut off from them if he knew. I remember this distinctly because it was my senior year and I was heavily involved in the LGBT center on campus because of SHADES, and it was National Coming Out Day, during the school's annual OUT Week. I was in the midst of going through a very uplifting week of speeches and events about the LGBT experience. I had even spoken at a gay rights rally earlier that day. I was on a "gay high," if you will.

Once I'd gotten home, I realized that I'd been telling everyone that week about how freeing it was to be an out and proud, black, gay man but I wasn't even out to everyone in my immediate family. So I picked up and phone and dialed my brother's number. After I told him he also got quiet. He said he'd had no idea (the first time anyone gave me that response) and proceeded to get choked up as he apologized for all the times he'd ever picked on me for being feminine or calling me a "sissy." I shed a few tears myself at his sincerity. It's a moment with my brother I'll always cherish.

As they say, time heals all wounds. Truer words have never been spoken when it comes to my parents. We are finally finding our way back to an open and affirming relationship. It's a slow and a deliberate process, but once we all decided to reopen lines of communication the healing ultimately began. They still have their faith and I still have my convictions, but we're no longer shutting ourselves off from each other emotionally.

It's a lesson that can also be used in other parts of my life and within the gay rights movement as a whole. Educating those who hate, as opposed to shutting them off completely, is the only way we're going to win the fight for equality.

I do often take a moment and think back on those times in high school and wonder why I didn't come out sooner. Maybe proudly and openly blazing a trail that wasn't there would have been a lot less damaging than bottling everything up inside me. Unfortunately, my surroundings didn't equip me with the strength to do so.

The black church and small rural towns are still two of the most homophobic areas in the American experience. I don't think members of these two communities understand the consequences of their hate. Especially the damaging psychological and developmental effects this hate can have on the youth in their communities. More and more gay teens are turning to suicide thinking it's the only escape. Hate is literally killing our youth. Every time a teacher ignores the problem, a bully is validated. Every time a televangelist says being gay is an abomination, hate is justified. And, every time a politician votes for anti-gay legislation, the roots of inequality grow stronger.

As a young adult, I quickly grew a thick skin and surrounded myself with supportive voices. I become a person who could confidently combat bullying and homophobia, be it from the local pastor who doesn't allow LGBT people in his church, an employer who threatens to fire anyone who's openly gay in the workplace or a landlord who refuses to rent to same-sex couples. However, not all kids grow up to be so strong and the fact of the matter is they shouldn't have to. Change is possible, but we must start transforming these communities of hate into communities of inclusion, if only to ensure that our gay youth have a chance at a healthy and self-determined adulthood.

LOGAN SHERMAN

21. MASCULINE OF CENTER

PREFACE

In order to describe my experience as an LGBT student in public schools, I put together several snapshots of my K-12 school career that hold particular significance to me. I left out many individual instances of bullying, but the general mood at each point in time reflects the types of experiences I was having and my fluctuating relationship with school. On the flipside, I could not include the stories of every person who touched me and supported me during my K-12 school career, but I do note that there are numerous faculty and peers that I remember fondly, many of whom still make up my network of support today. Their encouragement has made a world of difference to me and I am forever grateful that I didn't feel I had to go it alone.

I met my first bullies…

on bus 59. I was in the first grade and spent roughly an hour a day going back and forth from school on that bus. Its seats were hard plastic with chewed gum wedged into all the corners, and it was in that venue that I committed my earliest offenses.

At the age of seven, I decidedly hated the color pink and proudly wore Band-Aids on my latest playground battle wounds. My hair wasn't too long, and it wasn't too short. When I picked out my clothes in the morning, I went for the fit of my cousin's hand-me-down clothes because I liked the way his blue jeans hung loose around my legs. If someone had asked me to describe my style back then, before I was ever told any differently, I simply would've said I was comfortable. What I didn't know yet was that there were words for people like me, and I was going to wear a title like a nametag on my shirt throughout grade school. I would never have to work for it, but I wouldn't be able to shake it off either. At seven, I was slowly becoming visible.

And she saw me. She lived down the street from me and was my age, but she was in the other first grade class. My stop was before hers on the bus route, but because she was one of the last stops and the bus was mostly full, she ended up sitting down next to me. Her blonde hair was forever pulled into a neat ponytail and she was the kind of girl who spent recess trying not to get her skirt dirty or a run in her tights. I'm not sure I did much to provoke her; maybe she just didn't like the looks of me.

I had gotten a new pair of sneakers that weekend, and to my great excitement they were the kind that lit up when I walked. I remember wearing them around the house Sunday night with the excuse of breaking them in, but truthfully I just liked

C. Boske & A. Osanloo (Eds.), Students, Teachers, and Leaders Addressing Bullying in Schools, 123–132.

the way they lit up- whether I was bounding down the hallway or leaping off the second to last step on the stairs. She noticed them on the bus when she sat down that morning. "Light-up flowers on your shoes? Those are for babies," she informed me, "And how come your shoes have flowers? You don't even look like a girl. You're a tomboy." She had two older brothers and was much more sophisticated in the ways of the world than I was. I could feel my cheeks going red for having thought that those shoes were a good choice the day before. I sat next to her uncomfortably as she laughed, unsure how to respond. I hadn't thought of myself as a tomboy before, but in one word she had summed me up and practically handed me an instruction manual of what I could and could not get away with. Tomboys, I supposed, should not be wearing flowery light-up shoes. When I got home and informed my mother that I needed a different pair, she told me I was going to have to wait another six months.

The next few weeks weren't much better. She made a game out of my new shoes. Every day when she got on the bus she'd kick at my feet until we got to school, lighting my shoes up over and over again. If I had regretted the shoes before, then this continuous reminder sealed the deal. Not being the athletic type, she had a habit of missing my shoes half the time and giving me swift kicks to the ankles or shins instead. Fed up, I repeatedly asked her to stop. Her counter-move was to outnumber me by involving the kids sitting in seats around us. "Tomboy, tomboy!" they leered, "Why do you dress so weird? How come you think you're a boy?" At the end of each bus ride, I clambered off with both my legs and ego feeling more than a little bruised. The assigned seats policy that was instated after the fifth graders in the back of the bus got too rowdy meant that changing seats wasn't an option, and the times I tried to defend myself only served to fuel their game. With no end in sight and a growing dread toward school every morning, I finally took my parent's advice and approached my teacher after our class had walked to the cafeteria for lunch. My teacher listened to me with the kind of patient eyes that only someone who is surrounded by seven year olds all day must have, and when I was finished she sent me off to eat my sandwich with a solution in mind for the next day. On the bus ride home, I almost didn't feel her kicking at my feet.

Instead of going out for recess after lunch the next day, my teacher came into the cafeteria and put a gentle hand on my shoulder, steering me back toward the classroom. Inside, I came face-to-face with the girl from the bus. She wasn't smirking and didn't look put-together the way she normally did. Her face was pale and her eyes were burning red and wet, like she had been crying. She kept one hand on her stomach and the other trembled by her side. "I wanted...to say...I'm sorry," she got out before bursting into tears. The other first grade teacher placed a hand on her shoulder and urged her to continue. "And...you wanted to say that you're going to behave yourself on the bus from now on, isn't that right dear?" the teacher prodded. "Y-yeah, I'm sorry. It won't happen again," the girl finally managed. Her face was turning progressively whiter, as if she was so upset she was making herself sick. Then she tugged the teacher's hand toward the bathroom connecting our two first grade classrooms and promptly threw up the contents of her lunch before beginning to sob all over again. My teacher gave me a sideways smile and suggested I go outside and play with the rest of the class now, and then reassured me that everything would be fine from there on out. The girl wasn't on the bus that afternoon, and the next morning she didn't say a word. Without her provoking them, none of the other kids gave me a hard time either. As I climbed down from the bus and made my way into school that morning, I thought maybe tomboys could wear shoes with light-up flowers after all.

The summer before seventh grade, I became the only girl on the football team.

I can think of a handful of movies about a girl joining an all-boy sports team and becoming the star of the show. At first, none of the guys respect her, but via miraculous athletic feats she earns a place for herself on the team and at the end of the day she becomes something like a hero.

As much as I would love to claim that story as my own, it would be a far stretch from reality. On the first day of practice, I walked into the middle school gym with a water bottle in one hand and my paperwork in the other. As I made my way toward the bleachers where the rest of the players sat, I could feel every pair of eyes in the room turn toward me. True to my nature, I felt my face going red.

Let me be clear: I was never the star of the show. I hadn't been much of a football-watcher before I joined the team, so I was trying to learn the game as I hit the ground running. I pushed myself harder than I ever had before during workouts, and all while wearing football pads and a helmet in the sweltering August heat of Cleveland, Ohio. I hit the tackle bags and did pushups and ran laps just like everybody else. The only "special treatment" I got was the use of the girls' locker room, and that was only about two thirds of the time. I would frequently have to hunt down a janitor during summer practices in order to have the locker room door unlocked so I could get to my cleats, pads and helmet. I would inevitably end up being late to practice and have to run laps and stretch on my own. The team was divided into its own little cliques, but I didn't fit well into any of them. For the most part, I felt alone.

The boys I played football with did not treat me like a member of the team. Many of them made fun of the way I looked or the fact that I was out there in the first place. I was either too manly or I wasn't "man" enough. Some of them weren't so sure I should play because they didn't want to hit a girl, and some of the boys went out of their way to try to hurt me during tackling drills. I remember one particular practice when one of the biggest guys, who also happened to be one of the biggest assholes, gave me a late hit from behind at the end of a drill. He smashed me into the ground and we slid forward with him on top of me, crushing my arm. I hopped up, tears springing to my eyes, and went to the back of the line. The boy in front of me turned around, looked at the damage, and said "Damn, that must've hurt like hell." It certainly had, and I visited the trainer quietly that afternoon once everyone else had left. I knew better than to give anyone a reason to think I wasn't strong enough to be out there. Admitting pain felt comparable to bleeding in a tank of sharks.

Some of my teammates were disrespectful in other ways. It's not unusual for teammates to give one another a smack on the rear end after a nice play, and in fact that's generally accepted as locker room behavior. However, some of the boys on my team took it way too far and after a couple incidents, I had had enough. I was walking back toward the school after practice when one of the boys smacked my butt. "Nice job today, Sherman," he taunted, something mean-spirited about his grin. I spun around to face him and his friends, all of whom had fallen silent and were looking at us in awe. "Don't touch me," I said. I began walking toward the school again. "Don't touch me, don't touch me," they began to mock in falsetto voices. I was furious, but I didn't have a whole lot of options. I took my cleats off, dropped my things in my locker, and called it a day. I'm not sure what I could have done to earn their respect, but that day didn't come. These types of incidents happened pretty regularly for my entire football career.

My presence on the team was also noted by classmates. The population of the school had mixed responses. Sometimes I would have girls come up to me and say "I want to do what you're doing, I really admire you." Other times, like in my gym class, I could overhear their whispers about how strange I was. The walks down the hallways between classes were my least favorite because they were unregulated and overcrowded. It was not unusual for a group of boys to give me a hard time and I'm fairly sure that seventh grade was the year my "Savannah the Man" nickname developed along with my reputation as a lesbian. It felt like most of the people around me had an opinion about whether or not I should be playing, and all of them felt the need to voice it to me.

The faculty at the school also had mixed responses. Certain teachers brought it up in conversation with me, letting me know they thought highly of me. Others could not get it through their heads that when I was wearing a football jersey on game day, it was not because it was my boyfriend's but rather because I was going to be playing a game that day.

I learned a lot through my experience of playing football. I pushed the limits of my comfort zone all the time and couldn't afford to be as shy as I had been before. I began to realize that I was much stronger than I had given myself credit for. There was a constant struggle to prove myself capable on and off the field to my parents, my friends, and my peers. The bullying was getting progressively worse, but I was simultaneously beginning to develop a strong sense of self. I was gaining confidence and I was doing it the hard way.

When I kissed her for the first time, I knew.

I felt it deep down in the places I had been burying it for so long. It was the summer after eight grade, a long way off from the first time someone had questioned my sexual orientation. I had already gone through my brief homophobic stage and was now friends with the bisexual girls who had put me off initially. I saw no fault in them for their same-sex attraction, I simply told them it wasn't for me.

I was attending one of my neighbor's birthday parties. She had a bunch of girls out in her driveway with a fire going and lawn chairs set out. When I took a seat, I couldn't help but notice who I was sitting across from. I had passed her in the hallways in school and sat one table over from hers at lunch all of second semester. Maybe it was because she was so unique, her hair always a different color, her body housing significantly more piercings than most girls her age, but I had been curious about her. She tended to catch my eye, and there was something about the way I felt when we made eye contact. I wanted an excuse to talk to her.

I spent a good deal of the night goofing around with friends, but my gaze kept falling on her across the fire. My train of thought was interrupted when the birthday girl came up to me and asked me to read the text message she had just gotten. It was from the girl on the other side of the fire, and it said something like "who's the attractive person sitting across from me?" It took me a second to realize that she was talking about me. I felt my face turning red and my heart beginning to beat a little faster. "I think someone's got a crush on you," the birthday girl teased. The word spread quickly to the couple friends I was sitting near, and immediately they began to interrogate me. "Do you like her? Do you like girls? Are you a lesbian?," they prodded. My hands were sweaty and I felt panicky, unsure what to say. My orientation had been questioned over and over, quite publically, for years. I was used to denying it, but part of me knew that there was something about that girl. I played it off and tried avoiding their questions, and eventually they let it go and dispersed. I looked down to check my phone for a second, and when I looked up again she was right in front of me. She asked if she could sit down, and stumbling over words, I managed a yes. I made awkward conversation with her, unsure of how to approach the situation I was in. I was curious about her, but we were in a group of people and I had never let myself play with the idea of being interested in a girl so explicitly before. It was getting late and I was psyching myself out, so I decided to call it a night.

Turns out the story didn't end there, because the girl slept over at my neighbor's house that night. The next day, as I walked my dog past the house, the birthday girl came outside and informed me that my admirer was upset because I had rejected her. I dropped my dog off at home and went to my neighbor's basement to talk to her. The birthday girl let us be, and that was when I finally ended up alone with her.

I sat next to her on the couch and she stared at her feet, saying something about how she thought I was cute but it didn't matter because I was straight. "So...what if I'm not straight?" I ventured. I became hyper aware of how close we were, and when she turned her face toward mine I knew what was coming. When we kissed, I felt adrenaline pulsing through me and I thought, "Oh, so *this* is what it's supposed to feel like." She wasn't my first kiss, but it was the first time it had felt right. I was comfortable and I didn't have to think.

When I walked home, I couldn't wipe the smile from my face. I felt jittery, like I had done something forbidden and wonderful, like I had discovered a whole new way of seeing. I didn't know exactly what I had just done, but I knew I wanted to do it again.

Except the next day, reality hit me like a brick wall. Admitting that I liked kissing her meant that I would have to label myself a lesbian. For reasons I could not articulate at the time, I couldn't bring myself to claim that title. In the weeks to come, I got pressure to come out from the girl, my neighbor, friends, and so on. Why couldn't I just admit it, they asked. They called me closet case and teased me, and the more I thought about it the worse I felt. I had dipped my toes in the water, and that was a step for me. It was exciting and came naturally, and I was terrified. I had gotten a taste, but then I promptly turned around and slammed the closet door. Whatever was going on, I was not ready to say.

Call me faggot one more time.

I was walking down the steps at the end of a lunch period, talking with my friend. We had just gotten out of an especially boring health class and were ready for a break. It was Wednesday and the air around us was heavy with the scents of cafeteria food, perfume, and teenagers. We rounded the bend in the stairs and headed down toward the crowd of students waiting outside of the cafeteria. A boy I didn't recognize, probably a senior, glanced up at me and something flashed across his face. He began to tap on the shoulders of his buddies, pointed at me and called out "Hey, there's a faggot!"

A hush fell over the crowd as they registered the loud noise. My friend next to me went quiet and I stopped mid-step. That's when the laughing started. The people at the bottom of the stairs were looking up at me and laughing. The lunch aide, the adult stationed in the hall as chaos control, looked back and forth between me and the boy but didn't say anything. I finished walking down the stairs, my face red and my confidence rattled. The boy disappeared in the crowd as the bell rang and I began walking to the cafeteria, but something about that moment stuck with me.

The past week had been particularly rough. Every day I was dealing with some new instance of bullying. I had gotten called a faggot, dyke, a man, and so on in the hallways. I had been walking to the bathroom during a class period and kids in a classroom had pointed at me in the hall and asked "What is that? She looks like a man." If nothing else, I had assumed the hallways would be safe when they were empty. My experience in the bathrooms themselves were incredibly uncomfortable. I didn't feel physically threatened, but convincing myself it was worth coming to school was becoming a struggle. I wanted to blend in and get by, but being masculine resulted in all too much visibility for me. I had come to terms with the fact that I was attracted to girls and would openly admit I was gay, but I certainly wasn't asking for trouble. The way my school was handling the experiences I was having as an LGBT student consisted of turning a blind eye to the bullying and providing no support or resources or even addressing the fact that they had LGBT students in the school. The environment was anything but welcoming.

That night, March 24th, nine days after my 15th birthday, I finally came out to my parents. I was visibly upset by the incident from school that day, and by the end of the night I let them know that I was, in fact, interested in girls. It was no surprise to them, but at the same time I don't think it was an easy thing to hear. My presentation and identity had been a point of friction at home before I came out, and to this day that is still the case. However, I knew I needed to be honest with them in order to begin to address the issues I was having at school.

I went on to take over the Gay-Straight Alliance, a grassroots club that was struggling to take off, and established a safe meeting space every Monday for LGBT students and allies. My hunch had always been that the school was lacking allies, but after publishing a school-wide survey through the English department, I came to a very different conclusion. Many people considered themselves allies, the problem was that no one felt comfortable speaking up against the instances of bullying they were witnessing. To address this fear, I had teachers sign a makeshift ally contract in exchange for safe zone signs, which they could then display in their classrooms to indicate to students within those doors, they would be treated with respect and humanity regardless of their orientation or identity. These teachers allowed themselves to be marked as allies and agreed to speak up when they heard anti-LGBT speech and slurs. A visible network of student and faculty allies began to grow within the high school I had dreaded entering everyday during the first few years of my career. Suddenly, I was getting permission from the administration to bring in adult LGBT-identified community members to show the students that they did, in fact, have options for their futures. Every Monday, the Gay-Straight Alliance met and discussed topics ranging from individual identities to recent progress in the United States. Slowly but surely, the environment in my high school was becoming safer. By the time I graduated, it was a very different school than the one I had walked into four years prior.

I could feel it in the back of my throat before I ever said it out loud.

I used to play guitar with my best friend at Dewey's Coffee in Shaker Square. Dewey's is the kind of place where the walls hold years of good conversation and always smells like a bittersweet mix of coffee and popcorn. I remember the night she came inside and sat down during one of our songs. I couldn't stop myself from glancing over at her for the rest of the show. When she came up to talk to me at the end of my set, I thought it was too good to be true. When she ended up going back to my best friend's house with us, I thought surely it was a stroke of luck. When she put her number in my phone at the end of the night, I told myself not to get my hopes up.

Our first date was out-of-a-movie perfect. I spent most of it trying to figure out whether or not she was actually interested in me, but our goodnight kiss was my answer. A few dates later we went to an art show and ran into a bunch of people we knew, all of whom were curious about us. We were holding hands, so were we together? Well no, not exactly, we would say, awkwardly glancing at one another. That night we figured we had nothing to lose, and she asked me, "Does this mean we're girlfriends?" I was caught off-guard by how uncomfortable I felt being called her girlfriend. It was like putting on a pair of shoes that were a couple sizes too small. I felt restricted, and within a few days I opted to be her significant other instead of her girlfriend.

I began sorting through the parts of myself I couldn't wrap my head around over the course of many late-night phone conversations with her. We shared a common interest in creating safer schools for LGBTQ students and frequently discussed the implications and limitations of sexual orientations and gender identities. As I reflected on myself, I began to connect my relatively new, expansive LGBT-related vocabulary with situations and feelings I had faced in the past, with who I was at the present. We built a safe space in which we could tear apart our most ingrained thoughts and tendencies and began to view ourselves more clearly. She made me feel validated and we supported one another. Somewhere in those hours on the phone I was slowly piecing myself together into something I could make sense of.

I think it was a natural progression. One night she wanted to know my middle name, and I had to explain to her that even though over a decade and a half ago my parents named me "Savannah Elise Sherman," I had never embraced my given name. That night was the first time I ever thought about changing it. It was such a clear solution, but it never dawned on me until then. I began to think about a middle name that would suit me in the weeks to come, sometimes tossing one her way to see what she thought. She never liked anything I came up with, but she was sensitive to the process I was going through. I began to explain it as a masculinity thing. I was called a tomboy when I was little, but I think the truest explanation of me is that I had possessed this masculine energy for as long as I could remember, and I felt a misalignment between my name and the way I was. I didn't think it was my parents' fault: realistically, I was a curve ball of a child and they couldn't have known any better. All I knew was that Savannah Elise was going to follow me everywhere, on paperwork and applications and certificates, and I didn't want to be Savannah Elise my whole life.

Once I gave myself the freedom to explore choosing a name that fit, I found that I was surrounded by opportunities I never thought I had. I felt a new sense of hope when I began to imagine living in a way that would finally make me feel comfortable. I stopped worrying about what my family or peers would say for a brief moment and let myself imagine what it would be like to have my clothes hang the right way on my body, to feel like I fit inside myself, to be called by something other than what I had been known by for the better part of 17 years. The more I thought about it, the more in tune I became with myself and, gradually, I began to articulate the way I had always felt.

I was laying in a half-conscious state, just drifting off to sleep. My best ideas tend to come when I'm nearly asleep, too tired to get up and write them down. It was in one of those states, out of the blue, that it came to me. Logan. I rolled it around in my head. It was gender neutral, but it leaned masculine. It was kind of soft around the edges and short, simple. I don't know exactly how I knew, but it fit in a way that my given name did not. When I called my girlfriend the next day, I had a different type of energy about me. She was quiet for a minute when I told her the name, but for the first and only time, she gave me a positive response. For whatever reason, it fit me perfectly.

Being Logan was my best kept secret. I never let on that anything was different in high school or at home, but every time I made the 45 minute drive to her place, all my walls came down. I loved the way it sounded when she called me by my chosen name, like she was really seeing me and acknowledging my presence. Attempting to make up for years of lost time, I practiced writing my name on any and every scrap of paper I came in contact with. When no one was in earshot, I would say it aloud to myself, the name feeling forbidden and slightly foreign on my tongue. Somewhere inside me, I began to recognize that I couldn't just forget about this.

Figuring myself out had been a process, and in the meantime the world around me was spinning forward. I was beginning to get college acceptance letters and the future became a very real concern. As meaningful as my relationship had been for me during my senior year in high school, the fact that none of our potential colleges lined up made me think that maybe I didn't want to stay in my relationship as long term as I had once thought. Our breakup was difficult, and I told myself that I was never going to mention my chosen name, Logan, to another soul. For whatever reason, I actually believed I could bury that part of myself and all the memories associated with it.

Turns out this was a naive assumption. I found myself needing to tell the people I was closest to about who I was in a way that I hadn't vocalized before. I explained to them that I didn't feel like a girl. On the other hand, I didn't think I wanted to be a boy either. It was most accurate to say that I fell into some non-traditional space. I was fortunate in that my close friends were not only understanding but, by and large, supportive. I began to go by Logan with an ever-increasing number of friends along with my preferred gender pronouns, either they/them/their or he/him/his. Later on, due to the difficulty some people have with gender neutral pronouns and their arguably less-personal feel, I opted to go with masculine pronouns more often. However, I only use masculine pronouns because I am masculine, not because I'm male.

The more people that knew, the more terrified I felt. It was no longer an option to dive back into the closet, no matter how often I considered doing so. At the end of the summer, after my parents had moved me into my dorm room and left me alone at college, my RA (resident assistant) swapped the nametag on my door and I finalized my decision to go by Logan 24/7 at Ohio State University. I had deliberated back and forth for the entire summer, but in the end I thought about how happy I was when I was going by Logan and knew in my heart that moving to Columbus was my window of opportunity. A fresh start was literally being placed in my hands, and trying to avoid the inevitable seemed silly. I felt a newfound freedom and comfort introducing myself as Logan, and no one batted an eye because they had no reason to assume there was a story behind my name. I told all of my professors my preferred name and then avoided contact with kids from my hometown, all-in-all adding up to my successful "name change" in the first few months of school. When my parents called to check in, I told them all about rugby and my classes and my new friends, but I failed to mention my new name.

Parents' weekend rolled around and, in a last-minute panic, I sent them an email the week before with a letter I had spent the past month revising over and over again. The letter explained that I had always felt masculine and like something about me did not quite fit. I had embraced a trans* identity, I said, but for me, it wasn"t so much a female-to-male concept but rather that I fell outside the gender binary. I explained dysphoric feelings I was having and this sense that there was an incongruence between my mind and body. Finally, I talked about my preferred gender pronouns and the reason behind a name change. Within a few hours I got a call from home, and I was sure it would be the end of my family life as I had known it.

In some ways, I was right. My family dynamic has changed since then. It's only been a few months so far, but my younger brother has accepted me with open arms and calls me Logan now. As for my parents, it is a day-to-day process that we've been sorting through. I know it's been hard on them, but in the end I feel it is most important for me to lead a meaningful life and be honest with myself. I value my family, but my own mental health prevents me from trying to hide who I am in order to please them. After dealing with so many years of bullying and intolerance in school, the last thing I want to do is attempt to live up to others' expectations and try to blend in or change my character. It's not a quick process to go from knowing your daughter of 18 years, Savannah, to relearning your oldest child, Logan. We are all at our own stages in the game, but I'm willing to give it time.

Back in grade school they called me a tomboy and picked on me. I went on to break some social norms in middle school and play on the boys' football team, exposing myself to more bullying but ultimately gaining self-confidence. By the time I was in high school and ready to explore my sexual orientation and gender identity, I no longer felt comfortable going to school every day without feeling like I had a safe zone. Although I ended up having to build one for myself, I became aware of my ability to lead and fight for respect even through the intolerant speech and fear I felt in the process. All my life I have been getting questioned. Why do you dress like that? Are you doing this for attention? Why can't you just be gay? Are you a boy or a girl?

I know enough by now to tell you I'm not either.

BRADLEY RHODES

22. I WAS PRIME PICKN'

High school was the most difficult period of time I have experienced thus far in life. Since I was not on the sports team, a cheerleader, or an over achiever on the academic level, I was treated as the low tier nonexistent scum of the school who had no place being there not only by fellow class mates, but by some of the teachers as well. Due to my weight and quiet nature, I was prime picking for people to let them know what they thought of me. I did not fall under any of the categories listed. I had a large chest and being a male got me a lot of unwanted attention. Often, I would hear "You have C sized tits and you're a guy" or "You have larger boobs than the girls." Of course, it would always be followed up with the collective laugh of others. All I could do was try my best to ignore them. However, when you hear the same thing over and over each day, it begins to stick in your mind. You begin to take what people say to heart. People soon began to question my sexual orientation and asked me, "Are you gay? I bet you're a faggot. I have $5.00 that says you're a queer." One altercation I remember took place during study hall. Someone came over to me and asked, "Do you even know what a vagina looks like? I bet you've never seen one. You probably like looking at dick anyway, you're just a fag." Though I knew around the age of 15 that I was gay, I denied it every time it was brought up to me. The last thing I needed was to give everyone another reason to remind me on a daily basis of how different and inferior I was to them. Of course, trying to repress my sexual orientation has led to some issues of its own. I also had my fair share of being spit on, having food thrown at me, and having people draw obscene things on the my clothes, but those things faded over time. Yet, they still left emotional problems that I am still trying to recover from to this day.

My choice of clothing was very poor, resulting in a lack of style. It's not that I didn't have the money, but rather, I lacked the understanding of what to wear. During gym, I often wore shorts far too small for someone of my size. I soon earned the name "Short shorts Brad" and was reminded how large my thighs were. People would make sounds of thunder when I wore those horrible shorts. After weeks of that, I stopped wearing shorts during gym and carried sweat pants regardless of the temperature. I would make sure to never expose my body in the locker room. I began wearing two sets of clothes each day. I could just take off one set to participate during gym so I would not fail. And in time, I found my own method of changing clothes under my current clothing. During the summer, it was almost unbearable, but I would rather sweat and suffer in 90 degree weather while wearing an extra

C. Boske & A. Osanloo (Eds.), Students, Teachers, and Leaders Addressing Bullying in Schools, 133–138.

set of clothes instead of subjecting myself to the agonizing torture of revealing my body to the other boys during gym. I grew to hate my body and was reminded every single day that I was overweight and that I was disgusting due to it. Of course, my way to combat the negative feelings was to eat. Thus, an endless cycle was created. I began wearing heavy hoodies to cover up my body. It was something that made me feel more comfortable during school. It was something that would hide what I was so ashamed of. It didn't matter what the weather was like or what season it was, my hoodies were the shell of protection against the insults from others.

I never really had anyone in my life to stand up for me. My father was out of the picture and my mom was working 80 hours a week to support her drug-addicted husband and myself. It was bad enough that each day of school I was reminded of my failing grades; the fact I was still in freshman level classes as a junior; and the fact majority of the kids in school did not like me. But then I had to go home, only to be told how worthless I was by my step-father. He reminded me every single day that I was a fat, useless burden to everyone around me and that everyone would be so much better if I was out of the picture. I was told that the only reason family members let me come around was because they felt sorry for me. Some of what he said felt true to me, because I had come to Ohio when I was 10 and have always been the black sheep of the family. I was never really the favorite and felt like if it came down to it, I would be the last choice if someone had to choose between me and another. My step dad made sure each day he would do anything in his power to remind me how much I was hated. He would set his speakers up and play them at full volume; he would step outside of his room as soon as I went outside of mine; he would laugh at me when I walked by; he would stare at me until I left; he was constantly blaming me for things I never did; he stole money from me; he stole games from me; he used my things to support his drug habit and eventually, he got my mom addicted to drugs as well. He took the only person in my life who actually cared about me away. He used her for her money and got her addicted to prescription pills. The cops were called twice during their relationship, because he was becoming violent towards me and I was becoming violent towards him. I was at a point where I was alone in the world and I had no place that felt safe.

It was finally at that point I came to the thought that my life was not worth living. I had held a knife to my wrist many times, but was always too scared to follow through. I figured it would be easier to hang myself. I tied a rope around my neck and began tightening it so I could not breath. I didn't last long before I undid the knot and realized that I did not want to die. I did not want to believe that this was what life really was – just and endless cycle of self-hate and being reminded each day that I are of no use to anyone. That day, I made it my goal to survive. Nothing else mattered to me.

I found something that helped me along the way and still to this day it helps me cope with day-to-day life. I found the internet and connections that could be made across the world. I found games that took me to places where I was in control of how things went. I met people who saw me for my personality and not my weight. I met people who have stuck with me for many years, who I still talk to on a daily basis, people who listened to me when I was having a bad day and people who would lend me there shoulder when I had no one else. I finally had a life where I felt important, where I was happy and where my life mattered. I can't explain how it feels to feel like I was no use to someone. My online friends became my new life, my new family and that was the only time when I felt happy. Staying up for 12 hours locked in a small room did not matter to me, because the people I talked with saw something in me that no one else did. They saw another human being who was living on this earth just like them. They respected me just as I respected them. Finally, I had a place where I could smile and laugh. Living on the other side of the world as these people became a problem. My sleeping patterns began to revolve around them. I would be up until 4:00 a.m. and then go to school at 7:00 in the morning. I would often sleep during class, because of how little sleep I would get, but at least I knew when school was over I could return to a place where I could be happy.

In my last year of school, some teachers began to notice my lack of participation. As I said, my only goal then was to survive. My education was of no concern to me and it was showing. Thankfully, there were a few teachers who saw something in me that to this day I still do not see in myself. They saw someone who could succeed at whatever I decided to put work into. My Spanish teacher Mrs. Franks would have me come to her class every day during study hall and work on things with me ranging from English to science. She pushed me each and every day to try my best to apply myself and learn that hard work pays off. She was more or less a mother figure for me at the time. I appreciate every single day she spent trying to help me. My math teacher helped me each day to solve problems relating to math. She stood up for me when someone would throw something at me or spend 10 minutes poking me with a pencil just to bother me. Though I still failed many classes, at least those teachers did their best to try and help me. I can never thank them enough for all they did for me. I also bumped into my history teacher one day. I had failed her class three times and began lashing out on the few days I did attend, because I just wanted to be left alone. After everything I had done (or not done in terms of work), she still smiled and greeted me with "Hi, Brad!" To know that even after I failed as a student, that a teacher could forgive me, made me realize that there are people out there who can be understanding and forgiving.

I was soon approaching 18 years of age and with my grades, I would need to be in high school for another year to even have a chance at graduating (assuming I passed my classes). It was senior year. I finally stopped listening to what others were saying about me. Maybe it's because it had slowed down as they found other people to torment or maybe they just grew up. I don't know. I do remember being in math class, however, and I was discussing something with another student. Someone sitting in a different row began mocking me and laughing. I responded with a snarky remark. And before I knew it, I had the majority of the class screaming at me for the things I said. One of the kids came over to me and told me how bad he wanted to punch me in the face. He kept pacing back and forth to my desk and at the front of the room. I have no idea why the teacher did not stop any of this, but at that point, I grew to learn some teachers do not care, especially if the one threatening another student is the reason your cross country team is so successful.

On January 21st, the day before my birthday, there was a lunch special. Everyone wanted Egg McMuffins. I was one of the last people in line and soon found myself only having three minutes to eat by the time I sat down. The bell rang. I was trying to finish my meal when the principal approached me. She told me I needed to leave. I asked her if I could finish as I had just gotten my meal. She said, "We have strict time schedules and you can look in the agenda if you forgot them." I asked her if she was going to refund the money I spent since I was not even half way done eating. After arguing with with her for a few minutes, she finally pulled me into her office. I was given a lecture on the rules set in place. She said, "Just because you think you're better than everyone else does not mean it's true." I finally got tired of listening to her and let her know that things went on in this school far worse than someone trying to finish their lunch. I told her people did not abide by the dress code and that I could walk out into the office and point out the three girls at the front desk who were in tank tops and booty shorts, yet nothing was being said to them. I could point out the kids on their cell phones during class. I could point out the teachers allowing it and encouraging it. She finally responded, "I don't know if this is how you get what you want at home, but it does not work here." I knew then I would not be going back to school the next day. I would be 18, and at that point, I just stopped listening and snapped. I had been called stupid by other teachers. I was mocked and called cupcake, because I had eaten a Hostess cupcake during lunch. I was called an ape, and I was sure as hell not going to have some lady act as if she knew what went hon in my household. She sent me to the vice principal. I was lectured yet again and constantly told to shut up when I tried to plead my case. I knew it was hopeless to try, so all I could do was sit and listen.

After I dropped out of school, my step dad was still around. Thankfully, it only lasted for a few months. There was a final altercation in which he called my mother a cunt and pushed her. This led me to going ape-shit. I grabbed a fire poker and went off on him. As he tried to get to my mom, because she was calling the police, I grabbed his shirt. I held him away from her for awhile. She was able to lock herself in the room and contact the authorities. They made it out to our house, but said they could only take him in if I went as well, because I threatened my step dad. I told them I was willing to be locked up if he was locked up as well, but my mom did not want me in a cell. I think that was really the last strain on their relationship, because shortly after that, my mom and step dad divorced.

On his last day in the house, he woke me up by beating on the door. He told me, "You better be careful, because I will always be able to find you." Even though I've not seen him in five years, I still feel as if he is always lurking around waiting to do something to me. However, I was able to survive, despite how broken I was. I was no longer in school, where I was reminded how ugly and unappealing I was. I no longer had to deal with someone at home who hated me. I no longer had someone trying to break me down on a daily basis. I survived. I made it through the worst time of my life, but those times left scars on my mental well-being.

As time moved on, I realized all of the negative things people said to me were always on my mind. I could not get rid of the words "you're fat", "you're worthless", and "you will never amount to anything." Those words carried over every day, every morning when I awoke, and in every interaction with people. Still to this day I hate myself. I look in the mirror and hate everything I see. In my eyes, I was everything those people said to me.

I've been on medication for anxiety and depression for over a year. The medication doesn't fix the internal problems I deal with, just the symptoms. I have to prepare weeks in advance before I go outside or I will have a panic attack. When I step outside, I feel like everyone is looking at me as though I am an object of disgust and hate. Needless to say, I don't go out often. I spend most of my time inside my home, only going out when it is absolutely necessary. For five years now, my routine has been the same each and every day. I wake up, go downstairs, log onto my computer, and waste away the day until I fall asleep. I do have occasional times where I have to go out into the world, and thankfully, I have medicine to help keep my anxiety at bay. I have been seeing a counselor for year; yet, I still feel I have nothing to offer the world. And if I had just been able to end my life, I wonder, "Could I have avoided everything?"

I do often ask myself, "Would it have been worth it to just give up? To take the only life I have?" I can honestly say, "No, it would not be worth it." Although I have insecurities, self-hate, depression, anxiety, trust issues, no self-esteem, and lack of desire, the one thing I do have is a small thread of hope I will one day be content with my life. I will one day love who I am. I don't know if that day will ever come, but I will not stop reaching for that day. I have one life to live. Although it has not been the best life so far, I must continue working towards finding that place of inner peace, acceptance, and happiness.

Not everyone functions the same way, but I feel that if I had more support during high school, I would have been able to succeed. Although I had a few teachers help me along the way, it was too little, too late. Sometimes we can tell if someone is struggling, and other times it may be more difficult to know. If each person just took the time to ask others on a personal level., "Is there anything I can help you with?" and form a bond of trust, then it would help someone going through what I went through. I know it's not possible to do it for each student, but it's important for teachers and principals to know the kid who is quiet, failing classes, not participating, and who doesn't seem to fit in with others might have things going on inside or outside of school that are less than the ideal situation.

It might be helpful for teachers to ask students if they would like to come to your class during study hall. This might be a good way to steer them on the right track. Maybe suggest a student see a counselor. One major word of advice-make sure the counseling team knows what they are doing for the students.

It seems as though education is not at the top of the United States' agenda. If I had a counselor during high school, who was decent at their job, it might have made my hell a little more bearable. Instead, I had a bunch of counselors who seem to have gotten their Ph.D. from a cereal box.

The need for a child to have a decent education should outweigh the need for a school to appear at the top of the charts. A teacher or counselor's job is to ensure a child is in a safe environment where he or she can learn. And with my experience, a lot of teachers seem to forget that. I understand some students can be unruly or troublesome, but that is when teachers might consider necessary disciplinary action. Your job is not to make them feel stupid, but to help them learn, to become a smarter and better person.

I wish I could give you the answers to fix people's problems around bullying, but I have yet to find answers myself. The only thing I can say, is in time, things become easier to deal with. There are people out there who you can turn to even if you do feel alone. I also want students to know even if it feels no one is in your corner rooting for you, know I am cheering for you. I will always be in it cheering. I may never meet you or speak to you, but I know what it feels like to feel worthless. I am sorry if any of you have to go that. We have one shot at this life, and in the end, I know students can reach a place of happiness and contentment. Every single person on this earth lives differently and has different stories to share. No one will ever replace another person, will ever walk in another's shoes, or will see life in the same way. Each step we take is unique to that person. Life cannot be replicated in any way shape or form by someone else. To me, everyone is special and all stories should be heard. No matter a person's your gender, race, ethnicity, sexual orientation, or who that person is, know you are loved. As long as people are not hurting others, everyone deserves happiness in their lives. I will always be in the corner rooting for everyone, waiting for people to conquer the world, and take it by storm. Each of us need to realize how truly amazing we are. Although students may not see it in themselves, I hope they will someday realize how strong they are and that they have made it this far. I love all of you and I wish all of you only the best.

MANDY A. CENKER-MILLER

23. BULLIES IN DIAPERS

Techniques to Extinguish Bullying Behaviors in Young Children

The scream is ear-piercing. So loud, I am sure my neighbors heard it. My then one-and-a-half year old son is tormenting his older sister. He got mad, grabbed the first thing he could, which happened to be her arm, and bit down as hard as he could. I ran into the room and pried his jaw apart to release her. He glares at her with a gleam in his eye, as if he was saying he was not finished with her. I was not surprised at his behavior as he hit, kicked, bit, smacked, and charged at almost every child with whom he came into contact. I kept brushing it off as him being a boy, but I changed my mind that day. If I did not do something, my son was going to be a bully.

As a teacher, I am constantly inundated with how important it is for teachers to be aware of bullying behavior in the classroom and in the halls. As a teacher of students with special needs, I have the duty to teach my students how to handle bullying by advocating for themselves, but I also am the one who listens, and when they are the victims I contact administration. I know how important it is to keep bullying out of the classroom to maintain a safe learning environment for all students.

School districts have anti-bullying curriculum and character education as well as harsh consequences for school-aged children, but what happens when the bullies are still in diapers? How can we stop the behaviors at a young age to prevent bullies in our elementary schools?

CHARACTERISTICS OF PRESCHOOL BULLIES

For many children, preschool is the first time they have interactions with children their own age. Therefore, preschool may be the first place that adults and professionals can assess and identify difficulties in social interaction with peers (Vlachou, Andreou, Botsoglou, & Didaskalou, 2011). At this particular age, some researchers argue that the term "unjustified aggression" might be more proper for describing "bullying" in early years (Vlachou et al., 2011) due to the fact that peer aggression during early childhood has been found to differ from that identified in middle childhood and adolescence in terms of the stability of the victim role (Monks, Ortega Ruiz, & Torrado Val, 2002). Children are the victims of unjustified aggression by others

C. Boske & A. Osanloo (Eds.), Students, Teachers, and Leaders Addressing Bullying in Schools, 139–148.

when they are attacked physically, verbally, or psychologically without there being a justifying reason or motive for the act (Vlachou et al., 2011).

Bullying is a complex issue. No one knows exactly what makes some kids want to torment others and no two bullies are alike, making it difficult to pin down what triggers the aggression (Seiler, 2010). Preschool aged children are capable, however, of displaying different forms of bullying such as verbal, physical, and social exclusion (Vlachou et al., 2011) without there being a social conflict between the participants (Monks et al., 2002).

When a preschooler uses the phrase, "Give it to me! I want it!" all of the time, they are typical of a preschool bully as the child thinks they are in charge and uses the rules to suit his or her own purposes (Ucci, 2004). Bullies often exhibit their excessive power when adults are not watching and other children usually do not know how to counteract the use of power because it seems out of the ordinary (Ucci, 2004). It is important to note, that early childhood bullying occurs at approximately the same rate among males as females (Burkhart, Knox, & Brockmyer, 2012). Furthermore, research suggests preschool girls deliver more relational aggression than boys, who are more likely to display physical aggression (Vlachou et al., 2011).

Many young children have some degree of difficulty in learning social activities such as sharing. Preschool bullies have these characteristics in addition to others. Due to the cognitive development of a young child, it is best to notice and take swift action in order to eliminate the bullying behaviors.

TENSIONS

With the increase of bullying, cyberbullying, and bullying behaviors, states have taken the initiative to protect children and enact anti-bullying efforts. There is no federal law that specifically applies to school bullying however, according to the U.S. Department of Health & Human Services (2013), all fifty states have anti-bullying laws and/or policies. The Department analyzed all current state laws and found eleven key components common among many of the laws that help to define bullying and to what constitutes bullying on school grounds.

Additionally, anti-bullying law, in general, "directs every LEA (local education authority) to develop and implement a policy prohibiting bullying." This policy includes reporting bullying behaviors; investigating and responding; maintaining written records; sanctions; and referrals for the victim, perpetrators, and others to counseling or mental health services as appropriate. The laws also include a plan for notifying students, students' families, and staff, of policies related to bullying, including the consequences for engaging in bullying (U.S. Department of Health & Human Services, 2013). Because of state laws and anti-bullying policies in places, school personnel are under pressure to comply with these efforts as well as maintaining a safe learning environment for each student. Bullying behaviors are not tolerated at any age in the school environment, including preschoolers.

As an educator, I felt the tension of the behavior expectations at school as well as the need for compliance of state laws and policies. It was my duty to help my son reverse the bullying behaviors in order to eliminate the tension but also prepare him to be respectful of his peers, school personnel, and maintain a safe learning environment for his class.

REVERSING THE BULLYING BEHAVIORS

Luckily, my son has a mother who is an educator and trained administrator who recognized the signs of a preschool bully. Along with my husband, family, and pediatrician, I set out to put in a plan in place to find the cause of his bullying. He had a reputation at the babysitter's house, the church nursery, and among his cousins as the "bad" kid due to his behaviors. I had to create a plan that extinguished his current behaviors and taught him replacement behaviors. I also had to be sure to include prevention, as I do not want him to ever revert back to his bad habits. I knew it would take time, but changes made at an early age benefit everyone in the long term (Ucci, 2004). The following is a comprehensive list of all of the interventions the team put into place. The time line was over a six-month period but was maintained a year and a half later.

Early Intervention Services

In 1986, congress amended the IDEA law for students with special needs to include special education benefits and programming for infants and toddlers as the value to providing early educational programs was identified (Rothstein & Johnson, 2010). I was referred by our pediatrician to Help Me Grow, which is Ohio's early intervention program for infants to age three. Help Me Grow provided two early interventionist that came to our house and completed the Battelle Developmental Inventory, 2nd Edition, a standardized assessment of key developmental skills in young children. It measures adaptive, personal-social, receptive communication, expressive communication, gross motor, fine motor, perceptual motor, and cognitive areas. We knew he had a communication delay, but he also qualified in the personal-social domain, which confirmed my suspicions of his behavior difficulties.

Because of his eligibility to participate in their services, we were assigned a speech language pathologist/early interventionist as well as a service coordinator until he turned three. We met twice a month, mostly for his speech sessions, but also discussed how his lack of speech development was contributing to his bullying behaviors. The professionals taught my husband and me different ways to help him communicate with his peers. He was taught two word phrases as well as picture charts to help him communicate his wants and needs, which prevented a melt down because we did not understand. Simple sign language was introduced and taught to everyone who came in contact with him so he had the choice to communicate with words or signs depending on his level of stress.

Immersing in Play

Research has long documented the benefits of play in early childhood. Play with peers enhances social understanding and relationships among preschool children as they explore issues of control and compromise while negotiating the choosing of roles (Ashiabi, 2007). Such negotiations help children explore issues of control and compromise and communicate with each other more effectively to resolve conflicts associated with peer interactions (Ashiabi, 2007).

Although I am an educator, I knew very little about early childhood development outside of my motherly instincts, but as a licensed K-12 teacher I did know how important play is to the young child. I also knew that I was not going to shelter him from his peers until he was "cured". Play for him was very frustrating and usually when he exhibited his bullying behaviors. His aggression peaked when he was at the babysitter's house where he was often labeled "the biter." After realizing his frustrations with the children at the babysitter's house, I removed him and was fortunate to have my mom watch him full time. His sister stayed at the babysitter's so it was just him and his grandmother. He needed the one on one comfort of a family member where he could make mistakes and have a loving adult guide him in the right direction.

I re-introduced playing with peers in a very systematic way with a thorough plan of action. I began taking him to the church nursery during Sunday service, which was one hour a week. At first, I sat with him to monitor his behaviors. Eventually, I allowed myself to leave for the whole hour. We also began to see his cousins, who are a few years older, once a week for about three hours. Yes, if you add it up, that was only four hours of play a week with peers, excluding play time with his sister. In time, we increased the amount of play, allowing as many play opportunities as possible. We took him to the local playground, McDonald's (with a play area), birthday parties, and church activities, to immerse him in play with a trusting adult present to help if he needed intervention.

My son had to learn the differences between appropriate and inappropriate play. He needed to be provided with structured play experiences in which he could learn from other children and be reminded of self-regulation. My husband and I have apologized many times to moms and dads because of his aggression toward their children. We never explain or justify his actions however, we say "sorry" and remove him from the situation.

Positive Expectations

Children tend to learn as little or as much as their parents or teachers expect. Parents who set high expectations will obtain greater results then with low expectations. The odds are greater that what you want to happen will happen because you will be expending energy to see that this will be so (Wong & Wong, 2001). I had to take a step back and re-evaluate my expectations for my son. Even at the tender age of one he was hearing me say, "We can't even go there because he will hit one of the kids." My negative expectations were in turn leading him to continue his aggressive behaviors. I changed my "he will never be a nice kid" into "I know you can play nice with your friends" and many, many more times "I love you." It takes just as much energy to achieve positive results as it does to achieve negative, so why waste the energy on failing when that same amount of energy can help him succeed (Wong & Wong, 2001)?

Praise

An increase in praise can result in an increase in desirable behavior and a decrease in undesirable behavior. The praise should be immediate and specific, describing the exact nature of the behavior being rewarded as well as being delivered every time an appropriate behavior is displayed (Niesyn, 2009). Every time I see my son hand someone a toy, pick up after himself, ignore his sister when she is bothering him, and go to his room by himself to calm down, I praise him. At the grocery store, I praise him for sitting nicely in the cart or for holding my hand in the parking lot. I praise him for everything he does correctly. At first, it takes work to remember to praise after everything that is done correctly, but it comes naturally after practice.

Preschool

Finding a preschool that meets the needs of the family is quite challenging especially when the preschool finds out the child has a unique need. Parents of children with unique needs often have difficulty finding a provider capable of and willing to take care of their children as well as locating a program that support the family's approach to discipline, learning style, and other personal factors (Glenn-Applegate, Pentimonti, & Justice, 2010).

When I began to think about which preschool would be the right fit for my son I compared every local preschool toured numerous facilities, and determined which one I would not patronize. I made my decision and I was going to fight to get him in. I wanted a preschool that had a mission of providing a quality education using best practices for students who live on the margin. I did not want a staff that would put in him time-out every five minutes, or use words that my son would mistake as fighting words. I looked at the consistency of discipline, the years of experience of the teaching staff, and how they handled children with unjustified aggression.

At the meeting to determine if he would get into my preschool of choice my husband and I had to fight for his acceptance. After a long discussion is was decided he would go, and it was one of my more proud moments as a mother. I knew his acceptance would change our lives. My plan of action to change my son's bullying behaviors would be backed by a fantastic preschool staff who supported our efforts and our family beliefs about discipline.

Creating Safe Spaces

The idea of "safe spaces" has been commercialized into many different programs for educators to create classrooms where students can freely express their ideas and feelings, particularly around challenging areas such as diversity, cultural competence, and oppression. Safe spaces do not refer to physical safety rather a climate, regardless of location, that allow students to feel secure enough to take risks, honestly express their view, and share and explore their knowledge, attitudes, and behaviors. Staff members who provide this space have the characteristics that include: welcoming discussions, approachable, and supportive (Holley & Steiner, 2005).

Taking the safe space ideas from the research, one can tailor a safe space for an aggressive preschooler to just about anywhere as long as a supportive adult is present. Aggressive preschoolers need to know there are people who care for them, and provide a social and emotionally supportive environment regardless of their behaviors. The person providing care to aggressive preschoolers should be willing to allow the child to make mistakes, yet be protected from psychological and emotional harm (Holley & Steiner, 2005).

My son has two physical safe spaces, his room and the car, that he relies on when he is feeling aggressive. In certain places, such as family members houses or places with minimal external stimuli, he is able to use a corner, the bathroom, or a separate room as his space as long as my husband or I are with him. In his situation, he is partial to spaces where the physical safety of the space is evident as well as the emotional safety.

In the beginning of the interventions, my husband would put my (our) son in time-out in his room for a couple of minutes when he became aggressive. The difference between our time-outs versus typical time-outs is we never called them "time-outs." After the time-out was over, my husband would put our son in time-out. He would also provide ways my son could have done the behavior differently (*e.g.*, using his sign for more rather than steal from his sister). Sometimes, my husband would just listen to my son try and explain his side of the story. Having one of us present at the end of his time-out as an emotional support presented my son with the nurture he needed to calm down.

Because we did not negatively relate him going to his room, eventually he put himself in his room. He uses his room as a space to cry, throw things, jump, and scream. He has a two minute period to be alone and then we engage in reassuring conversation that ends with a smile and a hug. We say "I love you" and he resumes playing. Sometimes this cycle happens six times a day, sometimes only once. Regardless of the number of times it happens, the positivity at the end remains.

When we are out and he does not have his room, he knows he has safe space is in the car. If he starts to give off warning signs at the playground or at the store that he is going to be aggressive, we leave immediately. Removing him from the situation allows him to regulate in a private, safe space rather than being embarrassed in front of other children. This also allows us to have the positive conversations with him without the judgment of onlookers.

GETTING READY FOR THE RIDE

When a child is diagnosed with a special need, or starts exhibiting behaviors outside of the norm in comparison to peers the child's age, parents should get ready for the ride. That is, the roller coaster of emotions that follows knowing the child is not "typical." Not only does the parent have to process the interventions the child needs, but also the grief that will encompass them in throughout the process.

Teachers should be aware of the grieving process as they are often the middle man (mediator) between school and home. If the parent is in the middle of the grieving process, teachers can be faced with aggression and sadness from the family which adds to the stress of the school/home relationship. It is imperative the parent(s) feel supported. If necessary, have the school psychologist or counselor refer the parent(s) to a community-based resource that provides resources to parents who are having trouble understanding their child has a special need.

The following are techniques used by my family in order to help us overcome the grief associated with my son's diagnosis.

Allow for a Grieving Period

Researchers have long suspected that grief advances in stages, and now data suggests that a grieving person goes through five indicators: disbelief; followed by yearning; anger; depression; and acceptance. The grief indicators tend to peak in the order listed, and to take an average of about six months, suggesting that people who suffer longer may want to seek help in recovering (Maciejewski, 2007).

Some people may not agree that parents should grieve after discovering their child is a bully. I disagree. People react in many different ways. For me, I came from a family that was against bullying or any type of unfair treatment towards other. Because my son was not typical of our family behavior, it sent me spiraling into the grieving process. I was in disbelief for a couple of days, yearning for about a month, but anger and depression took much longer for me. Because I am a teacher of students with special needs, it hit me hard. I know what happens to students who are different. They are treated differently by their peers and many adults, although most adults will not admit treating students with special needs differently than typical students. I became depressed and angry at every adult who had an opinion about my son.

I used positive self-talk, meditation, and imagery to help in my transition to acceptance. When I finally accepted he was different, both in his speech development and his social-emotional behaviors, I became strong. I wanted him to have the best intervention plan we could possibly create in order to prevent him from becoming a school-aged bully.

Support System

In order to facilitate change and allow for emotional support, I needed a support system for my family – a team of people who I rely on. I call them my team because they have truly been there with us when my son was at his worst. They gave us support when we felt defeated. There are people, including family members, who are not a part of this support system and are still a part of our lives. For those people, we respectfully did not talk to them about our plans or solicit any emotional support.

The two people we heavily relied on, whether they knew it or not, were our early interventionist/speech therapist and our service coordinator. They were removed enough from our family to be able to look at our individual situation with a critical lens. It was refreshing to bounce ideas off of another professional but also to have a team to support me and my husband during this journey. As a parent, you never want to have your child be the bully, but when it happens you go through emotions that are difficult to explain. I learned through my experiences with Help Me Grow that his behavior was going to change and I had the drive to make it happen.

Conversations and Building Bridges

When I began my coursework for my principal's license, one of the first classes was called "Leading for Social Justice." In this course, my professor taught me the importance of building bridges with the community and facilitating the conversations in order to create change. I started having conversations with other professionals who had experience with early childhood. I shared my son's difficulties and solicited their advice. For example, I wanted to know how the preschool team at our district's elementary school ran their program. My daughter was fortunate enough to be a peer model in our preschool that is designed for students with special needs. Because of the open relationship I had with her teacher, I was able to apply techniques at home that helped benefit both of my children.

I called the Parent Mentor office in our school district, shared my story, and was given options as to how to utilize their services. I asked my boss, the Director of Special Services, how he would handle some of the situations we faced as a family. Anyone I knew that had background knowledge in early childhood heard questions from me. These bridges have been built, used, and in some cases, have been crossed back and forth many times.

THE RESULTS

Recently, I had a conversation with a staff member in my son's preschool in which she informed me that my son was caring of the other students in his class and has strong play skills. I had flashbacks of his biting and hitting while she was talking. I looked at him as he smiled back at me and it brought tears to my eyes. I keep reliving that conversation as it is proof that all of our efforts paid off.

Do we have some bad days? Of course we do. The difference is the duration and type of aggression. He no longer bites and rarely hits and kicks. When he gets frustrated he tries to tell an adult about the situation rather than resorting to violence. He utilizes his safe spaces to help him self-regulate when he is upset and he knows we have positive expectations of him. By expressing praise, my son gets excited when he realizes he is doing something correctly and seeks our affirmation. He strives to play nicely and wants other children to play with him.

GENERALIZATION OF TECHNIQUES

With the exception of early childhood intervention, most of the techniques outlined can be generalized to school aged children. Early childhood intervention can be replaced with school based intervention, in which parents and teachers can request an evaluation of the child by the school psychologist. The school psychologist will determine if the child qualifies for special education services and if the behavior adversely impacts the child's educational performance.

If the child does not qualify for special education services, the parent can ask their pediatrician for a referral to a mental health professional to help in determining the cause of a behavior. If the behavior is severe, the mental health agency can assemble a team in order to provide the best care and outcome for the child. Regardless of the child's age, parents and teachers can also increase positive expectations, praise, and most important, create safe spaces for the child. Creating a constructive and encouraging relationship will allow the child to have place for healthy discussions rather than engage in bullying behavior.

FINAL WORDS

As a parent and a teacher who successfully helped change my son from a bully in diapers to a loving and caring preschooler, I leave you with some advice: trust your gut instinct and never give up. If your gut says something is off with the child, it is probably right. Quickly identify what is off, seek out the help to change it, find supports to help you, and forge on! It may seem like the interventions are not working, but do not give up. Some interventions may take a long time to achieve a change in behavior. It also may require different techniques to be utilized than you are currently using.

Do not be disappointed if interventions need to be changed. It does not mean you are a bad parent/teacher nor does it mean the child is not going to change. Give it time. Behaviors are not extinguished overnight. Be patient and remember the child needs your patience, determination, and the understanding that you are there for him or her no matter what the behavior.

Bullies in diapers, bullies in schools, and adult bullies all need the same amount of attention and love as everyone else. Are you going to help facilitate the change in them? Do you have the determination to rid the hallways of bullying behavior? Stay positive and create a change. Our children thank you.

REFERENCES

Ashiabi, G. S. (2007). Play in the preschool classroom: Its socioemotional significance and the teacher's role in play. *Early Childhood Education Journal, 35*(2), 199–207. doi:10.1007/s10643-007-0165-8

Burkhart, K. M., Knox, M., & Brockmyer, J. (2012). Pilot evaluation of the ACT raising safe kids program on children's bullying behavior. *Journal of Child and Family Studies, 22*(7), 942–951. doi:10.1007/s10826-012-9656-3

Glenn-Applegate, K., Pentimonti, J., & Justice, L. M. (2010). Parents' selection factors when choosing preschool programs for their children with disabilities. *Child & Youth Care Forum, 40*(3), 211–231. doi:10.1007/s10566-010-9134-2

Holley, L. C., & Steiner, S. (2005). Safe space: Student perspectives on classroom environment. *Journal of Social Work Education, 41*(1), 49–64. doi:10.5175/JSWE.2005.200300343

Maciejewski, P. K. (2007, June). Death shall have no dominion. *Atlantic Monthly*, (June), 34.

Monks, C., Ortega Ruiz, R., & Torrado Val, E. (2002). Unjustified aggression in preschool. *Aggressive Behavior, 28*(6), 458–476. doi:10.1002/ab.10032

Niesyn, M. E. (2009). Strategies for success: Evidence-based instructional practices for students with emotional and behavioral disorders. *Preventing School Failure: Alternative Education for Children and Youth, 53*(4), 227–234. doi:10.3200/PSFL.53.4.227-234

Seiler, W. B. (2010, September). Cruelty free offspring: Ways not to raise a bully. *USA Today*, 57–58.

Ucci, M. E. (2004, January). Bullying and the young child. *Child Health Alert*, 3–4.

U.S. Department of Health and Human Services. (2013). *Key components in state anti-bulling laws*. Retrieved January 1, 2014, from http://www.stopbullying.gov/laws/key-components/index.html

Vlachou, M., Andreou, E., Botsoglou, K., & Didaskalou, E. (2011). Bully/victim problems among preschool children: A review of current research evidence. *Educational Psychology Review, 23*(3), 329–358. doi:10.1007/s10648-011-9153-z

Wong, H. K., & Wong, R. T. (2001). *How to be an effective teacher: The first days of school*. Mountain View, CA: Harry K. Wong Publications, Inc.

24. BULLYING

The Synthetic Cool

Beneath the sordid umbrella of bullying, the possibilities of discussion are endless. Given this platform to speak on the subject, I find myself mentally stretched like a bit of butter over a large, coarse slice of bread. I lack the capacity to handle the magnitude of the subject. As an artist and comic-book writer, I could speak on the faux sense of liberation one bullied may feel as she/he gains their super-ability and pounds away at the foul perpetrator. As a father, I could touch on the lack of communication among parents in regard to locating solutions for our bullying problems. As a man of the community, I could speak on the lack of solidarity among parents/schools/organizations in creating a socially responsible living space for one another. So I find myself forced to choose what I will pitch from this mound. I choose to speak on the "COOL" and how it pertains to bullying.

It is much easier to describe cool than define it. "Cool" shifts depending on your location in space, place, and time. Some people learned the definition of cool in Miles Davis, John Coltrane, and/or the many players in hip-hop culture. Others may have learned it from James Dean, Steve McQueen, or rock' n roll. And let's not omit the ladies who had so much cool that it manifested itself even in times of gender oppression: Angela Davis, Etta James, Katharine Hepburn, and Betty Friedan, just to name a few. Our list of "who's who" of COOL is extremely extensive and consequently varies beyond cultural boundaries. So what happens to our variety of "Cools?" If you look closely you will see that "cool" rests on a crutch and that crutch is media. Television, music, the web and popular art forms have a way of flattening the many layers of cool like Adobe's Photoshop. Slowly but yet immediately, cool is approved, packaged, and syringed into our social bloodstream, occupying and conquering space as if it was there all along as a solid truth. At this moment cool no longer is something you play audience to. Instead it is a festivity you can partake in, but without the stage, the lights, the camera, the hype, and sometimes without even an audience. So what happens to cool when it has no platform? One creates a platform for it.

Many of us have experienced it, and for those who haven't, they only need to look at popular television. We create an in-crowd so outsiders can exist. But this is simple, right? We all know this, right? Sadly though, unlike movies and teen television shows, our reality with the in-crowd hurting, suppressing, and abusing the

C. Boske & A. Osanloo (Eds.), Students, Teachers, and Leaders Addressing Bullying in Schools, 149–151.

outsider often goes unresolved. You see, the member of the in-crowd often stands on a false sense of cool. To have the feeling of that rock star, that rapper, that athlete, that idol, the perpetrator must be looked up to and held in a position above another. Sometimes they can just purchase it with a jumping man on their sneakers or with the latest object which that one person had on that NEWEST thing. Other times it is more subtle. It is done with a whisper, a punch, a threat, with belittling another to the point where fear, control and all attention are bowed away. However, the position of this feeling of being cool isn't earned. The bully hates hard work. The bully loves the feeling of the cool, but will not suffer any consequences to get there. Becoming an idol and obtaining the status of cool is not accomplished by stepping on those who can only take the form of stairs. Instead, becoming that person to whom the status of real cool is given comes with a series of self-reflection, self-discovery, walking and competing with those who will hold you accountable and knowing that you are accountable for others. Sadly, bullies may never learn this, as they strut through the hallway and then through life thinking their glitter is gold. What could help one realize that their cool is counterfeit? What if we could redefine cool? Or re-learn and then re-teach it.

Being raised in the low-economic urban margins of the United States, I often witnessed programming put into place to save the hood hard-knocks-life children who are on their way to the prison and/or grave. I personally applaud the effort. I also wonder how this effort would work for the meek, degraded, afraid, and low-self-esteemed youth of our society. There is a prize for acting "BAD." You are the attention-grabber in every class. You gain a reputation in school and possibly on the streets. Organizations spend funds upon funds on you in hopes that you will go on the straight path. And then if you ever decide to turn it all around, you are celebrated as if the prodigal child has returned! On top of it all you are blessed and given the crown of cool, not knowing that this is cool in its perverted form. So what is there for the meek child? There is no stage for you in class. You are lucky to be mentioned by a teacher and even at those moments where your name is brought to everyone's attention, you lack the confidence to handle the sharp peer gaze. You will fade deeper into yourself and you will be lost believing that cool is something for the others and not meant for you. You will accept the role as outsider. So what do we do, as teachers, community leaders, caretakers and socially responsible people, for the outsider? We create a realm in which they can turn their life into a work of art. In opposition to the bullies who mimic false cool behaviors, we offer a place where the meek can live the cool in truth. We revisit Youth Voice, and Youth Voice in Project-based learning. We allow them to comment on the things they wish to learn and do. We allow them to speak life as if they lived and be human as they navigate their youth and its obstacles. We put our knowledge, our skills, and our names on the line to help them make radiant the aspects of their being that matter most to them. Like scripture, we highlight them in bright colors and allow the world to see what they have to offer. There is no medium or no one way to do this. We must be willing to design a place in ourselves that will allow the capacity and humility to kneel down and ask, "Who are you? What do you want to do, and how can I help you?"

The "COOL" can never be bought nor talked down to nor beaten into possession. It is the practice of finding our own thoughts, our own dreams and our own true selves where the cool resides. And this cool will never be synthetic.

Martinez E-B
Socially Conscience Visually Artist
Esperanza Hispanic Youth Leadership Program Coordinator

25. KATIE

As a young 25 yr old Lesbian being born in a very conservative, backward thinking town in Ohio is difficult. A lot of people say you choose to be gay, but I can say now as an out lesbian for a couple years that I was born this way. At a early age I knew I was different then other girls; and I didn't know how to take it or what to do. I just knew I would wake up every morning and wish I didn't exist. I was not normal. and I also knew my family and society wouldn't accept it. To my family and society I was not normal. I went to school every day and put a fake smile on and was made fun of because of who I was; I was a tomboy, I wore boy blue jeans and t-shirts and I loved getting dirty. I was called fag or dyke, you name it I was probably called it; all this bullying hurt me so much that a couple of times I thought of ending my life, but I put that fake smile on and pretended like it didn't bother me because I was too chicken to end my life. In 8th grade to be normal I dated my first guy, it was so weird because we both didn't know "what we wanted." We would talk on the phone and not actually talk because we didn't know what to say or talk about.

During the same time my uncle was diagnosed with cancer (in February 2004) and died in June of the same year. I became more depressed and somewhat suicidal because of all the bottled up emotions that I had. I saw a school counselor and talked to her about my uncle; parts of me want to scream out to her I'm gay and I need help, but I didn't because I was afraid of her judgment and all I knew was that I had to act normal. I started high school with the same emotions and with the same boyfriend. We broke it off my freshman year after I found out he was cheating on me with my best friend.

I graduated in 2008 and joined my local town Fire dept as a Firefighter/ Photographer; and I love every minute of being a Firefighter/ Photographer, helping people in their time of need. My mom was an EMT and my Grandpa on my Dad's side was a Firefighter when I was growing up, so I knew it was in my blood to help people. As a women Firefighter I got a lot of shit; the guys would tell me that a woman doesn't belong in a man's job – that I was not strong or smart enough. I took this bullying and let it push me to prove them wrong. With the help of my other sisters and brothers on the fire dept that believed in me, I worked my tail off, got off probation, and got my yellow helmet. It was the proudest day of my life. I was not out to anyone at the fire dept at the time and I decided that I would let a couple of people know, So, I Facebook messaged one of the girls on the fire dept that I knew, and told her that I was a lesbian. I messaged her and she told me that she never knew

C. Boske & A. Osanloo (Eds.), Students, Teachers, and Leaders Addressing Bullying in Schools, 153–156.

and that she was 100% in support of me and if I need help she was here for me. I felt good that I had come out; it felt like I at least kicked the closet door open to who and what I was.

I decided at the same time to come out to my ex-boyfriend that I still talk to every now again because he was in the Army. I told him in a text and he called me and said, "I knew there was something up when we were dating. I just couldn't put my finger on it. I support you and I am here for you. In fact, I know a girl for you; she is in my unit." He gave me the girl's number and I texted her. We started talking and then we dated long distance – she was my first girlfriend. I was so nervous and scared. Our relationship lasted a couple months. I broke up with her because I found out on Facebook that she was cheating on me and was getting married to this girl that was in the Army with her. It sucked because I loved this girl and I trusted her enough to spill my emotions to her. After this relationship, I decided to come out to my mom. I messaged her on Facebook and told her that I was gay and how I was feeling. The next morning she called me downstairs and told me I had no clue what I was talking about and that I was confused. She asked me, "have you ever had sex with either sex" and I told her "no" and she told me "you're confused, stop thinking like this and do not to tell anyone." I had so much emotion after that day that I decided to go back into the closet. That was until 2013 when I decided as a 25- year old that it was time to grow up and put my big girl pants on and come out AGAIN to everyone and anyone that would hear me.

I started by looking up a local support group and found one in the Akron area close to where I live. I went to the meetings and started to open up little by little even though it was really hard for me. For the first time in my life I felt supported and like I had enough courage and information to step out into the world as a lesbian.

My best friend Christa at work, asked me one day if I wanted to go to Columbus Pride with DJ, Tony, and her and I told her, "yes I would love to go!" She asked me if I had a problem hanging out with gays and I told her "no I don't." I wanted to tell her right there and then, "No I don't have a problem because I'm gay myself," but I didn't because I was scared so I waited until that night after work to text both her and Tony and tell them. I first texted Tony and he texted me back and told me that he never knew and that he would always be there for me. Then I was going to text Christa, but she texted me and told me that she knew and that she loves me, was here for me, was glad that I came out to her, and was more excited for me now than ever because this would be my first pride as an out lesbian. I was excited for my first pride because I never been to one, but I was also scared a little. However, I knew my friends would be there for me and wouldn't let anything happen to me. We left Friday after work and got a hotel. The next day was the parade. We left the hotel and headed up to the parade spot. On the way Tony gave me advice saying I would see a lot that I probably haven't seen before and that he was here if it got overwhelming. We walked a couple of blocks and then ran into the protesters right by the capital building. They had signs that I didn't bother reading because they were full of hate.

We walked by and found a spot to sit and have a drink; the parade start and my friend Christa came up to me and hugged me and said, "I love you girl" and I told her, "I love you too." The parade ended and we went to the festival, which was so big and full of people that we decided together that we would go back to the hotel and take a nap before going back out that night. We went back to the hotel, took a nap, and got ready for the evening out. We went to a couple of local bars, got some drinks, and then decided to hit the hay so we took a cab back to the hotel. I will always remember this cab ride because the cab driver had the radio going and the song on the radio was "It's Raining Men" by the Weather Girls and we all broke out singing it. We got back to the hotel, went to bed, got up the next day and headed home. I had the time of my life because for one weekend I got to be myself and be around friends that supported me for me. They don't know it at the time, but they saved my life with this trip.

I decided the following weekend I would go with one of my best friend's from work Kyle, whose partner is in the Navy as a MP, to Cleveland Pride. We drove up, parked, and walked around. We walked right into the protesters who had signs and were handing out the Bible. One of the protesters tried to hand Kyle a Bible, but Kyle told him "do not to reach for us" and the protester told us to "reach for the hands of God. He will save you!" I will always remember Kyle said back to him, "I don't need saving. I'm already in his arms and he doesn't hate me for being gay. He made me gay and he also helped me find the man of my dreams so fuck you."

I came back home from both of the pride parades with the courage of a lion. I told a couple of my other friends and one of my three sisters. I then decided to come out to my mom again because it had been a couple of years and I thought she needed to hear it again. I didn't have to wait long because the next day she came to me and said, "Are you gay?" and I told her, "Yes I am." She said that I was confused and that I was bisexual and I told her, "No mom, I am gay." She then asked me if I ever had sex with either sex and I told her no. She then said until I had sex I wouldn't know what I was. I told her, "I know who I am and that I am Katie – your lesbian daughter." She said no and I said yes. I tried to explain to her that just like you knew she was straight without have sex, I knew I was lesbian without having sex. She told me "Okay, I still think your bisexual" and I told her, "Okay you can think that." She asked me why I didn't come to her sooner and I told her because I was afraid I would get kicked out of the house. She told me I would never do that to you. I love you and support you. I just think you're confused a little. I told her I loved her and we hugged. I went to a couple of more support meeting and then decided I would start going to PFlag meetings. I went and loved it. I found more support and decided to become the public relations officer for PFlag. A couple months passed and my sister got married. When we were at the wedding my mom came up to me, hugged me and told me she loved me for who I was and wanted to know when I was going to find a wife to marry. I told her when I find her mom I will let you know. She told me, "Cool because I want to plan the wedding." I started to cry because my mom now accepted me as her gay daughter. Even though my life continues and I know that I am bound to have more struggles as a young lesbian, I remind myself that it will get better, that it will take time, and to keep my head up and be strong like God would want me to be.

PART 3

VOICES FROM EDUCATORS AND SCHOLARS
IN THE FIELD

BERNARD OLIVER

26. BULLYING

Schoolhouse and Workforce Considerations for Students and Teachers

Over the past several years, considerable attention has been devoted to bullying behavior in schools. Much of this research and reporting has focused on students as victims and perpetrators of schoolyard bullying. Nansel et al. (2013), Limber, Olweus, and Luxenberg (2013), and others have found that significant numbers of students (often as high as forty percent) have experienced bullying as a victim or perpetrator/bully.

While bullying maybe a daily part of life for significant number of students at all levels, there is little doubt that bullying affects student learning, school climate, and often is a precursor for more violet behavior(see Bullying at School, California State department of Education, 2003). Not only are victims significantly impacted by bullying, some researchers suggest that witnesses to bullying behavior also suffer severe reactions as well (Davies, Chandler, & Nolin, 1995). The U.S. Department of Education concludes that bystanders and school peers are likely to:

- Become worrisome about becoming a victim of bullying
- Worry about establishing friendship with the bully and/or victim
- Withhold evidence about bullying behavior because of social repercussions of being labeled a snitch
- Feel helpless
- Coerced into bullying behavior unwillingly

Clearly bullying behavior has a significant impact on the entire schoolyard population.

EXACTLY WHAT IS BULLYING?

Schoolyard bullying has been defined in several ways:

an individual is being bullied when he/she is the target of aggressive behavior by another student or students (for example, when others say mean things, deliberately and systematically ignore someone, physically hurt others, spread negative rumors, or do other hurtful things); when

C. Boske & A. Osanloo (Eds.), Students, Teachers, and Leaders Addressing Bullying in Schools, 159–168.

a power imbalance exists between the individuals involved and when the bullying behavior happens more than once…all three conditions must be present…

(OBPP, 2013; Limber, Olweus, & Luwenberg, 2013)

bullying is defined as inatential repeated hurtful acts, words, or behavior; such as name-calling, threatening and/or shunning committed by one or more children against another

(U.S. Department of Education, ED453 592)

a desire to hurt + a hurtful action + a power imbalance + repetition (typically) + an unjust use of power + evident enjoyment by the aggressor + a sense of being oppressed on the part of the target.

(Rigby, 2003)

The California State Department of Education further state that bullying

…may be physical (hitting, kicking, spitting, pushing) verbal (tormenting malicious teasing, name calling), threatening or psychological (spreading rumors, manipulating social relationships or promoting social exclusion, extortion or intimidation).

Other considerations regarding bullying behavior centers around those behaviors clearly identified as sexual in nature; racial or hate related; and/or purposeful hazing. These racial and gender specific bullying incidents are seemingly on the rise in our nations schools and universities (see for example the hazing incident involving band members at Florida A & M University).

HOW DO STUDENTS DESCRIBE HOW THEY ARE BULLIED?

One of the most descriptive measures of bullying methods used by students in the nation's schoolyards is the Olweus Bullying Questionnaire. Repeatedly from data gathered from this survey, students indicate they are bullied in the following ways:

- Verbal: a student is called mean names or teased in hurtful way
- Rumors: a student is the target of false rumors or lies
- Exclusion: a student is left out on purpose or completely ignored
- Sexual: a student is bullied using words or gestures with a sexual meaning
- Racial: a student's race is the focus of the verbal bullying
- Physical: a student is hit, kicked, or pushed
- Threat: a student is threatened or forced to do things against his/her will
- Cyber: a student is bullied via a cell phone or computer (especially social media avenues)
- Damage: a student has personal property taken or damage
- Another way: a student is bullied in any way not previously discussed (Limber, Olweus, & Luxenberg, 2013).

Although student-to-student bullying receives most of the attention in the educational bully context, there's an emerging research trend that suggests teachers are seen as bullies by students and parents as well.

Twemlow and Fonagy (2005) suggests that teachers bully students who have different levels of behavior problems. They define a bullying "teacher as one who manipulates or disparages a student beyond what would be a reasonable disciplinary procedure" (p. 2387). This pattern of teacher bullying students is seen as "...a pattern of conduct, rooted in a power differential that threatens, harms, humiliates, induces fear, or causes students substantial emotional distress." (McEvoy, 2005). In a related study identifying the forms of teacher bullying, Zerillo and Osterman (2011) identified two types of teacher bullying: denial of access and belittling. That is teachers make comments about student characteristics, academic abilities, culture etc. and deny them access to those normal procedural activities found daily in classroom structures (going to the bathroom, sharpening a pencil, changing seats, going to the library, etc.)

When students identify bullying behavior by teachers they tend to make the following observations:

- Teachers repeatedly punish the same child
- Humiliates students
- Spiteful to students
- Hurt students' feelings
- Makes fun of students
- Uses rejection
- Devotes negative attention to the same student
- Denial of bathroom use
- Excludes from programs/activities
- Ignoring students
- Makes comments about personal characteristices (weight, dress,etc.)
- Cultural comments about race, culture, religion, etc.
- Tendency to bully the whole class
- Make comments about family/home life (Twemlow et al., 2006).

Teachers seem to bully for a variety of reason. Holt (2010) suggests that teachers bully students because they might remind them of an unpleasant individual in their life; because of various types of envy; personal problems; job related frustrations; don't like minorities; affinity for physical force/aggressiveness; and other school/leadership based issues.

Teacher bullying, when accompanied by peer bullying creates a toxic classroom environment which has significant implication for student learning and behavior. This continually misuse of power impacts student discipline; relationships with students' evaluation of students' ability grouping; teaching/classroom practices; and procedural event in class that single students out (Twenlow, Fonagy, Sacco, & Brethour, 2006).

Workplace Bullying By Teachers, Administrators, & Staff

Perhaps the most understated problem in schoolhouse bullying is the teacher-to-teacher; administrator-to-teacher; teacher-to- staff, etc. This adult bullying behavior has serious implications for workplace culture and performance.

Workplace bullying has received considerable attention in the private sector over the past several years. So it is not only students/children who are impacted by bullying behavior, but adults who are perpetrators and victims of workplace bullying. Similar to schoolhouse bullying, workplace bullying is defined as follows:

repeated, health harming mistreatment of one or more persons (the targets)
by one or more perpetrators that takes one or more of the following forms:
verbal abuse; offensive conduct/behavior (includes non-verbal) which is
threatening, humiliating, or intimidating.
(Workplace Bullying Institute, 2006)

repeated, unreasonable or inappropriate behavior directed towards a worker,
or group of workers, that creates a risk to health and safety.
(Commission for Occupational Safety Health, 2010)

interpersonal hostility that is deliberate, repeated, and sufficiently
severe as to harm the targeted person's health or economic status. It
is driven by perpetrators' needs to control another individual, often
undermining legitimate business in interests in the process.
(Namie, 2003)

repeated, unreasonable actions of individuals (or a group) directed
towards an employee (or group of employees), which are intended to
to intimidate, degrade, humiliate or undermine; or ehich create a risk
to the health or safety of employees.
(Washington State Department of Labor & Industries, 2013)

Workplace bullying takes many shapes and forms, all of which have the potential for devastating affects on the workplace environment. The Safety & Health Assessment and Research for Prevention Program (SHARP) in the state of Washington identified the following types of workplace bullying as a serious threat to the working environment:

• Unwanted or invalid criticism
• Blame without factorial justification
• Being treated differently than the rest of your work group
• Exclusion or social isolation
• Being shouted at or being humiliated
• Excessive monitoring or micro-managing
• Being assigned unrealistic work duties/deadlines

The government of Western Australia divides workplace bullying behaviors into either covert practices or overt practices. These workplace-bullying practices are seen as follows:

OVERT BULLYING BEHAVIORS

- Abusive, insulting or offensive language
- Behavior or language that frightens, humiliates, belittles or degrades, including criticism that is delivered with yelling and screaming
- Inappropriate comments about a person's appearance, lifestyle, or family
- Teasing or regularly making someone the brunt of pranks or practical jokes
- Interfering with a person's personal effects or work equipment
- Harmful or offensive initiation practices
- Isolation of workers from others
- Physical assault or threats

COVERT BULLYING BEHAVIORS

- Overloading a person with work or not providing enough work
- Setting/constantly changing timelines that are difficult to achieve
- Assigning tasks below and/or above the ability level of the worker
- Isolation or ignoring practices
- Purposefully denying information, resources, etc. related to job performance
- Unequal treatment in access to job related entitlements

WORKPLACE BULLYING OF TEACHERS

Workplace bullying of teachers and administrators continues to receive more attention in the school workplace based upon the significant ramifications that student-to-student bullying seems to have on student learning and development and the emerging instances of school related violence incidents that are possibly elated to bullying and workplace climate. International studies in Turkey and England indicated that over 50% of the teachers sampled experienced bullying and that bullying behaviors were common occurrences sighted in conversations with teachers (Cemaloglu, 2007; Davis, 2008; Morrison, 2008).

WHAT DOES WORKPLACE BULLYING LOOK LIKE FOR TEACHERS?

Riley, Duncan, and Edwards (2010) identified four categories of bullying behaviors faced by teachers: workload assignments; work conditions and environment; diminished professional standing; and personal confrontations. In addition, these researchers found that teacher demographics (age, gender, experiences, race, etc.) and school characteristics (size, location, etc.) were also related to the types of bullying behavior that teachers experienced. The top ten items affecting teachers who were consulted in this study were as follows:

- Your mental or physical health has been affected by the behavior toward you
- Tasks are set with unreasonable or impossible targets or deadlines
- Recognition, acknowledgement and praise are withheld
- Your concerns about unfair treatment bullying and harassment are dismissed
- Frozen out/ignored/excluded from decision making
- Lack of opportunity for face-to-face discussion to take place
- Undermining of your personal integrity
- Area of responsibility are removed or added without consultation
- You are ignored or excluded
- You are exposed to an unmanageable workload

In a major investigation of workplace bullying, the Houston Independent School District interviewed teachers at the elementary, middle and high school levels to get a sense of how teachers viewed bullying behavior. Although not comprehensive, the following list provides an illustration of teacher statements that pointed to bullying behavior:

"she's never been professional and is always mad"
"_____needs to hire better people"
"screams at teachers in front of everyone"
"retaliates with the evaluation if you disgust her"
"tells co-workers they need to retire and constantly calls them to the office because of what someone said"
"publicly told a teacher that if she can't follow directions then think of another profession to work in"
"the principal targeted older teachers for negative comments"
"if you don't like it, retire"
"shows teachers records to the entire staff"
"assigns extra duties for retaliations"
"makes fun of teachers"
"gives public reprimands to teachers"

These are just a few of the comments teachers provided that indicated bullying behavior on the part of the perpetrator.

Although one would assume that all teachers seem to hold a the same positions in educational settings relative to responsibilities; duties, etc.; there is evidence that strongly suggests that there is an imbalance of power that exists among educators in the school workplace which lead to undermining and/or subjugation of other teachers. This imbalance of power also leads to bullying behaviors b those teachers deemed to have power within the schoolhouse. These sources of power include positional power; relationship power; resources power; psychological power; knowledge power; delegated power; and the power of personality.

Clearly the impact/effects of bullying have severe consequences for both the victim and the perpetrator. We know from the workplace bullying literature that the effects of bullying leads to stress, anxiety, loss of sleep, emotional attacks, depression, incapacity to teach, absenteeism, strains of family relations, and in some cases physical injury and the potential for more violent behaviors.

Clearly from the research on schoolhouse bullying and workforce bullying, teachers who are bullied suffer the same fates as students who are bullied in the schoolyard. These personal attacks create psychological and emotional damage, which impacts the quality of instructional and school life for students and teachers. Of a more serious nature is the possibility of violence and suicidal behavior that has surfaced in the past few years. Given the emerging severity of bullying in the schoolhouse, what strategies can be identified to curb this serious threat to school safety for children and teachers.

How Should Schools Respond to Bullying in the Schoolhouse Workplace?

Research and the recent public/tragic events tied to schoolyard and workplace bullying strongly suggests that school districts, schools, leaders, teachers, parents and students give serious attention to the adoption of comprehensive strategies to address bullying.

Several agencies have adopted comprehensive training modules to assist school districts in the development of responsive bullying prevention programs (see for example the U.S. Department of Health and Human Services; Health and Safety Authority Headquarters in Dublin, Ireland; the National Education Association of Education; and the Department of Commerce in The Government of Western Australia).

Bullying is a serious threat to school and organizational safety which has the potential to inflict serious harm to children and school educators. As such, a comprehensive prevention/intervention plan must be implemented and involve all stakeholders (children, teachers, parents, administrators, other school staff and community members). Such a plan should include the following:

- An initial needs assessment/awareness survey or questionnaire regarding bullying behavior
- A parental/community awareness plan
- Professional development for teachers and school staff to understand schoolyard and workforce bullying
- Professional development/awareness training that focuses on gender, race, sexual orientation and other status characteristic associated with bullying
- Implementation of curricular and/or deep learning strategies for students and parents to enhance their understanding and awareness of bullying
- Policy and procedures that clearly spell out bullying behavior and consequences

- Identification of behaviors that might have a bullying effect on students and teachers
- Clearly identify roles/connections to community agencies for support
- Make available counseling and support services for teachers, students ad parents
- Include orientation for parents, students and teachers
- Provided protection for all involved with clearly spelled out sanctions
- Include a workplace civility policy that identifies unacceptable behaviors and include school-wide posters highlighting schoolhouse civility

In summary, to create a bully free schoolyard and workplace environment, school, districts must integrate the tenants of a bully free environment into policies procedures, and district culture. The impact on teacher and students is to critical/ harmful and potentially dangerous to leave unanswered.

Table 1. Major Forms of Teacher Bullying

Personal Confrontation

- Questioning decisions of instruction, students, etc.
- Questioning procedures
- Belittling behavior
- Undermining work
- Impact on mental emotional physical health
- Criticism
- Personal integrity

Diminished Professional Standing

- Withholding praise, recognition
- Withholding feedback, regarding performance
- Excluded from interactions
- Ignoring behavior
- Diminished responsibility/career advancement

Workload

- Unrealistic timelines
- Assigned tasks not related to job
- Increased workload

Work Conditions/Environment

- Invasion of personal space
- Conversation focusing on termination/changing jobs
- Isolation in the workplace and professional development
- Teasing/sarcasm
- Denial of request for training, leave, etc.
- Conflicted messages regarding entitlements (Riley, Duncan, & Edwards, 2010)

REFERENCES

Armstrong, P. (2011). Budgetary bullying. *Critical Perspectives on Accounting, 22*(7), 632–643.
Batsche, G. M., & Knoff, H. M. (1994). Bullies and their victims: Understanding a pervasive problem in the schools. *School Psychology Review, 23,* 165–165.
Blase, J., & Blase, J. (2004). The dark side of school leadership: Implications for administrator preparation. *Leadership and Policy in Schools, 3*(4), 245–273.
Bradshaw, C. P., & Figel, K. (2012). *Prevention and intervention of workplace bullying in schools.* Washington, DC: National Educational Association.
California Department of Education. (2003). *Bullying in schools.* Sacramento, CA: Author.
Cemaloglu, N. (2007). The Relationship between Organizational Health and Bullying that Teachers Experience in Primary Schools in Turkey. *Educational Research Quarterly, 31*(2), 3–28.
Cemaloglu, N. (2011). Primary principals' leadership styles, school organizational health and workplace bullying. *Journal of Educational Administration, 49*(5), 495–512.
Commission for Occupational Safety and Health. (2006). *Dealing with bullying at work: A guide for workers.* Western Australia: Author.
Davis, B. (2008). The silent treatment. *Times Educational Supplement,* 10–17.
De Wet, C. (2010). The reasons for and the impact of principal-on-teacher bullying on the victims' private and professional lives. *Teaching and Teacher Education, 26*(7), 1450–1459.
De Wet, C. (2011). The professional lives of teacher victims of workplace bullying: A narrative analysis. *Perspectives in Education, 29*(4), 66–77.
Einarsen, S. (1999). The nature and causes of bullying at work. *International Journal of Manpower, 20*(1/2), 16–27.
Feldman, S. (2004). Teacher to teacher: Bullying prevention. *Teaching Pre K-8, 34*(6), 6.
Fox, S., & Stallworth, L. (2008, March). *Defining workplace bullying: Issues of pervasiveness, power, and triviality.* Work, Stress, and Health 2008 Conference, Washington, DC.
Frazier, K. N. (2011). Academic bullying: A barrier to tenure and promotion for African-American faculty. *Florida Journal of Educational Administration and Policy, 5*(1), 1–13.
Glasner, A. T. (2010). On the front lines: Educating teachers about bullying and prevention methods. *Journal of Social Sciences, 6*(4), 537.
Kauppi, T., & Pörhölä, M. (2012). School teachers bullied by their students: Teachers' attributions and how they share their experiences. *Teaching and Teacher Education, 28*(7), 1059–1068.
Kennedy, T. D., Russom, A. G., & Kevorkian, M. M. (2012). Teacher and administrator perceptions of bullying in schools. *International Journal of Education Policy and Leadership, 7*(5).
Korkmaz, M., & Cemaloglu, N. (2010). Relationship between Organizational Learning and Workplace Bullying in Learning Organizations. *Educational Research Quarterly, 33*(3), 3–38.
Lewis, D., Sheehan, M., & Davies, C. (2008). Uncovering workplace bullying. *Journal of Workplace Rights, 13*(3), 281–301.
Limber, S. P., Olweus, D., & Luxenberg, H. (2013). *Bullying in U.S. schools: 2012 status report.* Center City, MN: Hazelden Foundation.
Maguire, M. (2001). Bullying and the postgraduate secondary school trainee teacher: An English case study. *Journal of Education for Teaching: International Research and Pedagogy, 27*(1), 95–109.
McEvoy, A. (2005, September). Teachers who bully students: Patterns and policy implications. In *Teachers who bully students.* Presentation to the conference on persistently safe schools–Philadelphia (September 11–14).
McKay, R., Ciocirlan, C., & Chung, E. (2010). Thinking strategically about workplace bullying in organizations. *Journal of Applied Management and Entrepreneurship, 15*(4), 73–93.
Morrison, N. (2008). You're not alone. *Times Educational Supplement, 4786,* 2–5.
Namie, G., & Namie, R. (2003). *The bully at work: What you can do to stop the hurt and reclaim your dignity at work.* Naperville, IL: Sourcebooks, Inc.
Nolin, M. J., Davies, E., & Chandler, K. (1995). *Student victimization at school: National center for education statistics – statistics in brief (NCES 95-204).* Washington, DC.
Olweus, D. (1993). *Bullying at school: What we know and what we can do.* Wiley-Blackwell.

Olweus, D., & Limber, S. P. (2009). The Olweus bullying prevention program: Implementation and evolution over two decades. In S. R. Jimerson, S. M. Swearer, & D. L. Espelage (Eds.), *Handbook of bullying in schools: An international perspective*. New York, NY: Routledge.

Quiroz, H. C., Arnette, J. L., & Stephens, R. D. (2006). *Bullying in schools: Fighting the bully battle*. National School Safety Center. Retrieved online on May 5, 2008.

Randall, P. (2004). *Adult bullying: Perpetrators and victims*. New York, NY: Routledge.

Riley, D., Duncan, D. J., & Edwards, J. (2011). Staff bullying in Australian schools. *Journal of Educational Administration, 49*(1), 7–30.

Schat, A. C., Frone, M. R., & Kelloway, E. K. (2006). *Prevalence of workplace aggression in the US workforce: Findings from a national study*.

Smith, P. K., & Sharp, S. (1994). *School bullying: Insights and perspectives*. London, UK: Routledge Press.

Tehrani, N. (Ed.). (2001). *Building a culture of respect: Managing bullying at work*. CRC Press.

Tehrani, N. (2012). *Workplace bullying: Symptoms and solutions*. Hove, UK: Routledge.

Terry, M. L., & Baer, A. M. (2013). Teacher-on-student bullying: Is your Massachusetts school district ready for this test? *Northeastern Law Journal, 5*(1), 107–130.

Ttofi, M., & Farrington, D. (2009). What works in preventing bullying: Effective elements of anti-bullying programmes. *Journal of Aggression, Conflict and Peace Research, 1*(1), 13–24.

Ttofi, M. M., & Farrington, D. P. (2011). Effectiveness of school-based programs to reduce bullying: A systematic and meta-analytic review. *Journal of Experimental Criminology, 7*(1), 27–56.

Twemlow, S. W., & Fonagy, P. (2005). The prevalence of teachers who bully students in schools with differing levels of behavioral problems. *American Journal of Psychiatry, 162*(12), 2387–2389.

Twemlow, S. W., Fonagy, P., Sacco, F. C., & Brethour, J. R. (2006). Teachers who bully students: A hidden trauma. *International Journal of Social Psychiatry, 52*(3), 187–198.

U.S. Department of Education. (1998). *Preventing bullying: A manual for schools and communities*. Washington, DC: Author.

Waggoner, C. (2003). Teachers behaving badly. *American School Board Journal, 190*(8), 29–31.

Zerillo, C. (2010). *Teachers and bullying developing a deeper understanding of teachers' perceptions of teacher-to-student bullying*. Ann Arbor, MI: ProQuest LLC.

Zerillo, C., & Osterman, K. F. (2011). Teacher perceptions of teacher bullying. *Improving Schools, 14*(3), 239–257.

Zirkel, P. (2008). Bullying. *Principal, 84*(4), 6–8.

Bernard Oliver, Professor
School of Human Development & Organizational Studies
College of Education
University of Florida
Gainesville, Florida

KIMBERLY MEREDITH

27. THE POWER TO MOVE OTHERS

Dancers Addressing Bullying

Being bullied is an embodied practice. When the bullying is physical (such as in the case of pushing, kicking, or punching), the embodied experience is clear. However, even when the bullying is social (such as rumours or social revenge) or verbal (such as teasing and name-calling), the effects are physical as it is often physical characteristics that are the focus of taunts and it is the body that experiences the resultant emotional pain. How, then, does the body respond to bullying? Sadly, we know all too well destructive physical responses as bullied youth turn to aggressive violence or self-harm as embodied means to express or to end the emotional anguish that they often cannot or will not effectively put into words. However, not all physical responses are destructive. As a dance educator and a multiliteracies researcher, I have witnessed deeply moving physically-creative responses to bullying. Rather than respond through destruction, these young artists respond through creation. They address their lived experiences of bullying by using music, gestures, and words to create choreographed meaning, identity, and hope. This chapter focuses the description of two of these danced responses to bullying: "O for Overcoming" created by seventeen-year-old Josh for his peer-judged high school hip hop competition, and "L for Love" created by 24-year-old hip hop dancer Madoka as she reflects on her own high school experience in response to "O for Overcoming". Through their words, music, and movements, we can understand the necessity, potential, and pedagogical method of providing our youth with opportunities to construct meaning physically and creatively to respond to and transform their emotional, physical, and social experiences.

Theoretical Inspirations: The data from this chapter comes from a video ethnographic research study examining the meaning-making processes of young dancers. In theorizing their creative work, this study draws on the literature of multiliteracies (New London Group, 2000), specifically transformative multiliteracies pedagogy (Cummins, 2009). This pedagogy seeks to embrace literacies beyond the written word and transformative practices beyond the reproduction of privileged genres to maximize students' identity investment (Norton, 2000) and cognitive engagement. The danced texts are understood to be identity texts (Cummins, 2011) as they are invested with and negotiate the value of the identity of their maker. Furthermore, this study draws on a social practice perspective to examine how the

C. Boske & A. Osanloo (Eds.), Students, Teachers, and Leaders Addressing Bullying in Schools, 169–188.

young dancers fight for the right to "speak" (Bourdieu & Thompson, 1991) and the power to impose reception (Norton & Toohey, 2004) through their gestured utterances as they negotiate their place in the fields (Bourdieu & Thompson, 1991) of the high school and global hip hop social spheres. Finally, in order to explore the rich gestural mode, this study draws on the work of Pippa Stein (2008), who conceptualizes bodies as "repositories of knowledge" that are "not always knowable in and through language" (p. 151). These social practices and multiliteracies theories can provide insight into how dancers move beyond the limits of words to create knowledge about bullying that is inexpressible in words alone.

Methodology: In order to honor the power of not only the verbal, but also the non-verbal meaning-making processes of these dancers, the creation, performance, and reflection of their dances was recorded using video ethnographic methodology, and transcribed and analyzed through a developing multimodal discourse analytic process. Participant and researcher-recorded videos were collected of the freestyling, designing, and performance process with dance interspersed with talk about the dance. When the performance was complete, I asked both Josh and Madoka to teach me their dances so that I could delve more deeply into their kinesthetic communication. Finally, I created an edited video combining all of these sources for Josh's *O for Overcoming* [https://vimeo.com/85000420 (password: overcoming)]. It was this video that Madoka saw at a dance workshop that inspired her to create *L for Love* and her own edited video to explain and share her work [https://vimeo.com/85202826 (password: love)].

Because I have taken a social practice approach to this study, I have analyzed the creative process, performance, and interviews (Talmy, 2008) as interactive occasions in which the designer and other interlocutors draw on multimodal resources to actively co-construct meaning, identity (Norton, 2000), and power (Cummins, 2011). To examine these practices, I draw on Bakhtin (1989) and other discourse analytic perspectives (Gee, 1999; Georgakopoulou, 2007). However, here I write with the intention to inspire teachers, students, and educational researchers to address bullying through the power of dance. With this aim in mind and with space limitations, I limit the in-depth discourse analysis and instead focus on providing the context, content, and conversation of each piece. The context describes when, where, why, and how the piece came to be produced. The content is a multimodal description of the dances, attempting to capture in words and images what was once powerfully produced in movement and sound. Links to the videos are provided and readers are greatly encouraged to leave the confines of this printed page to experience these works as they were intended to be viewed. Finally, the conversation provides necessarily brief excerpts from the deep discussions I have had the pleasure to engage in with these artists about their work. The excerpts chosen here focus on how these works address bullying. The chapter then ends with pedagogical implications, suggesting ways forward as students, teachers and the research community seek ways to effectively address bullying by inspiring physical creation rather than physical destruction.

O FOR OVERCOMING: THE CONTEXT

In the spring of 2011, I was studying the meaning-making processes of seventeen-year-old Josh as he prepared a routine to be performed for the judgment of his peers in his school's student-voted "So You Think You Can Dance" competition. From the beginning of the process, the social pressure was clear as Josh spoke of his indecision about entering the contest, battling between his fears of inadequacy performing before a jury of his peers and his fears of regret should he miss this opportunity to express himself. In interviews, he expressed anger at the lack of support he was receiving from his peers who compared him to other dancers and said he was "not good enough." In particular, when he saw one student walk by, he says he experienced a "jolt of anger" that he channeled into the emotional arc of his piece. In this environment of hostility, fear, anger, inspiration and hope, Josh free-styled to various songs, then selected and mixed his music. Over the course of five days, he choreographed and performed the routine. When he positioned himself in the center of his school gym to perform in front of hundreds of his peers, he heard a single male voice call out "lame" just before the music began. The audience was nearly silent during his performance, and cheered loudly at the end. He received 47 votes from his peers and placed third of ten competitors. After the performance, Josh continued to re-work the piece for a second out-of-school performance and continued to participate in interviews exploring various aspects of its production. While it began as an unnamed piece with the only expressed purpose of winning a dance competition, by the end of the six-week meaning-making period Josh had titled it *O for Overcoming* and could speak at length about its significance as a self-reflective piece about how he finds his inner power to overcome his fear of the judgment and bullying actions of his peers and just be himself.

O FOR OVERCOMING: THE CONTENT

Josh describes the flow of his dance as follows: "hurt, anger, stress, this is me" (Josh, interview, 2011). To achieve this flow, Josh has used GarageBand to mix together two songs: the acapella version of Eminem's "Lose Yourself" from the *8 Mile* soundtrack and Deadmau5's dub-step styled "Raise Your Weapon". In these music choices, Josh intertextually draws on the power of Eminem and his story of overcoming and finding his voice portrayed in the story of a rapper who struggles and eventually succeeds in a free-style battle in the movie 8 Mile. In addition, Deadmau5's "Raise Your Weapon" provides Josh with a contrast between the bass-infused angry call to "raise your weapons" and the strings-infused lyric-less sections that suggests calm and peaceful resolution. Below, a description of the dance intersperses Josh's words describing the emotional arc of his piece with the corresponding lyrics and my own description of his movements in an attempt to put to the page the power of the meaning he created on the stage.

Josh begins seated in a chair at the back of the gym at the furthest point away from the audience. He wears dark jeans and a dark sweatshirt with a hood hanging down the back. His elbows rest on his knees, head down (see Figure 1, below).

Part 1: Hurt

Figure 1. Okay, so first he's starting to panic *Figure 2. "Would you capture it?/Or let it slip"*

Josh: Okay, so first part he's starting to panic.
Eminem: Look. If you had one shot. / Or one opportunity. / To seize everything you ever wanted. / In one moment. / Would you capture it? / Or let it slip.

On the lyric "look", Josh raises his head. He then raises his right hand to his head and lowers his head to meet it, touching his head self-consciously. He rubs his palms on his knees, as though they were sweaty. He half stands, but does not get fully to his feet before he reaches his left hand back to grasp the chair once more, looking away from the crowd and sitting down again. Even as he sits down, his right hand hits downward, urging action. Then he stands again once more, slowly, and takes one tentative step forward with his right leg before turning back again to the left, while his right hand again hits downward (Figure 2). It is as though his left and right side of his body are debating—his left side wanting to run and hide while his right side urges him on.

Part 2: Panic

Figure 3. And he's starting desperate moves *Figure 4. "But the words won't come out"*

Josh: And he's starting desperate moves.

Eminem: Yo. *(Musical accompaniment- repetitive guitar hits)* / His palms are sweaty / Knees weak / Arms are heavy / There's vomit on his sweater already / Mom's spaghetti/ He's nervous / But on the surface he looks calm and ready / To drop bombs / But he keeps on forgetting / What he wrote down/ The whole crowd goes so loud / He opens his mouth but the words won't come out / He's choking how / Everyone's joking now / The clocks' run out / Over / Blaoh! / You better-

On the lyric "Yo", his left hand hits downward decisively, followed by a mirroring on his right, as though the two side of his body and two parts of his mind are finally in agreement and ready to fully seize the moment. He takes four steps towards the audience/camera, looking directly at them. He then mimes the meaning of the fear-full lyrics, interpreting them in a literal but stylized way, facial expressions alternating between fear/uncertainty and flashes of determination/aggression. This section ends with the following movements: On "he opens his mouth but the words won't come out," he steps back and forth to the rhythm of the words while his right hand covers mouth and his left hand stretches outwards and tenses as though both reaching and struggling. On "come out," right hand flies from face to hit left hand. On "he's choking how," both hands go to his throat. A full body roll causes hands to be removed and then forcefully returned to throat. On "everybody's joking," he takes two steps backwards, hands in fists, eyes wide, mouth partially open seemingly in fear/panic. On "clock's run out", runs downstage, stage left. On "time's up", right foot sharply right to left while hands palms open to audience sharply left to right. Jumps into air on "over". Lands jump in crouched position and punches toward ground with right hand on "blaoh!" (Figure 5).

Part 3: Power

Figure 5. Like he punches the ground   *Figure 6. Founds a weapon*

Josh: Kind of a switch of emotion. Like he punches the ground. Founds a weapon. And he discovered like- his punch can- He discovers it. And he founds that he has a weapon now so he's like- Like he has power.

Deadmau5: raise your weapon. / *Audible breath* raise your weapo:n. *Piano chords begin.* /And it's over.

On Deadmau5's first "raise your weapon," *his right hand reverberates from the punch by moving upwards towards the sky in a wave motion while body follows, returning to a standing position; head follows hand as though mesmerized (Figure 6). On Deadmau5's audible breath and sustained* "raise your weapo:n," *his right hand is re-energized and continues waving motion as he takes two upright steps backwards and four steps forward. On the piano chord, his left hand takes up the waving motion while body leans to the right and head follows the left hand. On* "and it's over," *both hands hit sides of thighs and coordinate in a wave as he takes one step back and second step to squarely face audience. His body tenses as right leg takes a step forward and body follows as though unfamiliar power is coursing through body.*

Part 4: Anger

Figure 7. And that made him angry   *Figure 8. At first*

Josh: So I guess that's just discovering his power. And then now when he discovered it. He realizes what he can do and that made him angry. At first. And the like really intense part- really angry part…

Deadmau5: How does it feel now / To watch it burn. *Drum beat drops* / Ripping though like a missile. (Burn burn burn) *Dubstep bass run.* / Ripping through my heart. *Dubstep bass three hits.* / Rob me of. *Dubstep rapid hits. Dubstep bass three hits.* / This lo:ve. *Dubstep run.* / Raise your weapon. *Dubstep bass three hits. Dubstep bass run.* / Raise your weapo:n. *Dubstep bass three hits.* / One word. *Dubstep rapid hits.* / And it's over.

This section is full of fast, powerful, aggressive movements including sweeping leg movements, raised fists, kicking (Figure 8), breaking hand-cuffs, rapid robotic movements on the rapid dubstep hits, break-dance floor work (6-step and coffee grinder) (Figure 7), shooting a bow-and-arrow, and punching motions. The majority of these motions are directed towards the audience. Finally, on "and it's over," *Josh ends the section by bringing his hands together at his waist as though holding a ball of energy that he then propels out towards audience and ends with his arms intertwined tightly together pointing at audience.*

Part 5: This is me

Figure 9. Just chill down I guess   *Figure 10. And then just sway*

Josh: And then that's just- Just chill down I guess. Like chill down but... I don't need to be angry. I mean just because yeah- I'm just doing this. Just let me do this. Like it's just getting back to what I really wanted to do... Live, dance. Live, laugh, learn, dance. And that's just like what I learned. Get something from me.

Deadmau5:   *Lyrics and bass drop away. Music shifts to piano, drums, and synthesizer.*

Begins by releasing his arms and moving into more flowing, rotational movements. Ends with feet planted side by side, body crouched and hands touching feet. Begins to rotate knees. Body follows and hands slowly make their way up the body to the chest, head back to face the sky. On the final piano note, bounces on heels as hands open wide.

Josh: And then just sway. The swaying is just calming I guess.

Deadmau5:   *Drums drop away, leaving only a final sustained piano note.*

Sways left right left right left, slowly moving towards audience as arms sway above head, palms open and facing inwards.

Josh: I guess that sound just reminded me of... It looked like- it sounds like you just watched something and you're just starting to wake up from a dream kind of thing. Like an insight is just about to come up. Go in you. Like pop up.

Deadmau5:   *Piano drops away, replaced by a sustained synthesizer note.*

Takes four steps towards audience as hands lower to sides. Gazes directly at audience.

Josh: And then "you can do anything you set your mind to." And that's it. That's the point... That's cool. That is the point. /.../ Yeah like all that hurt, anger, stress, this is me. Kind of made into that one point kind of combined. Into that conclusion.

Eminem: You can do anything you set your mind to man.

175

Steps on right foot towards audience, raising right hand to right temple. Pushes right hand quickly towards audience while spinning on feet to face away from the audience and walk away as the music and performance end.

O FOR OVERCOMING: THE CONVERSATION

During a break from one of his choreography practices, Josh sits on the counter at the back of the studio and starts to talk about wanting to "affect people" with his performance:

Josh:	I wanna affect people. So why. Why would I think that I would want to affect people. *(L hand gestures palm up towards Kim)*
Kim:	Why?
Josh:	Why? *(L hand gestures palm up to the side)*
Kim:	Why?
Josh:	Because this school is so bad. *Laughs as L hand fingers curl in. Hand to chin.* No this school is just so close-minded. *(Looks around to R, L hand to L temple)* Um. Even um the arts *(looks back at camera)* is not really supported- I don't know they are just too scared. It's all about like (1.5) emotions are not talked about I guess. There are so many people who are just like *glances right* "you're so gay" like "it's gay- it's really gay *(looks at camera)* to have emotions isn't it. It's so gay...." *Glances down.* Yeah. And it's- it's all about- like... [inaudible] I guess like if I expose myself it's like I'm sacrificing *Raises arms up and open like the end of his dance.*
Kim:	Yeah. [That's really brave-
Josh:	[just to- just for- like to even just affect some people. *Arms down.*
Kim:	Mm hm. And does that feel brave or? What does that feel like to you?
Josh:	(1.0) When I think about it like- like it's nothing. It shouldn't be anything. It should be like *hands to chest* okay I'm just another human being, I need to give to the world, right. *(arms open)*
Kim:	Mm hm.
Josh:	I just need to give- *(arms open again from chest)* I just need to give something *(hands touch temples and open)*
Kim:	Mm Hm.
Josh:	So that at least they'll get like- *hands to temples* they'll think about *it (R hand gestures out from R temple and drops to lap).* Other than not do anything about it and just- yeah. Like it shouldn't matter. *(L hand to chest)* Like when you really think about it *(L hand opens)* but like- *glances L.*
Kim:	Mm hm.

176

Josh:	On the other hand *(smiles)*, when I'm really stressed- hey *(R hand waves at peer)*- when I'm really stressed *(leans chin on L hand)* like yeah. Like I just get- I think the other... the other view?
Kim:	What do you think? If you're stressed.
Josh:	Um. ... I don't know... like... like nothing is... like I just think really sad thoughts like no one is really getting affected *(L hand touches neck)*
Kim:	Mm.
Josh:	There's not really a change- there's not really a change and you're just- you just made yourself *looks R.* Yeah and you feel lonely *(looks at Kim, smiling)* I guess when I'm stressed I feel lonely and I feel like no one really understands anything and there's no point. Or when I'm tired. *Leans chin on L hand, smiling. Looks L.*
Kim:	Yes.
Josh:	But yeah. I'm not tired I'm happy And it's just like yeah, whatever just expose! *(Raises both hands from chest in bouncing motion from end of dance and claps hands above head)* Expose *(rests hands on head)* like this is me like *(gestures out from chest)* this is- this is what you can do
Kim:	Mm hm.
Josh:	Yeah. *Looks at camera.*

L FOR LOVE: THE CONTEXT

I presented the edited mini-documentary version of Josh's "O for Overcoming" during a dance and expression workshop on board the Japanese NGO, the Peace Boat. 24-year-old hip hop dancer Madoka was in the audience. After the presentation, she approached me to thank me and to tell me that she was inspired to dance. She spent the subsequent hours dancing until she was exhausted, then recording her voice explaining why she was dancing, then mixing the soundtrack that combines sounds from 17 different sources, and choreographing a piece in response to "O." Finally, inspired by the video I had edited for "O for Overcoming", Madoka created her own video. Separately, she sat down with me to teach me the dance and talk about the meaning of her piece.

L FOR LOVE: THE CONTENT

In her video, Madoka begins with a series of black slides with white writing in Japanese and English (translated by a friend) to explain her inspiration:
After watching the video clip of Josh, I was immediately inspired to dance, / I wanted to hear about his life, so I asked Kim to tell me more / I understood every word Josh said, as if they were words coming out of my own mouth / Words are just

177

things you try to match together with what you feel instinctively so that you can communicate your feelings, but they don't express your raw emotions. / I bought an English book at the Shop on the 6ᵗʰ floor and tried to study, but my heart wasn't in it. / I've always felt that things get more and more lost when you try to put your emotions in words, so I've never been good a speaking, neither in Japanese or English. / I'm not good at expressing things with words. / Words are limited. / That's why I dance. / Everyone interprets a dance differently, but if everything goes well, dance or music or art has the power to make other people understand the problems we are currently facing. / ... / Even if society doesn't see value in something or someone, you can become a strong and gentle person if you see your own worth. / And if you can manage to express your thoughts, whatever they are, even a little bit, you have the power to move others.

What follows is a slow-motion video of her dancing her "L" choreography with subtitles in Japanese and English explaining the meaning of each section of the dance. Below I have combined Madoka's interpretation of her dance with audio cues from the complex mix she created and my own description of her movements in an attempt to recreate the power of her expression on the page as it was intended on the stage.

Madoka begins at center stage. She is wearing a bright red oversized t-shirt, over-sized black pants, and a silver peace symbol on a black string around her neck. Her hair is loose and she begins with her head down

Part 1: Innocence

| *Figure 11. The dance begins with the sound of a breath* | *Figure 12. My life begins with ... a heartbeat* |

Madoka: The dance starts with the sound of a breath / ONE LOVE represents the true nature of humans. / My life begins with the sound of a heartbeat.

Track: *Sound of inhale, exhale* (from Wade Robson's "Power") followed by the voice "One love" (from Radius's "Zion 1"), two hard drum-like hits (from beatboxing 2 sound effect), electronic sounds overlayed with breathing sounds (from Shinji's "Dance Box), and a man's voice says "power," followed by a brief silence (from Wade Robson's "Power")

At the sound of breathing, Madoka remains still, feet apart, head down, hands at her side at centre stage. On "One love," she raises her right hand index finger, back of hand towards the audience, then reaches the same hand to the sky and then both hands to her heart. On the two hard drum-like hits, she does two chest isolations with hands over her heart. On the electronic sounds, she pivots slowly to the right, raising left hand to her head and extending her right arm behind. On the breathing sounds, her head raises for the first time and then lowers again sharply as though noticing something. On "power," Madoka faces the audience and reaches both hands above her, palms open. She then closes her hands into fists and pulls them into her centre, crouching forward in a pose of potential energy.

Part 2: Confusion/Frustration

Figure 13. I don't understand English　　　　*Figure 14. Feelings of frustration*

Madoka:　The alphabet sounds mean I don't understand English.
Track:　　A synthesized-sounding voice says the English alphabet A-Z over beat boxing and ends with an exagerrated exhale "aaah" (from the Gospellers' "Iroha"/いろは)

The first part of this section is marked by powerful and dynamic movements as the alphabet is chanted over beat boxing. Around the letter "P," however, it shifts into a demonstration of confusion and frustration: She raises her right hand close to her right ear, then shifts body away from hand at ear. She looks right as the right hand raises again by her right ear and opens and closes like a talking mouth; repeats on the left. Both hands cover her mouth. Then both hands cover her ears and her body contracts at the waist, head down and ears covered. She then stands again, raising her right hand in a fist. On the final exhale sound, Madoka leaps up and lands on the left leg while propelling right arm forward as though throwing something to the ground in frustration.

Madoka:　Why can't I understand the people that are so important to me? / Feelings of frustration. / Step by step.
Track:　　Clear clicking sounds / Rapid clicking sounds followed by the voice "now walk" and the sound of rapid steps (from a beat box track)

Madoka walks in a circle, head down, dropping weight exagerratedly onto alternating feet while alternating hands raise and drop from lowered head. On rapid clicking sounds, she rapidly circles her hands into her centre as though gathering something together. On the voice "now walk", she raises her right hand. On the sound of rapid steps, she moves towards the audience with rapid steps.

Madoka: Why is the world not eaqual (sic)? / Why? / Be free
Track: Various beat boxing sounds ending with a zoom and the soun d of moving air (from an unnamed beat box track)

On the beats, he opens her stance to the audience and raises both arms out to the side, palms up as though questioning or balancing. Her whole body contracts down for two beats and up for a beat followed by two steps back, still with arms raised to sides. On the zoom, she brings her hands together in front of her head and draws a large question mark shape ending in a crouched position, head down. On the sound of moving air, her arms extend out and move in a synchronized flying motion three times.

Part 3: Strength

Figure 15. I realize my own strength   Figure 16. The dance is... full of power here

Madoka: The noise signals the time when I realize my own strength.
Track: *Two clicks followed by three bursts of white noise, a sudden violent crunch sound, and drum beats (all from unnamed free sound effect)*

On the two clicks, both hands are thrown forward and then to ears. Her body contracts rhythmically to bursts of white noise, moving towards a crouched position, hands on ears. On the sudden violent crunch sound, her entire body quickly contracts in a crouched position. On the drum beats, her feet jump out to a wide stance, hands open by sides, head remains lowered. On next beat, feet shuffle forward right left, hands raise to shoulder height, head raises and eyes gaze upward.

Madoka: Power. / A voice says From this time. / I think that the starting point for life is always now, the moment that you're in / The dance is really intense and full of power here. /Heartbeat.

Track: Techno-style energetic pulses with rapid drum beat followed by a rapid rewind sound and four strong drum hits. "From this time" followed by dubstep bass with occasional vocalizations such as "yeah!" (all from Flush's "Losers' Dubstep")

Arms remain open at shoulder height as entire body lowers quickly and then raises slowly with tension in arms as though lifting something large and heavy. Arms come together up to the right, head raised upwards as though receiving. On rapid rewind sound, arms pull repeatedly into centre rapidly as though gathering. On four strong drum beats, her entire body hits four strong poses. As the voice says "from this time," legs jump together and right index finger taps left wrist twice as though indicating a watch. Gathering motions to the left and right. Hands raise above head, body contracts down momentarily and then bursts forward on "yeah!" leaping towards audience on right leg while hands extend upwards and outwards followed by a section including more powerful gathering movements and several intense chest isolations like heart beats.

Madoka: But you can't beat strength with strength.
Track: A beat of silence followed by a voice saying "You ready?" and the beat dropping again in a percussive series of various beats ending with an audible exhale.

Spins and ends with feet together, left hand supports right elbow as right hand covers mouth, forcing head back slightly. Freezes for a beat of silence and the voice "you ready?" As the beat drops, moves back into powerful movements. Finally looks up and to the right as right hand goes to chest. Four chest isolations with hand pulling away from chest on each beat. Rapid arm movements end with right arm covering head while left arm wraps around centre to cover stomache. On audible exhale, entire body contracts.

Part 4: Pain

Figure 17. Coping with ... bullying at school   *Figure 18. I feel I can't go on living*

Madoka: I confront different obstacles and feel lost. / Coping with punishments and bullying at school, verbal abuse, and losing loved ones. / I feel like I can't go on living.

Track: Clicking sounds interspersed with bass hits followed by four gunshot sounds (from unnamed free sound effects)

On clicking sounds, body slowly raises up and left arm joins right arm covering face and seeming to protect head. On bass hit, contracts suddenly downwards as though punched in the stomache. Raises again on more clicks, hands covering face, and contracts again on another bass hit. On the four gunshot sounds, extends right arm and then punches in to centre as though punching self. Repeats left, right, left, contracting on each hit.

Part 5: Love

*Figure 19. I hear the voice
that says "I love you"*
        *Figure 20. I return to my
original nature, with love*

Madoka: Then I hear the voice that says "I love you" and remember that there's love there. / I return to my original nature, with love. / I become myself again and regain hope. / I love you.

Track: I luv U. *Four rhythmic breaths.* I luv U. I luv U. I luv U. I luv U *(altered voice). Bass and drum beats.* I- I- I- I- I. *Bass and drum beats.* / I- I- Lu-Luv U- U- U. *Bass and drum beats.* / I luv- luv- luv- luv U- U- U. Yo! / I luv U- U- U- U (from Dizzie Rascal's "I Luv U")

Stands upright on "I love you", *left hand to forehead. Chest isolations on rhythmic breaths. On second* "I love you," *raises right hand to ear. On third* "I love you," *raises left hand to ear. As bass drops, body rolls and hands release. Various sharp moves continue, including pointing to and popping her chest on* "I," *searching motions on* "luv," *and pointing to her audience and smiling on* "U." *On final* "I luv U- U- U- U," *right hand forms half heart on* "I", *left hand forms half hears on* "luv," *and the two come together on* "U." *Heart raises and lowers on repeated* "U-U" *and breaks apart on final* "U" *as Madoka takes two steps back on left and right.*

Part 6: Expression

Figure 21. Some things can't be put into words   *Figure 22. Drawing*

Madoka: Afterwards, I hold my hand over my mouth like I'm beatboxing to show that some things can't be put into words. / Notice / Dancing. / Recorders, / pianos, music. / Drawing. /You can expres yourself without words.

Track: *Silence followed by* "Uh. Uh. Let's go, Uh let's go let's go. Uh let's go" followed by two percussive hits. (source unclear) *Then beat boxing interpersed with two vocalized* "doo doo doo doo" *sections and one vocalized* "oooooooop" (from Justin Timberlake)

Looks up on first "uh". Gestures both arms in rapping motions to the rhythm of the words. On two percussive hits, right arm grasps bottom of shirt and airs out twice. As the beatboxing begins, moves percussively with weight shifts before standing upright, hands covering mouth. More weight shifts before both arms raise and then slowly descend on exhale. After rapid hand motions, her right hand touches her right shoulder and looks right as though noticing something there. Steps right left right with body rolls accentuated by hands rising and falling representing dancing. Feet pause and hands go to mouth miming a recorder on "doo-doo-doo-doo". Repeats body roll motions before feet pause and hands extend forward miming a piano on "doo-doo-doo-doo". Repeats the searching motion from earlier in the dance. On "oooooop", right hand draws heart shape in air as weight falls to the right in two steps ending in a contracted position with head down. Rapid arm movements and Madoka stands facing front.

Part 7: Be the Change

Figure 23. I let go of all pretenses   *Figure 24. Be the change*

Madoka: At the end, I let go of all pretenses and open myself to change. / Be the change.

Track: "Be the change- change- change" (Madoka's recorded and altered voice)

Raises left hand to face as though holding a mask. On the first "change", takes a lunging step to the right, leaving hand extended to the left as though removing a mask. On the second "change", looks down to the right. On the third "change", drops to the ground.

The final slide after the dance is white writing over black: "This is everything I've got."

THE CONVERSATION

Madoka is sitting crossed-legged on the floor in a dance studio where she has been teaching me "L for Love" and practicing a new dance. Her right rests across her right knee and her left hand rests on the left side of her head pensively as we talk about her creative process, which I have just summarized as "the meaning comes first, then the movement and then the sound". I ask her where in the process words come, and she says that words are "optional". This leads to a discussion of living in a verbal-centric world. I then ask about school.

Kim: How about school?

Madoka: School? *Small smile. /… /* I hate it. *Leans back and laughs.*

Kim: [I know, but heh heh why? Because of words or (0.5) no?

Madoka: *[Sits back up. L hand brushes hair from face and briefly to chin. Hands come together, elbows resting on knees. M. Sways slightly L and R as hands fidget. Head looks R.* Well. School (1.0) likes everyone to be the same. *(Hands open)*

Kim: I see.

Madoka: *Only Japan? (Hands gesture up and drop)* I don't know but- *hands gesture in, out, down and around.* Well. If you are different from everyone *(hands as though holding a ball)*, you get bullied *(L thumb in)* or you get discriminated against *(L index finger in). Looks R.* But when you get bullied, *(L hand sweeps out and to chest)* if you can't say it in words, *(L hand to lap, R hand opens and closes like mouth at chest aimed up. Ends closed)* inside you *(R hand touches chest)* there is just sadness, *(R hand cuts down twice)* and there is no choice but to bear it. *(R hand closes in a fist)*

Kim: [M.

Madoka: *[Nods slightly, fist still at chest.* But the teachers don't notice anything, they don't do anything *(R thumb opens and returns to fist at chest). R thumb taps chest.* Just (1.0). *Glances L. Nods. Slight shrug R. Smiles.* There is no meaning. Heh. *R hand drops to lap. Smile fades.*

Kim: M.

Madoka: There was no meaning. (*Glances R, up, straight*)

Kim: M.

Madoka: *Nods twice. °Nods twice° Um. Glances R. Heart- About a person's heart (Hands cycle forward.) Hands fold. Eyes glance down. There is no thinking.*

"INSTRUCTIONS FOR A BAD DAY": INSTRUCTIONAL INSPIRATION

The voices of these young dancers are clear. Through their embodied literacy and the words they found in conversation around these danced works, Josh and Madoka communicated to me the pains and pressures of their emotional journeys touched by bullying. They simultaneously demonstrated that the power of their chosen art to not only express these emotions, but also to transform their positioning in the field of their peers. Both constructed their identities as change-makers overcoming obstacles to express their true selves, and Josh shifted his identity to victor, not victim, while Madoka created her identity as "Dance Messenger Madoka," a survivor of high school pain now connecting with a global network of dance artists. Their voices call for educational change: for schools where "emotions are ... talked about" (Josh) and there is thinking "about a person's heart" (Madoka). As an educator and researcher, I understood the need and the promise of projects that allow youth to express their pain in empathetic connection with their peers. On Anti-bullying Day (February 28th, 2012), Canadian poet Shane Koyczan released a new poem: "Instructions for a Bad Day." This was a piece written to help youth find the strength to make it through difficult days. At Boogaloo Academy, I worked with the *Heart Mind Body Collective*, including Josh, to create a piece for the Vancouver Biennale's art education project. When I first played the poem for the dancers, I had them lie down and close their eyes. After that first listen, we sat in a circle and each dancer shared their personal connection to the words they had heard. With the ground rules that they would not be interrupted and that what they said would not be repeated outside the room, many cried as they shared stories of bullying, depression, fear, anger, and pain. It became clear that everyone had a story. Through the hugs that followed the sharing, I could feel a sense of depth and togetherness.

The next step was for each dancer to select the lines that they most connected to, emotionally and physically. They did this first by listening to the poem several times as they walked and freestyled in the space. Then they wrote their name on a sticky-note and placed it beside the lines they were drawn to. Through open discussion, the dancers reached a consensus on who would dance which line by balancing their own expressive needs (dancing the line they most liked) with the needs of the piece (ensuring that all lines were covered). In practice sessions, I offered the group an overall vision for the piece and a simple common piece of choreography. They begin frozen like the Walking Figure statues they are interpreting with rust-colored cloaks wrapped tightly around them. As the music begins, they all begin walking in straight lines, making 90 degree turns. They are instructed to stare directly ahead, avoid eye-contact, and to walk as though they were headed to a meeting. Then, when their chosen line is spoken, they come to the front of the stage area, remove their cloak—revealing the pink t-shirts (the youth symbol of the fight against bullying) with one chosen word or phrase from their poem taped on with black electric tape, and interpret their line with their own choreography. At the conclusion of their section, they walk to the back of the stage area and begin a simple 8-bar piece of my own contemporary choreography repeated until the end of the piece. By the end of the piece, all of the dancers were wearing pink shirts and dancing movements reflecting peace, calm, openness, and freedom in unison. Finally, they took eight steps forward, elbows at their waist and palms open as though carrying something. On the words "be calm," they stretched closed fists toward the audience. On "open each palm slowly now," they released first their right and then their left fist, allowing their hands to float down to a resting position at their sides. On "let go," they raised their open palms and outstretched arms to the audience as a gesture of offering.

CONCLUSIONS AND PEDAGOGICAL IMPLICATIONS

Josh Ongcol's "O for Overcoming", Madoka Suzuki's "L for Love", and the Heart Mind Body Collective's "Instructions for a Bad Day" are three examples of young dancers addressing the pain of bullying, reaching out for empathy, and transforming their worlds. They are bold statements written in music, movements, and words that take the pain of past experiences and use it to paint a powerful expression in the present and project a future of promise and passion. Through his honesty and expression, Josh sparked the flame of inspiration in Madoka to dance her own message. This flame grew to the roaring fire of hope that is Heart Mind Body's *Instructions for a Bad Day*. Since the first performance for the Vancouver Biennale, the piece has been performed multiple times, most recently as the opening act for Shane Koyczan and at a local TEDx youth conference. Madoka joined the group for these latter two performances, meeting Josh and bringing this story of international inspiration and hope full-circle.

It is my hope as an educator and arts advocate that these pieces reach as wide of an audience as possible. Just as Madoka was inspired to create "L for Love" through viewing Josh performing and discussing "O for Overcoming", there are young dancers everywhere looking for that message of hope and inspiration to speak their own voice and create their own statement. Students can be offered the opportunity to view and respond to the videos here in dance, words, art, music, or a combination therein. They could create their own video and upload it onto the web to inspire youth with their own stories of overcoming and inspiration. The process described above for the creation of Instructions for a Bad Day may inspire other educators to engage their students in the creation of similar work. The key elements can be summarized as an inspirational stimulus (a poem, song, or perhaps one of the videos mentioned), an atmosphere of open sharing and trust, and the freedom and ownership of expressing self-selected sections. Creating any opportunity for embodied expression can open the door for our students to find the dancer within themselves and to express the stories and emotions that they cannot necessarily put into words. Dance is a powerful medium to address bullying because it goes beyond words to express the emotions that are at the heart of the effects of abuse of unequal power relations. If given the opportunity to move, our students have the power to move others and to move our learning communities beyond bullying to a place of empathetic connection, embodied inspiration, and transformative expression.

VIDEO LINKS

"O for Overcoming": https://vimeo.com/85000420 (password: overcoming)
"L for Love": https://vimeo.com/85202826 (password: love)
"Instructions for a Bad Day": http://www.youtube.com/watch?v=xRLQ54WNGaU (original); http://www.youtube.com/watch?v=isy58pZvJiQ (with introduction)

Other Related Inspirational Video Links (chosen by Josh and Madoka)
"With a Piece of Chalk": http://www.youtube.com/watch?v=mBZAFJ-Q6Mw A young boy experiencing bullying and abuse discovers dance as a way to change his situation.
"If You are in a Shell": http://www.youtube.com/watch?v=elILetNPyr4 Harry Shum Jr. choreographed this piece to a voice over about being a shell in high school and finding the way out through dance and drama.

TRANSCRIPTION CONVENTIONS

steps right	non-linguistic mode (gesture or sound)
()	overlaps with previous utterance
[	two speakers' talk or gestures overlaps at this point
=	no interval between turns ('latching')
?	interrogative intonation
(2.0)	pause (silence and/or stillness) timed in seconds
(.)	small untimed pause
awa::y	prolonged syllable, sound, or movement
why	emphasis or stressed word or syllable or gesture
REALLY	word/gesture noticeably stronger than surrounding talk/gestures
°yes°	word/gesture noticeably softer than surrounding talk/gestures
<I have to>	words/gestures noticeably faster than surrounding talk/gestures
heh heh	laughter syllables
R	right
L	left

K. MEREDITH

REFERENCES

Bourdieu, P., & Thompson, J. B. (1991). *Language and symbolic power*. Cambridge, MA: Harvard University Press.

Cummins, J. (2009). Transformative multiliteracies pedagogy: School-based strategies for closing the achievement gap. *Multiple Voices for Ethnically Diverse Exceptional Learners, 11*(2), 1–19.

Gee, J. P. (2011b). *An introduction to discourse analysis: Theory and method*. London, England: Taylor & Francis.

Geertz, C. (1988). *Works and lives: The anthropologist as author*. Stanford, CA: Stanford University Press.

Georgakopoulou, A. (2007). *Small stories, interaction and identities*. Amsterdam, The Netherlands/ Philadelphia, PA: John Benjamin's Publishing.

New London Group. (2000). A pedagogy of multiliteracies: Designing social futures. In B. Cope & M. Kalantzis (Eds.), *Multiliteracies: Learning and the design of social futures* (pp. 9–37). London, England: Routledge.

Norton, B. (2000). *Identity and language learning: gender, ethnicity and educational change*. Harlow, England & New York: Longman.

Norton, B., & Toohey, K. (Eds.). (2004). *Critical pedagogies and language learning*. Cambridge, UK: Cambridge University Press.

Stein, P. (2008). *Multimodal pedagogies in diverse classrooms: Representations, rights and resources*. New York, NY: Routledge.

Talmy, S. (2010). Qualitative interviews in applied linguistics: From research instrument to social practice. *Annual Review of Applied Linguistics, 30*, 128–148.

RYAN SCHOENFELD AND JEFF DINSE

28. DARE GREATLY TO ENHANCE YOUR SCHOOL'S CLIMATE THROUGH ACCEPTANCE, RELATIONAL TRUST, AND CREATING A SENSE OF BELONGING

INTRODUCTION

The chapter submission will include the context of the work that had a significant impact at a western New York junior high school. Greater depth and specificity will be added to the chapter, as pragmatic strategies and approaches to enhance school climate in any school are expanded.

SETTING THE CONTEXT

The proposed chapter is a pragmatic approach to enhancing the culture and climate of a school through the implementation of a program aimed at celebrating the diversity and uniqueness of the school population (students, staff, administration, and community). I have been working as an educator in the small-city school district of Lockport, New York for the past twenty years. The Lockport City School District has become more diverse over time. It currently has just over 5,000 students: 54% in poverty, 24% minority, 13% students with disabilities, along with a steady increase of English language learners. I was the North Park Middle School assistant principal for three years in the early 2000s. Eleven years later I returned as principal. The building transitioned to a junior high school, serving almost 800 seventh and eighth graders. The school's reputation has historically been depicted as a tough school, on the outskirts of lower town, with many student behavioral issues.

At our first faculty meeting, I dared greatly by sharing personal information and being brutally honest. I started by presenting my complete biography, so the staff would gain a better sense of who I am and why I have a fire in my belly as a leader. We laughed a bit as I shared childhood pictures, shed a couple of tears while informing them of the tragic loss of a close friend, Stephen Mulderry, on 9/11. I also told them of my dad's near-death experience just last year. I was present as he battled the West Nile virus, in a foreign country, at the age of 72. After sharing my biography I went on to explain what people said when they learned I was going to be the new principal at North Park. Many sighed and said things like, "Oh, how do you feel about that?" It was almost like they were expressing their condolences.

C. Boske & A. Osanloo (Eds.), Students, Teachers, and Leaders Addressing Bullying in Schools, 189–192.

Then I firmly explained to the staff that my focus was to enhance the culture and climate of our school, improve our reputation in the community, and promote an inclusive culture that provided all students an opportunity to participate in a great educational experience. After the meeting I returned to my office and before noon I received supportive emails from staff members I barely knew. The first was from social studies teacher Jeff Dinse. The subject line was "Great Start." He stated that his first impression was that I hit it out of the park.

During the first full week of school I was asked to join a social studies department meeting. That meeting began the grassroots effort of enhancing the North Park culture and climate. Dinse, a dedicated and highly creative educator, suggested a school-wide video of students and staff to the backdrop of Miranda Lambert's song "All Kinds of Kinds." Jeff's technological and creative prowess, along with his commitment to produce a high quality video within a couple of days, paid off. The video went viral on YouTube and was highlighted on all major western New York news stations. To view, go to www.allkindsofkinds.org/stopbullyingvideo and access "Part 1: Introduction." The work was presented at Lockport's board of education meeting and screened at the Buffalo Movie and Video Makers club.

BEYOND THE VIDEO

The first expansion of the work was to increase involvement from the approximately 70 students and staff in the initial video to our entire learning community. We created a picture path in the hallways in an effort to include all North Park students and staff. Each person held a sign with a word or words that best described their kind then their picture was taken, printed out, and displayed. Within a couple of weeks, a picture path of over 700 pictures extended throughout our school. Parents and community members added their pictures. The path strengthened "relational trust" among members of our learning community (Day, 2009). Soon after a 29- minute, five-part "Stop Bullying" video and instructional downloads were posted to our new website (see www.allkindsofkinds.org) in an effort to share our work with other educators. As attention and notoriety from the viral video was attained, along with observing the positive impact in our building, Jeff and I recognized that it was the most profound thing that we had ever done in all of our years in education. Our efforts to expand this work are ongoing. We are steadfast in creating an opportunity for many other schools and organizations to benefit from this type of work.

IMPACT OF THE "ALL KINDS OF KINDS" WORK

During the first 10 weeks of school, the learning environment and public perception of North Park improved exponentially. The determination to bring diversity issues from the periphery to the mainstream dented the current habitual modes of practice (Gudykunst, 2003). The positive change was palpable. During the first half of the school year, student discipline referrals decreased dramatically: in-school suspensions were down from 122 to 88, and out-of-school suspensions dropped from 96 to 21. There were almost half as many suspensions this year. Moreover, superintendent hearings, when a student is suspended for more than five days, went from 12 to zero. Our staff attendance this year was 24% better. In general, the student attendance rate at North Park is always good, around 95%. There was a peak in attendance during the viral video period and remained commensurate with past years. Recently, students and staff were asked to give testimonials about the "All Kinds of Kids" work and the feedback was overwhelmingly positive.

LITERATURE

Having recently completed my third graduate level degree, it was apparent to me that building positive relationships within educational institutions and the workplace are paramount. The original and subsequent "All Kinds of Kinds" work is supported through scholarly literature.

The "All Kinds of Kinds" work carried out at North Park was driven by the concept of "daring greatly" (Brown, 2012). Seventh-grade social studies students were exposed to the concept of "daring greatly to be the kind that you are, and to face your fears and challenges." This instructional approach was later made into a 12-minute instructional video, "Part 4," for other educators to utilize as a powerful social emotional learning (SEL) and anti-bullying lesson.

Choice Theory's seven caring habits—supporting, encouraging, listening, accepting, trusting, respecting, and negotiating differences—are all firmly represented in the "All Kinds of Kinds" work (Glasser, 1998). An internal profile for each student was obtained via a student survey given during health classes (Erwin, 2012). We are driven by our genes to satisfy five basic needs: survival, love and belonging, power, freedom, and fun. Through this activity students and staff were able to stretch the initial "what kind are you?" to a deeper understanding of themselves and how to appropriately meet their highest basic needs at school and home. The survey was developed as a pragmatic approach to self-assessment, through the ranking of word clusters in each of the five basic need categories. Additional activities are currently being implemented within health classes to broaden this learning opportunity.

Intentionally, the focus on improving the culture and climate took precedent over academics at North Park. Researchers found that school principals matter to school achievement, accounting for almost five percent of overall variation in pupil scores (Leithwood & Riehl, 2003). A meta-analysis of 317 SEL studies yielded an average of 11–17 percentile points (Erwin, 2010). Moreover, a study of levels of trust within 200 Chicago public schools revealed that among 100 schools that found success academically—eight percent in reading and 20 percent in math—had relational trust, whereas the 100 schools that did not have relational trust had virtually no chance of improving either reading or math (Bryk & Schneider, 2003, p. 43).

REFERENCES

Brown, B. (2012). *Daring greatly: How the courage to be vulnerable transforms the way we live, love, parent, and lead*. New York, NY: Gotham Books.
Bryk, A., & Schneider, B. (2003). Trust in schools: A core resource for school reform. *Educational Leadership*, 40–44.
Day, C. (2009). Building and sustaining successful principalship in England: The importance of trust. *Journal of Educational Administration, 47*(6), 765–780.
Erwin, J. (2010). *Inspiring the best in students: Improving academics and character through social-emotional learning*. Alexandria, VA: ASCD.
Glasser, W. (1998). *Choice theory: A new psychology of personal freedom*. New York, NY: Harper Collins Publishers.
Gray, S., & Streshly, W. (2008). *From good schools to great schools: What their principals do well*. Thousand Oaks, CA: Corwin Press.
Gudykunst, W. (2003). *Cross-cultural and intercultural communication*. Thousand Oaks, CA: Sage Publications.
Johnson, L. (2006). Making her community a better place to live: Culturally responsive urban school leadership in historic context. *Leadership and Policy in Schools, 5*, 19–36.
Johnson, L. (2007). Rethinking successful school leadership in challenging U.S. schools: Culturally responsive practices in school-community relationships. *International Studies in Educational Administration, 35*(3), 49–57.
Leithwood, K., & Riehl, C. (2005). What we know about successful school leadership. In W. Firestone & C. Riehl (Eds.), *A new agenda: Directions for research on educational leadership* (pp. 22–47). New York, NY: Teachers College Press.

AMANDA HUDNALL

29. THE QUIET ROAR

Bullying within our schools is an issue, that if not acknowledged, could lead to disastrous outcomes for young people. My experience with regards to bullying began as a student and has evolved, but is still present in my function as a teacher. As a child, I was different. I was not a typical "tomboy" in the sense of dress or mannerisms, but I preferred playing with GI Joe figures as opposed to Barbies, and my friends were always male. As an adolescent, I spent my time mowing lawns and fishing rather than hanging out at the mall or spending time on the telephone.

My friends have always been primarily male throughout all phases of life. This presented me with challenges as a secondary student. Female students could not understand how or why I was consistently "hanging out with the boys" rather than the other girls. As a result, I was not accepted by the girls in my age group at all. I was labeled a "whore" five years prior to losing my virginity. I was larger than most, so the nickname assigned to me by other students was 'cottage cheese', among other more vulgar names. I ate my lunch alone in the bleachers above the gym so that I did not have to endure the taunts of the other girls in the cafeteria. Some days my one female friend Lola would sit with me there, and I recall her and I sharing a sense of isolation within the school.

Looking back, I realize this feeling of isolation was as much perpetuated by the adults in the school as it was by the students. The "popular" kids in my high school were a very small and elite group characterized by a higher socioeconomic status than most and a great pride in material objects such as designer label clothing and shoes. These were the same students who were favored by almost every teacher, and placed on pedestals by our principals and community members active within the school. As a result, I was able to achieve academically at school, but I did so in a quiet manner with very little engagement, and was rarely acknowledged or recognized by the staff at the school.

The worst I have ever felt about myself was during my 9th and 10th grade years of high school. The other girls had decided at this point to refer to me as a particularly vulgar name and had constructed an entirely false story to go along with it. Our teachers had also heard this story, and did nothing to acknowledge that the popular girls were doing anything wrong when they referred to me in class by the name, as the name itself was a word that had both harmless and vulgar meaning depending on its context. I went from being an "A student" to being an "A student" who despised

C. Boske & A. Osanloo (Eds.), Students, Teachers, and Leaders Addressing Bullying in Schools, 193–197.
© *2015 Sense Publishers. All rights reserved.*

not only going to school, but individually despised the feeling I experienced upon entering each individual classroom.

Luckily, there was one teacher, a Mrs. Fearn from Spain, who decided that I was a student worthy of something more than was recognized. She invited me to join her in teaching kindergarten students from Guatemala English each afternoon after school. Through this experience, I not only acquired a functional knowledge of the Spanish language that serves me well to this day, but I was also able to discover an alternative pathway through the Post-Secondary Education Program that allowed me to exit the small town high school two years ahead of schedule and graduate with enough college credit to be considered a sophomore in my undergraduate program at Kent State University.

My recollections of the reactions of adults in these types of situations are negligible outside of the subtle reinforcement that occurred through their refusal to address the offenders. I recall also the realization that in all cases it was a mistake to share the challenges I was facing with the teachers that I knew at the time. Now, more than twenty years later, I still recall the additional hurt I felt when the teachers in many cases acted as if it were my fault that I had done something to provoke the torment and harassment from the other girls. I do not recall one incident where an adult was supportive or took any action to improve the situation. As a result of this, I feel that now as a teacher I am especially cognizant of when this occurs among my students. Students do not hide their actions in many cases, because we have existed in a society that says "kids will be kids" or "girls are just mean.". These are excuses that allow adults to dismiss the responsibility that they have to the children they serve.

I teach secondary level science courses at Telle Workman High School in the Northeastern United States. Looking back now, after seven years as a high school physics teacher, I am able to see very clearly that there is a major responsibility attached to becoming an educator that is not taught in teacher preparation programs, nor openly discussed in my current professional setting. Teachers are charged with ensuring the intellectual growth of their students. This mandates that teachers be open to all students and unwilling to pass judgment on them based on the opinions of others. This means that teachers not only have an obligation to care about their students as people, but also to be willing to act accordingly in all situations.

As a teacher and an adult, I believe adults within our schools are ultimately responsible for not only the safety, but the happiness and welfare of all children whom we serve while they are under our care at school. I also believe that the primary influence on school protocol should be the perspectives of the children attending. I would even go as far as to say that in many cases, the voices of the children should be the ONLY ones we assign great value to.

Our students in this country are mandated to attend primary and secondary educational facilities. As such, adults should be cognizant of the fact that while they are in school, children have an innate right to sense that they are secure and cared for. Parents in general certainly assume this to be true. Unfortunately, this is not representative of the reality that children face daily while in school. Both of these concepts require that the adults whom are present have a fundamental appreciation for students, regardless of their age group. Teachers are tested in both content and pedagogy prior to becoming certified to teach. Why is there not an ethical component to this testing? While it seems outrageous to say so, there exists a need in teacher preparation programs to analyze simple concepts such as "Is the candidate kind?", "Does the candidate demonstrate patience and compassion with young people?", and "Does the candidate display racist tendencies or attitudes?"

While I would suspect there would be much controversy surrounding the elimination of teacher candidates based on the analysis of these questions, the end result would be that students overall would be treated much better at school. I define 'much better' as to mean that they would not be intimidated or bullied by their teachers, they would feel a sense of trust and respect with all teachers, and that they would not be further victimized or marginalized due to the attitudes and actions of their teachers. It is unfortunate, but I can testify to the fact that students are not treated in this manner in a lot of cases. I have worked with phenomenal teachers who were compassionate and kind to students on a regular basis as well as strong content teachers. However, I have also worked with teachers who seem to truly despise teenagers, those who regularly curse at students, those who are obvious racists and make no attempt to hide that fact, and those who even articulate to children that they "are not here for the students, they are here for their paycheck." In each of the aforementioned cases, children were hurt and felt a sense of isolation at school as a result.

I tend to be the teacher who hears these types of reports in our school, as the children come to me when they are upset. What does a classroom teacher do when they have no authority to question other teachers? I have supported the child in every scenario, but there are limits to the type of support that an individual teacher can offer. I cannot force people to be kind, nor confront the racism that I see in others publicly within my professional environment. What results is that children are mistreated at school, and the institution itself reinforces this with policies that enforce the idea that "the teacher is always right." The teacher is NOT always right. There is no need for children to be subjected to inappropriate treatment in a compulsory system of education. Additionally, student learning is severely and negatively affected when this occurs. How is a child to learn from someone whom they know does not respect them as a human being? And if the student is able to conform enough to at least be successful in terms of their grade, then I would question how much additional, higher level learning would have been possible in a supportive environment. Our students are already graduating high school with a level of education that requires remedial courses to be taken upon entry into undergraduate university programs. How much of this could be eliminated if we were able to include those three simple questions in the requirements for teacher licensure?

Another aspect to this discussion is centered on the fact that so much of the bullying, done by both children and adults, stems from race. The demographic data now available clearly suggests that within a very short time, those who identify as Caucasian will be the racial minority in our country. Knowing the current racial minority population is the emerging majority is central to the field of education, especially if the education that is provided in this country is to remain relevant. Culturally responsive teaching practices urges children be valued as individual resources for knowledge bases be included in the curriculum and policies within American schools.

There exists a stark contrast in this philosophy and the general philosophy that exists in our schools currently. In general, it seems that current practitioners view children through the lens of a deficit model, seeing them as being in school to simply receive information, rather than as holding information of value themselves, or as contributors to what takes place in the classroom. Our minority student populations, those who will soon outnumber the white, middle to upper class students, are those whose needs we must strive to accommodate the most, in the hope that our educational system will evolve into one that is more student-centered, and acknowledging of the fact that we must move beyond the illogical practices of the past. Racism is an example of one of these practices.

The literature that is available, and promoted through Global Education networks, states that relative to other nations in the world, American students are graduating very poorly prepared for the predicted job market of the 21st century. This job market is predicted to be primarily digital in nature, and will require a whole new set of skills from our students if they are to be competitive. They are going to compete and collaborate with individuals from diverse regions of the world, thus requiring not only enhanced technological capabilities, but also the ability to communicate effectively across cultures, investigate and analyze the world they live in and possess both the ability and initiative to formulate and facilitate action plans that will address the needs of the future. These are not skills currently taught as part of our curriculum. However, at the same time, they are skills that can be incorporated into any content area curriculum and pedagogy, simply through the inclusion of a global perspective into content, and an enhancement of the expectations and products placed on children in our classrooms.

At the heart of all of this is the acceptance of ALL children. We, as educators, must move beyond the willingness to place judgments on children based on race, socioeconomic class, gender, sexual orientation or any of the other qualifiers prevalent in today's system. The oppression that has taken place throughout the history of our country has been consistent enough to have now become buried in the institutional protocol not only in education. But in other aspects of society such as housing, legislation and the correctional system just to name a few. Our task now is to recognize this systematic and institutionalized bias and act to change it. Most importantly, however, we have a responsibility to recognize our own bias, and those being practiced in our educational protocol. This is the arena we have the most access to as educators, therefore this is where we can affect the greatest change.

I am of the position that what will result will be truly revolutionary in terms of the experience and preparation provided to the youth in our country. However, teachers must act first. We must ourselves become culturally proficient, and develop the technology skills needed to teach our students. At this point, this requires proactive measures on the part of teachers. There are various grant programs funded both privately and through our federal government that support such efforts. There are university programs focused on global education and cultural knowledge, and there is very little encouragement and seemingly little promotion of these programs in my experience. However, this does not mean that teachers cannot accomplish their goals for themselves, we simply must seek out initiatives and programs aimed at common themes, and be proactive in our pursuits of them. If these concepts were enacted in our schools, as one day I hope they will, there would be no issue of bullying in our schools in my opinion. If adults and youth alike truly respected the diversity that exists among human beings, there would not be racial tensions in schools, or students not wanting to attend classes due to the treatment they receive while in the facility. I would challenge every educator who reads this: Are you ready for the future in your classroom or school? Are you prepared to help eliminate the inequities that we sometimes unknowingly reinforce within our schools? What will YOU do about it?

LAURA MERRY AND JOANNA ROYCE-DAVIS

30. LOOKING TO THE FUTURE – EXPLORING THE NEED TO ADDRESS BULLYING IN HIGHER EDUCATION

Transitioning from high school to college life may be more difficult for some students than others, with many first year college students withdrawing before completing their degree (Parker, Summerfeldt, Hogan, & Majeski, 2003). Social integration or a sense of belonging and the related friendships that college students experience in their first year of college may have a major impact on their adjustment and become an important factor in finishing their first year (Kuh, Kinzie, Buckley, Bridges, & Hayek, 2006; Pittman & Richmond, 2008). Achieving an understanding of how this issue is situated alongside the other challenges that students experience in persisting through their degree programs has served as the foundation for much of the research on student success, including the early work conducted by Tinto (1999).

Tinto's work has continued to resonate and be affirmed by more recent studies that account for the role of campus climate (Reason, 2013; Tinto, 2006, 2007), social and cultural capital (Yosso, 2005), and a sense of connection and belonging (Kuh et al., 2006) as critical to the persistence of students from both majority groups and social identities that are historically underrepresented in higher education. The work of Astin (1993) that documents the role of involvement in student success is also relevant for considering factors that may be critical to student outcomes. Research findings to date have taught us that colleges and universities can contribute to student success by designing learning experiences and support structures to: (1) encourage student commitment and engagement; (2) develop expectations of students while also providing them with the tools necessary to navigate the resources of a given campus culture; (3) support students in ways that are culturally relevant and that intentionally support persistence; (4) provide feedback through proactive advising and progress mapping; (5) encourage student involvement both in and outside of the classroom; and (6) promote student learning and the pursuit of excellence overall (Reason, 2013; Tinto, 1999).

As we consider the linkage between support and involvement with student success, it is also important to understand that some students may have prior negative experiences that prevent their involvement and connectedness in school. Research to date has also suggested that self-esteem may be a major factor in student success, as the level of an individual's self-esteem will often dictate whether they are able to reach out to develop the relationships with others that ultimately facilitate

C. Boske & A. Osanloo (Eds.), Students, Teachers, and Leaders Addressing Bullying in Schools, 199–217.

involvement (Smokowski & Kopasz, 2005). A correlation between the levels of self-esteem an individual has and their reported happiness also exists. Individuals who report low self-esteem are more likely to have feelings of insecurity and depression, whereas individuals who are described as having high self-esteem are often more secure and are more likely to develop strong relationships with others (Baumeister, Campbell, Kreuger, & Vohs, 2003).

With a documented relationship between self-esteem and student success existing, understanding what inhibitors to an individual's self-esteem might look like can assist educators in identifying students who may be at risk allowing these educators to respond accordingly. A sense of belonging at all ages is linked to academic success where positive social acceptance contributes to increasing positive feelings about self and enhances self-efficacy. The self-confidence that is often the extension of healthy self-esteem also assists students to learn how to cope in difficult situations and may also promote engagement in social activities (Pittman & Richmond, 2008).

INTRODUCTION TO BULLYING

As we seek to understand how universities can improve student success, we need to simultaneously understand what might be inhibiting some students from feeling a sense of belonging and initiating involvement with their universities. As a part of this examination, colleges and universities need to consider what factors may disrupt this relationship development process. In the K-12 environment, bullying is regarded as a serious personal, social and educational problem affecting many students each day as they pursue their education (Ahmed & Braithwaite, 2004). In contrast, little visible discussion amongst universities with regard to the existence of bullying on college campuses and the role it may have in affecting student success has taken place. This lack of attention to bullying may be due to college administrators being reluctant to address an issue that may be viewed as counterproductive to their marketing strategies and recruitment of students; may create legal exposure; or may be difficult to address effectively (Coleyshaw, 2010).

Research on the frequency and experience of bullying has focused primarily on the K-12 setting, with little attention paid to bullying in the higher education arena. Bullying on K-12 campuses is seen as an aggressive and unprovoked behavior that is inflicted on individuals who are presumed to be weak (Whitted & Dupper, 2005). Statistics on bullying gathered by DoSomething.org (2013) indicate that in the course of a year, approximately 3.2 million students are victims of bullying, that an estimated 160,000 teens will miss school to avoid being bullied and that bullying has been linked to approximately 75% of school-shooting incidents. This report also indicated that one out of every ten students are at risk of dropping out school as the result of being victims of bullying, with a number of victims of bullying also becoming victims of suicide. Further, in a study conducted on bullying in U.S. Schools compiled by Limber, Olweus, and Luxenberg (2013) in conjunction with the Hazelden Foundation, it was documented that the highest prevalence of bullying occurred in the third and fourth grades. These students reported being victims of bullying two or three times a month, with many of them reporting feeling afraid of being bullied again.

While bullying continues to be an issue affecting many students at K-12 campuses across the U.S., the research and attention paid to bullying in K-12 environments has resulted in schools discovering the critical importance of addressing the issue and developing campus-wide anti-bullying strategies and policies that are implemented widely and systemically assessed (Smith, Ananiadou, & Cowie, 2003). In addition, research has shown that schools that have anti-bullying policies in place and show that they are serious about containing and controlling bullying, are more likely to be successful places for students to learn (Ahmed & Braithwaite, 2004).

Students continuing from high school to college may be entering campus environments where discussions regarding the impact and existence of bullying are not occurring. This lack of recognition by universities may be cause for concern for many incoming freshman who may have had experience with bullying during their K-12 educational experience. The following discussion intends to highlight that bullying is, at a minimum, a K-16 issue and one that deserves additional attention, as it likely is one of the invisible forces getting in the way of the shared goal of student success. It is not surprising that students who were bullied in K-12 tend to be a victim of bullying in college (Chapell, Hasselman, Kitchin, Lomon, MacIver, & Sarullo, 2006). As such, bullying is an issue that bridges both K-12 and higher education learning contexts and one that compels educators in both settings to become more knowledgeable and more fully equipped to address the issue. As a starting point, college campuses can learn a vital lesson from K-12 educators by understanding the impact that bullying has on students and its impact on their success and, later, their college experience.

LESSONS LEARNED FROM K-12 RESEARCH ON BULLYING

The research on bullying in the K-12 context has examined the effects of bullying on students and schools, as well as the most effective methods to address bullying. Likewise, prior studies (Good, McIntosh, & Gietz, 2011; Osterman, 2013; Dary & Pickeral, 2013; Adams, Lawrence, & Schenck, 2008) have focused on the role of school climate with student success, the lasting effects bullying can have on victims, bullying as a potential indicator for school violence, and the legal liability facing schools that do not address bullying. Together, findings reinforce the urgency of responding to bullying as a direct challenge to student well-being and student success.

School Climate and Student Success

High rates of bullying can have a negative impact on a school's climate, creating an environment of fear not only for the victim, but also for all of the students on the campus. A school climate that is affected by fear potentially disrupts academic and social learning outcomes for all students (Good, McIntosh, & Gietz, 2011). In turn, feelings of connectedness are a key dimension and predictor of student persistence and are aligned with an individual's sense of being accepted by peers and teachers (Osterman, 2000).

The role of school climate should be to provide a context for, expectations of, and structures to promote healthy, positive and connected relationships for each member of the campus and is seen as the most effective way to address bullying (Dary & Pickeral, 2013). Cohen, McCabe, Michelli, and Pickeral (2009) speak to the importance of communicating expectations for participation in campus community and with their findings, that school climate plays a major role in the development, learning and success of all students because it is one medium for communicating the types of behaviors that are acceptable on campus. Schools with positive environments are those that consistently and deliberately support students in being co-leaders and co-learners (Dary & Pickeral, 2013), which ultimately promotes student success as it challenges students to directly contribute to the development and maintenance of an inclusive, collaborative learning community where all learners are valued. These environments also empower students to name issues and be taken seriously and to co-craft solutions with invested educators.

Lasting Effects of Bullying

Groundbreaking research on bullying in K-12 sector conducted by Olweus (1993) brought attention to the power differences between a bully and victim, along with the lasting impact that experiences of bullying can have on a victim's future social interactions. This finding is echoed in findings reported by Adams, Lawrence, & Schenck (2008) who explored the continuation of bullying from K-12 to college and concluded that children who were bullied in middle and high school are more likely to experience a continuous effect of bullying that will follow them from one environment to the next. The authors postulate that these effects might ultimately be the contributing factor for students whom have experienced prior bullying that pushes them eventually to withdraw from college.

Some effects of bullying that follow victims from high school into college may include issues with feeling safe on campus, social isolation, abuse, alienation, and loneliness (Adams & Lawrence, 2011). All of these influences can have a major impact on students' overall success in the college environment. In particular, feelings of loneliness and experiences of isolation can impact their ability to develop the type of relationships that are crucial to developing a sense of belonging and connectedness (Adams & Lawrence, 2011).

More recent studies on the effects of bullying have examined the impact of the social pain that haunts many victims of bullying. The term social pain is used to describe the experiences of peer rejection or ostracism that victims of bullying feel (Vaillancourt, Hymel, & McDougall, 2013) and is also thought to be relived and re-experienced more easily than the physical type of pain. Additionally, in comparison to actual physical pain, for many victims of bullying, social pain lingers on through adulthood and ultimately impacts their social development and, potentially, their physical health. There appears to also be a link between childhood teasing and social anxiety with individuals diagnosed as having a social anxiety disorder often also reporting having been a victim of bullying or severe teasing (Roth, Coles, & Heimberg, 2002). Further, internalization of bullying effects can be a precursor to the development of related mental health issues, such as anxiety and depression. After continuous bullying, many victims also may continue to see themselves as outcasts and failures, which ultimately affect their ability to lead normal successful lives (Smokowski & Kopasz, 2005).

Bullying and School Violence

While we can only speculate why school shooting tragedies, such as the one at Columbine High School occur, research on school violence has identified a plausible relationship between being a victim of bullying and also being a school shooter (Hong, Cho Allen-Meares, & Espelage, 2011). In the aftermath of the Columbine tragedy, the school shooters were later described as being targets of bullying by their peers and it was revealed that both were undergoing counseling for depression and anti-social behavior related to loneliness and isolation. Similarly, in the aftermath of the college campus shooting at Virginia Tech in 2007, the shooter was believed to have been a victim of bullying in K-12 and college and similar to the case of the students at Columbine, the shooter at Virginia Tech had previously received treatment for an anxiety disorder that may be related to effects of bullying that he endured while growing up (Heilbrun, Dvoskin, & Heilbrun, 2009). In both of these instances, a student lacked a sense of relationship and connectedness to their school and peers and responded to their hurt by inflicting harm on others. While most cases of bullying do not result in these extreme outcomes, it is worth noting the potential long-term and widespread damage that may have an association with experiences of bullying.

Effectiveness of Anti-Bullying Policies

The Columbine tragedy sparked a public outcry for attention to be paid to bullying on K-12 school campuses and made it imperative that K-12 administrators take actions to address bullying through implementing zero tolerance anti-bullying policies across school districts in the United States (Hong, Cho Allen-Meares, & Espelage, 2011). However, it has been argued that zero tolerance anti-bullying policies are often ineffective and can be more harmful to victims as they impose a "one size fits all", often punitive approach in response to all incidents of bullying, rather than addressing bullying incidents one-by-one and in the spirit of investing in student learning about intent and impact and healthy relationships (Heibrun, Dvoskin, &

Heilbrun, 2009). Research findings to date suggest that effective anti-bullying strategies are those that focus on promoting an inclusive, globally conscious school climate that embraces individuals from a variety of backgrounds, social identities, body types, family structures, strengths and limitations, belief and value systems, and life experiences (Haeseler, 2010). Furthermore, effective anti-bullying strategies engage the entire school, with school administrators embracing the program and providing the necessary financial and administrative support to ensure that the anti-bullying program is actively and fully integrated into the school's curriculum (Whitted & Dupper, 2005).

TRENDS IN RESEARCH ON BULLYING IN HIGHER EDUCATION

Existence of Bullying on College Campuses

To date, minimal research has been conducted that examines the prevalence, frequency, and impact of bullying in the higher education setting. This limited attention to the effects of bullying on college students may be a holdover from earlier research that asserted that bullying did not persist from grade to grade and that as students matured, incidents of bullying decreased (Olweus, 1993). However, even as far back McDougall (1999), who performed a study of bullying at a higher education institution, discovered that among the staff and students who participated in the study, 9.6% had experienced some form of bullying at that institution. In more recent studies of bullying at a higher education institution, the prevalence of students describing either observing or directly experiencing bullying ranged from 60% of the participants reporting seeing student-on-student bullying and 44% of the participants reporting seeing teacher on student bullying (Chapell, Casey, De la Cruz, Ferrell, Forman, Lipkin, Newsham, Sterling, & Whittaker, 2004) to 37% of students reporting themselves being victims of bullying in both their K-12 and higher education experiences (Adams & Lawrence).

These studies of bullying in higher education institutions also sought to describe the effects of bullying endured by participants, with a large percentage of individuals reporting difficulty in developing relationships, utilizing coping strategies, and adjusting to being on a college campus (Adams & Lawrence, 2011). These findings have led researchers to conclude that bullying does exist on college campuses and that despite the early findings by Olweus (1999) that suggest that bullying decreases from grade to grade, in fact, bullying may indeed graduate from grade to grade and enter college along with its victims (Adams & Lawrence, 2011).

Cyber-Bullying on University Campuses

With the rapid development of technologies that are available to students of all ages, bullying has advanced from in person bullying to cyber-bullying. Cyber-bullying can be defined as an intentional act to harass someone through the use of cell phone or internet. Similar to traditional bullying, cyberbullying, is prevalent in the K-12 context with a steady trend showing movement of acts of cyber-bullying to college campuses (Schenk, Fremouw, & Keelan, 2013). Further, Beran, Rinaldi, Bickham, and Rich (2012) provided evidence that students who experienced bullying in K-12 also are likely to experience some form of harassment in a university setting.

Other recent studies exploring cyber-bullying on college campuses point to rates of cyber-bullying that parallel the prevalence of face-to-face bullying. Recent studies by Walker, Sockman, and Koehn (2011) and MacDonald and Roberts-Pittman (2010) describe 54% of participants reporting knowing someone who had been cyber-bullied and 11% reported being victims of cyber-bullying themselves and 38% of the participants reporting knowing someone who had been cyber-bullied, 22% being victims of cyber-bullying and 9% admitting to being a cyber-bullying, respectively. With the effects of cyber-bullying being similar to that of face-to face bullying, results from these studies should be encouragement for universities to take notice of the possible existence of cyber-bullying on their campuses and to develop strategies to prevent it.

Absence of Anti-Bullying Policies in Higher Education

Universities have been hesitant to specifically address bullying, possibly because, until recently, they have been immune from the liability associated with actions of their students (Duncan, 2010). However, the expanded implementation of Title IX now holds schools liable for gender-based, peer-on-peer conduct, which means that immunity may cease to exist. With the increase in Dear Colleague letters and aligned responses of the Department of Education and Department of Justice to campus-based issues, it is likely that it is only a matter of time before the specific issue of bullying as an issue of harassment and campus climate on college campuses is highlighted. While many universities potentially will address incidents of bullying using the focus on harassment and campus climate provided by Title IX and the related Dear Colleague guidance, this is not an effective way to address all bullying on college campuses as it is not inclusive of all potential victims, nor do the related mandates address the K-12 carry over effects that appear to be an added challenge of bullying.

K-12 educators have assisted us to more fully understand the lasting effects of bullying that continue to jeopardize student success (Dary & Pickeral, 2013). With the employment of anti-bullying strategies, schools are able to improve the climate of a school and also assist each student to achieve academic and social outcomes. Without specific anti-bullying policies, many first year college students who bring a prior experience of bullying with them to college may not know who to turn to report bullying experiences in their new learning environment (Duncan, 2010). Like their K-12 colleagues, universities need to be concerned with bullying on their campuses as unaddressed bullying incidents can lead not only to reduced persistence of students and retention rates, but also to more severe acts of violence, such as school shootings (Duncan, 2010).

Emerging Practices for Addressing Bullying in Higher Education

Given the evidence that bullying follows students from K-12 to college contexts and that cyber-bullying is an increasing threat to student learning and experience, higher education also is compelled to respond (Heilbrun, Dvoskin, & Heilbrun, 2009). Some strategies that proactive universities have implemented include addressing bullying as a campus-wide initiative, with staff and faculty being trained to recognize, address and discuss incidents of bullying as they see them and to not wait to take action (Hughes, 2001). Others have addressed bullying using approaches similar to those best practices used in the K-12 environment, which involve approaching bullying from an intervention, prevention and enforcement stance. This would include establishing anti-bullying programs that provide resources to increase awareness of bullying, as well as providing programs and assistance to students who may be dealing with bullying (Duncan, 2010). By developing this approach to bullying, universities have the opportunity to influence development of a positive school climate that promotes mutual respect across all members and that, as a result, enhances the potential for each student to experience success across campus.

To further illustrate the existence of bullying in the higher education arena and to support previous research conducted on the topic, the authors of this chapter determined that conducting a pilot study at their institution would provide further insight about the existence of student-on-student bullying in higher education. Due to time constraints, the availability of a convenience sample, and the multiple instructional roles that educators in training often play, the authors chose to limit the participants of the study to be students in the School of Education.

PILOT STUDY

An additional consideration when responding to bullying in a systemic way is to understand the bullying experience of educators in training, including Student Affairs educators who often serve as first line intervention in college settings. By first describing the experience of the individuals who soon will serve in teaching and leadership roles in K-12 classrooms and schools and in Student Affairs at colleges and universities and then next developing curriculum that situates learning in both their experience (Baxter-Magolda, Creamer, & Meszaros, 2010) and in effective pedagogy, progress may be made in bridging the "knowledge and response gap" that still exists in regard to bullying across educational environments. This pilot study begins to map the first question that asks about the personal relevance of bullying to educators in training by documenting the frequency and prevalence of this experience in a cohort of students enrolled in undergraduate and graduate educator training programs at one medium- sized private comprehensive university.

METHOD

This pilot study utilized an anonymous survey to initiate engagement with educators in training and to begin to document their experience. Survey methodology was chosen because of its inherent ability to provide anonymity and confidentiality to participants, a particularly important characteristic of the methodological approach for this project given the sensitivity of the topic and the typical intimacy of educator training programs.

Instrument

A survey of 20 questions composed of open-ended and multiple choice answers were developed based on the models provided by prior research and questions specific to the experience of educators in training (Appendix A). The multiple-choice portion of the survey utilized a four-point Likert scale. Open-ended questions asked respondents to provide definitions of bullying and hazing.

Procedure

Participants were invited to participate in the study through a classroom announcement by one of the researchers, as well as through email correspondence generated by Survey Monkey. Participants were provided with informed consents via email. The survey and request to participate was sent directly to the participants by Survey Monkey. Responses to the survey were anonymous as no identifying information was requested of the respondents.

For this pilot study, students enrolled in the School of Education of a medium size, comprehensive university were invited to participate in the survey. A total of 123 students were invited to participate in the survey, with 44 students (36%) of the population responding to the survey. This response rate is consistent with the average response rates of 35.7% found in organizational survey research (Baruch & Holtom, 2009). Of those students completing surveys, 13 identified as undergraduate K-12 teachers in training and 31 identified as graduate students working on degrees that would qualify them to work in higher education settings. Among the 44 respondents, 33 identified as female and 11 as male. Respondents ranged in age from traditional-aged to non-traditional aged, as would be expected in a typical educator training program.

DATA ANALYSIS

The text associated with each of the open-ended questions was analyzed using the approach to narrative analysis described by Chase (2005) and Reissman (2008). Narrative analysis focuses on the individual and collective accounts of particular phenomena and considers language as a tool for understanding how individuals make

207

sense of specific constructs and related experiences. Narrative analysis often is used to describe how constructs, such as bullying, are ascribed meaning by participants.

Qualitative analysis provided the framing for interpreting the quantitative analysis used in this study. Each item survey item that used a Likert scale items was analyzed using descriptive statistics and used to triangulate qualitative findings.

FINDINGS

Definition of Bullying

Participant definitions of bullying shared similar elements across gender, social identity, and class standing. Examples of participant definitions included: bullying as an action that can create domination over one person by utilizing physical or mental abuse; making one to feel bad or uncomfortable in a way that is demeaning and uncaring; using someone's characteristics, beliefs, behaviors, etc. against them so as to cause harm; and targeting an individual because they are different from yourself through physical and verbal abuse. Dimensional differences in definitions became apparent when definitions of those who had reported being bullied were contrasted with the definitions of those who had not been bullied. Those participants who had not been bullied were more likely to focus on the intent of bullying behavior and seemingly had a lower threshold for labeling behavior as bullying. Also, participants who had not been bullied were more prone to describe bullying as an action - "Putting somebody down"; "Making fun of somebody or making them feel bad"; "Picking on somebody"; and "Bothering somebody."

In contrast, participants who had been bullied had a broader and more intense set of criteria that appeared to guide their definition and labeling of bullying. Students who had been bullied were more likely to reference bullying as a repetitive behavior of sustained duration. They also more often described the personal nature of bullying and more frequently pointed out that bullying occurred as a response to "difference and being different"; was "based on social identity"; and was used to "isolate." Finally, students who had been bullied more often named the impact of bullying, describing the physical and emotional hurt that was the result of a bullying experience.

Perceptions and Experiences

Safety at current institution. The survey items were then sequenced to first ask respondents to identify how important campus climate was in their decision about which college to attend with 35 of the 44 participants strongly agreeing or agreeing that campus climate played an important role in their decision. Likewise, 41 of the

44 participants noted the importance of campus climate to their continuing success at their current institution. Further survey results on the importance of campus climate are summarized in Table 1.

Table 1. Summary of Findings – Safety at Current Institution

	Actual Number Participants	Percentage of Participants
Importance of Campus Climate in Choosing Schools		
Very Important/Important/ somewhat important	35	80%
Didn't think about it	9	20%
Importance of Campus Climate at Current Institution		
Very Important/Important/ somewhat important	41	93%
Didn't think about it	3	7%
Safety of Campus at Current Institution		
Very Safe/Safe	38	86%
Somewhat Safe	5	11%
Not Safe	1	2%

Victims of bullying. Twenty six of the participants in the study reported being victims of bullying prior to coming to their current institution, with six participants reporting that they had been victims of bullying since coming to this institution. Of these six of students, four are graduate students. Though a small number of students overall, this statistic potentially indicates that these students have experienced bullying during a large portion of their educational career: K-12, undergraduate and now graduate life. Participants who reported having experienced incidents of bullying described being affected by the following types of bullying: physical, social exclusion, racial, sexual orientation and cyber-bullying. Additionally, two participants reported missing school or an event due to fear of being bullied.

Twelve students from the pilot study described witnessing another student being bullied, with eight students commenting that they took action by either stepping in to assist the victim or reported the incident to a Public Safety officer or a faculty/ staff member. For the four students who reported not taking action, the reasons provided included that they did not know what to do, were afraid to report it, did not want to get involved, the bully was their friend, thought nothing would be done if they reported it, 33% they did not think it was their business or did not know who to report it to. (See Table 2 for detail data on Victims of Bullying.)

Table 2. Summary of Findings – Victims of Bullying

	Actual Number Participants	Percentage of Participants
Victim of Bullying Prior to Current Institution		
Yes	26	59%
No	16	36%
Not sure	2	5%
Victim since Coming to Current institution		
Yes	6	14%
No	38	86%
Graduate	4	9%
Undergraduate	2	5%
Witnessed Bullying at Current Institution		
Yes	12	27%
No	32	73%

Perception of bullying. Participants were also asked whether they thought that bullying was a major issue facing colleges and universities, with 28 of the participants noting that they strongly agreed or agreed with this statement. When asked if they thought hazing behaviors are gateways to bullying behavior, 33 of the participants commented that they strongly agreed or agreed. (See Table 3 for detailed data on the perception of bullying.)

Table 3. Summary of Findings – Perception of Bullying

	Actual Number Participants	Percentage of Participants
Hazing as a Gateway to Bullying Behavior		
Strongly Agree/Agree	33	75%
Disagree	11	25%
Bullying as a Major Issue Facing Colleges/Universities		
Strongly Agree/Agree	28	64%
Disagree	16	36%
Interested in Learning more about Bullying		
Strongly Agree/Agree	28	64%
Disagree	16	36%

DISCUSSION

The findings from this pilot study support previous studies by others that document the existence of bullying in the higher education setting and should serve as notice to this university and others like it that the existence of bullying on university and college campuses still needs focused attention. Further, participants from this study also agree with research findings to date that suggest that school climate is a critical contributor to their success. While this pilot study represented a relatively small cohort of students at one institution, it is important to point out the concerning finding that 6 of the 44 participants who reported being bullied prior to coming to the university where this study took place also reported being victims since coming to this institution. This finding suggests that for some students bullying is a defining part of their educational experience and persists as they travel from educational setting to educational setting. Perhaps, what is most encouraging is that a majority of the participants in this pilot study were interested in learning more about how to address bullying and expected that the degree programs that were preparing them to work with students in K-12 and higher education contexts would explicitly address how to disrupt bullying behavior. This participant expectation, combined with the clear awareness of bullying as an issue, creates additional pressure for preparation programs to respond by embedding specific learning outcomes in program curriculum.

Educator Preparation Programs

While this study did not address how these experiences might be connected to the accountability for student safety and student success that these future educators will encounter when working in K-12 and higher education environments post-graduation, these findings do suggest a predisposition for many of these educators to be sensitized to and personally understand the challenges associated with bullying that their students might face. Findings from this study suggest that teacher and Student Affairs educator preparation programs may need to more intentional and explicitly include responses to bullying, including bystander training, as both a part of their student support structures and in their program curricula. To that end, bullying may impact directly the success of these educators in training and may also be key to the persistence and overall success of the students that they will eventually serve. In response, the curricular and co-curricular dimensions of educator preparation programs must include visible support for students who have experienced bullying themselves, while also providing them with the tools, knowledge, and resources to respond or intervene effectively in both their current environment and in the educational systems of which they will become a part.

Differences in definitions of bullying described in the findings between individuals who have experienced bullying with those that have not may reflect the more nuanced awareness of the short and long term impact of being bullied that

211

come with the experience of being a victim of bullying. That is to propose that those who have experienced bullying may be better able to recognize bullying as a process that may lead to the development of multiple significant impacts on the individual, including challenges with anxiety and self confidence, over time. This finding also reinforces the need for educator preparation programs. Ultimately, if bullying is not appropriately recognized and labeled, then the ability to intervene is compromised.

Implications for Higher Education

As stated previously, the current trend has been for research on bullying to be primarily focused in the K-12 context, with little research performed to date on the trend –and impact- of bullying in higher education. The research conducted for this pilot study points to some of the impacts that bullying may have not only for the students who have been victims of bullying, but also for the school environment as a whole. Many universities, such as the one used in this pilot study, do not yet have specific anti-bullying policies or procedures. Rather, reported incidents of bullying are being addressed through more general student conduct and harassment policies. Since the pilot study revealed that there are students who have endured bullying since coming to their current university, this serves as evidence that the current methods used to address bullying may be not sufficient on their own.

How Can Universities Help?

Universities can begin to help victims of bullying by having transparent conversations about bullying on campuses and assessing the effects that bullying may be having on their specific student populations. These conversations can then continue with the students through incoming freshman orientations, where the topic of bullying is discussed openly and the expectations of community, care, and respect as essential conditions for learning and student success are clearly stated. Addressing bullying during orientations helps to set the stage for incoming students as to how students at a university are expected to behave, as well as serves as a venue to inform those students who may have been bullied prior to entering college that the university takes this issue seriously and understands the impact it can have on their student success.

Recommendations for Future Research

As this pilot study has indicated, higher education institutions could benefit from many practices that K-12 colleagues and systems have in place to address bullying to assist their students. This research only began to scratch the surface of the experience and consequences of bullying on college campuses as it only examined a small subset of students, at one university. Future studies on bullying in higher education could include conducting a campus wide study on the prevalence of bullying that educators could use to more fully understanding the dynamics of bullying as a part of the larger campus climate, as well as within specific programs of study. In this same regard, future lines of inquiry should also explore how the dynanmics of bullying may occur differently based on institutional type, geography, and history. Further, future research in higher education should focus on how coping and resilience is developed for individuals who are currently experiencing bullying in institutions where bullying is not specifically addressed. Finally, during this period of increased scrutiny and calls for greater accountability, higher education has the opportunity – and the responsibility, to understand how bullying might detract from student persistence and overall student success.

REFERENCES

Adams, F. D., & Lawrence, G. J. (2011). Bullying victims: The effects last into college. *American Secondary Education, 40*(1), 4–11.

Adams, F. D., Lawrence, G. J., & Schenck, S. (2008). A survey on bullying: Some reflections on the findings. *NASCD News & Notes, 8*, 1–7.

Ahmed, E., & Braithwaite, V. (2004). Bullying and victimization: Cause for concern for both families and schools. *Social Psychology of Education, 7*, 35–54.

Astin, A. (1993). *What matters in college? Four critical years revisited. The Jossey-Bass higher and adult education series.* San Francisco, CA: Jossey-Bass.

Baruch, Y., & Holtom, B. (2008). Survey response rate levels and trends in organizational research. *Human Relations, 61*, 1139–1160.

Baumeister, R. F., Campbell, J. D., Krueger, J. I., & Vohs, K. D. (2003). Does high self-esteem cause better performance, interpersonal success, happiness, or healthier lifestyles? *Psychological Science in the Public Interest, 4*, 1–44.

Baxter-Magolda, M., Creamer, E., & Meszaros, P. (2010). *Development and assessment of self-authorship.* Sterling, VA: Stylus.

Beran T. N., Rinaldi C., Bickham D. S., & Rich M. (2012). Evidence for the need to support adolescents dealing with harassment and cyber-harassment: Prevalence, progression, and impact. *School Psychology International, 33*(5), 562–576.

Chapell, M. S., Hasselman, S. L., Kitchin, T., Lomon, S. N., MacIver, K. W., & Sarullo, P. L. (2006). Bullying in elementary school, high school, and college. *Adolescence, 41*(164), 633–648.

Chapell, M, Casey, D, De la Cruz, C, Ferrell, J., Forman, J., Lipkin, R., ... Whittaker, S. (2004). Bullying in college by students and teachers. *Adolescence, 39*, 53–64.

Chase, S. (2005). Narrative inquiry: Multiple lenses, approaches, and voices. In N. K. Denzin & Y. S. Lincoln (Eds.), *The SAGE handbook of qualitative research* (3rd ed., pp. 651–679). Thousand Oaks, London, & New Delhi, India: Sage Publications.

Cohen, J., McCabe, L., Michelli, N. M., & Pickeral, T. (2009). School climate: Research, policy, practice, and teacher education. *Teachers College Record, 111*, 180–213.

Coleyshaw, L. (2010). The power of paradigms: A discussion of the absence of bullying research in the context of the university student experience. *Post-Compulsory Education, 15*(4), 377–386.

Conn, K. (2011). Allegations of school district liability for bullying, cyber-bullying, and teen suicides after sexting: Are new legal standards emerging in courts? *New England Journal on Criminal and Civil Confinement, 37*, 227–246.

Dary, T., & Pickeral, T. (2013). *School climate: Practices for implementation and sustainability.* A school climate practice brief, Number 1. New York, NY: National School Climate Center.

DoSomething.org (2013). *Eleven facts about bullying.* Retrieved from http://www.dosomething.org/tipsandtools/11-facts-about-school-bullying

Duncan, S. (2010). College bullies – Precursors to campus violence: What should universities and college administrators know about the law? *Villanova Law Review, 55*(2), 269–320.

Good, C., McIntosh, K., & Gietz, C. (2011). Integrating bullying prevention into school-wide positive behavior support. *Teaching Exceptional Children, 44*, 48–56.

Haeseler, L. A. (2010). Stopping child bullying: Educators' diverse approaches for school improvement. *Journal of Human Behavior in the Social Environment, 20*, 952–962.

Heilbrun, K., Dvoskin, J., & Heilbrun, A. (2009). Toward preventing future tragedies: Mass killings on college campus, public health, and threat/risk assessment. *Psychology Injury and Law, 2*, 93–99.

Hong, J. S., Cho, H., Allen-Meares, P., & Espelage, D. L. (2011). The social ecology of the columbine high school shootings. *Children and Youth Services Review, 33*, 861–868.

Hughes, G. (2001). Examples of good practice when dealing with bullying in a further/higher education college. *Pastoral Care in Education, 19*(3), 10–13.

Kuh, G., Kinzie, J., Buckley, J., Bridges, B., & Hayek, J. (2006). What matters to student success: A review of the literature. Commissioned report for the national symposium on Postsecondary student success: Spearheading a dialog on student success. National Postsecondary Cooperative.

Limber, S. P., Olweus, D., & Luxenberg, H. (2013). Bullying in U.S. schools: 2012 status report. Hazelden Foundation, 1–20. Retrieved from www.violencepreventionworks.org

MacDonald, C. D., & Roberts-Pittman, B., (2010). Cyberbullying among college students: Prevalence and demographic differences. *Science Direct, 9*, 2003–2009.

McDougall, L. (1999). A study of bullying in further education. *Pastoral Care, 17*(2), 31–37.

Olweus, D. O. (1993). *Bullying at school: What we know and what we can do*. Oxford, UK: Blackwell Publishers.

Olweus, D. O. (1999). The nature of school bullying. In P. K. Smith, Y. Morita, J. Junger-Tas, D. Olweus, R. Cantalano, & P. Slee (Eds). *The nature of school bullying: A cross-national perspective* (pp. 28–48, xiii, 384 pp.). Florence, KY: Taylor & Frances/Routledge.

Osterman, K. F. (2000). Students' need for belonging in the school community. *Review of Educational Research, 70*(3), 323–367.

Parker, J. D. A., Summerfield, L. J., Hogan, M. J., & Majeski, S., (2002). *Emotional intelligence and academic success: Examining the transition from high school to university*. ERIC Clearing House.

Pittman, L. D., & Richmond, A. (2008). University belonging, friendship quality, and psychological adjustment during the transition to college. *The Journal of Experimental Education, 76*(4), 343–361.

Reason, R. (2013). Creating and assessing campus climates that personal and social responsibility. *Liberal Education, 99*(1), 10–23.

Reissman, C. K. (2008). *Narrative methods for the human sciences*. London & Thousand Oaks, CA: Sage Publications.

Roth, D. A., Coles, M. E., & Heimberg, R. G. (2002). The relationship between memories for childhood teasing and anxiety and depression in adulthood. *Journal of Anxiety Disorders, 16*(2), 149–164.

Schenk, A. M., Fremouw, W. J., & Keelan, C. M. (2013). Characteristics of college cyber-bullies. *Computers in Human Behavior, 29*, 2320–2327.

Smith, P. K., Ananiadou, K., & Cowie, H. (2003). Interventions to reduce school bullying. *The Canadian Journal of Psychiatry – In Review, 48*(9), 591–599.

Smokowski, P. R., & Kopasz, K. H. (2005). Bullying in school: An overview of types, effects, family characteristics, and invention strategies. *Children and Schools, 27*(2), 101–110.

Tinto, V. (1999). Taking student success seriously: Rethinking the first year of college. *NACADA Journal, 19*(2), 5–9.

Tinto, V. (2006–2007). Research and practice of student retention: What next? *Journal of College Student Retention, 8*(1), 1–19.

Vaillancourt, T., Hymel, S., & McDougall, P. (2013). The biological underpinnings of peer victimization: Understanding why and how the effects of bullying can last a lifetime. *Theory into Practice, 52*, 241–248.

Walker, C. M., Sockman, B. R., & Koehn, S., (2011). An exploratory study of cyber-bullying with undergraduate university students. *TechTrends: Linking Research and Practice to Improve Learning, 55*(2), 31–38.

Whitted, K. S., & Dupper, D. R., (2005). Best practices for preventing or reducing bullying in schools. *Children and Schools*, *27*(3), 167–175.

Yosso, T. (2005). Whose culture has capital? A critical race theory discussion of community and cultural wealth. *Race, Ethnicity, and Education*, *8*(1), 69–91.

Laura Merry & Joanna Royce-Davis
University of the Pacific

APPENDIX A

Survey Sample Questions:
1. How do you describe your gender?
2. What is your status at Pacific?

   a. undergraduate
   b. graduate or professional student

3. How do you define campus climate?
4. As you were researching schools to attend, how important was campus climate in your decision?

   a. Very important
   b. Important
   c. Somewhat important
   d. Didn't think about it

5. How would you rate Pacific's campus climate with regard to being a safe learning space for all campus community members?

   a. Very safe
   b. Safe
   c. Somewhat safe
   d. Not safe

6. How important is campus climate to your success here at Pacific?

   a. Very important
   b. Important
   c. Somewhat important
   d. Didn't think about it

7. Define hazing
8. Define bullying.
9. A number of studies now suggest that hazing behavior is a "gateway" to bullying behavior. How would you rate your agreement with this statement.

   a. Strongly agree
   b. Agree
   c. Disagree
   d. Strongly disagree

215

10. Have you been a victim of bullying PRIOR to coming to Pacific?

    a. Yes

    b. No

11. If yes, what type of bullying have you had to deal with? (Check all that apply)

    a. Physical (hit, slapped, pushed or kicked, etc.)

    b. Social (excluded from social events or ridiculed in front of other students)

    c. Racial (comments made based on race/nationality)

    d. Cyberbullied (harassed through social network sites, email or text)

    e. Sexual orientation harassment

    f. Other (Please describe.)

12. Have you been a victim of bullying AT Pacific?

    a. Yes

    b. No

13. If yes, what type of bullying have you had to deal with? (Check all that apply)

    a. Physical (hit, slapped, pushed or kicked, etc.)

    b. Social (excluded from social events or ridiculed in front of other students)

    c. Racial (comments made based on race/nationality)

    d. Cyberbullied (harassed through social network sites, email or text)

    e. Sexual orientation harassment

    f. Other (Please describe.)_____

14. In your life at Pacific, have you ever missed school or an event because you were afraid of being bullied?

    a. Yes

    b. No

15. Have you witnessed another student being bullied at Pacific?

    a. Yes

    b. No

16. If Yes, as a bystander, what action did you take, if any?

    a. I stepped in and tried to stop it

    b. I reported it to Public Safety

    c. I reported it a faculty/staff member

    d. I stood and observed

    e. I ignored it

    f. Other (Please describe.)

17. If you did NOT assist the victim who was being bullied, what was the reason?

    a. I didn't know what to do

    b. Was afraid to report it

    c. I didn't want to get involved

    d. The person who was the bully is a friend

e. Not sure that it was my business

f. I thought that nothing would be done if I did report it

g. Didn't know who to report it to

h. Other (Please describe.)

18. I believe that bullying is a major issue facing colleges and universities.

    a. Strongly agree

    b. Agree

    c. Disagree

    d. Strongly disagree

19. When you are having personal issues or are in need of guidance, who do you seek help from or who do you consult?

    a. Friend

    b. Parent

    c. Sibling

    d. Professor

    e. Residence Director

    f. Other (Please identify.)

20. If offered the opportunity to learn more about addressing bullying, I would participate.

    a. Strongly agree

    b. Agree

    c. Disagree

    d. Strongly disagree

KAREN ANDRUS TOLLAFIELD

31. THE ELEPHANT IN THE SCHOOL

Recognizing Bullying in Other Forms

Act as if what you do makes a difference. It does.

— William James

Is it possible to be a bully or witness bullying and not even recognize it? What is a bully? Many definitions exist, as bullying has become quite a hot button issue these days. Generally, however, most definitions describe the use of power to control or harm others repeatedly (StopBullying.gov, 2014). In this way, bullying is usually considered to involve one or more of the following types: emotional, verbal, physical, and cyber. Bullying is also usually associated with student-to-student interactions, but adult bullies do exist. It might be a boss or co-worker, or even a parent of a student athlete who berates the teammates or coach. It might even be a teacher or principal.

Can that be true? Do adult bullies exist in schools? How might that behavior manifest? Hopefully, gone are the days when dunce caps, banishment to the corner of the room, and hand whacking with rulers were common practices. However, Stuart Twemlow (2006) defines bullying by educators (or other adults) as the use of "power to punish, manipulate, or disparage a student beyond what could be a reasonable disciplining procedure" (p. 191). As an example, he describes the educator who deliberately uses sarcasm or shaming to humiliate a student. While this does occur, I believe that most educators would find this behavior abhorrent and never do anything to intentionally hurt a child physically or emotionally, and yet many of these same educators make choices throughout the day that, while not so blatant, may be perceived as a form of bullying by their students, especially those who identify outside of the norm in regard to sexual orientation or gender identity.

While not all educators have done the things I will be outlining, these practices do occur in schools across the country. My intention here is simply to increase awareness that some of the everyday choices we make as educators may be causing discomfort or harm to some of our students. Whether or not these choices are intentional or accidental, it is important that educators recognize bullying in all of its forms and make steps to change these practices.

C. Boske & A. Osanloo (Eds.), Students, Teachers, and Leaders Addressing Bullying in Schools, 219–224.
© *2015 Sense Publishers. All rights reserved.*

SCHOOL CLIMATE FOR LGBTQ STUDENTS

While the LGBTQ (lesbian, gay, bisexual, transgender, queer) community is more visible in society now than in the past, the American public education system continues to function under a predominantly heteronormative/heterosexist belief system (Blackburn & Smith, 2010; Crocco, 2001, 2002; Payne, 2007; Payne & Smith, 2012a, 2012b; Pinar, 2007; Thornton, 2004), meaning that any orientation other than heterosexuality is unnatural (GLSEN, 2011). Along with this belief, American schools promote the concept of a gender binary in which everyone is either male or female, and should fall into traditional gender roles. This belief system has basically gone "unchallenged in teaching materials for K-12" students (Thornton, 2004, p. 362) and renders LGBTQ students invisible unless they choose to disclose those identities (Lopez & Chism, 1993; Thornton, 2004).

When a student identifies somewhere along the LGBTQ spectrum, school can be a lonely and/or a terrifying place. Educators must be held to a higher accountability far beyond that of high stakes testing results. If students are to learn to the best of their abilities, educators must be able to ensure their safety, both physical and emotional. In order to do this, we must begin to recognize bullying for what it is.

"HIDDEN" BULLYING PRACTICES

Most educators think they know what bullying is and are quick to stop it. Sometimes, however, when the behaviors involve students who identify within the LGBTQ community, these lines may begin to blur for various reasons. Some adults feel that being LGBTQ is a choice and they do not "agree" with these choices. This belief system often leads to the assumption that if the student being bullied would just not "flaunt" their choices, they would be fine. Others hesitate to get involved for fear of rousing suspicions of their own sexuality, don't feel comfortable countering what a colleague has said or done, or fear for their job if they speak out against school policies.

In this chapter, I have detailed some of these instances in hopes that you will begin to think about your school situation and work to make whatever changes might be necessary. If you are already aware of these issues, this chapter will help support you as you work to end bullying in your school.

Exclusion from the Group

Intentionally excluding students from a group is one abuse of power that bullies may use (StopBullying.gov, 2014). Most educators would never think of excluding any child, but exclusion happens in several ways within individual classrooms and on a school-wide basis, and is usually based on the heteronormative and gender binary belief systems mentioned earlier.

School Policies. While an increasing number of schools are becoming more inclusive to students who identify in the LGBTQ community, we still see exclusion of students in this group across the country. The most common instances involve school-wide policies of banning these students from enjoying the same privileges as their non-LGBTQ counterparts.

When same-sex partners are not allowed at school functions (i.e., prom), or there are gender specific roles (i.e., homecoming king and queen, girls not allowed on the wrestling team), schools are not treating all students equally (the same as other students) or with equity (in accordance to what the students need). Many schools also ban the formation of student clubs that address LGBTQ issues, commonly called Gay-Straight Alliances or GSAs. Although the "federal Equal Access Act of 1984 requires public schools to allow GSAs to exist alongside other non-curricular student clubs" (GLSEN, 2011, p. 18), there have been examples reported nation-wide of schools working their way around this by deciding to cancel dances and/or all extra-curricular clubs. There have also been GSAs that could not form because no educator would take on the advisor role that schools require.

Another issue in schools relates specifically to students who identify as transgender (gender identity differs from their physical sex at birth, U C Berkeley, 2014) Recently, there have been numerous news stories about transgender students of all ages and their families facing "unique challenges at school, such as difficulty accessing gender-segregated areas, including bathrooms and locker rooms" (Greytak, Kosciw, & Diaz, 2009, p. ix). When schools react negatively to these students, they are making it clear that transgender identity is not recognized as valid. The Gay, Lesbian & Straight Education Network's (GLSEN) 2011 national survey of LGBTQ students reports that compared to other students identifying on the LGBTQ spectrum, "transgender students faced the most hostile school climates (p. xix). Greytak, Kosciw, and Diaz (2009) also found that "such harassment, assault, and challenges negatively affects transgender students' abilities to engage in their education" (as cited in Blackburn & Nelson, 2014, p. 16).

Curricular Choices. Diversity awareness and acceptance seem to be more commonplace in the classroom than they were just a few years ago, and educators need to be sure to include materials specific to their student population whenever possible. This does not only include religious, racial, or cultural differences, however. Those students who identify somewhere on the LGBTQ spectrum, or may come from same-sex households, rarely see themselves reflected in any of the books or other curricular materials educators choose. In this way, they may feel excluded from the classroom as they see educators making efforts to include materials that reflect the diverse religious, racial, or cultural backgrounds of the other students in the class. Also, the needs of some of these students are rarely addressed in the health curricula and they may feel excluded in these classes, as well. These are more examples of how the heteronormative belief system thrives in schools and continues to render these students and their families invisible.

221

Classroom Practices.   Some educators do not realize how often gender separation and stereotyping occur in the classroom since these practices have been part of education for as long as anyone can remember. While many students pay no mind to this, some do and feel uncomfortable for a number of reasons. One of the most ubiquitous conventions used in elementary classrooms is that of stereotyping genders through colors and materials, which Wardy (2014) calls our "pink culture" (p. 21). For example, when educators make distinct choices to put all the girls' names on pink or purple nametags (or on tags with images of butterflies, princesses, sparkly things, etc…) and boys' names on tags of blue or red with images of trucks, or different sports, they are letting their students know that they have predetermined beliefs about them and may not see them as individuals. Educators must remember that all children do not fit into those stereotypes and may be uncomfortable with them. This holds true for children who simply have interests other than those typically assigned to their birth gender (e.g., girls who like sports or boys who like ballet), but is especially frustrating or uncomfortable for those students who may identify as the opposite gender to which they were born and feel once again excluded from a group with which they would prefer to identify.

Color-coding is not the only practice that may cause discomfort for students based on stereotyping, however. Throughout the grade levels, some educators separate students into groups by gender, thinking that girls and boys may feel more comfortable discussing certain topics within their own gender groups. Once again, these educators are basing decisions upon their own perceptions or level of comfort and not that of the students. The same thing occurs when educators create assignments based on gender. I have talked with students who told me about an assignment in which they were instructed to choose a character from the book they were reading and write from that character's point of view. This became a problem for one of the students who identified as transgender because the educator wanted the girls to choose a female character and the boys to choose a male character. Again, this practice assumes that all students identify with their birth gender in all situations and this is simply not the case. Wardy (2014) calls for more "gender neutrality" (p. 5) in order to allow children to demonstrate their individuality and feel comfortable in the world.

The previously mentioned stereotyping can apply to students who do identify in their birth gender, but simply do not always follow what are typically "female" or "male" interests and behaviors. When students identify outside of our societal norms as transgender or genderqueer (not identifying exclusively within society's binary of male and female, UC Berkeley, 2014), having to "side" with a gender they are perceived to be can cause great discomfort.

Another uncomfortable situation may arise for those transgender or genderqueer students who specifically ask educators to refer to them by their preferred gender pronouns (PGPs), and those educators do not honor those requests. Using the personal pronouns associated with birth gender (she, her, hers; he, him, his) when a transgender or genderqueer student asks you not to may feel dismissive to those students and it separates them from other students who are accepted for who they are.

Personal Choices.   Most educators would intervene and address many instances of bullying when they witness it personally or are made aware. For example, educators break up fights in the halls or reprimand students who may be calling other students fat, ugly, or stupid. On the other hand, as mentioned earlier, some educators do not intervene or address certain aspects of bullying (hearing students calling someone "gay" or teasing someone about their appearance / interests if they are usually associated with the opposite gender) for various reasons. Often, these educators say it is just part of growing up and is not bullying. Sometimes, educators will even put the onus on the bullied student by telling them not to wear certain clothing or make-up, or walk so "swishy" in order to avoid the problems. When adults tell students to "man up" or not be such a "wuss," they are reinforcing gender stereotypes and not taking into consideration that there is not one right way to express yourself.

Whether these educators believe that this is all part of growing up, are uncomfortable getting involved in these issues, or actually blame the bullied student, they need to realize that all teasing and name-calling can have adverse effects, and by not addressing these issues, they are excluding these students and telling them their feelings do not matter.

There are times when educators witness these events and choose not to get involved for completely different reasons. They may fear that they their own sexual or gender identity may be questioned or that they will incur the wrath of certain parents. They may not feel strong enough to stand up to other teachers or administrators by questioning policy or ways in which situations have been handled. As educators, we must remember that our actions speak louder than our words and each person can make a difference.

SUMMARY

Bullying in schools is such a problem that 44 states have mandated the implementation of anti-bullying programs over the last several years (Davis, 2011). Most of these programs deal with student bullies, but do not examine the school culture that fosters these behaviors and do not adequately address the needs of the LGBTQ students and their families. While these issues must involve all stakeholders in a joint effort, progress in this area can begin today if individual educators turn the magnifying glass upon their own practices and make immediate changes that can make such a difference in helping their students feel welcomed and comfortable in their classrooms. Please visit www.glsen.org for resources to help support your efforts.

REFERENCES

Blackburn, M. V., & Nelson, R. (2014). Policy work on behalf of gender creative kids in schools. *Ohio Voices* (pp. 16–20). Retrieved from http://www.octela.org/_resources/newsletter/Spring-2014.pdf

Blackburn, M. V., & Smith, J. M. (2010). Moving beyond the inclusion of LGBT-themed literature in English language arts classrooms: Interrogating heteronormativity and exploring intersectionality. *Journal of Adolescent & Adult Literacy, 53*(8), 625–634.

Crocco, M. S. (2001). The missing discourse about gender and sexuality in the social studies. *Theory into Practice, 40*(1), 65–71.

Crocco, M. S. (2002). Homophobic hallways: Is anyone listening? *Theory and Research in Social Education, 30*(2), 217–232.

Davis, M. R. (2011, February 4). State cyberbullying laws range from guidance to mandate: Measures seen as ranging from effective to mere window dressing. *Edweek*. Retrieved from http://www.edweek.org/dd/articles/2011/02/09/02cyberbullying-laws.h04.html

GLSEN. (2011). *The safe space kit: Guide to being an ally to LGBT students.* New York, NY: Gay, Lesbian & Straight Education Network.

Greytak, E. A., Kosciw, J. G., & Diaz, E. M. (2009). *Harsh Realities: The experiences of transgender youth in our nation's schools.* New York, NY: GLSEN.

Kosciw, J. G., Greytak, E. A., Bartkiewicz, M. J., Boesen, M. J., & Palmer, N. A. (2011). *The 2011 national school climate survey: The experiences of lesbian, gay, bisexual and transgender youth in our nation's schools.* New York, NY: GLSEN.

Lopez, G., & Chism, N. (1993). Classroom concerns of gay and lesbian students: The invisible minority. *College Teaching, 41*(3), 97–103.

Payne, E. C. (2007). Heterosexism, perfection, and popularity: Young lesbians' experiences of the high school social scene. *Educational Studies, 4*(1), 60–79.

Payne, E. C. & Smith, M. (2012a). Rethinking safe schools approaches for LGBTQ students: Changing the questions we ask. *Multicultural Perspectives, 14*(4), 187–193.

Payne, E. C. & Smith, M. (2012b). Safety, celebration, and risk: Educator responses to LGBTQ professional development. *Teaching Education, 23*(3), 265–285.

Pinar, W. (2007). *Intellectual advancement through disciplinarity: Verticality and horizontality in curriculum studies.* Rotterdam, The Netherlands: Sense Publishers.

StopBullying.gov Editorial Board. (2014). *What is bullying.* Retrieved from http://www.stopbullying.gov/what-is-bullying/definition/

Thornton, S. (2009). Silence on gays and lesbians in social studies curriculum. In D. J.Flinders & S. J. Thornton (Eds.), *The curriculum studies reader* (3rd ed., pp. 362–367). New York, NY: Routledge.

Twemlow, S. W., Fonagy, P., Sacco, F. C., & Brethour, J. R., Jr. (2006). Educators who bully students: A hidden trauma. *International Journal of Social Psychiatry, 52*(3), 187–198.

U. C. Berkeley. (2014). *Definition of terms. Gender Equity Center.* Retrieved from http://geneq.berkeley.edu/lgbt_resources_definiton_of_terms

Wardy, M. A, (2014). *Redefining girly: How parents can fight the stereotyping and sexualizing of girlhood, from birth to tween.* Chicago, IL: Chicago Review Press.

DARLA WAGNER

32. FIRST THINGS FIRST

A Middle School Model of Comprehensive Supports

A comprehensive system of support is essential to being proactive in addressing many student concerns and issues. Certainly we have not eliminated bullying in our middle school, but we do provide multiple approaches to make certain that students are aware of the expectations for a safe and positive culture and they know help and support are easily accessible. There is a collective commitment among our guidance counselors, social worker, administration, and staff to make certain that the most essential support to ensuring student health and happiness is the validation that he or she is recognized as an important person. The best way to help students feel a sense of importance and belonging is ensuring they have several go-to-adults in their lives. This concept is so important to being proactive in areas of bullying and self-harm, that at Brady Middle School we allocate time, resources and funding toward these supports.

Advisory: As is a common middle school practice, Brady Middle School provides students with an advisory program. Our program, PRIDE (Positive Relationships, Integrity, Dedication, and Excellence), is structured so that each student in our building belongs to a small group of 10–12 students and 1 teacher, known as the Pride Leader. Each PRIDE meets for 30 minutes each day. The mission of Pride Time is to develop a collaborative culture to meet the developmental, social, emotional, and academic needs of each Brady Middle School Student. Pride Time enables each student to establish a positive relationship with a faculty member and allows students to interact become part of a supportive group.

The basis of the program is that this teacher forms a strong supportive relationship with each of the students and their families. In addition, the Pride program incorporates lessons based on Covey's 7 Habits, provides a home base for student-led led conference preparation and delivery, as well as discussion and conversation that facilitates teamwork and good decision-making. Most of the students in our building identify their PRIDE Leader as the go-to-adult at school.

WEB: Where Everyone Belongs is a leadership program that provides extensive leadership training to our 8th grade students. WEB leaders then serve a leadership role with their younger peers. For the past three years, our 8th grade leaders have facilitated the 6th grade half day orientation by leading small groups of their peers through strategy based activities that help to build successful connections. In

C. Boske & A. Osanloo (Eds.), Students, Teachers, and Leaders Addressing Bullying in Schools, 225–228.

addition, the WEB leaders connect with their 6th grade groups throughout the year during the advisory program.

Guest Speakers: In addition to our advisory program, we intentionally allocate time and funds towards programs that enhance and build empathy, awareness, and respect. In partnership with the District Health and Safety Committee and our Parent Teacher Association (PTA), we have guest speakers to kick off our school year with an inspirational message. In the past few years we have had a range of speakers from song writers to football players, but all carry the same message of "make a positive difference." Likewise educating parents on topics of cyberbullying, social networking and other topics is an important part of our work.

Challenge Day: Every 7th grade student at Brady Middle School experiences Challenge Day. This program is a nationwide program with a mission to "provide youth and their communities with experiential workshops and programs that demonstrate the possibility of love and connection through the celebration of diversity, truth, and full expressions. The program is created to "build connection and empathy, and to fulfill our vision that every child lives in a world where they feel safe, loved and celebrated." (www.challengeday.org) Because the program requires one adult participant for every four students, it has increased our connections with parents and community. Perhaps best of all, it has mobilized adults across the school district and community in an effort to be a part of students lives in away that is supportive and nurturing.

Dancing Classrooms: In addition, all eighth grade students participate in Dancing Classrooms. The mission of this program is to build social awareness, confidence, and self esteem in children through the practice of social dance. Dancing classrooms is not about teaching ballroom dancing. The dance is a tool for getting the children to break down social barriers, learn about honor and respect, treat others carefully, improve self-confidence, communicate and cooperate, and accept others even if they are different. (http://dancingclassroomsneo.org/) For many of our students it is a way of leveling the playing field for students; everyone's level of learning is at that the same stage, everyone is socially awkward. They are in a public and vulnerable place and they grow together through it.

Daily Supports and Interventions: Even with supportive programs and explicit lessons designed to teach student empathy and compassion, we still have the daily work of helping adolescents apply these principles to their daily lives. Our response to issues of disrespect, racism, and harassment has many layers. Certainly there are times when school consequences remove students from their classrooms or building, however, we also layer that consequence with supports and interventions that help to change behaviors.

Behavior Contracts: One of the most difficult aspects of providing an anti-bullying atmosphere is helping students change their response to incidents and inappropriate behaviors that occur among adolescence. The most helpful strategy we have implemented is a Behavior Contract. Frequently, guidance counselors are able to facilitate a conversation between two middle school students who have been unkind to one another in some way or another. Sometimes, however, students need space and time. The behavior contract provides structures for students to be successful at eliminating interaction with another student. This one page document outlines expectations for the student and it empowers that student to take appropriate action(s). As I take a child through the process of completing the behavior agreement, we role play how to respond if someone tries to engage in conversation about the other student. We also role play the way in which the student report issues to a teacher. The document also includes a review date, at which time the counselor or myself will sit with students and review how the agreement is working.

Use of this document has eliminated the issues of students fearing that "reporting a bullying issue will only make it worse". In addition, it provides a student who is being treated unkindly from feeling a like a victim, by providing clear and specific responsibilities that empowers that student to take action.

BEHAVIOR CONTRACT

Student Name_____   **PrideLeader**_____

I will avoid potential conflict with _____by not talking to or about this student.

I will not approach this student when he or she is alone or with others.

If _____approaches me, I will remove myself from the situation and report immediately to an adult.

If _____talks to me, I will report immediately to an adult.

If_____makes me feel uncomfortable or unsafe in any way, I will report to an adult.

The adult I feel most comfortable reporting these issues to is_____
_____.

If that adult is not available, my back up plan is _____

_____.

I understand that the guidelines set up in this agreement are designed to help me be more successful at school.

I understand that by following this agreement it will help prevent potential conflict with

_____.

I understand that choosing not to follow the guidelines will result in consequences, including, but not limited to a call to parents, detentions, AEP, and/or other disciplinary actions.

_____   _____
Signature of student   Date   Signature of parent   Date

_____
Signature of administrator   Date
and/or supervising adult

Review of agreement to occur on _____.

Creating a safe and nurturing learning environment free from bullying is an impossible task, but increasing the opportunities for children and adolescents to understand how to make situations better is our responsibility. It requires a multi-tiered approach of support and education. It requires a commitment of time and resources. It requires putting first things first.

DICKSON S. PEREY

33. A CASE STUDY OF THE GAY-STRAIGHT ALLIANCE'S PRESENCE AT A PUBLIC URBAN HIGH SCHOOL

INTRODUCTION

Problem Statement

More conscious efforts have been made to give lesbian, gay, bisexual, and transgender (LGBT) students more equitable rights in safeguarding and empowering them from bullying, harassment, and discrimination. In recent years, it has become a topic that many educators have come to experience as more students are coming to terms with their sexual orientation at an earlier age and expressing themselves at schools without shame and/or secrecy. A research report developed by the Task Force on Bullying (2013) was presented at the American Educational Research Association's (AERA) annual meeting in April 2012, which identified a series of 11 briefs, highlighting considerations in addressing bullying in schools. The state of affairs of bullying and the lesbian, gay, and bisexual (GLB) community was highlighted and given more attention since this population is reported to be under-researched. As more students are coming out of the closet in schools, acceptance and understanding towards these minority students is varies considerably depending on individual school sites. The growing body of research showing that LGBT youth are at higher risks for depression, suicide, and substance abuse compared to their heterosexual peers (Heck, Flentje, & Cochran, 2011; Reis & Saewyc, 1999; Toomey, Ryan, Diaz, & Russell, 2011) gives reason to look at this issue more deeply.

Significance of Problem

In urban education, equity-related legal and policy issues continue to develop. There has been attention placed on the legal rights and safeguards for LGBT students. In creating and maintaining equitable educational environments for all students, LGBT students have gained legal rights, are part of the conversation and cannot be left behind. Countless acts of documented violence against LGBTs have taken place in public schools throughout the United States (GLSEN, 2013). Until recent times, few educational policies and specific safeguards existed to protect this at-risk population from bullying, harassment, and targeted violence. In a comprehensive review of literature, Black, Fedewa, and Gonzalez (2012) outline the effects of

C. Boske & A. Osanloo (Eds.), Students, Teachers, and Leaders Addressing Bullying in Schools, 229–243.
© *2015 Sense Publishers. All rights reserved.*

safe-school programs and policies on the social climate for sexual-minority youth in 17 scholarly articles. Their journal article reviewed the relationship between safe-school programs or policies, the effects on LGBT youth, and the importance of needs assessments to support this at-risk population. Their work echoes findings from The Gay, Lesbian, Straight, Education Network (GLSEN) 2011 National School Climate Survey that indicated that LGBT students are more vulnerable in relation to homophobic remarks, physical harassment, assault, and lack of comprehensive policies that safeguard students from harm (Kosciw, Greytak, Bartkiewicz, Boesen, & Palmer, 2012). Since schools are moving toward improving climates and ensuring all students (particularly LGBT) are safe from discrimination, harassment and bullying, it is critical to explore the legislative protections and appropriate supports for LGBT students in public schools. In the United States, California is one of sixteen states that have passed anti-bullying and/or nondiscrimination laws protecting LGBT students in schools (GLSNE, 2013). How did these safeguards come about? What tools could urban public schools use to safeguard and support LGBT students and/ or their allies?

Purpose of the Study

LGBT students who are coming to terms with their sexual identities are often isolated and alone with their feelings. To address this concern in a pro-active manner, an ongoing student-initiated and student-run movement has taken the form of Gay-Straight Alliances (GSA) on high school campuses throughout the United States. The purpose of this collective case study will be to explore the influence that the GSA has for visible LGBT students and straight allies at Delightful High School (DHS), a psdoeneum for an urban high school in metropolitan Los Angeles. The research question for this case study is: How do school stakeholders perceive the Gay-Straight Alliance in relation to a safe school climate? A research sub-question aims to uncover how the GSA promotes a safer school climate, particularly anti-bullying, for LGBT students and their allies. For this study Black, Fedewa, and Gonzalez's (2012) definition of a school climate is used which looks at the "quality and character of school life" (p. 322). The qualitative approach utilized is a case study using narrative inquiry techniques to generate data to assign value on how a GSA is part of a social movement for civil rights and equity in the communities it serves.

LITERATURE REVIEW

In a review of literature, the development of safe-schools laws and policy documents that explicitly safeguard LGBT students from bullying and harassment based on their actual or perceived sexual orientation and/or gender identity, a number of advances at the federal, state, and local levels have taken place, affording some protections for this minority group. Full equality has not yet been achieved for this class of citizens, but there is growth and expansion of protections to this community. The creation of the United States LGBT Equality Caucus and the California Legislative Lesbian, Gay, Bisexual and Transgender Caucus has contributed to legislation designed to protect LGBT students from anti-gay harassment in schools.

Inclusive Public Policy

Federal. The impact of the First and Fourteenth Amendments have shaped legal mandates safeguarding LGBT students at the highest level (Biegel, 2010). The safeguards and policies that help protect LGBT students have roots and connections to the civil rights movement of the 1960s and the *Brown vs. Brown of Education* (1954). Additionally, in contemporary cases regarding LGBT students' right-to-be-out in public schools, the 1969 U.S. Supreme Court decision *Tinker v Des Moines Independent Community College District* provides protections to K-12 students' freedom of expression under the First Amendment (Biegel, 2010).

Title IV of the Civil Rights Act of 1964 allows federal prosecution of an individual who "willingly injures, intimidates or interferes with another person...because of a person's race, color, religion or national origin" (Civil Rights Act, 1964, Sec. 245, subsection (b)) and is one of the original laws that helped protect six federally mandated life activities such as attending school. In its original form, this act did not cover sexual orientation; however, continual expansion through Title IX of the Education Amendments of 1972 broadens protections based on gender. In 1996, an additional amendment to Title IX indicated that public schools in the nation must ensure that abuse cannot take place against same-sex students. Before this case, no other legal proceeding in federal court challenged repugnant acts against out or perceived LGBT students. This case victory helped open the doors for other cases to have legal standing—including, but not limited to—*Flores v Morgan Hill Unified School District* (2003) and *Ramirez v Los Angeles Unified School District* (2004).

Additionally, the highly publicized and heinous murder of Matthew Shepard, an openly gay student who attended the University of Wyoming, ignited outrage from political communities that wanted an effective response regarding hate-crime legislation. Years later, The Matthew Shepard and James Byrd, Jr. Hate Prevention Act, passed on October 22, 2009 by Congress and signed into law President Barrack Obama, expanded the existing United States federal law to cover "actual or perceived gender, sexual orientation, gender identity, or disability" and dropped the prerequisite that the victim be engaged in one of six federally protected activities. This provided opportunities to states to follow suit and pass laws that specifically safeguard sexual orientation from bullying and harassment in schools. Unfortunately not all states have adopted such laws.

California state laws. California has adopted several important laws that reflect the emerging rights of LGBT students in public schools. A slew of reform reports from different levels of the government have increased awareness of crimes and injustices to LGBT students in schools and helped improve school climates, particularly urban schools. Although discrimination had taken place against LGBT students for several years prior to the release of such reports, the intolerance to injurious acts is diminishing with increased awareness. As one example, *Hate-Motivated Behavior in Schools: Response Strategies for School Boards, Administrators, Law Enforcement, and Communities*—a 1997 report from the California Dept of Education and the Alameda County Office of Education —specifically emphasized safeguarding gender identity and sexual orientation and created talking points about hate-motivated behaviors in schools. This and many other publications initiated problem recognition for lawmakers, which Marshall and Gerstl-Pepin (2005) state is an opening of a policy window.

Since California is one of the largest states in the union, the *California Student Safety and Violence Prevention Act of 2000* (Assembly Bill 537) was especially bold in its explicit adoption of sexual orientation and gender into law, further protecting students from discrimination and/or harassment in schools. The adoption of this law took place through with the work of the first openly gay CA legislative policy actor CA State Senator Sheila Kuehl. When she was elected to the California legislature, she led by authoring and championing the California Education Code Section 220 amendment to ensure that all students and staff in public schools have the same right to a safe learning environment. California law was important inspiring for other states to follow suit.

Kuehl's leadership in California as the founding member of the LGBT Caucus made way for additional laws affecting public education, including the *Safe Place to Learn Act* (Levine, 2007), *Students Civil Rights Act* (Kuehl, 2007) and *Seth's Law* (Ammiano, 2011). These recent California laws open doors for increasing safeguards for LGBT students. Interestingly enough, as noted with the dates of passed legislation, it took several years for the public's mood change towards LGBT equality and respect to shift.

Local school district context. In investigating local school district context, the Los Angeles Unified School District (LAUSD) began its explicit commitment to safeguarding LGBT students in October 1998 with a LAUSD Board Resolution that looked "To Enforce the Respectful Treatment of All Persons." Since LAUSD is the second-largest school district in the nation, this explicit measure impacted educational policy and gave room for other school districts to take action.

To support schools in their work for equality, LGBT advocacy groups and allied groups helped define policy communities for safeguarding LGBT students in schools. The American Civil Liberties Union (ACLU) (1920), originally created to frame free speech, helped open the door for specific LGBT groups like Lambda Legal (est. 1973), Human Right Campaign (HRC) (est. 1980), Gay, Lesbian, and Straight Educator Network (GLSEN) (est. 1990), Gay-Straight Alliance (GSA) Network (est. 1998) and Parents, Friends for Lesbians and Gays (P-FLAG) (est. 1972) along with other advocacy work to carry out focused initiatives in defending the rights of LGBT students who experience mistreatment and injustices that impede their learning and development in schools.

The right to be out and the right to have a student organization like GSA on public school campuses have grown over time. Political factions from various interest groups have challenged student expression rights in court cases. Since federal law mandates equal access for K-12 clubs, affirmative policies towards LGBT rights opened up for these students in the 1990s. Religious and societal persecution of LGBTs in mainstream media outlets (television, print, film, etc.) creates policy communities that identify problems and mobilized political interests for LGBT protections. In supporting schools around the nation, GLSEN's organized efforts and focus on research helps politicians and others interested in public policy.

In 2012, a comprehensive LAUSD bulletin, Bullying and Hazing Policy (BUL-5212.1), responded to a rash of highly publicized LGBT youth suicides and social media bullying and harassment affecting school-aged children. This bulletin helped identify the problems experienced in schools, drew alignment with both federal and state laws, and further allowed protection for LGBT students experiencing bullying and discrimination. In the most explicit board approval from a large public school in 2011, the LAUSD Commission on Human Relations, Diversity, and Equity adopted the Lesbian, Gay, Bisexual and Transgender and Sexual Orientation Resolution requiring all schools to be proactive in decreasing anti-LGBT language and bullying. This board adoption corresponded with the passage of California's SB48, the Fair Accurate Inclusive Respectful (FAIR) Education Act, further instituting policies which impact LGBT students and their communities.

Concept Map

The concept map (Figure 1) used to design this study illustrates the intricate underpinnings of a school system's procedural safeguards for LGBT students and how daily interactions influence an individual school climate. Modeled after the image of an automobile fan belt in an engine, this representation shows the interconnectedness among 1) significant issues and factors that have a part in developing safeguards for LGBT students and their allies; 2) how one specific school and its staff deal with everyday occurrences that may increase or decrease the warmth of the school climate for LGBT students; 3) specific roles and duties that educators at DHS view as essential to creating a hostility-free environment for LGBT students and their allies. Like an engine, several parts must run in unison to help a vehicle move forward. The main components of this three-part system are:

- *The Drive Shaft* (largest gear on the lower left-hand side) component represents comprehensive issues that affect all persons in the educational system. The areas that are included are federal, state and local laws, school district policies and procedures, and community groups serving the LGBT community. It is considered a "big influencer" and the strongest drive as an essential part of the whole. It is the slowest moving part in the system.

- *The Alternator* (medium gear on the upper right-hand side) component represents the institution that houses students to learn in a safe, inclusive environment. In this specific case, it is the case study school site. Like the drive shaft, it is also a moving part in the system, illuminating a range on a color continuum to indicate if the school is reacting to situations affecting the school site in a positive or negative manner. The continuum ranges from light to dark in relation to the LGBT-affirming school climate. The color shift indicates how the school deals with daily impacts to LGBT issues and incidents.
- *The Tensioner* (smallest gear on the lower right- hand side) component represents the educators working at the schools. A host of professional educators inform and bring about social change in schools as they implement policies with or without the influence of anti-gay bias, harassment, discrimination, or judgment to LGBT students and their allies. They react to daily situations relevant to LGBT students in school sites in a responsible, informed, and enlightened fashion to bring about change in the entire organization. As the fastest-moving part of the system, it is an important grassroots component that keeps the system tight and in proper functioning order. Influentially interacting with the school and its students, it is also the least permanent, most mutable, and changeable.
- *The Belt* (large black line that joins all parts of the system together) component is an ever-changing, everlasting bond that continually is transformed. Specific issues, concerns, achievements, and rewards that may affect a school system and specifically affect LGBT students change throughout school year.

Within the school system, a two-way arrow indicates communication and policy safeguards that influence what happens politically within the system. Outside of the system are outside influences represented as lighting bolts. These outside concerns influence the structure of the school system with anti-LGBT bias and harassment.METHOD
This study approaches the research question through a social constructivism and LGBT advocacy/participatory lens. Looking to understand the complexity of different viewpoints in the school community, steps were taken to gather multiple sources of information to understand community needs using a collective case study approach.

Context and Participants

Setting. This study was conducted from March 2013 to April 2013 at a high school called Delightful High School (DHS), situated in a large, comprehensive public urban school district in Southern California. According to information from California's Department of Education Dataquest website (2013), the total student enrollment in the 2012–2013 school year at DHS is about 1,000. The school features a district

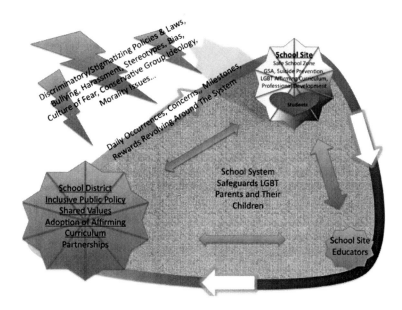

Figure 1. Concept map – School system safeguards for LGBT students and their allies

integration program with a diverse student population of 7% African American, 25% Asian, 8% Filipino, 58% Latino, and 2% white, comprised primarily of lower-to-middle-class families. Over half of the school is deemed socioeconomically disadvantaged. It is difficult to gauge how many students identify as part of the LGBT community at the school or the district; however, evidence in literature points out that in high school student populations, 4.5% are identified as LGBT students (Resi & Saewyc, 1999).

Sample. This study used a purposeful sample to generate an array of perspectives on the cultural dynamics at DHS. Included in this sample were leaders from the DHS student organizations including GSA, the Black Student Union (BSU), Associated Student Body (ASB), the school's principal, and a parent of a LGBT student. GSA members and students who supported the GSA were also part of this purposeful sample. These participants were selected based on their involvement with an annual school wide event called the Day of Silence. This activity allowed students to bring awareness to an effort to decrease anti-LGBT slurs, bullying, and harassment through a series of creative activities.

Participation in this study was voluntary. Two elected officers of the GSA and the school principal were formally interviewed and tape-recorded for later review. These interviews were structured with predetermined, open-ended questions, and lasted no more than 30 minutes. A parent of a LGBT student was solicited through e-mail with predetermined, open-ended questions. Other student leaders were involved in this study through GSA creative writing and art activities and informal interviews. Informational interviews were short and concise to provide depth and validation to formal interviews. All stakeholders were interviewed at the school site, either in an office or at the regularly scheduled GSA meeting.

The DHS GSA. The aftermath of a violent act against a lesbian student in 2005 prompted the DHS grass-roots community campaign called "Not at Our School." This campaign involved friends of the victim taking a stand against the violent act by creating signs of support declaring "no violence due to sexual orientation at our school." The following year, GSA developed into a student-run organization that works within the school community to promote equality and acceptance of all students at DHS. GSA attempts to reduce anti-gay violence, harassment, and discrimination by educating the school community about homophobia, using appropriate language, and encouraging a greater degree of understanding from students and school personnel. It also provides a safe place for LGBT students to connect with one another.

At the beginning of the school year, GSA met every week during lunch. As the year progressed, the group became smaller, but the core group of students continued to meet on Mondays and Wednesdays to talk about growing up as a LGBT teen and exploring issues that affect the community. The DHS GSA has sustained membership growth and grew to partner with other groups on campus by sponsoring activities. Day of Silence, an anti-bullying movement sponsored by the Gay, Lesbian Straight Education Network (GLSEN), is an annual event produced by the GSA, which brings awareness and actions to end anti-LGBT slurs and harassment.

Data Collection Procedures

Data collection began in March 2013 and continued through the following month. It consisted of four components: observations, interviews, documents, and audiovisual material. As an observer-participant, every attempt to be as neutral as possible when observations were conducted. It was difficult to embrace the role since many of students wanted to ask questions regarding school-related matters during formal and informal observations. Through a collection of data sources, qualitative data was analyzed through a variety of means to gauge whether or not the presence of the GSA at DHS had any effect on school safety and anti-bullying measures and promoted a positive, warm climate for LGBT students and their allies.

Observations.   Formal observations began with an evidence checklist, which looked for LGBT-affirming literature, signage, and brochures posted at DHS in hallways and school offices. A school map captured location of the artifacts and helped determine their frequency. A compilation of words that sent an affirming message about inclusive community values and positive school climate towards LGBT youth helped develop codes and themes for the study on 3x5 cards. Photographs using a smartphone captured unique artifacts in the school that illustrated an affirming stance in accepting LGBT students and their allies by the community. Preceding the community scan, formal observations with an evidence checklist took place during structured (classroom) and unstructured (student break periods) times during and after the instructional day.

Informal observations continued through the study where a notebook was used to document observations in staff meetings, GSA meetings, advisory classrooms, and unstructured times before, during and after school. Each observation was a short snapshot lasting no more than 30 minutes on five different occasions during the five-week time period.

Semi-structured and informal interviews. Semi-structured interviews of two elected student leaders from GSA and the high school principal were conducted and recorded. A set of open-ended questions guided the interviews. On-the-spot guided questions helped enrich the conversations and provide deeper context. Students participating in GSA activities were informally interviewed through casual conversations. By interviewing these students, themes and stories of what they understood about the presence of GSA on the campus was revealed. Each semi-structured interview was no more than 30 minutes. Questions gauged experience, opinions, values, feelings, and knowledge for participants which are listed below:

- How does the presence of the Gay-Straight Alliance (GSA) at Delightful High School (DHS) help promote a safe school climate for LGBT students and their allies? (both student leaders, principal)
- How would DHS be a different place if there were no GSA on campus? (both student leaders and principal)
- What does an LGBT or straight ally do in response to an anti-LGBT situation at DHS? (both student leaders only)
- When there is a controversial topic that comes up regarding LGBT issues, how do you address them? (principal)
- What is difficult or easy about being part of a LGBT or straight ally at DHS? (one student leader)
- Does having a GSA at DHS allow you to feel empowered to fight for equality for LGBT? (one student leader)

Each semi-structured interview was transcribed. The first interview with the 2012–13 GSA president was transcribed in it's entirety. Interviews with the second GSA leader and the principal were transcribed as close as possible. Interviews were recorded using a Voice Memo application on a smartphone. Field notes were also used to help document the process. One interview using e-mail with a parent of an LGBT student at DHS was used. Three questions via e-mail to gain a parent perspective helped triangulate data.

Text-based data documents. The following documents were analyzed: (a) a local school district policy bulletin, (b) two local school district board resolutions on the status of lesbian, gay, bisexual and transgender issues in schools, (d) Day of Silence reflection letters from GSA members, (e) Ending the Silence art activity, and (f) a mainstream news article highlighting the school's GSA. Items A-C were accessed through the central school district website, Items D-E were collected from student participants during the study time frame, while Item F was retrieved from the mainstream news outlet's archives. These sources of information were appropriate for my study as I was able to triangulate data sources through multiple means and these helped provide a rich texture for the data analysis.

Audio-visual artifacts. A televised news broadcast was collected during the study and used to gain understanding about the school culture at DHS. The Day of Silence, an annual school-wide anti-bullying awareness event organized by GSA, was featured on a local new station in April 2012. A newscaster on-site, who interviewed three students and a counselor at DHS, documented the footage. The interview quotes from the news footage were transcribed and later analyzed like an interview transcript.

Coding and Data Analysis

At the stage that could be classified as "thinking about things," followed an analysis continuum in generating meaning from raw data, turning it into descriptive statements and generating interpretation through open coding, categorization, integration and interpretation (Miles & Huberman, 1994). Data collected from observations, semi-structured and informal interviews, text-based documents, and audio-visual artifacts were compiled and kept as separate groups. The artifacts were collected in separate file folders and used consistent methods to generate themes and codes. To begin the first stage of data analysis, open coding took place to look at common concepts that described an idea, an expression, a feeling or thought that related with my research question and concept map. The methods used for all data were: 1) highlighting key words, 2) computer charting with color codes, and 3) notes analysis. The initial list included key words like *alliance, perspectives, misunderstood, non-violent, togetherness, action, affirming, acceptance, relationships, resolution*, etc. to identify descriptions of GSA's influence (or lack thereof) on the school campus. Document transcripts were reviewed several times. A review of information that supported affirmations as well as limitations was sought. Categories were developed after codes were reviewed and five turned up: *Stakeholders, Network, Results, Difficulties, and Safety Net*. At this point, an alignment of descriptive sentences from transcripts and text to help identify emerging themes was utilized through inductive analysis.

Validity, Reliability and Trustworthiness

Data triangulation and peer checks were embedded throughout the data collection.

As an employee at the school site for over 10 years had both positive and negative aspects regarding validity. Participants could review and confirm the study's accuracy. As a observer-participant, a depth of historical context of the school climate, values and leadership structure helped bridge context to the case study. Daily informal interactions with study participants helped keep perspectives fresh.

In this study, the researcher had a dual role as observer-participant and professional educator working intimately with the stakeholders at DHS. Member checking for personal bias took place with participants. Second opinions regarding data collection helped with validity. In order to establish internal reliability and trustworthiness, multiple sources of data collection validated findings through triangulation. Several sources of permanent documents including local school district board resolutions, policy bulletins, an article published in a newspaper, emails from community resources, and GSA materials and student-created flyers helped enhance the study.

FINDINGS

Toomey, Ryan, Diaz, and Russell (2011) found several associations between GSA presence and positive well-being for LGBT young people and aligned with findings in this study. The observations, interviews, and creative work samples showed support for the idea that the GSA's presence at the high school was influential in the cultural, social and political climate of the institution. The broader themes that developed from this study were 1) Freedom of Expression, 2) Supportive Network, 3) Education, 4) Awareness.

Freedom of Expression

Freedom of Expression was a common theme in the data sources, which was interpreted as "the ability to be yourself." This theme suggested that stakeholders felt empowered to express their point of view without repercussions. Interviews with different stakeholders revealed evidence from all levels.

- "I never worked at a high school with so many out gay boys in particular and I think part of the reason why we have so many…is…they feel safe to be out and that is critical." (School principal)
- "With a GSA in the school, everyone in the school, from students, teachers, staff, parents, administrators, coaches, are all in a position to reflect on their attitudes about LGBT people. Attitudes come out in the open and are discussed." (Parent of a LGBT student)

A critical exploration of expression was documented in the GSA's Day of Silence event that took place during the study. GSA members produced the event. In a writing activity, reflective responses generated from a free-response question, "What does Day of Silence mean to you?" were collected. Regarding Freedom of Expression, one student wrote:

- "Day of Silence is a day of solidarity in which we engage in moments of silence for our fallen rainbow warriors. It is very important because while we honor memories of our brave brothers and sisters, we are also supporting those still courageously fighting." (GSA member)

Supportive Network

Supportive network was the most widely recognizable theme. The data indicated that interconnectedness exists among stakeholders. This connection helps safeguard LGBT students and their allies at all levels. A review of explicit and inclusive laws and policies asks school districts in the California to safeguard LGBT students from bullying and harassment in public schools. Schools in California are also asked to include fair, accurate, inclusive, and respectful portrayals of LGBT citizens in instructional lessons. Quotes from interviews indicated:

- "We are fortunate enough to work in a district that is very supportive of promoting LGBT awareness and making sure that schools are safe for LGBT students.there is support behind any decisions that I make…. I think it's about being courageous and being open." (School principal)

At the school level, the GSA leader indicates how a supportive network is embedded in the structure of the school. The development of positive relationships with adults is notable and expressed this way:

- "Personally when I have issues I talk to either one of my counselors or talk to one of my teachers, which I see as friends as well, that's how friendly people are here." (Student leader)

The GSA's Day of Silence demonstrates the school's willingness to "stand up for others" as frequently noted in a creative writing activity. The GSA president in 2011–12 was interviewed on camera and illustrated the supportive network that exists at the campus:

- "I remember being 15 and telling my mom, I would rather have cancer than be gay…. It was so amazing seeing all of these kids this morning just going to the table to get some tape. It was like, wow these kids are actually interested; they want to be a part of it.To look during the assembly, to see all those kids standing there. If no one got saved today, I did." (Student on national news)

Education

Education refers to the temperature of the school climate towards LGBT students and the hidden curriculum that encompasses community values (or does not value) norms about LGBT safeguards against victimization. The awareness that LGBT students are part of the fabric of the school is important as it creates transparency and acknowledges the diversity of the community. There is a sense that educating the school population regarding LGBT issues is valued and can be addressed openly, as is evident in these responses:

- "Not only CAN we talk about it, or ok to talk about it, we should be talking about it." (School principal)
- "Everyone is able to take a stand in terms of supporting LGBT youth. It allows the LGBT students to be open about who they are and enjoy life in their own skin. For some kids DHS becomes their home – the place where they can be who they are in safety." (Parent of an LGBT student)

Evidence indicates that education happens at many levels in the school and the classroom. In a newspaper article highlighting the passage of the California FAIR Education Act in 2011, a DHS teacher was interviewed and asked about his ideology in including LGBT's contribution in the United States in the social science curriculum. The response was favorable:

- "I'm a history teacher and this is history. It's part of the narrative. You can't remove it." (Social Studies Teacher)

Awareness

Evidence suggests that the GSA's presence is helpful in providing a safe space for LGBT students and their allies. There is an understanding about the structure that exists at the school for reporting incidents that may create harm.

- "I talk to my counselor and resolve it, like I said. And it ends up being, some type of misunderstanding where people are just judging by the way. You know people have their own perspectives on things, uhhh, yeah; I end up resolving it in the end." (Student leader)

Even with procedural safeguards, there is still room for growth at the school. This theme reveals an awareness of the values of students and administrators at the school and whether actions take place to safeguard students. A student was called a denigrating term during a classroom activity, spoke up about it to the class, then sought advice from adults on campus to address the matter:

- "I got my comments and I was going through them, and a lot of them had good compliments, and then I see one that says, mmm, Faggot…. And it really got to me. And usually I try not to let words get to me because of my, you could say, my temper problem. …first thing I did as soon as class was over, I came to my counselor, showed him the paper, and talked about the situation and mmm, the principal was involved and it mmm got sorted out. And in the end, I didn't really find out who it was, although I had a sense and as well as the principal, but I kind of just dropped it afterwards…. (Student, GSA president)

CONCLUSIONS AND IMPLICATIONS

Improving the school climate, reducing anti-LGBT slurs and language that harasses and targets students who are out or perceived to be LGBT is a challenge. At the school and district level, there is staunch and active support to safeguard students from harassment and bullying; however, implementation of LGBT protections can be difficult even in an inclusive environment like DHS. Consistent reporting of issues and concerns and having front-line staff in the classrooms or school hallways are a concern, students who declare, "That's so gay" or use other derogatory words create a hostile school environment. Likewise, students can fear retaliation for disclosing this information and therefore just let the acts go on unnoticed. It is perceived that LGBT harassment still exists at a school like DHS. Continuing to follow comprehensive district anti-bullying harassments policies is suggested. An active effort to continue working on reducing anti-LGBT slurs and stigmas is also suggested. Continuing to support GSA activities is suggested, as it helps bring about freedom of expression, a supportive network, education, and awareness to a broad audience. With the passage of the California FAIR Education Act, looking at ways to implement this law needs to be considered and discussed. Finding LGBT-inclusive resources is necessary.

Unfortunately, even with explicit policies and numerous district bulletins that specifically outline how schools shall implement safeguards, some educators struggle with their personal LGBT bias. Continual professional development would be helpful in order to increase awareness of and reduce expressions of LGBT bias.

REFLECTION/ISSUES AND CONCERNS

At the close of this study, I was reminded why I do the work toward helping LGBT students have a voice. I just ended a very touching conversation with one of the students I interviewed earlier in this study. The student is the GSA president at DMHS. I held a counseling session with him for close to an hour after the study was completed. We chatted about a slew of issues and concerns he had about the relationship with his boyfriend, family matters, and general concerns about school. Additionally, he described incidents of harassment directed at him that spanned years that he never disclosed to anyone until that point due to shame and guilt. Our conversation was informal in nature, but I was able to able see the impact that bullying and harassment had taken on this student's dignity. His role in the GSA was influential in developing a positive self-image and regard in growing up as a member of the LGBT community. With tears welling up, he shared, "If it wasn't for you, I would not be the person that I am today."

As a high school counselor, I see firsthand how laws and policies help safeguard LGBT students. Over the years, I have seen how responsive school district staff is at addressing concerns about acts of violence that were outlined in my review of literature. As a school GSA advisor, I have called the school district to resolve concerns from students and parents about LGBT issues. Laws specifically outlining what is acceptable and not acceptable at the local school context empower professionals who have an interest in social justice and progressive educational philosophies to educate and inform students about anti-LGBT stereotypes, bullying and harassment. Safety is the number-one concern for students, especially LGBT students.

REFERENCES

American Educational Research Association. (2013). *Prevention of bullying in schools, colleges, and universities: Research report and recommendations.* Washington, DC: American Educational Research Association.

Biegel, S. (2010). *The right to be out: Sexual orientation and gender identity in American's public schools.* Minneapolis, MN: University of Minnesota Press.

Black, W. W., Fedewa, A. L., & Gonzalez, K. A., (2012). Effects of safe school programs and policies on the social climate for sexual-minority youth: A review of the literature. *Journal of LGBT Youth, 9*(4), 321–229.

Flores v Morgan Hill USD, 324 F.3d 1130 (9th Cir. 2003).

GLSEN. (2013a). *School climate in California* (Research brief). New York, NY: GLSEN.

GLSEN. (2013b). *Enumerated anti-bullying laws by state.* New York, NY: GLSEN.

GLSEN. (2013c). *School climate in California* (State snapshot). New York, NY: GLSEN.

Heck, N. C., Flentje, A., & Cochran, B. N., (2011). Offsetting risks: High school gay-straight alliances and lesbian, gay, bisexual, and transgender (LGBT) youth. *School Psychology Quarterly, 26*(2), 161–174. doi:10.1037/a0023226

Henkle v. Gregory, 150 F. Supp. 2d 10767 (D.Nev.2001).

Kosciw, J. G., Greytak, E. A., Bartkiewicz, M. J., Boesen, M. J., & Palmer, N. A. (2012). *The 2011 national school climate survey: The experiences of lesbian, gay, bisexual and transgender youth in our nation's schools.* New York, NY: GLSEN.

Miles, M., & Huberman, A. (1994). *Qualitative data analysis: An expanded sourcebook* (2nd ed.). Thousand Oaks, CA: Sage Publications.

Nabozny v. Podlesny, 92 F.3d 446 (7th Cir. 1996).

Reis, E., & Saewyc, E. (1999). *Eighty-three thousand youths: Selected findings of eight population-based studies as they pertain to anti-gay harassment and the safety and well being of sexual minority students.* Seattle, WA: Safe Schools Coalition of Washington.

Toomey, R. B., Ryan, C., Diaz, R. M., & Russell, S. T. (2011). High school gay-straight alliances (GSAs) and young adult well-being: An examination of GSA presence, participation, and perceived effectiveness. *Applied Developmental Science, 15*(4), 175–185.

Dickson S. Perey
California State University
Los Angeles

YOONA LEE, MALCOLM W. WATSON AND KI-HAK LEE

34. THE RELATION OF PHYSICAL DISCIPLINE TO BULLYING BEHAVIORS ACROSS DIFFERENT FAMILIES AND ETHNICITIES

No single cause leads to a child becoming a habitual bully, but research has provided us with information on several antecedent factors that seem to lead to bullying behaviors. Harsh or frequent, parental physical discipline is one of those factors. According to Barboza, Schiamberg, and Oehmke's (2009) review, adolescent bullies tend to be reared with a lack of parental involvement and warmth (Olweus, 1993) and with authoritarian parenting, in which parents use a lot of physical discipline and power assertive techniques (Bowers et al., 1994; Rodkin & Hodges, 2003). Children and youth whose parents use physical discipline are at a heightened risk of using bullying behaviors themselves (Baldry & Farrington, 2005; Schwartz et al., 2000; Schwartz, Dodge, Pettit, & Bates, 1997). Results from the research of Espelage et al. (2000), among bullies from middle school students, parental physical discipline was positively related to bullying behavior.

Using a longitudinal study, Schwartz and colleagues (2000) assessed pre-school boys' parental home environments, including physical discipline, and their subsequent behavior in elementary school. They found that a harsh home environment helps to create bully-victims, who are children who bully and also get bullied. It appears that parental corporal punishment causes children to develop emotional deregulation, leading to children becoming easily angry and to bully others. According to Hong, Espelage, Grogan-Kaylor, and Allen-Meares (2012)'s review of parental maltreatment, including physical types toward children, and its relation to school bullying, parental use of physical punishment is related to emotional deregulation, which impedes the ability of a child to develop healthy models of attachment leading to healthy peer relationships.

This brief review of some of the literature indeed shows that parents who use harsh discipline, particularly physical discipline (i.e., corporal punishment), have children who are more prone to developing into bullies. Yet, the literature on parental corporal punishment is not at all clear as to the universality of such a relation. Although a limited knowledge has been known regarding bullying predicted by physical discipline and ethnic-cultural variations (Hong & Espelage, 2012), it seems to be the case that people in different ethnicities or cultures perceive and use parental discipline in different ways (Whaley, 2000; Zhai & Gao, 2009) and with different degrees of negative consequences (e.g., Eamon, 2001; Sheehan & Watson, 2008).

C. Boske & A. Osanloo (Eds.), Students, Teachers, and Leaders Addressing Bullying in Schools, 245–259.

Might it be the case that in some cultures, in which corporal punishment is the norm and is even expected of caring (Landsford, 2010), diligent parents that the outcome may not lead to increased child bullying or other aggressive behaviors. If this cultural difference is true, then what might be the process whereby aggressive parental behaviors lead to less aggressive ends in children? Or does physical parental punishment in fact lead to negative consequences regardless of culturally different family environment? We intended to address these questions.

Though there is a general agreement in both Eastern and Western cultures that physical and sexual abuse are the most severe types of parental abuse (e.g., Lee, Jang, & Malley-Morrsion, 2008), subtle cultural variation still exists, as noted above, in the perception and effectiveness of physical discipline. Those in Western cultures tend to regard physical discipline as parental rejection or lack of control; whereas those in non-Western cultures tend to view physical discipline as indicative of responsible parental involvement (Landsford, 2010; Whaley, 2000; Zhai & Gao, 2009). For example, for East Asians who were raised with an emphasis on cohesive family environments based on a collectivist focus in a culture of relational collectivism (Brewer & Chen, 2007; Oyserman, Coon, & Kemmelmeier, 2002) physical discipline could be considered a loving and concerned parenting technique which is much better than neglect. Lee, Jang, and Malley-Morrison (2008) found that Koreans are less likely to view physical discipline and more likely to perceive neglect as a form of abusive behavior than are European Americans.

Depending on the cultural contexts in which parenting occurs, specific parenting behaviors may have different effects on children's perceptions, responses and outcomes (Lansford, 2010). In terms of effectiveness, in general, physical discipline has been associated with higher externalizing behaviors and disorders (See Gershoff, 2002, for a review). However, in the past two decades, as we mentioned, researchers have found that this effect of parental discipline may not be universal across cultures. This questioning of the universality of the discipline-externalizing behaviors relation was first based on the weaker relation that was found between physical discipline and behavior problems for African Americans as compared to European Americans. There was generally a more frequent use of physical discipline in Hispanic and African American families (e.g., Deater-Deckard et al., 1996; Sheehan & Watson, 2008) but with fewer negative outcomes of children's externalizing behaviors than in European American families (e.g., Eamon, 2001; Sheehan & Watson, 2008). Meanwhile, there was no association between discipline and subsequent aggression in African American children (Gunnoe & Mariner, 1997; Polaha, Larzelere, Shapiro, & Pettit, 2004; Whaley, 2000) and in Asians (Le et al., 2005). Regarding Asians, specifically, little is known about whether the association would be weaker, stronger, or the same as compared to other ethnic groups. Interestingly, authoritarian parental style (including physical punishment), which was detrimental for European American adolescent outcomes (Steinberg, Mounts, Lamborn, & Dornbusch, 1991), was more likely than authoritative parental style to result in better academic achievement among East Asians (Leung, Lau, & Lam, 1998).

Surprisingly, family environment, which affects the essential manner in which parents use punishment in different ethnic cultures, has largely been ignored in research. Thus, in our study we wanted to examine whether family marital status, as one of the most representative characteristics of family, moderates the relation of physical discipline to children's bullying behaviors within ethnicity and between ethnicities. Unmarried mothers are more vulnerable to mental health and behavioral problems than married mothers, and this factor may have an effect on poor parenting and children at risk of poor developmental outcomes (DeKlyen et al., 2006).

Previous research showed that the use of more physical discipline has been closely related to some aspects of the family environment, such as family size (Flynn, 1994; Pinderhughes et al., 2000; Xu et al., 2000), mother's employment status (Weis & Toolis, 2010; Roehling et al., 2005), and marital status (DeKlyen et al., 2006; Loeber et al., 2000; McCabe et al., 1999; Pinderhughes et al., 2000; Xu et al., 2000). In terms of marital status, the lack of a partnership had an influence on parent's use of corporal punishment. It was found that single and separated or divorced parents use more physical punishment on their children than do married parents (Loeber et al., 2000; McCabe et al., 1999). Moreover, Ceballo and McLoyd (2002) investigated stressful environmental conditions within African American single mothers related to social support and parenting strategies and found that when these mothers' surrounding environments were inferior, the relation between lower social support and use of verbal and physical punishments were stronger.

Regarding bullying behaviors, structure of one-parent families has also been positively related to bullying involvement (Flouri & Buchanan, 2003; Spriggs, Lannotti, Nansel, & Haynie, 2007). By contrast, we assumed that the status of being married and having two parents in the house could buffer the association between physical discipline and bullying behaviors. According to the U.S. Census Bureau, Statistical Abstract of the United States (2012), in 2010, marital status by ethnicity showed the highest frequency of people being married in Asian, followed by European, African, and Hispanic Americans (66%, 59%, 54%, and 39%, respectively). The ethnic differences in marital status could be significant across ethnicities and also have an impact on the association between physical discipline and bullying behaviors across ethnicities.

The primary goal of the study reported below was to examine how marital status moderates the association between mothers' use of physical discipline and children's bullying behaviors within ethnicity and between ethnicities. It included a sample of major racial/ethnic groups made up of Black, White, and Hispanic Americans, and East Asians.

In this study, we attempted to determine whether and how individual- and ethnic-level marital statuses influence the relation between mother's physical discipline and child bullying behaviors. First, we examined differences within families in an ethnicity to determine whether marital status moderates the association between mother's use of physical discipline and children's bullying behaviors. Thus, the first research question was to assess whether marital status can buffer the negative

247

impact of physical discipline on bullying behaviors within families. Second, we examined whether level of marital status did indeed differ across ethnicities and whether these differences would explain any significant variation across ethnicities in the association between parent punishment and children's bullying behaviors. The second research question was to investigate whether ethnic-level marital status across ethnicities would moderate the relation between physical discipline and bullying behaviors.

METHOD

A total of 729 children from 7 to 13 years of age and their mothers were sampled from five race/ethnic groups (i.e., White, Black, and Hispanic Americans, Koreans, and Chinese). The data used in this study were drawn from the Springfield Child Development Project (SCDP), a longitudinal study of aggression and bullying behaviors and other risk behaviors in middle childhood and adolescence in the U.S., and from samples of Chinese and Korean parents and children: The total sample was 23% Black, 19% White, 18% Hispanic, 32% Koreans, and 8% Chinese. The U.S. sample (from the SCDP) consisted of a community-based, representative sample of 440 mother-child dyads from the city of Springfield, MA (See the sampling procedure from Watson, Fischer, Burdzovic Andreas, & Smith, 2004). This current study used a total 438 mother-child pairs from the baseline assessment (T1). Some zip codes were over-sampled to obtain a more equally balanced representation of African American (38%), Hispanic American (29%), and European American (32%) children.

For the East Asian samples, Chinese and Korean families were recruited in their own countries. The Chinese sample was interviewed by a professional researcher and was drawn from those living in the city of Fuzhou, Fujian where the economic environment is similar to that of the U.S. sample from Springfield, MA. Ninety-five children (64 nine-year olds and 31 ten-year olds) were selected from fourth-grade classes in an elementary school. After screening the father's reported surveys, 55 Chinese families were used. The Korean sample, along with the Chinese sample, was collected to obtain an expanded and more generalizable East Asian sample. Like the Chinese sample, 236 children in elementary school, ages 7 to 13 years, were recruited by teachers from locates at Dong-Tan in Korea where the economic situation was also similar to the U.S. sample from Springfield, MA.

Regarding measures used in this study, physical discipline and married status were completed by mothers, but children completed the measures of bullying behaviors. Two proficient bilingual assistants helped the translation processes by translating from the original English versions of all measures into Korean and Chinese. Afterwards, these measures were back-translated into English and were compared to the original versions in order to achieve the equivalence of meanings, tenses, tones, and intonations. Then, the measures in the two language versions reconstructed concurrently.

Fighting behavior (Guerra & Slaby, 1990; Slaby & Guerra, 1988).   For bullying behaviors, children were asked 6 questions about bullying which included physical-related bullying behaviors (e.g. "Do you hit and push other kids?", "Do you try to pick fights with other kids?"), and verbal-related bullying behaviors (e.g. "Do you call other kids' names or say mean things?", "Do you say that you can beat up other kids?"). The frequency for each question was indicated using a 4-point scale (0= "never"; 1="sometimes"; 2="often"; 3="almost always"). This scale had Cronbach alpha values of .87 for the entire sample, .74 for Blacks, .63 for Whites, .82 for Hispanics, .72 for Koreans, and .67 for Chinese. Thus, the scale was shown to have a fairly high degree of internal consistency and reliability.

Maternal discipline.   The Conflict Tactics Scale (CTS) (Straus, 1979; Straus & Gelles, 1990) was used to assess the disciplinary practices that the mother used with her child. This measure, which has been used with many families and has been shown to be reliable and valid (Straus, 1979), was completed by the mother. The CTS was originally a 19-item questionnaire, split into the three subscales of reasoning, verbal discipline, and physical discipline, using 7-point scales. They ranged in terms of severity of discipline. In this study, I did not include reasoning and extreme forms of physically abusive assault, such as burned/scaled the child, threatened to use a knife or gun, or actual use of abusive assault. Items with higher numbers mean more frequent use of the discipline from "never" to "20 times in the past year." The physical discipline methods that were eventually included in this study were pushing/grabbing/shoving, slapping/spanking, kicking or hitting with a fist, hitting the child with something, and beating (5 items). Cronbach alpha values were .64 for the entire sample, and. 58 for Blacks, .60 for Whites, .53 for Hispanics,. 75 for Koreans, and. 75 for Chinese.

Marital status was assessed by the following question: "Are you married, widowed, divorced, separated, or have you never been married?" In this study, single parent status (including widowed, divorced, separated, and never having been married) was coded as 0 and married status was coded as 1.

To analyze the data of individuals nested within the same ethnic groups, multilevel model is appropriate for our analysis; data supports individuals nested within the same ethnicities that could share similar parenting practices and family environment in same ethnic history and backgrounds. In this study, we used Hierarchical Linear Modeling (HLM, Raudenbush, Bryk, & Congdon, 2010) that is capable of analyzing nested, hierarchical data. For example, in this data set, individuals who shared the same ethnic group's background would be nested within the same ethnicities. Two-level multilevel models are possible: the level-1 model investigates differences within families in the same ethnicities, and the level-2 model investigates differences across ethnicities. However, small number of level-2 unit, five ethnicities raises the concerns for the violation of distributional assumption for ethnic group-subsample level variations. Thus, in this study, we employed two complementary analytic approaches: parallel multilevel and fixed effects models based on multilevel

249

analysis. The analytic plan was based on the robustness suggested by Gershoff et al. (2010). Based on Gershoff et al.'s (2010) suggestion, we used a fixed effects model which does not account for any ethnic group-subsample level variations along with a multilevel model, because fixed effects model does not suffer from the same distributional concerns for any ethnic-level variations. Thus, we can use the benefits (i.e., analyzing nested data) and reduce the costs of using a multilevel model (i.e., a small number of level-2 unit, the five ethnicities at ethnicity-level analysis).

As previous studies conducted by the same methods pointed out (e.g., Lansford et al., 2005; Gershoff et al., 2010), the small subsamples of ethnicity cannot research for generalization of any ethnicity subsample differences directly to the given ethnicity used in this study. Instead, we investigated how different marital status between ethnicities would be related to the association between physical discipline and bullying behaviors. For the research question 1 and 2, the final multilevel model's significance was confirmed with that of a fixed effects model.

For the first research question, we tested whether family marital status moderates the association between mother's use of physical discipline and children's bullying behaviors (individual-level analysis). A within ethnicity-level equation included main effects of the mother's physical discipline and marital status along with the interaction between the two variables, with child age and gender as control variables.

For the second research question, as a preliminary analysis, different group-frequencies of marital status across ethnicities was tested using Chi-square test of independence for categorical variable of the marital status. And then, we tested whether the associations between physical discipline and bullying behaviors vary across ethnicities. If the variations exist, the variations might be explained by the ethnic-level group variable of marital status. Descriptive statistics was presented in Table 1.

Table 1. Descriptive Statistics for Study Variables for the Total and Subsamples

	Sample Mean (N = 729)	Black (N = 168)	White (N = 141)	Hispanic (N = 129)	Korean (N = 236)	Chinese (N = 55)
Predictor:						
Physical Discipline	2.67 (3.14)	3.25 (3.12)	2.41 (2.83)	2.05 (2.34)	2.43 (3.33)	3.98 (4.11)
Age	9.82 (1.83)	9.93 (1.93)	9.75 (1.95)	10.14 (2.09)	9.73 (1.69)	9.31 (0.47)
Gender (female)	48.6%	45.2%	47.5%	40.3%	54.2%	56.4%
Bullying behaviors	4.45 (3.42)	2.87 (2.80)	1.90 (2.03)	2.56 (3.06)	7.22 (1.79)	8.40 (1.97)
Married Status	66%	27%	72%	37%	97%	100%

Note. Means are presented with standard deviations in parentheses.

RESULTS

Research Question 1 (within Ethnicity)

Would the harmful effect of physical discipline on bullying behaviors decrease when it happens in the families who have both parents instead of single parent? Research question 1 examined whether marital status within an ethnicity moderates the association between mothers' use of physical discipline and children's bullying behaviors. The main interest of research question 1 was the significance of the interaction terms, and the interaction between physical discipline and marital status was significant in bullying behaviors; the significant interaction demonstrated that marital status moderates the association between mother's use of physical discipline and children's bullying behaviors, $\gamma_{\text{physical discipline*marital status}} = -.15$, $p<.05$. The interaction result of marital status in the multilevel model was also consistent in the fixed effects model, $\gamma_{\text{physical discipline*marital status}} = -.15$, $p<.10$.

The significant interactions of marital status are presented in Figure 1. Use of physical discipline was more strongly associated with children's bullying behaviors in the families with single parent status as compared to married status. In addition, although the slope was attenuated if families had a married status, more frequent use of physical discipline was still associated with a higher level of children's bullying behaviors.

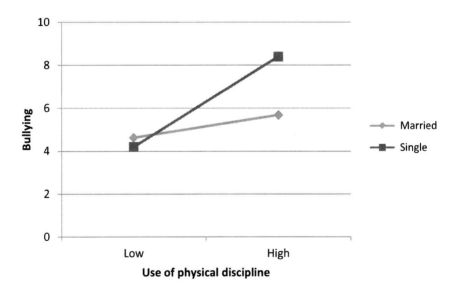

Figure 1. Multilevel regression within an ethnicity predicting child's bullying behaviors from physical discipline moderated by mother's marital status contolling for child age and gender

Research Question 2 (between Ethnicities)

Would ethnic-level marital status buffer the harmful effect of physical discipline on bullying behaviors across ethnicities? To address research question 2, first we tested whether the ethnic groups would differ in marital status. Chi-square test for independence results demonstrated that there were significant differences in marital status between the ethnic groups; $\chi^2(4, N=729) = 293.05, p<.001$: 72% of married status in European Americans, 27% in African Americans, 37% in Hispanic Americans, 97% in Koreans, and 100% in Chinese. Also, there were significant variations in the associations between physical discipline and bullying behaviors across ethnicities, $\gamma_{physical\ discipline}=.12, p=.06$. Fixed effects models also supported a significant slope for the association between physical discipline and bullying behaviors, $\gamma_{physical\ discipline}=.09, p<.05$, which means that more frequent use of physical discipline was associated with more bullying behaviors (in the average slopes across ethnicities). Of interest, there were significant variations for the slopes of association between use of physical disciplines and bullying behaviors across ethnicities, $^\wedge\sigma^2_{physical\ discipline}=0.01, p<.05$.

To explain the ethnic-group level variations across ethnicities in the slopes, each level-2 group variables of marital status was entered. Results from the multilevel model and fixed effects models are presented in Table 3. As expected, the significant moderating effect of marital status in the association between physical discipline and bullying behaviors was consistent in the multilevel models, $\gamma_{physical\ discipline*marital\ status}=-.21, p<.05$ and in the fixed effects models, $\gamma_{physical\ discipline*marital\ status}=-.21, p<.10$. As control variables, age effect on bullying behaviors was not significant; whereas gender effect on bullying behaviors was significant in all models in bullying behaviors—females showed less bullying behaviors than males. Although the main effect of ethnic-level marital status was not the main interest of this study and there were significant main effects of marital status on bullying behaviors across ethnicities. It means that group-level marital status can explain the variations across ethnicities in bullying behaviors (as revealed by the intercept at Figure 2). The implication will be addressed about this result in discussion.

DISCUSSION

The goal of this study was to examine how family marital status moderates the association between mothers' use of physical discipline and children's bullying behaviors between families in an ethnicity and between ethnicities.

First, can marital status buffer the negative impact of physical discipline on bullying behaviors within families? Within families, the research question 1 asked was whether each family variable moderates the relation of mother's use of physical discipline to children's bullying behaviors (individual-level). The moderating effect of marital status on the association between physical discipline and bullying behaviors was supported. More frequent use of physical discipline was strongly associated with

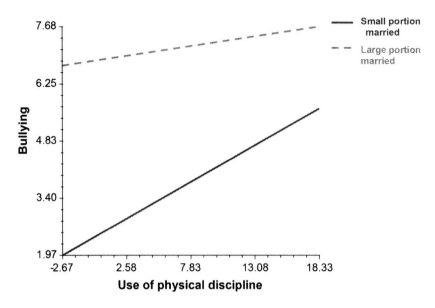

Figure 2. Multilevel model plot of the link between mother's use of physical discipline and child's bullying behaviors as moderated by ethnic group-level marital status controlling for child age and gender
Note. Large portion of single and both parents refer to ethnic group whose married status is at the top 25% position (broken line) and the bottom 25% (solid line), respectively

more children's bullying behaviors in families having a higher frequency of single mothers than in families having a higher frequency of both parents. When physical discipline was administered by mothers who were married, the detrimental impact of the physical discipline on bullying behaviors was attenuated. Although there has been previous research that showed the positive relation between physical discipline and marital status (DeKlyen et al., 2006; Loeber et al., 2000; McCabe et al., 1999; Pinderhughes et al., 2000; Xu et al., 2000), little is known about the moderating effect of family marital status on the association between physical discipline and children's outcome. While using a sample of major race/ethnic groups made up of Black, White, Hispanic, and Asians, we extended previous research by showing the buffering effect of the status of being married on the relation of physical discipline to children's bullying behaviors.

Second, we asked whether ethnic-level marital status (i.e., ethnic groups with more or less marriage in families) would buffer the harmful effect of physical discipline on bullying behaviors. We also found that ethnic group-level marital status moderates the association between mother's use of physical discipline and children's bullying behaviors (ethnicity-level analysis). As preliminary steps, we found significant differences in ethnic-family variables across ethnicity subsamples, and there were significant variations across ethnicities in the associations between physical discipline and bullying behaviors. Finally, consistent findings across multilevel and fixed effects models showed that ethnic-level family marital status moderated the association between physical discipline and bullying behaviors. Ethnicity groups with a large portion of married mothers showed a weaker relation of physical discipline to bullying behaviors.

To our knowledge, the ethnic-level family environment has not been examined as a moderator of the association between physical discipline and externalizing behaviors across ethnicities. In the current study, marital status was a significant moderator to buffer the negative effect of physical discipline on bullying behaviors between ethnicities as well as within an ethnicity. Within families, when physical discipline is used, if the family has both parents present, the negative effect of physical discipline was attenuated. Moreover, the associations were weaker among ethnic subsamples with a large portion of mothers who were married than among ethnic subsamples with a large portion of single parents. Consistent with the U.S. Census Bureau's (2012) report, marital status of the population as sampled by ethnicity in this study showed some variation: the highest frequency in the married status was found in the East Asian samples (100% of the Chinese, 97% of the Koreans), followed by White, Black, and Hispanic Americans (72%, 37%, and 27%, respectively). Thus, this study suggests that marital status should be an index for consideration when evaluating the effect of physical discipline on children's adjustment between ethnicities.

There is some evidence that implies greater endorsement of physical punishment in East Asians, including Chinese and Koreans, than in American samples (e.g., Mercurio, You, & Malley-Morrison, 2006; Zhai & Gao, 2009). Theoretically, these results may reflect another aspect of collectivism for East Asians, the so-called vertical collectivism that emphasizes a hierarchy, based on authority ranking and parental duty along with children's low level of self determination of activities, rather than a horizontal equality within family members (Triandis & Gelfand, 1998). By contrast, those people living in more individualist cultures may consider the egalitarian family environment versus parental control as a healthy parenting and childrearing styple for achieving the ultimate goal of child autonomy and independence (Rothbaum et al., 2000), and thus they may be less likely to use physical discipline than in collectivist cultures (e.g., Mercurio, You, & Malley-Morrison, 2006; Zhai & Gao, 2009).

However, from our results, we can speculate that under the high normativeness of parents being married and living together in the most collectivist cultures in our sample (100% of the Chinese, 97% of the Koreans), their higher use of parental punishment would buffer the negative impact of physical discipline to bullying behaviors as compared to individualists who showed the relatively low level of parents being married in this study (72% of European Americans, 37% of African Americans, and 27% of Hispanic Americans). When we consider the previous study that showed no association between harsh discipline and subsequent aggression in Asians (Le et al., 2005), our results shed light on why previous research has shown the link in some ethnicities (e.g., ethnicities in the U.S.) but not others (e.g., ethnicities in Asia).

Regarding the results of research question 2, the main interest of this study was to investigate group differences in the moderating effects of marital status, how ethnic group-level marital status influences the association between physical discipline and bullying behaviors, rather than the group differences in the main effects of marital status on bullying behaviors represented by varying intercepts in bullying (Figure 2).

However, the results have important implications for further study. In terms of the intercepts shown in Figure 2, the higher intercepts were found in ethnic groups with higher proportion of married status, and can be explained by the pattern of Korean and Chinese families used in the study. Korean and Chinese families had the largest portion of married both parents living together. According to Figure 2, the ethnic groups who had a large portion of both parents, represented by the ethnic groups of Korean and Chinese in this study, showed generally higher levels of bullying even when physical discipline was rarely used, and, also, their levels of bullying were consistently high regardless of physical discipline (i.e., despite a possibly greater buffer effect, higher levels of bullying in general).

Figure 2 also reflected relatively higher levels of bullying in Korean and Chinese groups. The bullying levels in these ethnic groups (i.e., M=7.22, SD=1.79 for Korean and M=8.40 and SD=1.97 for Chinese) were almost 1 standard deviation higher than the entire sample mean (M=4.45, SD=3.42) (See Table 1). This pattern of bullying levels was consistent with the finding by Nesdale and Naito (2005) about bullying levels in Japanese participants based on collectivism, and Australians, based on individualism. Nesdale and Naito (2005) found that Japanese participants, who were more collectivistic than the Australian participants based on their results of individualism-collectivism scores, showed a greater likelihood of bullying than Australians. Their review showed that peer attitudes and behaviors are crucial factors in the actual incidence of bullying behaviors in school, and one of the critical factors was the student's desire to be similar to and be biased toward the in-group. The Japanese, who have strong values of interdependency, cohesion, and harmony (Triandis & Gelfand, 1998), were less likely to help victims when they were connected with a bully (Nesdale & Naito, 2005). Australians, who have values on being independent, unique, autonomous, separate, and individual (Triandis & Gelfand, 1998), were more likely to help a victim even though they were connected with the bully. These finding suggest a possibility that ethnic groups, who were raised with so-called relational collectivism (Brewer & Chen, 2007; Oyserman et al., 2002), are more likely to benefit from both parent status as a buffer between parental discipline and bullying behaviors but may also experience higher levels of bullying, greater pressure or interpersonal stresses driven by the cultural emphasis on relational aspects, and also view physical aggression used in bullying as not so egregious when done against someone not seen in the child's in-group.

These results of the intercept terms in bullying suggest that further studies need to consider the different ethnic groups' dimension of collective-individual orientation in comparisons, which has been the overarching framework in cross-cultural research (Markus & Kitayama, 1991; Triandis & Gelfand, 1998), in order to understand better the relation between the three variables of physical discipline, family variables, and bullying behaviors across ethnicities. In this study only two subsamples were East Asians, and they are known as collectivists. Thus, we recommend that future research includes diverse ethnic groups based on collectivism and consider the role of various family values on the relation of physical discipline to bullying behaviors in collectivist versus individualist ethnic groups.

Future Directions

There are many frameworks that could be used to examine possible moderators in cultural variations across ethnicities between physical discipline and children's adjustment. One of the limitations in this study was that the ethnicities used in this study can be also different in ecological contexts as well as the family contexts involving differences in religion and religiosity, legal statues and public policy, stress and social support, and socioeconomic resources (e.g., Gershoff, 2002a). Further study should attempt to separate out such elements to examine which specific and essential features in ethnic cultures, relate to differences in the effects of physical discipline on children's adjustment across ethnicities. Moreover, the Chinese sample had relatively small number of participants after screening out fathers' reported surveys, and there was little variation in marital status in the East Asian samples. Further study should investigate the relation of physical discipline and children's outcome variables and their moderating effects by using more equivalent sample sizes collected from diverse ethnicities.

CONCLUSIONS

This study examined whether physical parental punishment lead to negative consequences regardless of culturally different family environments. Our results showed that culturally different levels of marital status made the relation of physical discipline to bullying behaviors differ across ethnicities. Also, the family status of being married has a buffering effect on the relation of physical discipline to bullying behaviors in an ethnicity. In other words, individual-level and ethnic-level marital status each moderates the association between mothers' use of physical discipline and children's bullying behaviors, as shown in a sample of major racial/ethnic groups consisting of Black, White, and Hispanic Americans and East Asian ethnicities. Within families in an ethnicity, families who had married mothers showed a buffering effect on the relation of physical discipline to bullying behaviors as compared to families who had single mothers. Between ethnicities, there were weaker associations between physical discipline and bullying behaviors among ethnic groups with a large portion of married mothers. Our results shed light on why previous research has shown the more or less negative effect or lack of effect, of physical discipline on aggressive behaviors in some ethnicities but not in others. Regarding the results of the current study, more research should focus the different contexts in ethnic family relationships and environment where the physical discipline is administered and investigate what is considered as culturally appropriate discipline from what is considered as abusive behaviors from diverse perspectives in terms of children's adjustment.

Previous literature has shown that those in Western cultures tend to consider physical discipline as failure of parenting or parental rejection toward children; whereas those in East Asian cultures are more likely to perceive physical discipline as indicative of responsible parental involvement, instead of parental neglect. From this study, we can speculate that ethnic groups, who are raised in relational collectivism emphasizing family cohesion are more likely to show the relatively high proportion of being married in the family. And, in turn, the family status of being married has a buffering effect on the relation of physical discipline to bullying behaviors.

Cultural differences in ethnicities can't justify abusive behaviors or violence against children. However, the results of this study may help mental health professionals in education, and related policy-establishing groups to become more aware of ethnic differences in diverse family environments when they evaluate the influence of physical discipline on children's externalizing behaviors.

REFERENCES

Baldry, A., Farrington, D. (2005). Protective factors as moderators of risk factors in adolescence bullying. *Social Psychology of Education, 8*, 263–284.

Barboza, G., Schiamberg, L., & Oehmke, J. (2009). Individual characteristics and the multiple contexts of adolescent bullying: An ecological perspective. *Journal of Youth and Adolescence, 38*, 101–121.

Brewer, M. B., & Chen, Y. (2007). Where (who) are collectives in collectivism? Toward conceptual clarification of individualism and collectivism. *Psychological Review, 114*, 133–151.

Ceballo, R., & McLoyd, V. C. (2002). Social support and parenting in poor, dangerous neighborhoods. *Child Development, 73*, 1310–1321.

Deater-Deckard, K., Dodge, K. A., Bates, J. A., & Pettit, G. S. (1996). Physical discipline among African American and European American mothers: Links to children's externalizing behaviors. *Developmental Psychology, 32*, 1065–1072.

DeKlyen, M., Brooks-Gunn, J., McLanahan, S., & Knab, J. (2006). The mental health of married, cohabiting and non-coresident parents with infants. *American Journal of Public Health, 96*, 1836–1841.

Eamon, M. K. (2001). Antecedents and socioemotional consequences of physical punishment on children in two-parent families. *Child Abuse and Neglect, 25*, 793–796.

Espelage, D. L., Bosworth, K., & Simon, T. R. (2000). Examining the social context of bullying behaviors in early adolescence. *Journal of Counseling and Development, 78*, 326–333.

Flouri, E., & Buchanan, A. (2003). The role of mother involvement and father involvement in adolescent bullying behavior. *Journal of Interpersonal Violence, 18*, 634–644.

Flynn, C. P. (1994). Regional differences in attitudes toward corporal punishment. *Journal of Marriage and the Family, 56*, 314–324.

Gershoff, E. T. (2002). Corporal punishment by parents and associated child behaviors and experiences: A meta-analytic and theoretical review. *Psychological Bulletin, 128*, 539–579.

Gershoff, E. T., Grogan-Kaylor, A., Lansford, J. E., Chang, L., Zelli, A., Deater-Deckard, K., & Dodge, K. A. (2010). Parent discipline practices in an international sample: Associations with child behaviors and moderation by perceived normativeness. *Child Development, 81*, 487–502.

Guerra, N. G., & Slaby, R. G. (1990). Cognitive mediators of aggression in adolescent offenders: II. Intervention. *Developmental Psychology, 26*, 269–277.

Gunnoe, M. L., & Mariner, C. L. (1997). Toward a developmental-contextual model of the effects of parental spanking on children's aggression. *Archives of Pediatric and Adolescent Medicine, 151*, 768–775.

Hong, J. S., & Espelage, D. L. (2012). A review of mixed methods research on bullying and peer victimization in school. *Educational Review, 64*, 115–126.

Hong, J. S., Espelage, D. L., Grogan-Kaylor, A., & Allen-Meares, P. (2012). Identifying potential mediators and moderators of the association between child maltreatment and bullying perpetration and victimization in school. *Educational Psychology Review, 24*, 167–186.

Lansford, J. E. (2010). The special problem of cultural differences in effects of corporal punishment. *Law and Contemporary Problems, 73*, 89–106.

Lansford, J. E., Chang, L., Dodge, K. A., Malone, P. S., Oburu, P., Palmérus, K., & Quinn, D. (2005). Physical discipline and children's adjustment: Cultural normativeness as a moderator. *Child Development, 76*, 1234–1246.

Le, T. N., Monfared, G., & Stockdale, G. D. (2005). The Relationship of school, parent, and peer contextual factors with self-reported delinquency for Chinese, Cambodian, Laotian or Mien, and Vietnamese youth. *Crime and Delinquency, 51*, 206–212.

Lee, Y., Jang, M., & Malley-Morrison, K. (2008). Perceptions of child maltreatment in European Americans, Korean Americans, and Koreans. *International Psychology Bulletin, 12*, 13–16.

Loeber, R., Drinkwater, M., Yin, Y., Anderson, S. J., Schmidt, L. C., & Crawford, A. (2000). Stability of family interaction from ages 6 to 18. *Journal of Abnormal Child Psychology, 28*, 353–369.

Markus, H. R., & Kitayama, S. (1991). Culture and the self: Implications for cognition, emotion, and motivation. *Psychological Review, 98*, 224–253.

McCabe, K. M., Clark, R., & Barnett, D. (1999). Family protective factors among urban African American youth. *Journal of Clinical Child Psychology, 28*, 137–150.

Mercurio, A. E., You, H. S., Malley-Morrison, K. (2006). Reasoning about parental rights to physically discipline children in the United States and Korea. *International Psychological Bulletin, 10*, 12–13.

Nesdale, D., & Naito, M. (2005). Individualism-collectivism and the attitudes to school bullying of Japanese and Australian Students. *Journal of Cross-Cultural Psychology, 36*, 537–556.

Oyserman, D., Coon, H. M., & Kemmelmeier, M. (2002). Rethinking individualism and collectivism: Evaluation of theoretical assumptions and meta-analyses. *Psychological Bulletin, 128*, 3–72.

Pinderhughes, E. E., Dodge, K. A., Bates, J. E., Pettit, G. S., & Zelli, A. (2000). Discipline responses: Influences of parents' socioeconomic status, ethnicity, beliefs about parenting, stress, and cognitive–emotional processes. *Journal of Family Psychology, 14*, 380–400.

Polaha, J., Larzelere, R. E., Shapiro, S. K., & Pettit, G. S. (2004). Physical discipline and child behavior problems: A study of ethnic group differences. *Parenting: Science and Practice, 4*, 339–360.

Raudenbush, S. W., Bryk, A. S., & Congdon, R. (2010). *HLM 7: Hierarchical linear and nonlinear modeling.* Lincolnwood, IL: Scientific Software International.

Rothbaum, F., Pott, M., Azuma, H., Miyake, K., & Weisz, J. (2000). The development of close relationships in Japan and the United States: Paths of symbolic harmony and generative tension. *Child Development, 71*, 1121–1142.

Schwartz, D., Dodge, K. A., Pettit, G. S., & Bates, J. E. (1997). The early socialization of aggressive victims of bullying. *Child Development, 68*, 665–675.

Schwartz, D., Dodge, K. A., Pettit, G. S., Bates, J. E., & The Conduct Problems Prevention Research Group. (2000). Friendship as a moderating factor in the pathway between early harsh home environment and later victimization in the peer group. *Developmental Psychology, 36*, 646–662.

Sheehan, M. J., & Watson, M. W. (2008). Reciprocal influences between maternal discipline techniques and aggression in children and adolescents. *Aggressive Behavior, 34*, 245–255.

Slaby, R. G., & Guerra, N. G. (1988). Cognitive mediators of aggression in adolescent offenders: 1. Assessment. *Developmental Psychology, 24*, 580–588.

Spriggs, A. L., Iannotti, R. J., Nansel, T. R., & Haynie, D. L. (2007). Adolescent bullying involvement and perceived family peer and school relations: Commonalities and differences across race/ethnicity. *Journal of Adolescent Health, 41*, 283–293.

Straus, M. A. (1979). Measuring intrafamily conflict and violence: The conflict tactics (CT) scales. *Journal of Marriage and Family, 41*, 75–88.

Straus, M. A., & Gelles, R. J. (1990). *Physical violence in American families: Risk factors and adaptations to violence in 8,145 families.* New York, NY: Doubleday/Anchor.

Triandis, H. C., & Gelfand, M. (1998). Converging measurement of horizontal and vertical individualism and collectivism. *Journal of Personality and Social Psychology, 74*, 118–128.

U. S. Census Bureau. (2010). *Profile of selected social characteristics in the United States: 2006–2010 American community survey selected population tables.* Retrieved from http://factfinder2.census.gov/faces/tableservices/jsf/pages/productview.xhtml?pid=ACS_10_SF4_DP02&prodType=table

Watson, M. W., Fischer, K. W., Burdzovic Andreas, J., & Smith, K. W. (2004). Pathways to aggression in children and adolescents. *Harvard Educational Review, 74*, 404–430.

Whaley, A. (2000). Sociocultural differences in the developmental consequences of the use of physical discipline during childhood for African Americans. *Cultural Diversity and Ethnic Minority Psychology, 6*, 5–12.

Xu, X., Tung, Y., & Dunaway, R. G. (2000). Cultural, human, and social capital as determinants of corporal punishment: Toward an integrated theoretical model. *Journal of Interpersonal Violence, 15*, 603–630.

Zhai, F., & Gao, Q. (2009). Child maltreatment among Asian Americans: Characteristics and explanatory framework. *Child Maltreatment, 14*, 207–224.

MICHAEL J. SHEEHAN

35. ADDRESSING BAD BEHAVIOR WITH GOOD SCIENCE

Research Implications for School Policies and Intervention Programs

Aggression and violence among school-age children have long been of concern to developmental psychologists and educators, but recent highly-publicized events (such as the Columbine High School massacre of 1999 and the 2010 suicides of Phoebe Prince and Tyler Clementi) have led to a more refined focus on aggressive interactions. Earlier research on this topic had treated perpetrators and victims of aggression as largely separate entities (e.g., Bernstein & Watson, 1997; Olweus, 1978, 1993; Perry, Kusel, & Perry, 1988). However, the shooters at Columbine (to use an extreme example) were among those who, in addition to a tendency toward aggressive acts, can also be categorized by a tendency to be bullied by others. Olweus (1978) was among the first to identify children who can be classified as both aggressors and victims, though most of the research regarding this type of child has been more recent, perhaps due to increasing public awareness of and interest in school violence. In addition, research in this area has grown beyond its "Western" roots, gaining traction among researchers in nations such as China (Wang et al., 2012) and Taiwan (Hokoda, Lu, & Angeles, 2013).

The aim of this chapter is to review psychological research on aggressive behavior (including some of our own) to address several issues integral to our understanding of such interactions. Included in this review are several notable phenomena that have recently been uncovered: (1) aggressive victims, who are bullied by others in addition to behaving aggressively, are significantly worse off than their peers in a number of behavioral and psychosocial domains; (2) "pure" aggressors and "pure" victims tend to be more similar to each other than is often assumed, both in terms of antecedents of and outcomes related to their behavior, suggesting that addressing a child's mere *involvement* in aggressive behavior may be more important than determining their exact role as aggressor or victim; (3) classification as an aggressor, victim, or aggressive victim tends to be consistent over time, highlighting the need for early intervention; (4) numerous variables involving parents, neighborhood factors, and other aspects of the child's environment have been implicated in influencing these behaviors, such that any successful intervention program will necessitate action beyond school walls.

C. Boske & A. Osanloo (Eds.), Students, Teachers, and Leaders Addressing Bullying in Schools, 261–280.

PREVIOUS RESEARCH

Bullies/Aggressors, Victims, and Aggressive Victims: Defining Characteristics and Terminology Issues

According to a review by Pellegrini (1998), bullies are traditionally defined as children who systematically and repeatedly target another group of children (victims) using direct, indirect, physical, or relational aggression. They are generally older, bigger, stronger, and more dominant than their victims, and tend to be noncompliant and aggressive outside the school setting (Bernstein & Watson, 1997; Olweus, 1993; Pellegrini, 1998; Veenstra et al., 2007). Bullies typically use aggression to gain or maintain dominance status among peers, yet their behaviors tend to result in rejection by peers and being viewed as unpopular, except among small cliques of other bullies (Olweus, 1993; Pellegrini, 1998). Bullies' aggressive behavior has traditionally been viewed as proactive or instrumental, rather than reactive (Pellegrini, 1998; Perry et al., 1998; Schwartz, Proctor, & Chien, 2001). That is, bullies generally pick fights (usually with "easy targets") rather than responding to threats or attacks from others, and their aggression is goal-oriented, with the purpose gaining either something tangible (e.g., lunch money) or more abstract, such as higher dominance status (Pellegrini, 1998; Schwartz et al., 2001).

Pure victims, also referred to as "passive" victims (Olweus, 1978) or "low-aggressive" victims (Perry et al., 1988) are generally smaller, weaker, and less dominant than their peers (Bernstein & Watson, 1997; Olweus, 1978; Pellegrini, 1998). They tend to have low self-esteem and are insecure, sensitive, cautious, vulnerable, unpopular among and rejected by their peers, and, above all else, highly submissive (Bernstein & Watson, 1997; Olweus, 1993; Veenstra et al., 2007). There is also evidence that victims' poor social skills and high need for approval lead them to make continued attempts to interact with those who bully them, thus continuing the abusive relationship (Bernstein & Watson, 1997).

Most researchers have followed Olweus's (1978, 1993) criteria for bullying: that the victimization is repeated over time and there exists an imbalance of strength between the bully and victim. In many cases, however, frequent aggressive behavior does not fulfill these requirements. For example, research on prison populations (e.g., Ireland & Archer, 2004; Turner & Ireland, 2011) indicates that power imbalances can be unclear and subtle. Likewise, sexual assault and coercion (e.g., Oswald & Russell, 2006; Russell, Oswald, & Kraus, 2011) nearly always involves some degree of power imbalance, but does not necessarily involve repeated actions against the same victim. In these cases, where the criteria for being labeled a *bully* have not been met, the term *aggressor* is often preferred. Even leaving aside these more extreme examples, teachers, parents, and others familiar with school-age children are likely to recognize that not all aggressive students can be rightly considered to be *bullies*.

Similarly, a number of terms have been used to describe children who are both perpetrators and victims of aggression. Olweus (1978) originally referred to them as *provocative victims.* Others (e.g., Burk et al., 2011; Schwartz et al., 2001) have used the term *aggressive victims*, including recent attempts to identify *highly-aggressive aggressive victims* and *highly-victimized aggressive victims* (Giang & Graham, 2008). In addition, the term *bully-victim* is being used with increasing frequency (e.g., Espelage & Holt, 2013; Fanti & Kimonis, 2013; Strohmeier, Wagner, Spiel, & von Eye, 2010). As argued above, not all *aggressors* can be considered *bullies*, so it follows that an *aggressive victim* is not necessarily the same as a *bully-victim*. In spite of these concerns, however, these terms continue to be used more or less interchangeably throughout the literature. In addition, much of the research in this area, even when the term *aggressive victim* is used, has been and continues to be cited in efforts to identify and solve bullying problems in school settings. To avoid confusion and maintain consistency, the term *aggressive victim* (which the authors believe to be the more accurate and generally useful term) will be used throughout this chapter, even when referring to studies in which the term *bully-victim* is used.

Aggressive victims do not occupy a "middle ground" between pure aggressors and pure victims (Schwartz et al., 2001). Rather, they exhibit characteristics both similar to and different from both bullies (e.g., they tend to be reactively rather than proactively aggressive) and victims (e.g., although they are targets of bullies, they are not necessarily unassertive or submissive) in such a way that they are worse off than both pure aggressors and pure victims in many respects (e.g., they are unpopular among peers and tend to be psychosocially maladjusted).

Issue 1: Aggressive Victims Are Significantly Worse Off than Their Peers

Like victims, aggressive victims generally have lower self-esteem than non-victims, and tend to be anxious and insecure (Bernstein & Watson, 1997; Isolan, Salum, Osowski, Zottis, & Manfro, 2013). On the other hand, they are not submissive; instead, they tend to be hot-tempered and hyperactive, and display a hostile style of social interaction (Pellegrini, 1998; Toblin, Schwartz, Gorman, & Abou-ezzeddine, 2005). In addition to being victimized, aggressive victims tend to create tension, irritate and tease others, lose control easily, and attempt to fight back against their victimizers (Pellegrini, 1998; Perry et al., 1988; Schwartz et al., 2001).

Indeed, this tendency toward retaliation is a key factor for distinguishing aggressive victims from pure victims, who are more likely to respond to aggression by attempting to ignore the aggressor (Pateraki & Houndoumadi, 2001). Similarly, Kristensen and Smith (2003) found that, in response to hypothetical situations, aggressive victims were significantly more likely than victims to endorse externalizing behaviors (e.g., "Take it out on others," "Get mad and throw or hit something") to cope with being bullied.

Unlike the more calculated style of bullies and pure aggressors, aggressive victims tend to be highly emotional and impulsive (Fanti & Kimonis, 2013; O'Brennan, Bradshaw, & Sawyer, 2009) and have trouble controlling their emotions once they are aroused (Pellegrini, 1998; Schwartz et al., 2001; Toblin et al., 2005). This, in addition to aggressive victims' use of reactive aggression, in which they retaliate against real or perceived threats from others (Pellegrini, 1998), led Perry, Perry, and Kennedy (1992) to refer to them as "ineffectual aggressors." Other research on negative behaviors has yielded similar results, as aggressive victims have scored less favorably than aggressors, victims, and uninvolved peers on measures of misconduct and self-control (Haynie et al., 2001), externalizing behaviors (Kumpulainen et al., 1998), and hyperactivity (Gini, 2008; Toblin et al., 2005; Xu, Farver, Schwartz, & Chang, 2003).

Research has consistently found that aggressive victims face a number of social problems. Compared to their peers, including pure aggressors and pure victims, they score more negatively on measures of peer rejection (Schwartz, 2000; Veenstra et al., 2007), social acceptance (Andreou, 2000), and number of friends (Unnever, 2005; Xu et al., 2003). Some researchers (e.g., Schwartz et al., 2001) believe that this unpopularity may be an extension of the behavioral problems discussed above; the pattern of emotional dysregulation and impulsive behavior may lead peers to reject them and perpetuate peers' negative attitudes about them. In a study by Andreou, Vlachou, and Didaskalou (2005), aggressive victims reported significantly higher pro-bully attitudes than their peers combined with the fewest number of positive peer interactions (e.g., sharing, playing together). These results suggest that aggressive victims are less popular than their peers (including pure aggressors) not only because of their tendency toward and approval of aggressive behavior, but also because they are less likely than aggressors to behave in a positive, prosocial manner with their peers. The same difficulties in regulating behavior and emotion that leads other children to dislike aggressive victims also leaves them vulnerable to higher levels of emotional distress (Schwartz, 2000), neuroticism (Mynard & Joseph, 1997), narcissism (Fanti & Kimonis, 2013), anxiety (Isolan et al., 2013), and other internalizing symptoms (Haynie et al., 2001; O'Brennan et al., 2009). In addition, aggressive victims have lower levels of self-esteem (O'Moore & Kirkham, 2001) and poorer social perception skills (Burk et al., 2008) than their peers.

Kumpulainen and colleagues (1998) found that aggressive victims scored higher than their peers on self-report depression inventories and were more likely to exceed clinical cutoffs for behavior problems and receive referrals for psychiatric consultations. Rigby (1998) found similar results for male aggressive victims on a self-report measure of anxiety. Kaltiala-Heino, Rimpela, Rantanen, and Rimpela (2000) found that aggressive victims were significantly more likely to report symptoms of anxiety, depression, and somatic disorders, and were second only to bullies with respect to use of illicit substances and frequent excessive drinking. Other studies (e.g., Swearer, Song, Cary, Eagle, & Mickelson, 2001; Toblin et al., 2005) have found that aggressive victims and pure aggressors are more likely to be depressed than other children, and aggressive victims and pure victims are more likely to be anxious. It has been suggested that, given aggressive victims' increased risk on two psychopathological dimensions (i.e., depression and anxiety), they may be the most at-risk of any group involved in bullying, and may be most in need of help from intervention programs (Swearer et al., 2001).

Finally, in addition to having problems interacting with their peers at school, aggressive victims tend to struggle with school itself. Research has found that aggressive victims tend to perform poorly on measures of school refusal (Kumpulainen et al., 1998), school adjustment (Haynie et al., 2001; Nansel, Haynie, & Simons-Morton, 2003), and general academic functioning (Schwartz, 2000; Toblin et al., 2005; Xu et al., 2003). In addition, aggressive victims have reported negative perceptions of their school climate (Harel-Fisch et al., 2011; Nansel et al., 2003; O'Brennan et al., 2009), reporting low levels of teacher support (Berkowitz & Benbenishty, 2012), dissatisfaction with the way that teachers and staff address aggressive behavior (Swearer & Cary, 2003), and feeling disconnected, fearful, and unsafe (Berkowitz & Benbenishty, 2012; Bradshaw, O'Brennan, & Sawyer, 2008; Forber-Pratt, Aragon, & Espelage, 2013).

These results provide strong support for the idea that aggressive victims' dysregulated style of behavior is associated with negative functioning across a number of domains. In summary, aggressive victims seem to display the worst characteristics found in both pure aggressors and pure victims. As such, they have a tendency toward externalizing and other problem behaviors, are highly disliked and rejected by their peers, are more vulnerable to psychological disorders, and function poorly in academic settings.

Issue 2: The Importance of Involvement in Aggression, Regardless of Role

As noted above, a number of characteristics distinguish aggressors from victims, including aggressors' narcissism (e.g., Fanti & Kimonis, 2013) and endorsement of aggression and fighting behavior (e.g., Bradshaw et al., 2008), victims' vulnerability (e.g., Veenstra et al., 2007) and poor social skills (e.g., Fox & Boulton, 2005), and aggressors' social and physical dominance over their submissive targets (e.g., Bernstein & Watson, 1997; Menesini, Melan, & Pignatti, 2000). In many other respects, however, aggressors and victims are surprisingly similar to each other, and a number of studies have indicated that children's *involvement* in aggressive interactions, regardless of their specific role, is a significant predictor of negative outcomes.

For example, there are those who disagree with drawing any absolute distinctions between proactive and reactive aggression. Given that proactive and reactive aggression have been found to be highly correlated (Camodeca, Goossens, Terwogt, & Schengel, 2002; Dodge & Coie, 1987), it is not surprising that a number of studies (e.g., Camodeca et al., 2002; Ragatz, Anderson, Fremouw, & Schwartz, 2011) have provided evidence that aggressors and aggressive victims exhibit both styles of aggression. In some cases, pure victims (Fanti & Kimonis, 2013) and pure aggressors (O'Brennan et al., 2009) have shown tendencies toward impulsivity and reactionary behavior on par with aggressive victims.

Wolke, Woods, Bloomfield, and Karstadt (2000) found that all children in their sample who were involved in bullying (as bully, victim, or aggressive victim) were worse off than their uninvolved peers with respect to hyperactivity and conduct/ behavioral problems. Similar findings were reported by Burk and colleagues (2008) regarding temperamental dysregulation. Overall involvement in aggression has also been associated with negative perceptions of the school environment (Harel-Fisch et al., 2011), significantly lower academic efficacy and school involvement (Ozer, Totan, & Atik, 2011), and low social support from both peers and parents (Holt & Espelage, 2007).

Finally, researchers have established a connection between involvement in aggression and a number of problematic psychological and health-related outcomes. Aggressors, victims, and aggressive victims alike have been reported to display significantly more psychiatric symptoms (Kumpulainen, Rasanen, & Henttonen, 1999), tendencies toward suicidal ideation and self-injurious behavior (Espelage & Holt, 2013; Winsper, Lereya, Zanarini, & Wolke, 2012), somatic symptoms and health complaints (Rigby, 1998), and various symptoms of anxiety and depression (Holt & Espelage, 2007; Kaltiala-Heino, Frojd, & Marttunen, 2010; Rigby, 1998).

In summary, although perpetrators and victims of aggression are often treated as separate entities, similarities between them in various behavioral, psychosocial, and health-related domains suggest that intervention programs would be well served to target overall involvement in aggressive behavior, above and beyond simple labels.

Issue 3: Identification as Aggressor/Victim/Aggressive-Victim Is Consistent Over Time

In 2001, Schwartz and colleagues commented on the rarity of longitudinal research in this area. Those concerns are still valid today, as the large majority of studies rely on cross-sectional techniques. That said, a number of studies have addressed the stability of involvement in aggressive behavior over time. Nansel and colleagues (2003) found that nearly all students in their sample who were identified as aggressive victims in the sixth grade were still involved with aggression (as bullies, victims, or aggressive victims) in the seventh grade. Similarly, Kumpulainen and colleagues (1999) found that, although involvement in aggression declined somewhat over the course of their longitudinal study, aggressive victims were significantly more likely that aggressors and victims to maintain their involvement over time. More recent research on adolescents and pre-adolescents (Bettencourt, Farrell, Liu, & Sullivan, 2013; Strohmeier et al., 2010) has found good overall consistency among groups, with gradual decreases in involvement in aggression over time. On the other hand, Hanish and Guerra (2004) found that aggressors and victims became more prevalent over time and aggressive victims became less prevalent.

While these studies have reported somewhat mixed results, it appears that involvement in aggressive interactions with peers is reasonably consistent over time. Additional longitudinal research will be essential for a more complete understanding of relevant psychosocial issues. For example, Kochenderfer-Ladd (2003) found that victims and aggressive victims who faced greater peer rejection were significantly more likely than others to remain victimized. In turn, Burk and colleagues (2011) revealed that children who remain aggressive victims throughout elementary school face significantly greater difficulties related to academics and mental health as they approach adolescence. Understanding of such developmental trajectories can and should inform development of intervention programs within schools and surrounding neighborhoods.

Issue 4: Understanding of Parent/Neighborhood/Environmental Factors Is Essential

Much of the research on aggressive behavior and bullying among children and adolescents focuses on their behavior, social functioning, and abilities within the school context. This is not surprising, considering that much of children's interactions with their peers takes place within the academic setting. However, involvement in aggressive behavior is strongly influenced by factors related to the child's home and neighborhood.

For decades, researchers have consistently found that aggressive behavior is, in part, learned from parents and guardians (e.g., Eron, Huesmann, & Zelli, 1991; Weiss, Dodge, Bates, & Pettit, 1992). Numerous studies have linked harsh parenting techniques, including frequent physical discipline, to increased aggressive behavior in children (e.g., Lereya, Samara, & Wolke, 2013; Sheehan & Watson, 2008). Recent research has also linked negative parenting with peer victimization (e.g., Lereya et al., 2013). Duong, Schwartz, Chang, Kelly, and Tom (2009) found that aggressive children whose mothers used physical discipline were more likely to be victimized by their peers. In addition, research associating punitive disciplinary practices with negative, long-term academic outcomes discovered significantly worse effects among students experiencing peer victimization (Schwartz, Lansford, Dodge, Pettit, & Bates, 2013).

Similarly, involvement in bullying has been strongly linked to the authoritarian style of parenting, which emphasizes parental control and obedience to authority but is lacking in warmth and responsiveness to the child's needs (Baumrind, 1991). For example, Baldry and Farrington (1998) found that aggressors, victims, and aggressive victims in their sample were significantly more likely that their peers to have authoritarian parents. Similar results have been confirmed in a number of studies comprising an impressive variety of Western and non-Western samples, including children and adolescents in Australia (Ahmed & Braithwaite, 2004), Israel (Knafo, 2003), Colombia (Chaux, Molano, & Podlesky, 2009), Hong Kong (Lee & Wong, 2009), and Taiwan (Hokoda et al., 2006). It is likely the case that authoritarian parents' emphasis on power, tradition, and conformity leads their children to affirm these values within their peer group (Knafo, 2003), leading them to demand obedience from others through aggression, blindly accept their lower dominance status as victims, or some combination of both (i.e., aggressive victims).

Beyond disciplinary practices and parenting style, a number of other family variables have been identified as risk or protective factors for involvement in aggressive interactions. Burk and colleagues (2008) found that victims and aggressive victims were more likely than their peers to have negative relationships with their mothers, aggressors and aggressive victims experienced low levels of emotional expressiveness within the family, and aggressive victims were more likely to have been exposed to their mother's depressive symptoms. Conflict between parents and children has also been related to aggressive behavior in a reciprocal manner, such that high levels of conflict predict aggression and victimization, which in turn leads to increased conflict at home (Georgiou & Fanti, 2013). Finally, parental warmth, involvement, and support have been found to be protective factors against both bullying behavior (Georgiou & Fanti, 2013) and victimization (Lereya et al., 2013).

In addition, children need not be victimized in a direct way in order to experience the negative effects of violence. For example, Bowes and colleagues (2009) found that experiencing maltreatment in the home was related to involvement as an aggressor, victim, or aggressive victim, but so was witnessing domestic violence. Mustanoja and colleagues (2011) found that boys who witnessed domestic violence between their parents were more likely to be victims, and girls who were victims of violent crime were more likely to be aggressive victims. The link between witnessing domestic violence and aggression/victimization appears to be especially strong among children who struggle with other social, academic, and behavior problems (Voisin & Hong, 2012). Exposure to violence in the neighborhood has also been associated with bullying behavior (Bacchini, Esposito, & Affuso, 2009; Espelage, Bosworth, & Simon, 2000), whereas the availability of youth organizations and other services has been found to be a protective factor against such behavior (Molnar, Cerda, Roberts, & Buka, 2008). All these results underline the critical importance of understanding family and neighborhood characteristics when addressing the problem of aggression and violence in childhood and adolescence.

THE CURRENT STUDY

We conducted the following study with the aim of confirming, expanding on, and clarifying results from previous research through the use of a two-wave longitudinal data set and a diverse sample of children and their mothers. Using both cross-sectional and longitudinal techniques, we tested our hypotheses that: (1) aggressive victims in our sample are significantly worse off than their peers with regard to a number of behavioral and psychosocial problems (e.g., delinquency, social withdrawal); (2) we would find few significant differences between pure aggressors and pure victims; (3) involvement in aggressive interactions is stable over time, especially for aggressive victims; (4) risk factors within the family and neighborhood environment (e.g., harsh discipline, violence observed) are significantly related to involvement in aggressive interactions (as aggressor, victim, or aggressive victim).

Original Sampling Procedure and Participants

Data for this study were drawn from the Springfield Child Development Project, a longitudinal study of middle childhood and adolescence, focusing on antecedents of aggression and other problem behaviors. Sampling procedures for the original project were designed to produce a representative sample of all children living in the city of Springfield, MA, between 7 and 14 years of age. Rather than relying on potentially biased frames such as schools, the sample was compiled from Massachusetts street lists, a state-mandated census of potentially eligible voters. A computerized street list was obtained containing the names, addresses, ages, and employment status of all women between the ages of 25 and 44 years residing in the city (N = 4,518). This age range was selected so that mothers would be most likely to have eligible children. Recruitment letters and telephone calls were used to identify eligible women (mothers or legal guardians of children between 7 and 14 years of age), resulting in a final sample of 440 mother-child dyads (86.3% of the eligible families that could be contacted). If two or more children in the household were eligible, one child was chosen at random. The original sample consisted of 242 male and 198 female children. ZIP codes with greater proportions of minority residents were over-sampled to obtain a more equal representation of African American (38%), Hispanic (29%), and European American (33%) children (see Watson, Fischer, Burdzovic Andreas, & Smith, 2004, for more detail regarding the sampling procedure).

Participation in the study was entirely voluntary, and participants were given modest compensation for their time. Interviews were conducted in each family's home by professional research staff from New England Research Institutes, and each mother and child was interviewed separately. All participants (mothers and children) responded to a number of questionnaires assessing psychological and behavioral characteristics of the child, as well as characteristics of the family and neighborhood. Data collection for the baseline phase of the study (Year 1 of the study, hereafter called Y1) was conducted from October, 1995, through February, 1997, when the children in the sample ranged in age from 7 to 14 years. Follow-up interviews were conducted when the children in the sample ranged in age from 8 to 15 years. Every effort was made to interview participants in the same order. This procedure allowed for consistency of participant age and age ranges, as indicated by age means and standard deviations at both time points: Y1 (M = 9.92 years, SD = 1.99), Y2 (M = 10.98 years, SD = 1.99).

Measures

A variety of measures were used to assess the predictor and outcome variables included in the hypothesized models. Psychometric information can be found in the references cited in the descriptions of each measure.

Demographics. A demographic interview was completed by both mother and child. The current study used items addressing *age* and *sex* of the child and mother's *years of education* (used as a measure of socioeconomic status).

Aggressor/Victim status. Children's responses to the *Fighting Behavior Scale* (*FBS*: Guerra & Slaby, 1990; Slaby & Guerra, 1988), specifically the Aggressor Behavior and Victim Behavior subscales (6 items each), were used to assess participants' behavior as aggressors, victims, or both (using a multiplicative interaction function). Child participants responded to all 12 items (e.g., "Do you hit and push other kids?" "Do you get picked on by other kids?") on a four-point scale ranging from "almost never" to "almost always." The majority of research reviewed above used a set of dichotomous variables to determine the degree of children's involvement in bullying (as aggressor, victim, or aggressive victim). Typically, cutoff scores of +1 or 0.5 standard deviations from the mean have been used. Given the strong positive skew of the distribution in this sample on both the Aggressor and Victim Behavior subscales of the FBS, the less strict cutoff of +0.5 SD was used in this study.

Family & environmental risk factors. The *Conflict Tactics Scales (CTS)* (Straus, 1979; Straus & Gelles, 1990) were used to assess the disciplinary practices that the mother reported using with her child. The 19 items range in terms of severity of discipline from "discussed an issue calmly with your child" to "used a knife or fired a gun at your child," and range in frequency from "never" to "20 times in the past year" on a 7-point scale. The *Emotional/Verbal Discipline* subscale consists of 6 items and the *Physical Discipline* subscale consists of 8 items.

In addition to the *CTS*, five items addressing the frequency (ranging from "never" to "daily") of various disciplinary techniques (i.e., sending child to room, scolding/ yelling, spanking, reasoning, taking away privileges) were used to assess *Overall Discipline Frequency*.

The *Family Environment Scale, Form R (FES)*, a 45-item true/false questionnaire that has been used to study family dynamics for decades (Moos, 1990; Moos & Moos, 1986), was completed by the mother. For the current study, only the 9-item *Conflict* subscale was used, which measures the extent to which openly angry and aggressive interactions are characteristic of the family.

Violence Observed was measured using the *Things I Have Seen and Heard* scale by Richters and Martinez (1990), completed by the child. Twenty items ranged in severity from witnessing adults yell at each other to seeing someone get shot, and were answered on a five-point scale ranging from "never" to "many times." Seven items were excluded from the current study because they assessed the role of the child as a victim of (rather than a witness to) violent behavior (e.g., "I have been beat up").

Behavioral & psychosocial problems. The Achenbach *Child Behavior Checklist (CBCL)* is a standard assessment of several dimensions of behavioral problems and social competencies (Achenbach, 1991; Achenbach & Edelbrock, 1981). The CBCL-parent report consisted of an 83-item questionnaire (on a 3-point scale from "not true" to "very true") that the parent filled out concerning her child. Two subscales from this measure were used to assess problem behaviors: *Aggressive Behavior* (20 items) and *Delinquent Behavior* (13 items). To assess psychosocial characteristics and problems, four additional subscales from the CBCL were used: *Social Problems* (8 items), *Anxious/Depressed* (14 items), *Withdrawn* (9 items), and *Somatic Complaints* (9 items). The items on these subscales used the same 3-point response scale as the two subscales discussed above.

Attitudes toward aggressive behavior were assessed through children's responses to a 12-item *Beliefs about Fighting* (*BAF*) scale (Guerra & Slaby, 1990; Slaby & Guerra, 1988). The items on the *BAF* scale evaluated children's feelings toward aggression and their endorsement of aggressive behavior as an appropriate and legitimate problem-solving tool (e.g., "It's okay for you to fight with other kids" "It makes you feel big and tough to be a bully") using a four-point scale from "completely agree" to "don't agree at all."

Results

Behavioral & psychosocial problems. Multivariate analysis of variance at Y1 (using Bonferroni paired comparisons and controlling for age, gender, and SES) revealed several significant differences between groups: (1) Aggressors, victims, & aggressive victims showed significantly more aggressive behavior than uninvolved children, and aggressive victims were significantly more aggressive than victims, $F(3,423) = 13.76$, $p < .001$, $\eta^2 = .09$; (2) Aggressors and aggressive victims showed significantly more delinquent behavior than uninvolved children, and aggressive victims were significantly more delinquent than victims, $F(3, 423) = 8.43$, $p < .001$, $\eta^2 = .06$; (3) Victims and aggressive victims showed significantly more social problems than uninvolved children, $F(3,423) = 7.00$, $p < .001$, $\eta^2 = .05$; (4) Aggressive victims showed significantly more withdrawn behavior than uninvolved children, $F(3,423) = 4.32$, $p = .005$, $\eta^2 = .03$; (5) Aggressors and aggressive victims reported significantly more positive beliefs about fighting that victims and uninvolved children, $F(3,423) = 16.35$, $p < .001$, $\eta^2 = .10$. No significant differences between groups were found for anxious/depressed symptoms or somatic complaints.

Multiple regression analysis (controlling for age, gender, and SES) was used to assess relations between Aggressor/Victim Status at Y1 and negative outcomes at Y2. Results indicated that: (1) Aggressive victims at Y1 showed significantly more aggressive ($B = 1.32$, $p = .02$) and delinquent behavior ($B = .46$, $p = .04$) than their peers at Y2; (2) Victims ($B = .36$, $p = .09$) and aggressive victims at Y1 ($B = .71$, $p = .002$) showed significantly more social problems than their peers at Y2, whereas aggressors showed significantly fewer social problems ($B = -.54$, $p = .04$); (3) Aggressors ($B = .11$, $p = .02$) and aggressive victims at Y1 ($B = .08$, $p = .04$) reported significantly more positive beliefs about fighting than their peers at

271

Y2, whereas victims reported significantly less positive beliefs about fighting ($B = -.11, p = .002$). No significant results were found for anxious/depressed symptoms, somatic complaints, or withdrawn behavior.

Frequencies and stability over time. Using the method described above, 62 of the 440 children (14.1%) at Y1 were classified as aggressors, 118 (26.8%) as victims, 91 (20.7%) as aggressive victims, and 169 (38.4%) as uninvolved. At Y2, 41 of 391 children (10.5%) were classified as aggressors, 87 (22.3%) as victims, 50 (12.8%) as aggressive victims, and 213 (54.5%) as uninvolved.

A 4 X 4 chi-square test analyzing Aggressor/Victim Status Group at Y1 vs. Y2 (see Table 1) generally supported stability of the groups over time. Results were significant, $\chi^2(9, N = 391) = 127.20, p < .001$, with a medium effect size, *Cramer's V* = .33. Examination of frequencies at Y1 and Y2 indicated that the "uninvolved" group increased considerably in relative size over time while the "involved" groups decreased in size. However, comparison of observed and expected values in Table 1

Table 1. *Crosstabulation of aggressor/Victim status group at Y1 and Y2*

A/V Status Group Y1		Uninvolved	Aggressor	Victim	Aggressive Victim	Total
			A/V Status Group Y2			
Uninvolved	Actual Frequency	113	11	27	3	154
	Expected Frequency	83.9	16.1	34.3	19.7	
Aggressor	Actual Frequency	28	17	5	2	52
	Expected Frequency	28.3	5.5	11.6	6.6	
Victim	Actual Frequency	48	6	38	13	105
	Expected Frequency	57.2	11.0	23.4	13.4	
Aggressive Victim	Actual Frequency	24	7	17	32	80
	Expected Frequency	43.6	8.4	17.8	10.2	
	Total	213	41	87	50	391

also indicated that: (1) Members of all four groups at Y1 were overrepresented (compared to the expected values) in the same groups at Y2, suggesting overall stability across all groups, and (2) Aggressive victims at Y1 were significantly underrepresented in the uninvolved group at Y2, suggesting that aggressive victims are more likely than others to maintain their involvement in aggression over time.

Family & environmental risk factors. Multivariate analysis of variance at Y1 (using Bonferroni paired comparisons and controlling for age, gender, and SES) revealed several significant differences between groups: (1) Aggressive victims experienced significantly more frequent discipline than victims and uninvolved children, $F(3,423)$ = 8.85, $p < .001$, $\eta^2 = .06$; (2) Aggressors, victims, and aggressive victims experienced significantly more emotional/verbal discipline than uninvolved children, $F(3,423)$ = 7.36, $p < .001$, $\eta^2 = .05$; (3) Victims and aggressive victims experienced significantly more physical discipline than uninvolved children, $F(3,423) = 5.79$, $p = .001$, $\eta^2 = .04$; (4) Aggressors and aggressive victims reported observing significantly more violence in their home and neighborhood than victims and uninvolved children, $F(3, 423) = 28.89$, $p < .001$, $\eta^2 = .17$. No significant differences between groups were found for family conflict.

Multinomial logistic regression (controlling for age, gender, and SES) was used to assess relations between risk factors at Y1 and Aggressor/Victim Status at Y2. Relevant statistics can be found in Table 2. Results indicated that: (1) Victims at Y2 were significantly more likely than uninvolved children to experience frequent discipline at Y1; (2) To a marginally significant degree, aggressive victims at Y2 were less likely than uninvolved children to experience emotional/verbal discipline at Y1; (3) Aggressors and aggressive victims at Y2 were significantly more likely than victims and uninvolved children to observe violence in their home and

Table 2. Significant Risk Factors at Y1 Predicting Aggressor/Victim Status at Y2

Variable	Wald	p-value	Odds Ratio (95% CI)
Overall Discipline Frequency Victims >			
Uninvolved	9.66	.002	2.23 (1.34 – 3.69)
Emotional/Verbal Discipline			
Uninvolved > Aggressive Victims	2.94	.086	1.53 (0.94 – 2.49)
Violence Observed			
Aggressors > Uninvolved	20.50	< .001	4.95 (2.48 – 9.89)
Aggressive Victims > Uninvolved	13.76	< .001	3.48 (1.80 – 6.72)
Aggressors > Victims	9.88	.002	3.33 (1.57 – 7.05)
Aggressive Victims > Victims	5.58	.018	2.34 (1.16 – 4.74)

neighborhood at Y1. No significant results were found for physical discipline or family conflict.

CONCLUSIONS

The problem of bullying in schools has received considerable media attention in recent years, and it is clear that schools are taking the issue seriously by implementing policies designed to decrease these behaviors. Research on the effectiveness of bullying intervention programs (e.g., Frey, Hirschstein, Edstrom, & Snell, 2009; Karna et al., 2013) has produced a mix of positive, negative, and inconclusive results. Researchers have been both highly critical of popular but largely ineffective techniques, such as "zero tolerance" policies (e.g., Borgwald & Theixos, 2013) and highly supportive of evidence-based "whole-school" intervention programs (e.g., Wurf, 2012). Even programs that have been found to be effective to some degree have run into difficulties, including inconsistent results across age groups and evidence that positive changes in knowledge and attitudes about aggression do not necessarily lead to significant changes in actual behavior (e.g., Merrell, Gueldner, Ross, & Isava, 2008; Smith, Schneider, Smith, & Ananiadou, 2004; Ttofi & Farrington, 2012, 2013). Additionally, both teachers and parents may be unaware of bullying behavior (Holt, Kantor, & Finkelhor, 2009; Houndoumadi & Pateraki, 2001) or attempt to intervene in ineffective ways (Cooper & Nickerson, 2013; Lovegrove, Bellmore, Green, Jens, & Ostrov, 2013; Swearer & Cary, 2003). While significant progress has been made in addressing aggressive behavior in schools, it is clear that there is much room for improvement.

We hope that the research reviewed in this chapter, along with the new research findings presented, will contribute to a deeper and more complete understanding of aggressive interactions in childhood and adolescence, such that empirical evidence can be used to develop and improve upon school policies and programs designed to reduce such behaviors. Our recommendations for teachers, school officials, parents, and other concerned parties can be summarized as follows:

First, we should pay particularly close attention to *aggressive victims*. These children, who are both victims and perpetrators of aggression, have consistently been found to be worse off than their peers (including pure aggressors and pure victims) across a number of domains. The results of our own research are no different. In our sample, aggressive victims showed significantly higher levels of problem behaviors (including aggression and delinquency), positive beliefs about fighting, social problems with peers, and withdrawn behavior. It follows that these children are most in need of support and assistance from parents, teachers, and peers. If, however, an anti-bullying program focuses primarily on a simple dichotomy that identifies children as either aggressors *or* victims, aggressive victims could be misidentified or overlooked completely.

Second, we should recognize that pure aggressors and pure victims are quite similar to each other in many ways. The dominance/submission aspect of the relationship between these two groups is readily apparent, which leads to the assumption that they require separate treatment and intervention strategies. Numerous research results suggest that a focus on *involvement* in aggressive behavior, regardless of role, may be a more appropriate approach in many cases. For example, in our own sample, pure aggressors and pure victims differed significantly from each other only in terms of beliefs about fighting; unsurprisingly, aggressors indicated more positive attitudes toward aggression than victims. Otherwise, the two groups were not significantly different in terms of either externalizing behaviors (i.e., aggressive and delinquent behavior) or psychosocial problems (i.e., social problems and withdrawn behavior). Effective intervention programs should emphasize the idea that aggressors and victims face similar difficulties. Focusing only on the differences between these groups, rather than their shared *involvement* in maladaptive behavior, may serve to mask (or even exacerbate) these problems.

Third, it is important to recognize that both aggressive and victimization behaviors can be highly consistent over time. There is substantial evidence that these behaviors decrease with age, and that "uninvolved" students typically outnumber aggressors, victims, and aggressive victims. It is clear, however, that many students have difficulty changing their behavior, and that aggressive victims are particularly at risk for remaining involved in aggressive behavior over time. In light of this longitudinal evidence, it is essential that intervention programs begin as early as possible, apply age-appropriate strategies throughout elementary/ middle/high school, and, above all, emphasize a high degree of patience. These behaviors can begin early in childhood and prove considerably difficult to change; expecting a "quick fix" or providing inconsistent support is likely to bring about counterproductive results.

Finally, we must recognize that negative behaviors within the context of school may have their roots in the child's home and neighborhood environment. Through their choice of disciplinary techniques, parents can influence their child's aggressive interactions with peers. They may model aggressive behaviors as an effective means to get one's way, leading to an increase in their child's aggressive behavior; alternatively, their child may fall into a pattern of submissive behavior, increasing the child's risk of becoming a victim. Exposure to violence, even when the child is not directly targeted (e.g., intimate partner violence between parents, gang activity in the neighborhood), can have similar effects. Thus, the foundations for aggressive and victimization behavior may be established long before children begin school, and even the most well-intentioned attempts to curb bullying in schools may be in vain if children face a violent, unsafe environment when they return home. Teachers and school officials should work hand-in-hand with parents and community leaders to stay up-to-date on the most recent empirical research, recognize which students are most at-risk, promote efficacious parenting behaviors, and advocate for positive change in the communities they serve. Cooperation is essential; the problem of aggression and violence in schools is far too complex for schools to tackle on their own.

REFERENCES

Achenbach, T. M. (1991). *Manual for the child behavior cheklist/4–16 and 1991 profile*. Burlington, VT: University Associates in Psychiatry.

Achenbach, T. M., & Edelbrock, C. S. (1981). Behavioral problems and competencies reported by parents of normal and disturbed children aged four through sixteen. *Monographs of the Society for Research in Child Development, 46*.

Ahmed, E., & Braithwaite, V. (2004). Bullying and victimization: Cause for concern for both families and schools. *Social Psychology of Education, 7*, 35–54.

Andreou, E. (2000). Bully/victim problems and their association with psychological constructs in 8- to 12-year-old Greek schoolchildren. *Aggressive Behavior, 26*, 49–56.

Andreou, E., Vlachou, A., & Didaskalou, E. (2005). The roles of self-efficacy, peer interactions and attitudes in bully-victim incidents: Implications for intervention policy-practices. *School Psychology International, 26*, 545–562.

Bacchini, D., Esposito, G., & Affuso, G. (2009). Social experience and school bullying. *Journal of Community & Applied Social Psychology, 19*, 17–32.

Baldry, A. C., & Farrington, D. P. (1998). Parenting influences on bullying and victimization. *Legal and Criminological Psychology, 3*, 237–254.

Baumrind, D. (1991). The influence of parenting style on adolescent competence and substance use. *Journal of Early Adolescence, 11*, 56–95.

Berkowitz, R., & Benbenishty, R. (2012). Perceptions of teachers' support, safety, and absence from school because of fear among victims, bullies, and bully-victims. *American Journal of Orthopsychiatry, 82*, 67–74.

Bernstein, J. Y., & Watson, M. W. (1997). Children who are targets of bullying: A victim pattern. *Journal of Interpersonal Violence, 12*, 483–498.

Bettencourt, A., Farrell, A., Liu, W., & Sullivan, T. (2013). Stability and change in patterns of peer victimization and aggression during adolescence. *Journal of Clinical Child and Adolescent Psychology, 42*, 429–441.

Borgwald, K., & Theixos, H. (2013). Bullying the bully: Why zero-tolerance policies get a failing grade. *Social Influence, 8*, 149–160.

Bowes, L., Arseneault, L., Maughan, B., Taylor, A., Caspi, A., & Moffitt, T. E. (2009). School, neighborhood, and family factors are associated with children's bullying involvement: A nationally representative longitudinal study. *Journal of the American Academy of Child & Adolescent Psychiatry, 48*, 545–553.

Bradshaw, C. P., O'Brennan, L. M., & Sawyer, A. L. (2008). Examining variation in attitudes toward aggressive retaliation and perceptions of safety among bullies, victims, and bully/victims. *Professional School Counseling, 12*, 10–21.

Burk, L. R., Armstrong, J. M., Park, J.-H., Zahn-Waxler, C., Klein, M. H., & Essex, M. J. (2011). Stability of early identified aggressive victim status in elementary school and associations with later mental health problems and functional impairments. *Journal of Abnormal Child Psychology, 39*, 225–238.

Burk, L. R., Park, J., Armstrong, J. M., Klein, M. H., Goldsmith, H. H., Zahn-Waxler, C., & Essex, M. J. (2008). Identification of early child and family risk factors for aggressive victim status in first grade. *Journal of Abnormal Child Psychology, 36*, 513–526.

Camodeca, M., Goossens, F. A., Terwogt, M. M., & Schuengel, C. (2002). Bullying and victimization among school-age children: Stability and links to proactive and reactive aggression. *Social Development, 11*, 332–345.

Chaux, E., Molano, A., & Podlesky, P. (2009). Socio-economic, socio-political and socio-emotional variables explaining school bullying: A country-wide multilevel analysis. *Aggressive Behavior, 35*, 520–529.

Cooper, L. A., & Nickerson, A. B. (2013). Parent retrospective recollections of bullying and current views, concerns, and strategies to cope with children's bullying. *Journal of Child and Family Studies, 22*, 526–540.

Dodge, K., & Coie, J. (1987). Social-information-processing factors in reactive and proactive aggression in children's peer groups. *Journal of Personality and Social Psychology, 53*, 1146–1158.

Duong, M. T., Schwartz, D., Chang, L., Kelly, B. M., & Tom, S. R. (2009). Associations between maternal physical discipline and peer victimization among Hong Kong Chinese children: The moderating role of child aggression. *Journal of Abnormal Child Psychology, 37*, 957–966.

Eron, L. D., Huesmann L. R., & Zelli, A. (1991). The role of parental variables in the learning of aggression. In D. Pepler & K. Rubin (Eds.), *Handbook of developmental psychopathology* (pp. 169–188). Hillsdale, NJ: Erlbaum.

Espelage, D. L., Bosworth, K., & Simon, T. R. (2000). Examining the social context of bullying behaviors in early adolescence. *Journal of Counseling & Development, 78*, 326–333.

Espelage, D. L., & Holt, M. K. (2013). Suicidal ideation and school bullying experiences after controlling for depression and delinquency. *Journal of Adolescent Health, 53*, S27–S31.

Fanti, K. A., & Kimonis, E. R. (2013). Dimensions of juvenile psychopathy distinguish "bullies," "bully-victims," and "victims". *Psychology of Violence, 3*, 396–409.

Forber-Pratt, A. J., Aragon, S. R., & Espelage, D. L. (2013). The influence of gang presence on victimization in one middle school environment. *Psychology of Violence* [Advance online publication]. doi: 10.1037/a0031835

Fox, C. L., & Boulton, M. J. (2005). The social skills problems of victims of bullying: Self, peer, and teacher perceptions. *British Journal of Educational Psychology, 75*, 313–328.

Frey, K. S., Hirschstein, M. K., Edstrom, L. V., & Snell, J. L. (2009). Observed reductions in school bullying, nonbullying aggression, and destructive bystander behavior: A longitudinal evaluation. *Journal of Educational Psychology, 101*, 466–481.

Georgiou, S. N., & Fanti, K. A. (2010). A transactional model of bullying and victimization. *Social Psychology of Education, 13*, 295–311.

Giang, M. T., & Graham, S. (2008). Using latent class analysis to identify aggressors and victims of peer harassment. *Aggressive Behavior, 34*, 203–213.

Gini, G. (2008). Associations between bullying behavior, psychosomatic complaints, emotional and behavioural problems. *Journal of Paediatrics and Child Health, 44*, 492–497.

Guerra, N. G., & Slaby, R. G. (1990). Cognitive mediators of aggression in adolescent offenders: 2. Intervention. *Developmental Psychology, 26*, 269–277.

Hanish, L. D., & Guerra, N. G. (2004). Aggressive victims, passive victims, and bullies: Developmental continuity or developmental change? *Merrill-Palmer Quarterly, 50*, 17–38.

Harel-Fisch, Y., Walsh, S. D., Fogel-Grinvald, H., Amitai, G., Pickett, W., Molcho, M., ... Craig, W. (2011). Negative school perceptions and involvement in school bullying: A universal relationship across 40 countries. *Journal of Adolescence, 34*, 639–652.

Haynie, D. L., Nansel, T., Eitel, P., Crump, A. D., Saylor, K., Yu, K., & Simon-Morton, B. (2001). Bullies, victims, and bully/victims: Distinct groups of at-risk youth. *Journal of Early Adolescence, 21*, 29–49.

Hokoda, A., Lu, H.-H. A., & Angeles, M. (2006). School bullying in Taiwanese adolescents. *Journal of Emotional Abuse, 6*, 69–90.

Holt, M. K., & Espelage, D. L. (2007). Perceived social support among bullies, victims, and bully-victims. *Journal of Youth and Adolescence, 36*, 984–994.

Holt, M. K., Kantor, G. K., & Finkelhor, D. (2009). Parent/child concordance about bullying involvement and family characteristics related to bullying and peer victimization. *Journal of School Violence, 8*, 42–63.

Houndoumadi, A., & Pateraki, L. (2001). Bullying and bullies in Greek elementary schools: Pupils' attitudes and teachers'/parents' awareness. *Educational Review, 53*, 19–26.

Ireland, J. L., & Archer, J. (2004). Association between measures of aggression and bullying among juvenile young offenders. *Aggressive Behavior, 30*, 29–42.

Isolan, L., Salum, G. A., Osowski, A. T., Zottis, G. H., & Manfro, G. G. (2013). Victims and bully-victims but not bullies are groups associated with anxiety symptomatology among Brazilian children and adolescents. *European Child & Adolescent Psychology, 22*, 641–648.

Kaltiala-Heino, R., Frojd, S., & Marttunen, M. (2010). Involvement in bullying and depression in a 2-year follow-up in middle adolescence. *European Child & Adolescent Psychiatry, 19*, 45–55.

277

Kaltiala-Heino, R., Rimpela, M., Rantanen, P., & Rimpela, A. (2000). Bullying at school: An indicator of adolescents at risk for mental disorders. *Journal of Adolescence, 23*, 661–674.

Karna, A., Voeten, M., Little, T. D., Alanen, E., Poskiparta, E., & Salmivalli, C. (2013). Effectiveness of the KiVa antibullying program: Grades 1–3 and 7–9. *Journal of Educational Psychology, 105*, 535–551.

Knafo, A. (2003). Authoritarians, the next generation: Values and bullying among adolescent children of authoritarian fathers. *Analyses of Social Issues and Public Policy, 3*, 199–204.

Kochenderfer-Ladd, B. (2003). Identification of aggressive and asocial victims and the stability of their peer victimization. *Merrill-Palmer Quarterly, 49*, 401–425.

Kristensen, S. M., & Smith, P. K. (2003). The use of coping strategies by Danish children classed as bullies, victims, bully/victims, and not involved, in response to different (hypothetical) types of bullying. *Scandinavian Journal of Psychology, 44*, 479–488.

Kumpulainen, K., Rasanen, E., & Henttonen, I. (1999). Children involved in bullying: Psychological disturbance and the persistence of the involvement. *Child Abuse & Neglect, 23*, 1253–1262.

Kumpulainen, K., Rasanen, E., Henttonen, I., Almqvist, F., Kresanov, K., Linna, S-L., ... Tamminen, T. (1998). Bullying and psychiatric symptoms among elementary school-age children. *Child Abuse & Neglect, 22*, 705–717.

Lee, S. S., & Wong, D. S. (2009). School, parents, and peer factors in relation to Hong Kong students' bullying. *International Journal of Adolescence and Youth, 15*, 217–233.

Lereya, S. T., Samara, M., & Wolke, D. (2013). Parenting behavior and the risk of becoming a victim and a bully/victim: A meta-analysis study. *Child Abuse & Neglect, 37*(12), 1091–1108. doi: http://dx.doi.org/10.1016/j.chiabu.2013.03.001

Lovegrove, P. J., Bellmore, A. D., Green, J. G., Jens, K., & Ostrov, J. M. (2013). My voice is not going to be silent: What can parents do about children's bullying? *Journal of School Violence, 12*, 253–267.

Menesini, E., Melan, E., & Pignatti, B. (2000). Interactional styles of bullies and victims observed in a competitive and cooperative setting. *The Journal of Genetic Psychology, 161*, 261–281.

Merrell, K. W., Gueldner, B. A., Ross, S. W., & Isava, D. M. (2008). How effective are school bullying intervention programs? A meta-analysis of intervention research. *School Psychology Quarterly, 23*, 26–42.

Molnar, B. E., Cerda, M., Roberts, A. L., & Buka, S. L. (2008). Effects of neighborhood resources on aggressive and delinquent behaviors among urban youths. *American Journal of Public Health, 98*, 1086–1093.

Moos, R. H. (1990). Conceptual and empirical approaches to developing family-based assessment procedures: Resolving the case of the family environment scale. *Family Process, 29*, 199–208.

Moos, R. H., & Moos, B. S. (1986). *Family environment scale: Manual.* Palo Alto, CA: Consulting Psychologists Press.

Mustanoja, S., Luukkonen, A.-H., Hakko, H., Rasanen, P., Saavala, H., & Riala, K. (2011). Is exposure to domestic violence and violent crime associated with bullying behaviour among underage adolescent psychiatric inpatients? *Child Psychiatry and Human Development, 42*, 495–506.

Mynard, H., & Joseph, S. (1997). Bully/victim problems and their association with Eysenck's personality dimensions in 8 to 13 year-olds. *British Journal of Educational Psychology, 67*, 51–54.

Nansel, T. R., Haynie, D. L., & Simons-Morton, B. G. (2003). The association of bullying and victimization with middle school adjustment. *Journal of Applied School Psychology, 19*, 45–61.

O'Brennan, L. M., Bradshaw, C. P., & Sawyer, A. L. (2009). Examining developmental differences in the social-emotional problems among frequent bullies, victims, and bully/victims. *Psychology in the Schools, 46*, 100–115.

Olweus, D. (1978). *Aggression in the schools: Bullying and whipping boys.* Washington, DC: Hemisphere.

Olweus, D. (1993). *Bullying at school: What we know and what we can do.* Oxford, England: Blackwell.

O'Moore, M., & Kirkham, C. (2001). Self-esteem and its relationship to bullying behavior. *Aggressive Behavior, 27*, 269–283.

Oswald, D. L., & Russell, B. L. (2006). Perceptions of sexual coercion in heterosexual dating relationships: The role of aggressor gender and tactics. *Journal of Sex Research, 43*, 87–95.

Ozer, A., Totan, T., & Atik, G. (2011). Individual correlates of bullying behaviour in Turkish middle schools. *Australian Journal of Guidance and Counselling, 21*, 186–202.

Pateraki, L., & Houndoumadi, A. (2001). Bullying among primary school children in Athens, Greece. *Educational Psychology, 21,* 167–175.

Pellegrini, A. D. (1998). Bullies and victims in school: A review and call for research. *Journal of Applied Developmental Psychology, 19,* 165–176.

Perry, D. G., Kusel, S. J., & Perry, L. C. (1988). Victims of peer aggression. *Developmental Psychology, 24,* 807–814.

Perry, D. G., Perry, L. C., & Kennedy, E. (1992). Conflict and the development of antisocial behavior. In C. U. Shantz & W. W. Hartup (Eds.), *Conflict in child and adolescent development* (pp. 301–329). New York, NY: Cambridge University Press.

Ragatz, L. L., Anderson, R. J., Fremouw, W., & Schwartz, R. (2011). Criminal thinking patterns, aggression styles, and the psychopathic traits of late high school bullies and bully-victims. *Aggressive Behavior, 37,* 145–160.

Richters, J. E., & Martinez, P. (1990). *Things I have seen and heard: A structured interview for assessing young children's violence exposure.* Rockville, MD: National Institute of Mental Health.

Rigby, K. (1998). The relationship between reported health and involvement in bully/victim problems among male and female secondary schoolchildren. *Journal of Health Psychology, 3,* 465–476.

Russell, B. L., Oswald, D. L., & Kraus, S. W. (2011). Evaluations of sexual assault: Perceptions of guilt and legal elements for male and female aggressors using various coercive strategies. *Violence and Victims, 26,* 799–815.

Schwartz, D. (2000). Subtypes of victims and aggressors in children's peer groups. *Journal of Abnormal Child Psychology, 28,* 181–192.

Schwartz, D., Proctor, L. J., & Chien, D. H. (2001). The aggressive victim of bullying: Emotional and behavioral dysregulation as a pathway to victimization of peers. In J. Juvonen & S. Graham (Eds.), *Peer harassment in school: The plight of the vulnerable and victimized* (pp. 147-174). New York, NY: Guilford.

Schwartz, D., Lansford, J. E., Dodge, K. A., Pettit, G. S., & Bates, J. E. (2013). The link between harsh home environments and negative academic trajectories is exacerbated by victimization in the elementary school peer group. *Developmental Psychology, 49,* 305–316.

Sheehan, M. J., & Watson, M. W. (2008). Reciprocal influences between maternal discipline techniques and aggression in children and adolescents. *Aggressive Behavior, 34,* 245–255.

Slaby, R. G., & Guerra, N. G. (1988). Cognitive mediators of aggression in adolescent offenders: 1. *Assessment. Developmental Psychology, 24,* 580–588.

Smith, J. D., Schneider, B. H., Smith, P. K., & Ananiadou, K. (2004). The effectiveness of whole-school antibullying programs: A synthesis of evaluation research. *School Psychology Review, 33,* 547–560.

Straus, M. A. (1979). Measuring intrafamily conflict and violence: The conflict tactics (CT) scales. *Journal of Marriage and Family, 41,* 75–88.

Straus, M. A., & Gelles, R. J. (1990). *Physical violence in American families: Risk factors and adaptations to violence in 8,145 families.* New York, NY: Doubleday/Anchor.

Strohmeier, D., Wagner, P., Spiel, C., & von Eye, A. (2010). Stability and constancy of bully-victim behavior: Looking at variables and individuals. *Zeitschrift fur Psychologie, 218,* 185–193.

Swearer, S. M., & Cary, P. T. (2003). Perceptions and attitudes toward bullying in middle school youth: A developmental examination across the bully/victim continuum. *Journal of Applied School Psychology, 19,* 63–79.

Swearer, S. M., Song, S. Y., Cary, P. T., Eagle, J. W., & Mickelson, W. T. (2001). Psychosocial correlates in bullying and victimization: The relationship between depression, anxiety, and bully/victim status. In R. A. Geffner, M. Loring, & C. Young (Eds.), *Bullying behavior: Current issues, research, and interventions* (pp. 95–121). Binghamton, NY: Haworth.

Toblin, R. L., Schwartz, D., Gorman, A. H., & Abou-ezzeddine, T. (2005). Social-cognitive and behavioral attributes of aggressive victims of bullying. *Journal of Applied Developmental Psychology, 26,* 329–346.

Ttofi, M. M., & Farrington, D. P. (2011). Effectiveness of school-based programs to reduce bullying: A systematic and meta-analytic review. *Journal of Experimental Criminology, 7,* 27–56.

Ttofi, M. M., & Farrington, D. P. (2012). Bullying prevention programs: The importance of peer intervention, disciplinary methods and age variations. *Journal of Experimental Criminology, 8,* 443–462.

Turner, P., & Ireland, J. L. (2011). Officer attitudes towards intra-group aggression in young people and young adults: Does the reported motivation of an aggressor impact on intervention and support? *International Journal of Law and Psychiatry, 34,* 309–316.

Unnever, J. D. (2005). Bullies, aggressive victims, and victims: Are they distinct groups? *Aggressive Behavior, 31,* 153–171.

Veenstra, R., Lindenberg, S., Zijlstra, B. J. H., De Winter, A. F., Verhulst, F. C., & Ormel, J. (2007). The dyadic nature of bullying and victimization: Testing a dual-perspective theory. *Child Development, 78,* 1843–1854.

Voisin, D. R., & Hong, J. S. (2012) A mediational model linking witnessing intimate partner violence and bullying behaviors and victimization among youth. *Educational Psychology Review, 24,* 479–498.

Wang, H., Zhou, X., Lu, C., Wu, J., Deng, X., Hong, L., … He, Y. (2012). Adolescent bullying involvement and psychosocial aspects of family and school life: A cross-sectional study from Guangdong Province in China. *PloS One, 7.*

Watson, M. W., Fischer, K. W., Burdzovic Andreas, J., & Smith, K. W. (2004). Pathways to aggression in children and adolescents. *Harvard Educational Review, 74,* 404–430.

Weiss, B., Dodge, K. A., Bates, J. E., & Pettit, G. S. (1992). Some consequences of early harsh discipline: Child aggression and a maladaptive social information processing style. *Child Development, 63,* 1321–1335.

Winsper, C., Lereya, T., Zanarini, M., & Wolke, D. (2012). Involvement in bullying and suicide-related behavior at 11 years: A prospective birth cohort study. *Journal of the American Academy of Child & Adolescent Psychiatry, 51,* 271–282.

Wolke, D., Woods, S., Bloomfield, L., & Karstadt, L. (2000). The association between direct and relational bullying and behaviour problems among primary school children. *Journal of Child Psychology and Psychiatry, 41,* 989–1002.

Wurf, G. (2012). High school anti-bullying interventions: An evaluation of curriculum approaches and the method of shared concern in four Hong Kong international schools. *Australian Journal of Guidance and Counseling, 22,* 139–149.

Xu, Y., Farver, J. A. M., Schwartz, D., & Chang, L. (2003). Identifying aggressive victims in Chinese children's peer groups. *International Journal of Behavioral Development, 27,* 243–252.

CHRISTA BOSKE

36. BRIDGE BUILDING

Promoting Culturally Responsive Practices and Policies to Address
Bullying in K-12 Schools

Bullying is a pervasive problem within all grade levels across race/ethnicity, gender, socioeconomic status, ability, sexual orientation, native language, religion/beliefs/ faith, and immigration status. I became interested in this research over 20 years ago when I worked with young men ages 13 to 18, who were identified as emotionally disturbed. For most of these young men, they were imprisoned for crimes ranging from rape to aggregated assault to gang violence to theft to dealing illegal drugs. All of the young men received special education services due to their learning differences. Teachers and support staff often informed the young men they did not possess the same intellectual abilities as their public school regular education counterparts. I witnessed the abuse of power between teachers/staff members towards residents, residents towards other residents, and residents towards teachers and administration. The power differential often resulted in residents receiving negative consequences including extensive social isolation in time-out rooms, sexual and physical abuse, full-body restraints for verbal offenses, threats of possible imprisonment for divergent behaviors, and degrading comments made regarding their personal character and family. These extensive abusive occurrences inspired me to examine the wide-range of bullying experiences of students, teachers, and school community members across schools. There is limited research regarding teacher-student bullying in schools and its impact on student development, especially for vulnerable populations such as lesbian/gay/bisexual/transgender/queer (LGBTQ), Children of Color, children who do not conform to heteronormative gender norms, and children with learning differences (see Cook, Williams, Guerra, Kim, & Sadek, 2010; Meyers, 2008; Poteat & Rivers, 2010; Rose, 2010).

The purpose of this chapter is three-fold: 1) to examine bullying as a larger phenomenon of abuse and power differential with an inner-city Midwestern school community; 2) to investigate bullying between teachers and students; and 3) to promote culturally responsive bridge building for systemic change. I begin with a review of extant literature on bullying in schools. Next, I present the context for the case study and describe four incidents of bullying within one of the middle schools. The first case focuses on a young man who identified as a girl and "in transition." The second situation describes the experiences of a male Student of Color with

C. Boske & A. Osanloo (Eds.), Students, Teachers, and Leaders Addressing Bullying in Schools, 281–303.

learning differences who was bullied for his gender expression and perceived sexual orientation by a school leader. The third narrative centers on a veteran teacher physically bullying male Students of Color. The final incident focuses on a female veteran teacher bullying a sixth grade male Student of Color. Next, I describe the findings and make recommendations to address the complexities of bullying in schools through culturally responsive bridge building among educators, students, families, and community organizations.

BRIEF LITERATURE REVIEW ON BULLYING IN U.S. SCHOOLS

Although bullying embraces a range that varies in type and severity, there is limited research regarding trends, accurate reporting, contextualizing incidents, and use or abuse of power by the perpetrator(s). However, there is research regarding the impact of bullying on the development and well-being of children. Bullying is of significant concern, because it is often less visible or identifiable than other academic, social or emotional concerns. For the purpose of this chapter, bullying is defined as a form of unwanted or intentional aggression, harassment, abuse or violence. It is a systematic use of power including, but not limited to, physical aggression (i.e., pushing, shoving, punching, kicking, use of weapons), verbal aggression (i.e., using degrading language towards another person, humiliation, spreading rumors, name-calling), social aggression (i.e., exclusiveness), and cyber bullying (i.e., the use of social media to embarrass, harass, or abuse) (Espelage & Holt, 2012; Olweus, 1993; Vaillancourt, McDougall, Hymel, Krygsman, Miller, Stiver, & Davis, 2008; Wade & Beran, 2011).

Because the impact of bullying is often unidentifiable or invisible, there is an urgency to better understand the immediate and long-term impact bulling may have on children's development. The concern lies knowing most children spend at least 30 hours a week in school. The percentage of children bullied in schools for 12 to 18 year olds is approximately 28% (Robers, Zhang, Truman, & Snyder, 2012). Other studies suggest comparable percentages of students who admit to bullying peers (Wang, Iannotti, & Nansel, 2009).

Research regarding bullying suggests bullying is aimed at vulnerable student populations. These populations include children with learning differences, LGBTQ youth, and Black students. First, students with learning differences are twice as likely to be identified as victims and perpetrators as their general education counterparts (see Rose, Espelage, Aragon, & Elliot, 2011). This is often due to students being perceived as having low social and cognitive skills (Rose et al., 2011) and being socially rejected by their peers (Baumeister, Storch, & Geffken, 2008). Second, students who identify as LGBTQ experience homophobic teasing and derogatory language (Espelage, Basile, & Hamburger, 2012; Kosciw, Greytak, & Diaz, 2009; Poteat & Espelage, 2005; Poteat & Rivers, 2010). This group of students often encounters more victimization than their heterosexual counterparts (Espelage, Aragon, Birkett, & Koenig, 2008; Kosciw et al., 2009). Finally, students who identify as Children of Color, specifically Black children, are less likely to report bullying and victimization; however, Black youth experience more hostile acts than their White or Latino/a counterparts (Turner, Finkelhor, Hamby, Shattuck, & Ormrod, 2011).

Deepening understanding of bullying in educational settings provides opportunities for educators to create spaces for positive change. Dr. Stuart Twemlow, a psychiatrist and Director of the Peaceful Schools and Communities Project at Baylor College of Medicine's Menninger Child and Family Program, researches bullying in schools. Findings from his studies suggest a greater number of teachers than expected shared they bullied students at some point during their careers. However, there is limited extant research on this topic. Annual survey data from the National Center for Educational Statistics and Bureau of Justice Statistics do not include any questions on this issue; however, they do collect data regarding students bullying teachers. Tremlow (2005) and Espelage (2012) stress many school leaders, teachers, and support staff lack the training to address bullying, may not be aware of when or how to address it, and might not know ways to prevent bullying from occurring.

Although teachers and school leaders may lack the necessary training to address bullying in schools, it is also important to note a number of anti-bullying programs implemented in schools are unsuccessful. According to Tremlow (2005), sustainability is the key. Anti-bullying programs are not successful due to more complex issues such as lack of awareness to funding to faculty/administrator turnover. In regards to lack of awareness, teachers do not seem to understand that regardless of age, children who are bullied by teachers without the power to change teacher-student interactions, are at risk of poor attendance, achievement, and sense of self. Most children, especially small children, realize teachers and school leaders are in charge. Furthermore, children realize faculty and school leaders have the ability to interrupt bullying when they witness it or allow it to continue. However, some bystanders do not report bullying, because they fear retaliation or have conflicting loyalties with colleagues. Therefore, a canned curriculum for bullying prevention and intervention is not enough to address these issues. Those who are bullied are among the most vulnerable populations. These groups are vulnerable due to learning differences (Rose, Espelage, Aragon, & Elliot, 2011), race/ethnicity (Cook, Williams, Guerra, Kim, & Sadek, 2010), sexual orientation (Kosciw, Greylak, Bartkiewicz, Boesen, & Palmer, 2012; Russell, Kosciw, Hom, & Saewye, 2010), gender expression (i.e., traditional, heterosexual gender norms are expected for girls and boys) (Kosciw et al., 2012; Meyer, 2008), immigration status, native language, and religion/beliefs/faith. Historically, the extant literature has omitted, distorted or under researched the experiences of these student groups. There is a need to examine the bullying dynamics surrounding these marginalized school-age populations (Boske & Osanloo, in press, 2014).

Context of the Study

This Midwest school district was identified as the third largest urban school district in the state. The district served over 12,000 P-12 students. Over 98% of students

283

were Children of Color. The majority of Children of Color were Black (39%) and Latino/a (40%) with 2% of students identifying as White. Over 95% of students received free breakfast and free/reduced lunch. Approximately 5% of students were homeless and lived in nearby shelters. Approximately 27% of students transferred in and out of school district throughout the year. Most families lived in apartments and section 8 housing. The district's average daily attendance was 89%; however, the school in this case study reported more than 100 students might be tardy to school on any given day.

Ninety-nine percent of the students were Students of Color. Forty-five percent of students identified as Latino/a, 54% of students identified as Black, and 1% identified as White. Over 98% of students received free breakfast and lunch. The school experienced declining standardized test scores for two consecutive years and was placed on academic watch. Administrators and faculty were given one more year to improve standardized test scores before the state would issue a consultant to work with the teachers and administrators to improve students' test scores. Educators were asked to specifically focus on improving student achievement for Black and Latino/a students as well as students receiving special education services. Over 30% of these students were identified as needing individual education plans.

Over the last twenty-five years, the neighborhood demographics shifted from an all-White middle class to upper class neighborhood to a predominantly Black neighborhood with families living in poverty to a majority of Families of Color with an influx of recent immigrants from Mexico. Some of the faculty members were students when the school was identified as the "best school in the city", serving White, English speaking children from middle to upper class families. The support staff was comprised of People of Color, including police and truancy officers, and community counselor. The faculty included all White teachers and three People of Color. Two of the Teachers of Color grew up in the city and attended the public schools on the south side. The third Teacher of Color grew up in a southern state and moved to the Midwest as an adult. The remaining teachers were White. All of the remaining teachers spent their childhood in surrounding suburban areas within a 25 mile radius of the school. More than half of the teachers attended the school and/or district as P-12 students.

Disciplinary referrals ranged from not being prepared for class to disruption to disrespect to physical assault/fighting. Teachers submitted 1,097 office referrals in the first four months for 878 students. Over 70% of referrals were given to males. Eighty-two percent of referrals were given to Black males and 18% of these referrals were given to Latino males. Sixty-three percent of referrals for males were for "disruption", 30% for "disrespect," and 7% for physical assault.

METHODOLOGY

This study examined the overarching question: How do students, teachers, and school leaders in this Midwestern school understand teacher-student bullying? To do so, I utilized a case study approach. This methodology was particularly well-suited to this research because of the ways in which it affords the researcher an opportunity to investigate a contemporary phenomenon within a real-life context across multiple sources of data (Feagin et al., 1991; Yin, 1994). Data collected for this study consisted primarily of school district data (i.e., surveys, disciplinary records, attendance, and office referrals over two academic years), 60 minute interviews (i.e., one school leader, police office, truancy officer, counselor, 10 teachers, five teachers' aides, and one librarian), 67 field notes (i.e., school observations and school meetings), and surveys.

I Need to Use 'That' Bathroom

A 15-year old multiracial student was enrolled in the middle school mid-year. The administrators as well as the school guidance counselor, truancy officer, and school police officer met to discuss the student's situation. The student dropped out of middle school four times within the last three years. One of the administrators laughed and said, "This kid is a basket case and so is his family. He was prostituted for years and pimped out by his mother." The same administrator continued, "His mother supported her son dropping out of school, because he was allegedly harassed while he was attending here."

The team asked for clarification regarding the student's harassment claims. The administrator replied, "Michael's mother is a drug addict. She is strung-out on crack. She prostitutes her son so she can stay high. I have seen her on street corners and at the motel down the street walking up and down the boulevard. Michael is usually around the same area or at the park down the street. God only knows what that child has seen and experienced. Everyone in the community is aware of this."

A team member inquired about the support Michael and his mother received to address the alleged harassment. The administrator emphasized the school's responsibility to "take care of children in school, not outside of school." Discussions continued regarding the school's responsibility to "keep tabs" on students after school hours. One of the team members noted, "If Michael's mom wants to prostitute herself and her son, then let the police deal with it. We just have to deal with the fact that Michael's mom wants him back in school again. This has now become our problem again."

The guidance counselor noted the student was not "well received by the faculty." The student was described as "shy." The truancy officer laughed and said, "And yah...he wants to be called Michelle, not Michael and use the girls' bathroom." The team discussed how to address whether or not Michelle would be able to use the girl's bathroom, because, according to the student's record, Michelle was born a "boy", not a "girl." Other teachers shared concerns including, "Michael goes against my religious belief", "He needs to be cured from his disease" and "He's a freak." Another teacher reminded team members Michelle was hospitalized for psychiatric care a few years ago. One replied, "See, I told you he doesn't belong here."

When Michelle came back to school, she encountered several teachers who made comments regarding how she dressed. According to Michelle, one teacher said, "You don't look like a boy." She heard another teacher say, "You tend to wear a lot of black…what's that for? And what's up with the makeup?" When he asked to use the restroom, some of the boys told him he "talks like a girl" and "acts like a girl", but he is "just a fucking faggot" and "can't go into a girls' bathroom." Michelle explained to one of the administrators that he was physically pushed by the male students when she attempted to enter the girl's restroom. Michelle said, "I have been called queer, faggot, butt fuck, cock sucker, AIDS boy, reject, sissy, little girl, fuck up, and all sorts of stuff! Kids look at me and say stupid stuff like 'What the fuck is that?' Guys threaten to rape me, or tell me to suck them off, or something. And teachers say things and just stand there and act like they never heard a thing! I just don't think I belong in school. I don't like it there."

Upon her return to class, a teacher said, "Which bathroom did you use?" Michelle replied and pointed out into the hallway, "I used that one." The teacher clarified and asked, "Which one?" And Michelle responded by pointing to the girl's restroom. The teacher laughed and said, "You don't belong here." The teacher proceeded to write a disciplinary referral and told "Michael" to leave the classroom.

Michelle received a "warning" for choosing to use the "wrong" restroom. Michelle was informed to use the nurse's bathroom from this point forward. Michelle did not return to school for over a week. Upon her return, Michelle's mother accompanied her. The administrator said, "Your hair is even longer now and you are wearing even more makeup?" The truancy officer said, "I thought you were a girl." Michelle's mother was informed that "her son did not belong in a traditional public school due to his attendance issues." The administrator added, "And this school is just too hard for him." The team recommended he be placed in the "alternative school," so "he could come and go as he pleased" and "be with other students like him."

If You Didn't Act Like such a Faggot

Marquane was sent to the main office for disruption during lunch. He was accompanied by five girls who he identified as his friends and witnesses to the incident. Marquane was an eighth grade Black male student who received special education services as well as free breakfast and lunch. Marquane was sent to the office four times by his teachers for "not being prepared for class" and for "disruption." He informed the principal of the situation in the cafeteria. He said, "A bunch of girls keep talking about me and spreading rumors. They say that I'm gay and have sex with boys. I don't like it and I just want it to stop. Every time I go by them, they are always talking smack. I just keep going, but it's really getting to me now. It happens all the time." He pointed to the girls in the room and said, "They can tell you all about it too, cause they've seen it." Marquane started to cry. His friends in the office stood by his side. One girl put her arm around his shoulders. They informed the principal the girls Marquane was referring to often antagonized him in the hallway and during lunch.

These particular girls seemed to choose opportunities to approach Marquane when teachers were not around. Marquane asked the principal for help. The principal sat behind the desk and said, "If you didn't act like such a faggot, these things wouldn't happen to you." Marquane had tears roll down his cheeks. He did not respond verbally to the principal's comments. The principal said, "I think we are done here… you know what you need to do, Marquane. Go take care of your business and man up." Marquane reported the incident to his grandmother. His grandmother contacted the principal. After the conversation, the grandmother encouraged her grandson to "find more boys to be friends with so you don't find yourself in this situation at school with the principal."

I Dare You to Go through This Door

Jesus was a twelve year old Latino male student. He worked with three White teachers and one Black teacher (i.e., two males and two female teachers). Jesus was often tardy or absent from school. A truancy officer met with his parents regarding the school's concerns. Jesus had difficulty in most of his subject areas; however, he seemed to do well in music, art, physical education, and language arts. His language arts teacher was a Teacher of Color. Jesus met with his grade level team several times throughout the year for disciplinary purposes. He was often restricted from classroom field excursions and received detentions during lunch for missing work. During one of his classes, a 25 year White male veteran teacher began to publicly announce his low academic progress. He said, "I can't believe you don't know how to this problem. Do you know anything at all?" Jesus remained quiet. The teacher said, "Of course you don't know how to do this. Aren't you supposed to be in eighth grade now?" Jesus remained quiet. Some students started to laugh. The teacher did not request students to stop laughing. Jesus stood up from his desk. The teacher asked, "Where do you think you're going?" Jesus proceeded to walk towards the classroom door. The teacher stood in front of the doorway and stretched out his arm to block the door. Jesus stood in front of the teacher. He asked him, "Please get out of the way." The teacher said, "I dare you to go through this door." Jesus said, "I am going through this door. You can't stop me." The teacher said, "If you go through this door, then you have to go through me. I will have you arrested for assault." Jesus quickly moved under the teacher's arm and ran to the office. The teacher called down to the office and announced Jesus left the classroom without permission and he was in the process of writing an office referral. The teacher wanted Jesus suspended from school for "threatening a teacher", "disrespect", and "disruption."

This veteran teacher was approached by the principal. The teacher did not seem to understand how his behavior was possibly antagonizing the student. The principal also discussed the teacher's use of degrading language toward the student. The teacher replied, "If he doesn't want his business out there, then he should do what I expect him to do. I don't want him in my classroom. He doesn't belong there. He doesn't want to learn, so he needs to leave. It's not my job to teach someone who doesn't want to obviously learn."

Go Back to Africa Where You Belong

Tyrone was an eleven year old Black male student. He worked with four White teachers (i.e., one male and three female teachers) who identified as teachers with "middle class values." Tyrone's teachers urged him over the course of his sixth grade year to be more organized in school. He had difficulty keeping his locker clean and remembering which materials to bring to class. Tyrone's papers were often wrinkled, torn, and scattered around his work area. As his classmates moved from class to class, he was often marked tardy, because he spent time trying to gather his belongings before moving to his next class. One day, his female science teacher said to him, "I am sick and tired of you coming to class late and leaving all of your crap everywhere in this classroom." Tyrone did not respond to the teacher's comments. One of the students commented, "You make no sense, Ty." Someone from the back yelled, "You smell, Tyrone!" And another student said, "You are so dirty!" The teacher did not redirect the students' comments or inform them their behavior was not conducive with school policy; rather, the teacher said, "You are stupid and lazy!" Students looked around the classroom at one another. The room grew quiet. Tyrone lowered his head. He starred at his desk. The teacher announced, "Tyrone, you should go back to Africa where you belong!" Tyrone started to cry. He left the classroom without permission and headed to the office.

This veteran teacher of 15 years seemed to encourage students to make degrading comments to Tyrone by choosing not to redirect their behavior. The teacher informed administrators she made those comments; however, the teacher did not agree her behavior was inappropriate. The children in the classroom, at the time of the incident, confirmed the teacher's behavior. Students who made derogatory comments towards Tyrone were given four hours of school community service by the administration. In regards to disciplinary actions for the teacher, central office administration would not support any disciplinary action. The associate superintendent informed the building level administrators, "We have a hard enough time finding teachers to work in this district and work with *these* kids. We cannot afford to lose another one." As administrators, they were not allowed to document the incident in the teacher's file or comment on the situation in her annual evaluation. Both administrators were asked to "let it go."

Although administrators were concerned the incident had the potential to make the evening news, they believed the teacher's behavior was dismissed, because the student was a member of two vulnerable populations. Tyrone was a Student of Color and his family lived in extreme poverty. The school leaders decided to utilize the data they collected to examine how often vulnerable student populations experienced excessive discipline and what type of disciplinary actions were taken by teachers towards students.

FINDINGS

Although Black students were 45% of the total student population, they received over 78% of the total discipline for the entire school. The remaining office referrals were given to Latino/a students (21.5%) and White students (.5%). Furthermore, boys were 48% of the total school population; however, they received 79% of the discipline referrals. Office referrals for Black males ranged from "not having appropriate school supplies" (18%) to "disruption" (33%) to "disrespect" (38%) to "physical assault" (11%). According to the teachers' family contact records, 89% of office referrals for Black males were sent directly to the office versus disciplinary action taken in the classroom (i.e., warning, phone call home, grade level team conference). There were no records of "hate speech" or "discriminatory speech" between student to student or teacher to student.

According to the administrators, the incidents provided faculty and staff with opportunities to create meaningful dialogue around bullying; however, administration realized the need for faculty to deepen their understanding of cultural differences among teachers, students, families, and community. Tensions rose, because issues facing Children of Color seemed easier to address than issues facing students due to gender expression, gender identity, and perceived sexual orientation. Union representatives informed administration teachers were "taking sides" regarding the incident between the veteran teacher and Tyrone. Many teachers allegedly agreed with the choices the veteran teacher made towards Tyrone, because they shared similar beliefs regarding student behavior and expectations.

The superintendent approached principals across the school district and requested they participate in a state-wide Positive Behavior Intervention System (PBIS) pilot. This program emphasizes teachers and school leaders acknowledge when students demonstrate respectful behavior. In turn, students earn points, tickets, or credit to use towards donated prizes, school events, or extra time with adults/students in the building. Administrators decided to participate in the pilot, and hoped this program might provide teachers with opportunities to engage in meaningful dialogue regarding the alignment of the school's vision, mission, and student outcomes.

As a school community, they discussed the vision and mission of the school and presented data regarding student outcomes. Faculty were presented data regarding disciplinary actions taken throughout the school year. The office received 774 office referrals in four months. Out of these referrals, 389 out-of-school suspensions were given in four months. In addition, administrators calculated the number of minutes students missed from class due office referrals. The total number of hours students missed within four months totaled 2,235. The disciplinary referrals ranged from not being prepared to class to disruption to disrespect to threats to gang affiliation to physical assault/fighting.

School leaders facilitated discussions centered on the following: 1) What did it mean to be a teacher? 2) Why did teachers enter this profession? and 3) What did they expected from their colleagues regarding the improvement of student learning?

Throughout these discussions, school leaders realized how many teachers did not agree on "appropriate school behavior" for children as well as for adults. Teachers discovered their backgrounds often influenced what they deemed appropriate. Collectively, school leaders and teachers discussed how each of them brought their backgrounds and experiences to school and how those understandings influenced decisions made.

Teachers also shared how they understood the significance and implementation of inclusive practices. For most teachers, this was a difficult undertaking. Teachers seemed uncomfortable working with children who did not look like them or share similar upbringings. Children who experienced the most office referrals or reported being harassed by teachers at the middle school were Children of Color, children living in poverty, recent immigrants, boys, English Language Learners, and those who were ridiculed for their gender expression, gender identity, and perceived sexual orientation.

School leaders helped teachers understand the need to create positive learning environments for all children. At the time, the middle school was under state watch. They reported low standardized test scores for three consecutive years. The principal explained how often teachers verbally and physically harassed and excessively disciplined students, specifically Young Men of Color. White, middle class, English speaking teachers seemed to assume their colleagues agreed on "appropriate school behavior" as well as assuming children shared similar beliefs as their teachers and school leaders. Tensions rose when some teachers demanded children align their values and beliefs with them. School leaders discussed their expectations for student behavior. Some teachers admitted to purposely antagonizing students, because they wanted specific students to leave their classrooms. Throughout the process, school leaders discovered how often teachers engaged in bullying behaviors. They spoke with central office administrators about the dialogue occurring at the middle school. Central office personnel encouraged the building level leaders to collect data regarding teachers' perceptions. School leaders informed central office personnel they would only collect data if they could keep the participants anonymous and allow teachers, counselors, and staff members to voluntarily participate.

Administrators asked faculty, staff, and students if they would be interested in better understanding the culture and climate of the building. The majority of teachers expressed an interest in gathering the data. Students emphasized how often teachers did not seem interested in their insights. Administrators offered faculty an opportunity to facilitate conversations regarding the findings. They were also provided with two anonymous surveys: two open-ended questions and Likert scale questions with four possible responses ranging from never to sometimes to frequently to always with one open-ended question regarding behaviors they witnessed in school. Below are questions asked of adult school community members:

1. What does it mean to bully someone?
2. How often do you witness bullying during the school day?

3. How often do you stop the bullying during the school day?
4. Were you ever bullied as a child?
5. Were you ever bullied as an adult?
6. Do students bully students?
7. Do teachers bully students?
8. Do students bully teachers?
9. Have you ever bullied a student?
10. What have you observed?

Administrators informed families they were collecting data regarding students' experiences with bullying. All of the families gave permission for their children to participate. Students were asked four open-ended questions. They were also asked to respond to eight Likert scale questions with responses ranging from never to sometimes to frequently to always. Students the following questions via an anonymous survey:

1. What does it mean to bully someone?
2. How often do you witness bullying during the school day?
3. How often do you stop the bullying during the school day?
4. Were you ever bullied?
5. Do students bully students?
6. Do teachers bully students?
7. Do students bully teachers?
8. Have you ever bullied a student?
9. If yes, what happened? If no, please go to the next question.
10. Have you ever bullied a teacher?
11. If yes, what happened? If no, go to the next question.
12. If you have seen bullying in school, what did you see? If you have not seen bullying in school, you are finished with this survey.

Over 95% of the adult school community members participated. This included faculty, staff, and specials teachers. The administrators received 80 out of 89 completed anonymous surveys. Administrators received 875 anonymous student surveys, which was the entire school population. The administrators shared all of the responses with faculty and staff members in an all-school retreat. Findings suggested faculty who experienced bullying as children seemed more sensitive about students bullying students, teachers bullying students, and students bullying teachers. Those who experienced bullying seemed more aware of bullying occurring in school. Four out of 89 participants reported they were bullied by students. Forty-one teachers reported students bullied other students. These incidents included, but were not limited to, name-calling, using the word "faggot" or "gay" or "dyke" in the hallways and cafeteria, and pushing. Sixty-four adult participants documented they witnessed teachers bullying students. Sixty-seven students reported they had been bullied in school by other students. One hundred thirty eight students witnessed students bullying other students. Three hundred and eighty seven students witnessed teachers calling students names (i.e. dumb, stupid, gay), making threats to a student's academic progress, blocking students from leaving the classroom with their bodies.

Some students emphasized which students were often targeted. These students included students who did not conform to gender specific behaviors of "traditional" boy or girl roles, students who were thought to be "gay", students who did not academically perform well in school, students who attended class in special education classrooms, students who were socially isolated, and students who spoke a language other than English. Six students witnessed the principal telling a young Black male that "if he didn't hang out with girls and act like such a faggot, he wouldn't be bullied in school." Over twenty students identified specific teachers who "yelled at students", and while yelling at them, the teachers "spit on them" and "threw up their arms." Thirty-six students identified specific Black males who were often "picked on by teachers." Thirty-seven students chose not to report bullying incidents in school. These students stressed they did not think their teachers would address the behavior. Out of 67 students who reported being bullied, participants who identified as boys emphasized the need for boys to "take care of their own business", because their friends might ridicule them for relying on an adult to solve their problems.

As for teachers bullying students, 51 teachers, 13 staff members, and 387 students witnessed teachers bullying students. These incidents included, but were not limited to, teachers spitting on children, calling children names (i.e., stupid, dumb, worthless), calling students "gay" or "dyke", antagonizing students during class (i.e., telling students to "shut up", humiliating children by putting them down until children stop the targeted behavior, physically blocking doorways and daring students to push their way through, threatening to send students to prison, telling students they will never graduate from high school), and repeatedly disciplining the same student. Non-tenured teachers and first-year teachers were "afraid to report" teachers bullying students, because they did not want to "rock the boat" or "sabotage their chance to earn tenure."

The administrators shared the findings during a school-wide retreat. Most of the adult participants were surprised by the number of teachers-bullying-students incidents. Some educators walked out of the meeting. An administrator recalled an educator yelling, "This is bullshit!" The faculty member proceeded to leave the retreat and did not return until the following day. Educators, counselors, and support staff who were marginalized due to their race/ethnicity, religion/beliefs/faith, native language, gender expression, sexual identity, ability (i.e., mental and physical), and socioeconomic status (i.e., during childhood), noted they were not surprised by the findings. They emphasized the need for school community members to deepen their understanding of bullying. They urged their colleagues to reconsider why teachers engage in aggressive and abusive behaviors with children, especially children from vulnerable populations. Several of these faculty and staff members inquired about aligning the vision, mission, curriculum, expectations, and school policies to improve the learning environment for all children. School community members continued discussing the implications of the findings on student achievement, attendance, and social emotional well-being.

These authentic discussions led to the creation of the Multicultural Task Force. The purpose of the group centered on engaging in often highly personal discussions regarding values, beliefs, and responses towards marginalized populations. Members of the team included educators and staff who voluntarily joined the Multicultural Task Force. Of the 14 members, 12 identified as People of Color and two people identified as White. The Task Force membership included four security officers, a police officer, truancy officer, librarian, two administrative assistants, community psychologist, principal, assistant principal, and two faculty members. They discussed the racial and ethnic makeup of the Task Force. Despite the lack of faculty involvement, especially from school community members who identified as White, American citizens, able bodied and mind, middle class, and heterosexual, they decided to move forward with their project.

After reviewing three incidents of bullying by educators towards students, they concluded the need to directly address teacher-student bullying throughout the organizational culture. The Task Force offered opportunities for educators and staff members to participate in dialogue, data collection, analysis, sharing research, and promoting culturally responsive practices and policies. Members engaged in dialogue centered on challenging texts regarding sensitive subject areas including, but not limited to race, class, gender expression, White privilege, hegemonic practices, sexuality, heterosexism, learning differences, immigration, native language, religion/faith/beliefs, and diverse families.

Members spent several sessions choosing which areas to focus on and aligned the priorities with the findings from the school-wide surveys, disciplinary data, and three reports of teacher-student bullying. Together, they found meaning within the readings and contextualized findings from a myriad of studies to their middle school community. Members read for meaning and formulated new ways of knowing that generalized not only to their school practices, but to their personal lives. Several members reminded one another that schooling practices are related to issues of power and race. The key issue, therefore, from their perspectives was to deepen their understanding of who has the power to decide the nature of schooling, especially for children from marginalized populations. The three incidents of teacher-student bullying for Children of Color, children with learning differences, and a child who did not conform to "traditional" gender expressions associated with males, were made a priority within the Task Force.

They assessed the needs of the children and researched community organizations, including universities and colleges, who could provide additional resources and insights to promoting culturally responsive practices and policies. The National Association for the Advancement of Colored People, food pantries, Alcoholics Anonymous, museums, politicians, homeless shelters, local university and college scholars, Latino/a organizations, church leaders, and the Gay Lesbian Straight

Teachers Network all played a critical role throughout the dialogue and creation of an action plan to meet the needs of the community.

Their primary goal of the Task Force was to create a safe place in which collectively and individually, they promoted culturally responsive pedagogy, curriculum, and school policies. Members shared personal narratives from their professional and personal lives. Often times, members identified spaces in which they were marginalized due to race, class, educational attainment, family dynamics, learning differences, and perceived gender expression. The group concluded from analyzing the written narratives of teachers and students that children from marginalized populations often received a reduced and intellectually and emotionally inferior curriculum compared to wealthier peers in surrounding school districts. Ignoring these wider issues of policy, structural oppression, and discriminatory school practices was not an option. It was within the context of this recognition that Task Force members explored how the power differential between teachers and students, especially children from disenfranchised populations, were perpetuated to the extent of bullying students. Collectively, they examined broader issues of social class, ideology, and power within their inner-city school community.

They read books, journal articles, watched documentaries, and shared school data from their ongoing surveys to improve the school environment for all children. Collectively, they understood bullying children was not an acceptable practice. Members realized the need to socially mediate for new cultural practices situated and embedded within their broader school community. An emphasis was placed on specialized discourses of its participants. Together, they decided how to mediate access to such knowledge to manifest reciprocity in a more deliberate or formal manner. The disposition to critically question and redirect teaching practices, values, and beliefs were issues noted in Task Force sessions. They explored the purpose of teaching, recognizing the political and social constraints on an educator's work in schools. The time to process and develop these authentic collaborations was crucial to the group's ability to promote their efforts as cultural resources for their school community. Their level of engagement fostered opportunities for self-transformation, which expanded to the experiences within the Task Force to develop knowledge, skills, and a new group identity. Their new identity afforded them opportunities to work with school community members to conceptualize inclusive classroom environments. Their new understanding stressed the importance of classrooms as cultural settings. Members drew meaning from their new understandings of societal realities, personal histories, cultural practices, and facilitated new ways of perceiving and discussing students and their learning.

Within one year of actively engaging in this work, the Task Force assessed the school's disciplinary records. As a school community, they began by discussing the vision and mission of the school and presented data regarding student outcomes. The office received 442 versus 774 office referrals within the next school year's first four months. Out of these referrals, 182 versus 389 out-of-school suspensions were given within this time. The total number of hours students missed within four months totaled 1,232. The disciplinary referrals continued to range from not being prepared to class to disruption to disrespect to threats to gang affiliation to physical assault/ fighting; however, the number of referrals significantly decreased.

The bullying survey was distributed after the first year of implementing the Task Force. Over 99% of the adult school community members participated. This included faculty, staff, and specials teachers. The administrators received 87 out of 89 completed anonymous surveys. Administrators received 873 anonymous student surveys, which was the entire school population. The administrators shared all of the responses with faculty, staff, families, and students. Twenty-one teachers reported students bullying other students. These incidents included, but were not limited to, name-calling, using the word "faggot" or "gay" or "dyke" in the hallways and cafeteria, and physical contact (i.e., pushing or shoving). Eleven adult participants documented they witnessed teachers bullying students. Twenty-nine students reported they had been bullied in school by other students. Fifty-seven students witnessed students bullying other students. Seventy-eight students witnessed teachers calling students names (i.e. dumb, stupid, gay), publicly degrading students about their academic progress, and blocking students from leaving classrooms with their bodies.

Students who did not conform to gender specific behaviors of "traditional" boy or girl roles, students who were thought to be "gay", students who did not academically perform well in school, students who attended class in special education classrooms, students who were socially isolated, and students who spoke a language other than English were still noted as being bullied; however, the number of incidents significantly decreased. None of the students reported school leaders bullying students. Eleven students identified specific grade level teachers who publicly raised their voices at students while in class and made negative comments about their academic performance. As for teachers bullying students, 11 teachers, 3 staff members, and 78 students witnessed teachers bullying students. These incidents included, but were not limited to, teachers calling children names (i.e., stupid, dumb, worthless), calling students "gay" or "dyke", antagonizing students during class (i.e., telling students to "shut up", humiliating children by putting them down until children stop the targeted behavior, physically blocking doorways and daring students to push their way through, threatening to send students to prison, telling students they will never graduate from high school), and repeatedly disciplining the same student. Non-tenured teachers and first-year teachers noted the Task Force as a valuable resource to discuss these situations.

Within the first year of the Task Force, one teacher requested a transfer to another school. During the second year, five teachers chose to transfer to other schools in the district. They informed union representatives and administrators they chose to leave the middle school, because their values were no longer aligned with the values of the new school culture. After three years of engaging in this work with the Task Force, the middle school was removed from the state's academic watch list. Children of Color, children living in poverty, and children with learning differences were meeting or exceeding state standards. As the school experienced an influx of recent immigrants and English Language Learners, the Task Force was preparing to assess the knowledge and skills of faculty to meet the needs of this increasing student population.

DISCUSSION

Findings from this study suggest school community members deepen their understanding of bullying when they increase their self-awareness regarding beliefs, power, and privilege. The critical reflective process seemed to provide opportunities for school members to examine themselves in relation to others. As school leaders engaged in the reflective process, they became responsible for creating symmetrical and additive relations for authentic collaboration among school community members, especially vulnerable student populations (Espelage et al., 2008; Kosciw et al., 2009). They uncovered how often Children of Color, children living in poverty, children who did not conform to gender expressive norms, and children with learning differences experienced more victimization than their counterparts.

The authentic collaborative work among school community members and community members (i.e., universities, nonprofits) seemed to impact not only the school's disciplinary record, but also the academic success of students. As colleagues, they developed the capacity to contribute new ways of knowing to the group's intellectual endeavors in an effort to promote culturally responsive practices and policies to meet the needs of all children, especially those from underserved populations.

Their critical work needed time and space to develop authentic social networks. These networks played a significant role in systemically impacting students' academic, social, and emotional experiences in school. Their efforts became part of the social and cultural capital within the school. The action space of the Task Force promoted the intellectual abilities of school community members (i.e., children, families, educators, school leaders, and community members). Task Force members became resources for one another. They utilized their lived experiences and ways of knowing as the foundation for expanding the school's capacity to interrupt oppressive practices, expand new social practices, and systemically impact the way in which school community members understood cultural responsiveness.

The Task Force assessed the impact bullying played on student development as well as examined bullying behaviors by the perpetrators in an effort to reduce the number of incidents of bullying in school. Their insights situated their findings and work in the context of collegial and reciprocal relationships with others. There was a strong element of self-determination, of agency, throughout the Task Force. Their level of engagement supported efforts to increase participation, responsibility, and access to discourses as well as the development of new identities, skills, and knowledge. Their expanded participation was in deep contrast to their prior confining roles within the middle school. The direct contrast of the Task Force in relation to institutionalized practices encouraged a dynamic shift in understanding their new roles in promoting possibilities for systemic change. As a result, Task Force members mediated between teachers and students as well as the school-community-at-large. The key was to facilitate new relationships. These relationships developed due to new understandings and responses towards students, specifically, those who were marginalized because of their race, sexual identity, gender expression, class, and learning differences.

Although school leaders were faced with a possible state take-over due to an overwhelming emphasis to improve standardized testing, Task Force members emphasized the need for promoting culturally responsive learning to prepare teachers to meet the diverse needs of the student population. The dominant assumption guiding the creation and implementation of the Task Force centered on the belief that children, families, and educators were capable making informed decisions. These informed decisions emphasized the cultural strengths within marginalized populations (see Boske & McEnery, 2010; Gay, 2010). Such efforts challenged teachers' and school leaders' deficit interpretations. Their original interpretations suggested children from disenfranchised populations did not possess the necessary knowledge, skills, or values to be successful in school.

Findings also suggest school leaders created spaces for educators to collaborate with culturally aligned school community stakeholders in an effort to consider the influence of curriculum design, pedagogy, and school policy in creating an inclusive school environment. Issues of generalization, applicability, and adaptability were addressed within the school as well as within the extant literature shared with Task Force members. Each of these discussions fostered opportunities for members to better understand cultural diversity, their approaches and responses to marginalized populations, and assessing relationships between their data collection and contemporary school contexts. Members valued and understood the strong indications of promoting culturally responsive practices. Such efforts provided the school with vitality, energy, and flexibility in assessing and addressing the needs of those they served, especially those who were members of disenfranchised populations.

Their intent was not to request other schools replicate their Task Force; however, their efforts and outcomes may have encouraged school leaders and educators to adapt and recontextualize their school practices to new social conditions within school communities. Aspects of their Task Force collaborative work may be considered for school communities regardless of social location–but it is important to remember it all starts with a focus on the school as the primary unit of study. Their Task Force encouraged a reform effort that placed relationships at the center of their work. The key to facilitating this process lies in creating necessary safe spaces to think and talk about ways of understanding. All members must commit to the intellectual activities that emphasize the need for school community members to orient themselves to the goals of this work and find ways to create new structures and settings for authentic culturally responsive collaboration.

Although the work is not easy, educators and school leaders have the capacity to care and persevere. The primary goal of their work centered on critically examining their own lived experiences within their community, families, and society at large. They discovered how their new ways of knowing facilitated a self-transformation of their semi-private professional lives into the public sphere. These new public identities had the capacity to form new, authentic social networks that ultimately interrupted oppressive practices and policies. Their new identities became resources with the Task Force, inspired others, and addressed the tensions among themselves, others, and their work in schools. The sociocultural processes of this nested conceptual model (see Figure 1) afforded members to interactively co-construct change. It became more than innovation; rather, it was the development of new identities, both individual and school-community wide. The internalization did not simply imply a transformation of insights or perspectives from one member to another. The development and collaboration of all members from identifying the challenges to sharing their narratives to collecting data to analyzing findings to presenting information to researching possible solutions to promoting this work and conceptualizing the consequences for practice were critical to their evolving trajectories of participation. The process was intimately related to the development of new identities as professionals, and in some cases, as individuals (see Boske, 2011). The need for students, teachers, staff, school leaders, families, and community members to think collectively placed a high premium on respecting and understanding cultural diversity. Such efforts stressed the need to develop collaborative and reciprocal relationships with school community members. These relationships were at the heart of this work, their self-transformation, and self-promoted professional identities with the public sphere.

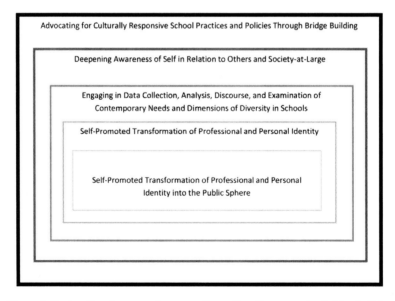

Figure 1. Sociocultural process for promoting culturally responsive bridge building

RECOMMENDATIONS

There is a need for school leaders to cultivate a school culture that centers on respect for self and others. One means of fostering this critical dialogue is to provide spaces for educators to consider bullying in all of its forms. Another possibility centers on the promotion of culturally responsive practices and policies through bridge building. Findings encourage school community members to reframe how they understand what it means to address bullying in schools by reframing the problem. Reframing may be the necessary precursor to gaining understanding, increasing critical consciousness, expanding personal knowing, and gaining resources to support a paradigm shift in addressing bullying in schools (see Boske, 2015). This paradigm shift encourages school community members to assess the culture and climate of the community and its members to provide spaces to examine the experiences of children, families, educators, school leaders, and community members.

The nested model suggests reframing begins from within. Rather than focusing on "anti-policy making", there may be a need to uncover deficit-laden beliefs as a means of engaging in reflective critical dialogue to promote culturally responsive practices and policies. For example, educators may believe schools serving low-income communities are incorrigible and that money spent on serving underserved populations is money wasted. Although reframing does not alter statistics or data related to student achievement or discipline, nor does it alter social trends (i.e., educational attainment, social mobility), reframing provides spaces to critically think about what influences the lives of those being served in school communities, the way in which people's beliefs impact which issues matter, whether or not circumstances should be changed, to what extent they feel they can change these realities, what they think they can do to make change; and finally, what they think promoting culturally responsive practices and policies means within that context.

Sometimes arguments to promote anti-bullying practices and policies require prescribed courses of action. In other words, people should do this first and this next. Being too rigid in the construction of reframing bullying policies may simply promote strategic chatter. In any given context, school community members (e.g., children, families, teachers, community organizational leaders, school leaders, staff, foundations, and others) are crucial to a civic alliance to reframing how we understand addressing bullying in schools. Such efforts may involve school community members spelling out their assumptions about race, class, gender, sexual orientation, ability (i.e., social, emotional, cognitive, physical), immigration status, native language, religion/beliefs/faith, family dynamics, and other dimensions of diversity. These opportunities may afford members with spaces to wrestle with their arguments, learn to consider context, and combine their arguments to attract and build bridges among themselves and others. The nested model exemplifies what might happen when ambitious, committed, and passionate people build bridges among themselves and others to assemble exceptional capacity for making meaningful change in schools actionable. Members play a critical role in giving cause to action by aligning themselves with viable actors interested in promoting similar beliefs. Bridging individuals, organizations, and resources, may create opportunities school communities to actively engage in addressing bullying through the promotion of cultural responsiveness.

In essence, bridging may create intersections for personal capacity–people who share similar beliefs; organizational capacity–people who work directly with school community members; civic capacity–people in positions of power willing and able to utilize their power and/or money to promote this work; and action capacity–people who utilize bridge building to address and interrupt oppressive practices and policies. Such efforts may be identified as bridging capital (see Putnam, 2000) or bridge building, a space to examine connections between prior lived stories, school communities, and the community-at-large to connect reform to deep local culture in more holistic and authentic ways (see Boske, 2012; Tooms & Boske, 2010).

These bridges may play an essential role in providing a political cover for those involved in promoting social justice and equity in schools. The act of bridging encourages actors to take greater risks themselves, and because of the power within bridging personal, organizational, civic, and action capacities, may warn off potential opponents of such reform (Comer, 2009; Henig & Rich, 2003). Although studies on bridge building are less abundant and often dismissed in the field of education (e.g., Boske & Diem, 2012; Tooms & Boske, 2010), research on bridge building suggests when communities mobilize around making schools better places for children, their efforts have the capacity to transform communities (i.e., Boske & McEnery, 2010; Lopez, 2001; Merchant & Shoho, 2010; Tooms & Boske, 2010). For example, Boske and McEnery (2010) found teachers and school leader who engaged in home visits reflected on the relationship between self and others, established meaningful home–school connections, rethought curricular practices, and promoted systemic school reform. In this instance, reform resulted in an impoverished inner-city school moving from on the brink of closing its doors to "excellent with distinction" in two years.

With regards to reconsidering how to define bridge building for migrant families, Lopez (2001) found that although families did not attend school functions, they were highly involved in their children's education by transmitting a strong work ethic that bridged home and school. Merchant and Shoho (2010) used the term *bridge people* to describe individuals committed to issues of social justice. These school leaders demonstrate how they create bridges between themselves and others to improve the lives of all of those with whom they serve. Similarly, Tooms, and Boske (2010) share first tellings of seminal educational leadership work to break through barriers of what scholars deemed "ordinary" day-to-day actions. These efforts centered on engaging in bridge leadership, which is rooted in the moral compass set firmly towards decisions made to address issues of equity and social justice in schools.

Making meaningful connections is essential to engaging in authentic bridge building. Moreover, it is important to note, the act of bridging does not prescribe a specific formula to engage in this work or limit this work to a specific level of impact. More importantly, bridge builders strive to acquire catalytic leadership at various levels, all of which are essential to constructing and implementing culturally responsive practices and policies.

Bridging encourages school community members to consider their alliance as a call to action. Considering the implications of the alliance urges school community members to look within, critically reflect on their ability and willingness to advocate for those who live on the margins, and promote meaningful relationships between school communities and communities-at-large. Culturally responsive bridge building may include, but is not limited to critically examining curriculum design, pedagogy, practices, policy, and inclusive decision-making. For those who work with youth, school leaders and teachers may need to consider the growing body of literature documenting the influence of hostile teacher-student relations, racial differences in bullying, and the impact of bullying on LGBTQ youth to better understand the experiences of vulnerable populations. There is a need for more research highlighting the cultural strengths of Children of Color and how those strengths impact a student's ability to overcome bullying, harassment, and victimization in school.

Researchers may consider examining the experiences of individuals from vulnerable populations including children with learning differences, LGBTQ youth, and Children of Color. For those who identify as LGBTQ, researchers may want to consider the lived realities of youth who are gender-nonconforming and Children of Color (Boske & Asanloo, in press). Although this case study focused on Black and Latino youth, other racial and ethnic groups may also be considered for future research studies as well as refugee and immigrant populations. Race and ethnicity may be considered across diverse socioeconomic groups.

CONCLUSION

There is an urgency for educators to examine how best to create culturally responsive practices and policies to provide safe learning environments all children. The sustainability of providing such spaces involves the creation of meaningful relationships among school community members, especially between teachers and students. Authentic bridging involves social and intellectual networks among members who share a vision. The action of bridging is crucial to sustaining the innovation of new public professional identities that promote cultural responsiveness in the face of adversity.

REFERENCES

Baumeister, A. L., Storch, E. A., & Geffken, G. R. (2008). Peer victimization in children with learning disabilities. *Child and Adolescent Social Work Journal, 25*, 11–23.

Boske, C. (2012). *Educational leadership: Building bridges among ideas, schools and nations.* Charlotte, NC: Information Age Publishing.

Boske, C. (2015). Preparing school leaders to interrupt racism at various levels within educational systems. *International Journal of Multicultural Education, 17*(1), 121–142.

Boske, C. (2011). Sense-making reflective practice: Preparing school leaders for non-text-based understandings. *Journal of Curriculum Theorizing, 27*(2), 82–100.

Boske, C., & Asanloo, A. (in press). *Living the work: School leaders, teachers, children, and scholars promoting social justice and equity work in schools.* United Kingdom: Emerald Publishing.

Boske, C., & Diem, S. (2012). *Global leadership for social justice: Taking it from the field to practice.* United Kingdom: Emerald Publishing.

Boske, C., & McEnery, L. (2010). Taking it to the streets: A new line of inquiry for school communities. *Journal of School Leadership, 20*(3), 369–398.

Comer, J. P. (2009). *What I learned in school: Reflections on race, child, development, and school reform.* San Francisco, CA: Jossey-Bass.

Cook, C. R., Williams, K. R., Guerra, N. G., Kim, T. E., & Sadek, S. (2010). Predictors of bullying and victimization in childhood and adolescence: A meta-analytic investigation. *School Psychology Quarterly, 25*(2), 65–83.

Espelage, D. L. (2012). Bullying prevention: A research dialogue with Dorothy Espelage. *Prevention Researcher, 19*(3), 17–19.

Espelage, D. L., & Holt, M. K. (2012). Understanding and preventing bullying and sexual harassment in school. In K. R. Harris, S. Graham, T. Urdan, S. Graham, J. M. Royer, & M. Zeidner (Eds.), *APA educational psychology handbook: Individual differences and cultural and contextual factors* (Vol. 2, pp. 391–416). Washington, DC: American Psychological Association.

Espelage, D. L., Aragon, S. R., Birkett, M., & Koenig, B. W. (2008). Homophobic teasing, psychological outcomes, and sexual orientation among high school students: What influences do parents and schools have? *School Psychology Review, 37*, 202–216.

Espelage, D. L., Basile, K. C., & Hamburger, M. E. (2012). Bullying experiences and co-occurring sexual violence perpetration among middle school students: Shared and unique risk factors. *Journal of Adolescent Health, 50*, 60–65.

Feagin, J., Orum, A., & Sjoberg, G. (Eds.). (1991). *A case for case study.* Chapel Hill, NC: University of North Carolina Press.

Gay, G. (2010). *Culturally responsive teaching: Theory, research, and practice* (2nd ed.). New York, NY: Teachers College Press.

Henig, J. R., & Rich, W. C. (2003). *Mayors in the middle: Politics, race, and mayoral control of urban schools.* Princeton, NJ: Princeton University Press.

Kosciw, J. G., Greytak, E. A., Bartkiewicz, M. J., Boesen, M. J., & Palmer, N. A. (2012). *The 2011 national school climate survey: The experiences of lesbian, gay, bisexual, and transgender youth in our nation's schools.* New York, NY: Gay Lesbian Straight Education Network.

Kosciw, J. G., Greytak, E. A., & Diaz, E. M. (2009). Who, what, when, where, and why: Demographic and ecological factors contributing to hostile school climate for lesbian, gay, bisexual, and transgender youth. *Journal of Youth and Adolescence, 38*, 976 –988.

Lopez, G. R. (2001). *On whose terms? Understanding involvement through the eyes of migrant parents.* Paper presented at the Annual Meeting of the American Educational Research Association, Seattle, WA.

Merchant, E., & Shoho, A. (2010). Bridge people: Civic and educational leaders for social justice. In C. Marshall & M. Olivas (Eds.), *Leadership for social justice: Making revolutions in education* (pp. 120–138). Boston, MA: Allyn & Bacon.

Meyer, E. J. (2008). Gendered harassment in secondary schools: Understanding teachers' (non) interventions. *Gender and Education, 20*(6), 555–572.

Olweus, D. (1993). *Bullying at school.* Oxford, UK: Blackwell.

Poteat, V. P., & Rivers, I. (2010). The use of homophobic language across bullying roles during adolescence. *Journal of Applied Developmental Psychology, 31*(2), 166 –172.

Putnam, R. D. (2000). *Bowling alone: Collapse and revival of American community.* New York, NY: Simon & Schuster.

Robers, S., Zhang, J., Truman, J., & Snyder, T. (2012). *Indicators of school crime and safety: 2011(NCES 2012-002/NCJ 236021).* Washington, DC: National Center for Education Statistics, U.S. Department of Education, and Bureau of Justice Statistics, Office of Justice Programs, U.S. Department of Justice.

Rose, C. A. (2010). Bullying among students with disabilities: Impact and implications. In D. L. Espelage & S. M. Swearer (Eds.), *Bullying in North American schools: A socio-ecological perspective on prevention and intervention* (2nd ed., pp. 34–44). Mahwah, NJ: Lawrence Erlbaum.

Rose, C. A., Espelage, D. L., Aragon, S. R., & Elliott, J. (2011). Bullying and victimization among students in special education and general education curricula. *Exceptionality Education International, 21*(2), 2–14.

Russell, S. T., Kosciw, J. G., Horn, S. S., & Saewyc, E. (2010). Safe schools policy for LGBTQ Students. *Social Policy Report, 24*(4), 3–17.

Tooms, A. K., & Boske, C. (2010). *Bridge leadership: Connecting educational leadership and social justice to improve schools.* Charlotte, NC: Information Age Publishing.

Twemlow, S. W., Fonagy, P., Sacco, F. C., & Brethour, J. R. (2006). Teachers who bully students: A hidden trauma. *International Journal of Social Psychiatry, 52*(3), 187–198.

Turner, H. A., Finkelhor, D., Hamby, S. L., Shattuck, A., & Ormrod, R. K. (2011). Specifying type and location of peer victimization in a national sample of children and youth. *Journal of Youth and Adolescence, 40*(8), 1052–1067.

Vaillancourt, T., McDougall, P., Hymel, S., Krygsman, A., Miller, J., Stiver, K., & Davis, C. (2008). Bullying: Are researchers and children/youth talking about the same thing? *International Journal of Behavioral Development, 32*(6), 486–495.

Wade, A., & Beran, T. (2011). Cyberbullying: The new era of bullying. *Canadian Journal of School Psychology, 26,* 44–61.

Wang, J., Iannotti, R., & Nansel, T. (2009). School bullying among adolescents in the United States: Physical, verbal, relational, and cyber. *Journal of Adolescent Health, 45,* 368–375.

Yin, R. (1994). *Case study research: Design and methods* (2nd ed.). Thousand Oaks, CA: Sage Publishing.

PAUL SALTZMAN

37. CONCLUDING THOUGHTS

President and CEO, Moving beyond Prejudice

We are all human. This must be our starting point. Overwhelmingly, I observe that people want to feel safe, to love and be loved, and to be healthy and live long. Yet, I must say that it still shocks me, yes, shocks me, to hear the statistics of how many children, teenagers and adults have been bullied or been bullies, been the target of prejudice or been the perpetrators of prejudice. We are messing with the very fabric of our society, wherever we may live; and this scares me.

I imagine that any reasonable person would agree that it is an ill society that is based in hatred and the suppression of others. Equally, I imagine that any reasonable person would agree that a healthy and enlightened society is based in compassion and the freedom of individuals to live in peace.

Yes, the solution is partly in education, and in a zero tolerance of bullying in schools, community groups, corporations, on the Internet, and everywhere. Yet, human behavior is individual: I decide what I believe, and feel, and how I act towards others; just as you decide what you believe, how you feel, and how you act towards others. This is why change truly begins within each one of us.

On the other hand, why look within ourselves? Why change at all? Why not love who you love, and hate who you hate? Why not be prejudice towards others? Why not bully others? Yes, we can say there is a moral and ethical responsibility to be fair, kind and decent to other members of society and, personally, I believe this. But many people don't think so much of others. They mostly think of what they want and need. What motivation is there for them to be decent, to not bully, to not be prejudiced?

Morgan Freeman speaks to this in *Prom Night in Mississippi,* the documentary film following his efforts, and the efforts of others, to change one thing in Charleston, Mississippi, where he lives. As late as 2007, in that town with one public high school and 2,100 people, there were two proms: A 'Black Prom' and a 'White Prom'.

On camera, Morgan speaks to the issue of why choose to not be prejudiced. "These are chains around our souls," he says. Meaning, it's for your own soul, for your own heart, for your own good to drop prejudices, to stop bullying. Moreover, you

C. Boske & A. Osanloo (Eds.), Students, Teachers, and Leaders Addressing Bullying in Schools, 305–307.

get to know and enjoy wonderful people who are different from yourself, thereby increasing your own enjoyment of life.

In the bigger picture, prejudice is likely the most pernicious, hidden pandemic on the planet, and it can be devastating and deadly—as Michele Josue shows in her powerful documentary film: *Matt Shepard is a Friend of Mine.*

Prejudice and bullying is shame-based behavior: if I feel good enough about me, I don't need to put you down. If you feel good enough about you, you don't need to put me down. And being shame-based behavior, prejudice most often remains buried in individuals, unseen and unhealed, until it bursts forth.

Almost all acts of bullying are predicated on prejudice. On the macro-level, it can lead to wars, clan rivalries, deaths of gays, Muslims, Hindus, Palestinians, Jews, Blacks, Whites and on, and on, and on.

Prejudice and its derivative, bullying, undermine safe-school environments, individual self-esteem and academic achievements, often resulting in poor marks and school dropouts. It's a disease that infects corporations, leading to inequities in promotions and in hiring and firing; and reducing productivity and self-esteem.

It leads to unhappiness, anti-depressants and job changes.

So, what's the science behind all this? It's the reptilian brain: fight or flight; and how the reptilian brain correctly alerts us to danger when we experience fear. Yet, the reptilian brain cannot distinguish between fear of annihilation and small fears, like being turned down for a date, or fear of a school exam, or fear of another student or a co-worker who's different than we are, but poses no danger.

For effective fight or flight, for survival, fear activates the reptilian brain to sever us from 1,400 of our upper brain functions—including logic, creativity, clear assessment of true danger, compassion and love. Under these conditions, compassionate listening, empathy and non-violent communication are impossible. This pandemic leaves no one untouched.

To date, the non-profit Moving Beyond Prejudice has screened the two documentary films, *Prom Night in Mississippi* and *The Last White Knight—Is Reconciliation Possible?* followed by audience discussions on prejudice and bullying for over 50,000 students of all ages, community groups, faith groups and corporations, internationally.

Our conclusion?

People of all ages, genders, races, faiths, nationalities, sexual preferences and so on, feel happiest, healthiest and most free when they feel good about others, not when they feel fear. They feel best when they are treated with respect by others. They even feel best when they treat others with respect. They feel happiest when they love rather than hate. They feel best about themselves when they are kind to others, rather than when they are bullying others.

So the most powerful reason to not be prejudiced, to not bully?

Try self-interest: your own happiness and joy in life!

Paul Saltzman was a civil rights volunteer with SNCC, the Student Non-Violent Coordinating Committee, in Mississippi in the summer of 1965. He is also the director and producer of 'Prom Night in Mississippi' and 'The Last White Knight— Is Reconciliation Possible?'

CONTRIBUTORS

Leah A. Bailey. I went to a private school in Ohio called "Northfield Baptist Christian School" for two years. When I left after 1ˢᵗ grade, I became a "new kid" at the best school in the world, "Valley Christian Academy." It was there where I experienced the bully and stayed until I became a freshman in high school. (9ᵗʰ grade, for those of you who don't know.) I am currently fifteen and my birthday is 3/31/99. Presently, I run track, my favorite color is pink, I love cats and dogs, I love drawing, my favorite number is twelve, and my favorite season is summer. I would like to be a teacher, or author because I love to write as well. I hope you enjoy this true story of mine. I would really appreciate if you read it and if you are reading this too. Thank You!

Anthony Michael Bias is an 18 year old graduating senior at Horizon Science Academy Cleveland High school with plans to attend Kent State University in the fall of 2014 for Zoology. He is also looking into a few writing minors to expand himself and his writing. Bias enjoys writing different forms of short stories, poetry, and music. His influences include people such as; Robert Frost, Tupac Shakur, Steven King, and James Patterson.

Chris Board. I live in Streetsboro, OH. I just turned 18 November 17th and I'm coming to the end of my senior year of high school. I live with my four siblings, my mother , and step dad. My father is currently incarcerated for seven years so I have been trying to be strong for him. I have been determined to go to college and I did it. I will be attending the University of Akron in the fall and I'm very excited to start my college journey. I will be the first kid in my family to go to college. I love sports. I kinda have a addiction to basketball. I couldn't stop playing even if I wanted to. I hope that I can play for Akron U next year so I'm dedicating my summer to prepare my body for Division 1 competition. I am very grateful I got a chance to share a piece of me with you. Writing this chapter was very difficult for me to do but I did it! Just remember, If you dream and believe, you will achieve greatness.

Angely Boske. I am 11 years old and in 6ᵗʰ grade. I am originally from Guatemala. When I was in elementary school, I was bullied by a group of girls and one boy. I stood up for myself and although I did this, those students continued to ignore me. Eventually, I could no longer deal with it, so my parents moved me to a better school in the same district. This chapter is about those experiences. My story is powerful and needs to be heard by students, teachers, families, and school leaders. They need to know how often this happens in schools. It needs to stop! I hope my chapter inspires you to realize that all students need to speak up and be heard, because every story matters.

Christa Boske grew up in a politically conservative small town community in the Midwest. She recalls questioning the exclusivity of religious practices and beliefs at the age of seven, and being shunned by the nuns. At an early age, she raised questions about race, class, religion, learning differences, sexual identity, gender expression, and immigration. Most people were not receptive to promoting culturally responsive practices and policies. However, Christa understood these challenges as opportunities to educate people. Christa identifies as "gay" and is the proud mother of her 11 year old daughter Angely. Mommy and me time is time she treasures most. Christa and her former partner separated after 15 years. Both of them continue their friendship and place Angely at the center of their lives. Last summer, Christa's new partner Wendy, Angely, and her were on the steps of the Supreme Court when D.O.M.A. was overturned. They were excited about sharing this historical moment as a family. Although it is not yet legal to be "married" in her current state, Christa and Wendy are getting married this summer in the presence of family and friends. They are legally getting married in a nearby state and hope their marriage will soon be recognized. As an Associate Professor and Program Coordinator of PreK-12 Educational Administration, Christa works to encourage school leaders to promote humanity in schools, especially for children and families from historically disenfranchised populations. Christa's line of inquiry focuses on the intersections of the cognitive and affective domains of school leadership with a particular focus on how school leaders transform their sense of self to lead in culturally responsive ways. Christa's most recent research has been published in journals including: *Journal of School Leadership, Journal of Research, Leadership and Education, International Journal of Multicultural Education, Journal of Cases in Educational Leadership, Multicultural and Technology Journal, Journal of Curriculum Theorizing, High School Journal, International Journal of Educational Management*, and *Planning and Changing*. She has also published over 20 book chapters. One of her more recent chapters, "Critical reflective practices: Connecting to social justice" Ira Bogotch and Carolyn Shield's (2014) *International handbook of educational leadership and social (in)justice*(Springer). Christa co-edited a book with Dr. Autumn K. Tooms (2010) titled *Bridge leadership: Connecting educational leadership and social justice to improve schools* (Information Age Publishing). She has two edited books published in 2012, which include: 1) *Educational leadership: Building bridges between ideas, schools and nations* (Information Age Publishing) and 2) *Global leadership for social justice: Taking it from the field to practice* (co-edited with Dr. Sarah Diem) (Emerald Publishing). Christa has two more books scheduled to be published in 2015 including this book, *Students, teachers, and school leaders promoting anti-bullying in schools* (Sense Publishing) (co-edited with Azadeh Osanloo) and *Living the work: Promoting social justice and equity work in schools around the world* (Emerald Publishing) (co-edited with Azadeh Osanloo).

Mandy Cenker-Miller is a Ph.D. student and graduate assistant in the K-12 Educational Administration program at Kent State University. She received her

Masters of Education degree from Malone University specializing in the teaching of students with special needs and her Educational Specialist degree in K-12 Educational Administration from Kent State University. After teaching students with mild to moderate learning differences for eight years, she decided to continue her learning at KSU, specifically on the preparation of school leaders as well as high education administration.

Aajah Chapman was born in the fall 4 minutes before midnight on October 19, 1998 at Maple Heights hospital in Maple Heights Ohio. My parents are Kelly Putnam and Alfred Chapman Jr. I am an only child. I'm 15 ½ years old and I'm a freshman. Active, adventurous, dependable and respectful would describe me. My favorite sports are volleyball and track. I enjoy hiking, bike riding, and horseback riding. I never skied before and I'm hoping to join the sky club my sophomore year. I'm presently in the Art Club, Global Leadership Club which raises money to build a science center in Ghana to teach the student about clean water source and proper sanitation skills, Beta Club which is a volunteer club, and Diversity Club. My favorite movie is "Freedom Writers" it's based on the book Freedom Writers Diary. It's about these high school students that were labeled "unteachable" until a teacher showed up and helped the turn their lives around by believing in them. She let them write stories about the troubles in their lives. She let their voices be heard by getting their stories published. That is why I was inspired to write about my story. I want my voice to be heard and I hope that students, teachers and parents realize that bullying is an issue and needs to be dealt with. It can cause so much damage in a person's life. I thank my mom for talking to me, and recognizing that there was an issue and taking action by talking to the principal and guidance counselor. I also thank her, her friends and my family and friends for their support and encouraging me to stay strong. I have been on the honor roll since sixth grade; I have perfect attendance since sixth grade. I have great plans and goals for myself. I know I'm wonderful person, I know I am somebody and I will not let bulling stand in my way!

Jeff Dinse, M.S. in Education, has been a seventh grade social studies teacher for 16 years in the Lockport City School District as well as the Kenmore Town of Tonawanda School District. He has been a volunteer assistant varsity basketball coach in his hometown of Wilson, New York for 13 years. In 1999, Jeff co-founded *Harbor Town Games Inc.* which produced the Master Guru board game and CD-ROM which is an interactive assessment tool based on the New York State Learning Standards. Jeff is also the co-creator of the "All Kinds of Kinds Program" and website designer.

Martinez E-B is a mixed media artist with an emphasis in painting. Martinez works primarily with themes related to identity through representation, urban stigmas and communal practices. He holds a BFA degree, with a Major in Painting from, The Cleveland Institute of Art. He has recently been commissioned, by Rid-All: Urban

311

Agriculture and Youth Education Group, to co-create, write and illustrate a 12 issue comic book series which is geared toward educating inner-city youth and general community about environmental sustainability. Since then, his writings and visuals for the comic book has been adapted into a live performance play at Cleveland's historic Karamu House. Martinez is also working on creating a course of study at the elementary level that will teach the importance of owning ones representation.

Jonathan Gill would grow up to serve in the United States Marine Corps during the time of Don't Ask, Don't Tell and its subsequent repeal, later deploying to Afghanistan in support of Operation "Enduring Freedom." It was there where he would come to terms with a long held secret, his queer identity. Knowing all too well what it means to face an adversary, without or within, Jonathan has dedicated his life to helping others face their own struggles in all that he does. From serving as a chapter leader in the LGBT service member's advocacy group *OutServe*, to assisting prominent anti-bullying advocates *GLSEN* form new chapters in North Carolina, Jonathan continues to accept nothing but victory for those who seek to discover their own victories and triumphs in their individual lives.

Amanda Hudnall is a high school Physics teacher residing in the Northeastern United States. She has served as an International Ambassador for the U.S. public education system to Ghana, holds a Master's of Education Degree in Curriculum and Instruction in Science Education and is currently pursuing a second master's degree in Educational Administration. As a hobby she exhibits Persian felines professionally with her mother, and pursues fields of interest outside of education such as biological anthropology, Mountain Gorilla conservation and many environmental issues and efforts.

Kiara Kane is 15 years old and a freshman in high school. She enjoys reading and drawing. She also enjoys learning Spanish. She is 4'11 and has brown hair and a Pitbull mix dog named Hunny Bun. Her mother and her rescued Hunny Bun in October 2012. She lives with her mother and sees her father on weekends.

Ki-Hak Lee is a Professor of Psychology at Yonsei University. He received his Ph.D. in School Psychology from Yonsei University. He worked as a President of the Korean School Psychological Association and as a Vice President of the Korean Psychological Association. His main interests are in the measurement of career development.

Yoona Lee is a postdoctoral fellow and an adjunct faculty in the Department of Psychology at Brandeis University, Waltham, MA. She received her Ph.D. in Developmental Psychology from Brandeis University and her master degrees in Psychology from Yonsei University, Seoul, Korea, and from Boston University, Boston, MA. Her major research interests include child maltreatment, child discipline, bullying behaviors, bullying intervention programs, and children/adolescent psychosocial behaviors in developmental and cross-cultural perspectives.

Kimberly Meredith is a lover of dance, writer of poems, educator of peace and researcher of empathy. She recently completed here PhD in Language and Literacy Education at the University of British Columbia. Her research focuses on creating connections through communication beyond language barriers, including through gesture or dance. She is currently a global English educator at Pearson College of the Pacific, a United World College that brings together students from 80 different countries to use education as a force for peace. She is also the founder of the Heart Mind Body Collective, a dance group devoted to using creative expression as a means to heal the whole self and build deep empathy.

Laura Merry earned her Master's of Art in Educational Leadership and Administration from the Gladys L. Benerd School of Education at the University of the Pacific in May 2014, and is currently a staff member in the Office of the President at University of the Pacific. The focus of her thesis was on bullying in higher education, which was inspired through observation of her youngest son dealing with issues of bullying.

Katie Miller was born and raise in Seville,Ohio where she is a triplet and a firefighter/photographer for her hometown. Katie is also the Vice President for Wooster Pflag and enjoys doing PR event where she can education people about the LGBT population.

Joan Mosyjowski is a 17 year-old senior high school student from Hartville, Ohio. After her crisis, she and her family found the support of Akron PFLAG and the Unitarian Universalist Church of Akron. Since then, she has been active in both organizations promoting outreach to LGBTQ+ youth who have had similar struggles. She has volunteered with PFLAG and teamed up with the Teen Pride Network to help bring regional youth together in a supportive environment. Through the Unitarian Universalist Church, she has taken on leadership positions in her church district and in the regional LGBTQ+ community. She is currently enrolled in an early college program at Kent State, and plans to attend Bowling Green State University after she graduates to pursue a degree in sociology.

Kim Mosyjowski is an artist by nature and education, a mother of two wonderful children who are gay and an equally wonderful child who is not, a gardener, and vermiculturalist. She serves as the president of the Akron chapter of PFLAG and is one of the founders of the Teen Pride Network, a prosocial organization for LGBTQ teens and their allies. She and her daughter, Joan, are active members of the Unitarian Universalist Church of Akron. Kim and Joan actively seek to change hearts and minds by telling their stories.

Bernard Oliver earned his B.S. in physical education and history at California State University, Hayward (now named California State University, East Bay) and his M.A. and Ed. D. at Stanford University in Teacher Education and Curriculum Development. Dr. Oliver's teaching experience includes service as a high teacher and coach; and university teaching experience at St. Cloud State University, University of Missouri, Kansas City, Washington State University, Syracuse University, The University of Texas at Austin, and the University of Florida. In addition to teaching, he has held leadership positions as Dean of the College of Education; Department Chair, Program Director and Assistant Superintendent for High School Education. His academic recognition includes being named the Kauffman/University of Missouri Professor and Endowed Chair in Urban Education; postdoctoral fellowships in leadership with the Bush Foundation; the Association of Southern Universities; Stanford University; Harvard University; and a Fulbright Fellow (Germany). Dr. Oliver has published and presented over 70+ articles focusing on leadership, college access/success; diversity; physical education; and more recently at-risk and dropout students. His professional service includes AERA; AAHE; AABHE; NCATE. AACTE; Holmes Partnership; UCEA; and ASCD. Dr. Oliver has four children and 12 grandchildren.

Azadeh Osanloo – Before joining the faculty of the Department of Educational Leadership and Administration at New Mexico State University, Dr. Osanloo received her doctorate in the Educational Leadership and Policy Studies Program, specializing in the Social and Philosophical Foundations of Education at Arizona State University. Her research addressed civic education in a post 9/11 climate focusing on the concepts of democracy, cosmopolitanism, human rights, and citizenship from theory to praxis. She has merged her work in civics and human rights with her new research agenda on collaborative systemic diversity-based interventions for bullying for middle schools. Prior to being in Arizona she taught in the New York City public schools working primarily with junior high school students in the South Bronx and jointly was a program director at the Harlem Educational Activities Fund - a not-for-profit that specialized in closing the gap between educational attainment and disenfranchised students. While in New York City she obtained her Master's in Public Administration from New York University's Robert F. Wagner School. In general, her research agenda focuses on issues of educational equity; educational leadership and policy; the philosophical foundations of education; diversity, multiculturalism, and human rights; and bullying interventions. She is currently the Stan Fulton Endowed Chair for the Improvement of Border and Rural Schools and has won the Dean's Awards for her teaching and service. Azadeh has four books due for publication in 2015 including this book, *Students, teachers, and school leaders promoting anti-bullying in schools* (Sense Publishing) (co-edited with Christa Boske); *Living the work: Promoting social justice and equity work in schools around the world* (Emerald Publishing) (co-edited with Christa Boske); *Handbook of Urban School Leadership* (Rowman & Littlefield) (co-edited with Muhammad

314

Khalifa, Noelle Witherspoon-Arnold, and Cosette Grant-Overton); and *Creating and negotiating collaborative spaces for socially-just anti-bullying interventions and innovations for K-12 schools* (Information Age Publishing) (co-edited with Cindy Reed and Jon Schwartz).

Dickson Perey is a native Southern Californian that has attended K-12 public schools and earned his Bachelors and Masters in public universities. Dickson is a credentialed public school counselor and is employed in a large metropolitan school district. As a doctoral candidate at the Charter College of Education at California State University, Los Angeles, Dickson's research interests include safe school climate, anti-bullying efforts and the role of the school counselor. Dickson is legally married to his husband and aspires to raise children.

Bradley Rhodes. I am 24 years old. I identify as a gay male. I was born in North Carolina. I grew up in a home in which the adults stressed the importance of "being with your own kind." If someone was involved in an interracial marriage, identified as a lesbian/gay/bisexual/transgender/queer (LGBTQ), was a Person of Color or identified as female, then that person was thought to be inferior to my All-American White family. At the age of 10, my Mom and Dad separated. I moved to Ohio with my mother. She married three years after we moved. I was emotional abused by my stepfather. Growing up, I was constantly told I was "worthless" and "would never amount to anything." Not only was I emotionally and physically abused at home, my peers at school constantly told me I was "fat", "undesirable", and "useless". Fortunately, my Mom divorced my stepfather. The abusive treatment by my peers pushed me over the edge. I dropped out of school. I was withdrawn and isolated myself. I used this opportunity to write about being bullied as a means to let teachers and school leaders realize the need to know their students and the lives they live. There is a need for all students, especially those who are "different", to be recognized and valued. Recently, I enrolled in Intensive Treatment Services, and I am in the process of building a strong, positive foundation, and will continue to work on my bright future.

Joanna Royce-Davis is the Dean of Students. She has the honor of partnering with talented educators in the Chaplain's Office, Counseling Services, Health Services, Academic Support Services, Leadership Development, and Assessment to cultivate the strength and potential of each of these key Student Life areas in maximizing opportunities for student learning and student success. In addition, Joanna has the honor of serving on the faculty of the Benerd School of Education and collaborating together with faculty and Student Life colleagues to support the development of future higher education leaders in her role as the Director of Pacific's graduate program in Student Affairs. Her research interests focus on leadership development, student success, and development of intercultural capacity.

Paul Saltzman was a civil rights volunteer with SNCC, the Student Non-Violent Coordinating Committee, in Mississippi in the summer of 1965. He is also the director and producer of "Prom Night in Mississippi" and "The Last White Knight— Is Reconciliation Possible?" He is currently the President & CEO of Moving Beyond Prejudice.

Ryan S. Schoenfeld, Ed.D. has been a practitioner in the field of education for 21 years (15 years in administration and 6 years teaching). His roles include; a special education aide, elementary teacher, coach, assistant principal, principal, and coordinator of K-6th grade mathematics and coordinator of 7th – 12th grade Science Technology Engineering Mathematics (STEM). Ryan attended many leadership conferences; including the International Successful Schools Project (ISSPP) Conference in Nottingham, England, his dissertation *Leadership and Sustainability During Changing and Challenging Times* was shared at the University Council of Education Association (UCEA) Conference in Pittsburgh, Pennsylvania and Denver, Colorado. He also served as a panelist at an ISSPP Conference in Boston College. As a graduate student, he presented *Narratives of Puerto Rican English Language Learner (ELL) Parents* at The Graduate Student Symposium at the University of New York at Buffalo. Ryan is the co-creator of the "All Kinds of Kinds Program".

Goldeia Shaw, I am in the eleventh grade. I live with my mother and my step-dad. I have four half siblings and two full blooded siblings. Four of them live with me. I like to paint and draw, cook, work, and help others. Those are my hobbies. Working is my whole life. I work at KFC so it's not entirely too difficult but there are its challenges. This book chapter is very important to me because I really want to let the teachers and schools know how bullying is more important than you think. I believe there are so many things teachers can do to help students dealing with this problem. We can talk to them and let them know that they are not alone. This one book can change the teachers and change the lives of all the students that are going through this experience.

Michael J. Sheehan is an Assistant Professor of Psychology at Quinnipiac University in Hamden, CT. He earned his B.S. in psychology at The Ohio State University and his M.A. and Ph.D. in Social Developmental Psychology at Brandeis University. Dr. Sheehan has taught a variety of courses in child and adolescent development, statistics, and research methods. His research focuses primarily on antecedents of aggressive behavior in children and adolescents, including the influence of parents (e.g., discipline), peers (e.g., social problems), and environmental risks (e.g., exposure to violence). Dr. Sheehan is grateful for the guidance of Dr. Malcolm Watson, his mentor and research collaborator, and the unconditional love and support of his wife, Jen, and his dog, Hannah.

Logan Sherman attends The Ohio State University where they are studying Mandarin Chinese, Women's, Gender and Sexuality Studies and Hospitality

Management. Logan has been active in creating safe schools through Gay-Straight Alliance leadership, GLSEN Northeast Ohio, and speaking engagements in high schools. As a high school student, Logan got involved on PFLAG Cleveland's board and are currently a board member of PFLAG Columbus. Logan is becoming increasingly involved in trans* and queer activism and hopes to continue to serve the LGBTQ community in the future. In their spare time, Logan enjoys playing rugby, being outdoors, and a good laugh.

Dwayne Steward is a nationally recognized journalist, activist and speaker. He was appointed in May 2013 to become to the City of Columbus' first LGBTQ Health Advocate at the Columbus Public Health Department in Ohio. He is also the founder and director of the Make It Better Foundation, a bullying prevention organization, and is founder of "Queer Minded," the top-rated LGBTQ news/entertainment talk show on TalktainmentRadio.com. He was also the founding HIV Testing Coordinator for the Greater Columbus Mpowerment Center in 2011. A federally funded initiative through AIDS Resource Center Ohio, the center works to combat the high HIV infection rate among black and Latino gay men. In 2010, he was published in the New York Times Bestseller "*It Gets Better: Coming Out, Overcoming Bullying and Creating a Life Worth Living*" edited by Dan Savage and Terry Miller, and continues to speak throughout the country on the devastating effects of anti-gay bullying. Dwayne received a Bachelor of Science in Journalism from Ohio University. He is a senior writer for Outlook Columbus (a statewide LGBT news magazine) and currently resides as Marketing Chair on the Board of Directors for Kaleidoscope Youth Center, a safe drop-in facility for LGBTQ youth ages 12-20. He is a lead organizer of Columbus Urban Pride, a social and educational organization geared towards creating inclusive spaces for LGBTQ people of color.

Karen Andrus Tollafield is a retired teacher with 30 years experience in the elementary and middle school classroom. She is currently a doctoral candidate at Kent State University studying the writing experiences of LGBTQ young adults during their K-12 schooling. Furthering her work as an Ally (supporter for the equality of LGBTQ rights), Karen serves as the LGBTQ Liaison for the Ohio Council of Teachers of English Language Arts (OCTELA) and a Safe Space Trainer for the Gay Lesbian Straight Education Network (GLSEN).

Jennifer Turley is an Intervention Specialist with a Master's Degree from KSU in Special Education. Jennifer completes her AUTISM Specialist Certification in Fall 2014, and continues to pursue her k-12 Administration Degree. Jennifer's daughter, Maddy, grew up noticeably different from her peers. Maddy and her parents were forced to fight against the female stereotypes that pervade our society, as well as advocate for fair treatment of LGBTQ youths in Maddy's school. Jennifer also attempted to start a GSA in a school in which she was employed, but was abruptly turned-down by the administration, who insisted that the town's inhabitants would never approve. This, as well as the struggle for her daughter's fair treatment, is what prompted her to pursue a degree in Administration. She continues to fight and advocate for the LGBTQ population wherever she works.

Edward Valentin-Lugo is a first year college student attending classes at the Cleveland Institute of Art (CIA). A private college of liberal arts located in University Circle, Cleveland, OH. It is one of the nations leading colleges of art and design. For a kid who arrived from Puerto Rico at a very young age, struggled to learn English, had no art courses in high school, and never expected to go to college, Lugo's path to CIA held plenty of obstacles. Esperanza, Inc., a Cleveland agency dedicated to supporting educational achievement among Hispanic youth, played a key role. Much of the credit for that change, according to Lugo, goes to his mentor, Martinez E-B, a 2012 graduate of CIA. The story that Lugo created in Esperanza was very tedious in Lugo's words. " How can I create a story where my audience can in some way relate with the main character?" He continues by stating, "What better way then by incorporating some of my personal emotions and thoughts in the main character that I create." This story that he created is also a story that he plans on continuing when he graduate from CIA.

Darla Wagner has been honored to work in the field of education for over 24 years. With a focus on instructional leadership, Darla has served as an Instruction & Learning Consultant for teachers across Northeast Ohio. She co-directed The National Writing Project at Kent State University for 10 years. Currently she is a building administrator for Orange City Schools and an adjunct professor at Ursuline College. Her publications and professional presentations include: "Hooked on YA Lit: A Book Group for Teachers and Librarians", *VOYA, 2009.* Co-authored with CJ Bott, M. Arnold, and J. Harr; "From Artist Teacher to Citizen Teacher: Reaching the Standards through Performance Arts in the Summer Institute at Kent State University" NWP Monograph series, National Writing Project Publication. 2005. Co-authored with A. Manna and N. McCracken; "A Safe Harbor: Writing: Groups in the Middle School Classroom", *English Journal,* spring2001; "A Picture's Worth a Thousand Words", *OCTELA Journal, fall 1999; and* NCTE Presentations (1999-2007): *Writing Groups in the Middle School Classroom, TeachingGrammar in the Context of Revision, Using Literature Circles to Address Issues of Social Justice,* and *Beyond the Standards.* Darla celebrates life with her husband Richard Wagner their four children, and one granddaughter.

Malcolm W. Watson earned his Ph.D. in Psychology from the University of Denver in 1977. He has been a professor of psychology at Brandeis University for 37 years. He has also been the Chair of the Psychology Department and Dean of the Graduate School of Arts and Sciences. His most recent research and articles are focused on antecedents of aggression in children and adolescents and factors protecting children from becoming aggressive and engaging in other risky health behaviors. His research has been funded by NIMH and NICHD.

CPSIA information can be obtained at www.ICGtesting.com
Printed in the USA
BVOW05*0925191115

426703BV00003B/8/P